kisiskâciwan

kisiskâciwan

*Indigenous Voices from Where
the River Flows Swiftly*

Edited by

Jesse Rae Archibald-Barber

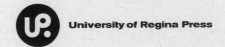

University of Regina Press

Printed and bound in Canada at Marquis. The text of this book is printed on 100% post-consumer recycled paper with earth-friendly vegetable-based inks.

Cover design: Duncan Campbell, University of Regina Press
Text design: John van der Woude, JVDW Designs
Proofreader: Kristine Douaud
Cover art: "Flowing Water" by Dieter Tracey / iStockphoto.

Library and Archives Canada Cataloguing in Publication

Kisiskâciwan : Indigenous voices from where the river flows swiftly / edited by Jesse Rae Archibald-Barber.

Includes index. Issued in print and electronic formats. ISBN 978-0-88977-542-8 (softcover).— ISBN 978-0-88977-543-5 (PDF).—ISBN 978-0-88977-544-2 (HTML)

1. Canadian literature (English)—Native authors. 2. Canadian literature—Native authors.
3. Canadian literature (English)—Saskatchewan. 4. Canadian literature—Saskatchewan.
5. Native peoples—Saskatchewan—Literary collections. 6. Canadian literature (English)—
21st century. 7. Canadian literature—21st century. I. Archibald-Barber, Jesse Rae, 1972-, editor

PS8235.I6K57 2018   C810.8'089707124   C2018-900974-8   C2018-900975-6

10 9 8 7 6 5 4 3 2 1

University of Regina Press, University of Regina
Regina, Saskatchewan, Canada, S4S 0A2
tel: (306) 585-4758 fax: (306) 585-4699
web: www.uofrpress.ca

We acknowledge the support of the Canada Council for the Arts for our publishing program. We acknowledge the financial support of the Government of Canada. / Nous reconnaissons l'appui financier du gouvernement du Canada. This publication was made possible with support from Creative Saskatchewan's Creative Industries Production Grant Program.

*For all those whose voices have been lost too soon
and for all those whose voices are still singing*

The prairie is full of bones. The bones stand and sing and I feel the weight of them as they guide my fingers on this page.

—*Sky Dancer Louise Bernice Halfe, from* Blue Marrow

Contents

Preface

Bringing this anthology to fruition has been an amazing learning experience, and it has been my sincere intent to honour the significant contributions that have been made to Saskatchewan literature by our Indigenous writers and storytellers.

While this anthology is the first of its kind in Saskatchewan, it was most certainly inspired by the great work of *Manitowapow: Aboriginal Writings from the Land of Water*, edited by Warren Cariou and Niigaanwewidam James Sinclair, and published by HighWater Press. When I attended the book launch in February 2012 in the Tower Atrium at the Forks Market in Winnipeg, I was astounded by the immensity of the work, and by all the writers and community members gathered together to celebrate the rich oral and written traditions of Manitoban Indigenous communities. It motivated me to finally begin a project that had been simmering in my mind for some time: to bring together the diverse Indigenous stories of my home province of Saskatchewan. Cariou and Sinclair's work helped me realize that this project was possible and something to celebrate.

It took me some time to figure out where to begin. Of course, I knew of the great Saskatchewan Indigenous writers; I had been reading and teaching their works for years, but I was still uncertain where to start—that is, until March of 2013 when I attended the book launch at the Artesian Performance Venue in Regina for *The Literary History of Saskatchewan*, edited by David Carpenter and published by Coteau Books. In the first chapter, "'Our New Storytellers': Cree Literature in Saskatchewan," Kristina Fagan Bidwell locates the earliest Indigenous writings in English in the lands now designated by Saskatchewan. I also found in this chapter the guiding image for the anthology with Bidwell's meditation on the Saskatchewan River: "with its deceptively slow-moving surface and its ever-shifting sandbars[, w]ith its permanence and its continual movement, the river is perhaps an appropriate metaphor for Aboriginal storytelling. Aboriginal traditional stories are the most ancient literature of this land. Yet they continue to change and shift and to speak to the realities of people today." Indeed, *kisiskâciwan*, which means "it flows swiftly" and is the Cree word from which the province derives its name, expresses the spirit and sentiment of this anthology, with the ongoing flow of traditions from the past into the present.

It took me another year to begin the work in earnest, and another two years of research and collecting materials. I confronted many complicated issues along the way, the first being what to include in the anthology. I found such an abundance of materials that I realized I would be able to include only a fraction of all of the great works available. I also had to confront the strange rectangular borders that outline the province, which of course do not reflect traditional Indigenous territories or the movements of cultures throughout history. Today, there are five main First Nations cultural groups in Saskatchewan—Cree, Saulteaux, Nakoda, Dakota, and Dene—in addition to the Métis, and a Lakota community near our southern border. Prior to the nineteenth century, though, there were several other groups that inhabited these lands at one time or another, including Slave, Beaver, Snake, Sarsi, Blackfoot, and Gros Ventres. However, as these groups are no longer based in the province, I made the choice to include only writers and historical figures, with a few exceptions, who descend from the nations still present in Saskatchewan. Even then, it was complicated at times to determine which writers to include in the anthology. Beyond the obvious choices of writers who were born, raised, and continue to live in the province, there are writers and historical figures who are not originally from Saskatchewan, but whose impact on our literature and history has been profound. Then there are those authors who were born in Saskatchewan but have not lived in the province for quite some time, and yet whose works speak deeply to their Saskatchewan roots. And even then, much material was not able to be included due to page length, and here I'm referring specifically to plays and critical essays. There are a few dramatic pieces and essays in this anthology, but I was not able to include anywhere close to an adequate sample, and many great playwrights, scholars, and historians are regretfully not represented here. Clearly, there is a need for an anthology specifically for drama, and likewise for critical essays, and it is my hope that more of these collections will be brought together in the near future.

What we do have here is a wonderful collection of oral traditions, early writings, speeches from historical leaders, stories from elders past and present, and poems and writings found in archives and magazines, in addition to contemporary fiction, poetry, and nonfiction by many of our established and emerging writers. With much consideration, and through extensive consultation with colleagues and community members, I made selections that I hope readers find informative and enjoyable.

There are so many people to thank for their support of this project. First, I would like to thank all of the authors of *kisiskâciwan*. Without their support, this anthology would never have happened—obviously because of their writings in the first place, but also because of their generosity, and the generosity of all the copyright holders, in donating their fees to help make this project possible. This was a heart-warming show of goodwill by our writers, and, in the spirit of giving back to our communities and following the lead set by Cariou and Sinclair, I will be donating the proceeds from this anthology to a special fund, administered by the Department of Indigenous Languages, Literatures, and Linguistics at the First Nations University of Canada, to help support Indigenous youth literacy and creative writing initiatives in the province.

I'd especially like to thank Warren Cariou for helping me navigate some of the many complexities of editing a project of this scope, and Randy Lundy for the many conversations about the elusive definitions of Saskatchewan Indigenous writing.

I would also like to acknowledge all of the individuals, organizations, and publishers who directly or indirectly contributed to making this publication possible: Belle Young and all the staff at the First Nations University of Canada Library; Belinda Daniels and the Saskatchewan Indigenous Cultural Centre; Lynda Holland and *The Dene Elders Project*; David Carr and the University of Manitoba Press; Valerie Nair and the University of British Columbia Press; John Agnew and Coteau Books; Jacqueline Gubiani and Fifth House Books; Jackie Forrie and Thistledown Press; Greg Younging and Theytus Books; Michael Barnholden and Kevin Williams with Talonbooks; Ronald Hatch and Ronsdale Press; Doug Cass and Susan at the Glenbow Museum Archives; Annie Gibson and Playwrights Canada; Rick Marcello with Kobalt Music; Stephanie Hanis and Todd Jordan with Paquin Entertainment; and Alison Jackson and Tomali Pictures.

I'd also like to thank my colleagues Arok Wolvengrey, Shannon Avison, Vincent Collette, Jan Van Eijk, John Corrigan, Jeremy Gow, and Joanne Arnott for their help in finding materials. And I'd like to express my heartfelt appreciation to all my family and friends for their unwavering moral support and encouragement.

Finally, I would like to acknowledge my deep gratitude to Bruce Walsh, Karen Clark, Donna Grant, Duncan Campbell, Morgan Tunzelmann, Wendy Whitebear, Kelly Laycock, and the rest of the staff at the University of Regina Press. Their enthusiasm for this project and their expert work on the design of the book has been astounding, and it has been an honour to work with them.

This is a beginning. There is more work to do—and more stories to share.

Introduction

In 1922, Rev. Edward Ahenakew was convalescing in a cabin on Chief Thunderchild's reserve. Thunderchild would often visit during the day and tell stories to pass the time. The stories were from the times of the great buffalo hunts, of the Sun Dance, of the times before the treaties. Ahenakew realized the importance of these stories and wrote them down in a manuscript. In one story, "A Winter of Hardship," Thunderchild recalls a winter that was particularly long and cold. The animals had gone away and the people were starving, wandering across the plains, searching for food and shelter. When all seemed lost, one night Thunderchild had a dream: when he looked to the south, he saw all green, and when he looked north, he saw all darkness. Thunderchild told his father about his dream, and his father affirmed that "dreams count," and to take the people and go south. It was a risky decision, but eventually the group arrived at a camp near an old Sundance ground. A short while later, Thunderchild was sitting alone on a hill when he saw something flickering over a big snowdrift. He walked over and located a pole sticking out of the snow with a piece of tattered cloth attached. He began clearing away the snow and found some buffalo hides, and when he lifted them up, he discovered a great cache of buffalo meat cut into pieces! And so the people ate, and so they survived.

For the past several years, I have been researching the history of Indigenous oral and written traditions. I found that many literary historians tended to mark the beginnings of modern Indigenous literature in Canada with the publication of Maria Campbell's *Half-Breed* in 1973. When I first read these theories, I must admit I felt a sense of pride, as Campbell is from Saskatchewan, and because I have Métis roots in the province. However, I also found that these same literary historians often characterized the period before the 1970s as a time of "voicelessness" for Indigenous writers and communities. Initially, this seemed like an intriguing, even seductive, idea, but I soon realized it to be another kind of postmodern romantic concept extended back over our history. While much of Canadian history has involved the oppression and displacement of Indigenous peoples, I knew that the voices of our ancestors had never been completely silenced, that the traditional stories, the teachings, the shouts of protests, the celebrations of life, the self-expressions, all these had always filled and still fill the communities. And when I looked in the libraries and archives, and when I talked with the storytellers, the writers, and elders, and artists, I found that there were hundreds, thousands, indeed countless stories out there, in decade after decade going back in time.

Many of the writings in this collection speak to us from across history, reminding us that the oral traditions, the memories of the people, reach far back into the depths of primordial times. And although these oral traditions are included here in their English translations, their meaning and significance carries through all the colonial transformations of our lands, through the era of the fur trade in Rupert's Land, through the treaties and settlements in the North-West Territories, and into the present-day province of Saskatchewan, where the more recent English writings in this collection continue to express the lives and stories of our Indigenous communities. With all this change, these writings undoubtedly express a colonial legacy filled with violence and oppression: western expansion, broken treaties, the clearing of the buffalo, disease and starvation, imprisonments and executions, removal to reserves, the pass system, the banning of ceremonies, the residential schools system, the loss of language, the "sixties scoop," the shortfalls in education, housing, and drinking water, the disproportional suicide and incarceration rates, and the ongoing stripping of resources from traditional lands. But the writings in this collection also speak to a history filled with the strength of individuals and communities, with resistance and empowerment, the reclaiming of traditions and ceremonies, the retaking control of education, the celebration of cultures, the search for identity, restored family connections, activism for land rights and conservation, and the creation of new forms of art and new ways of knowing.

The writings in this collection are just a small sampling of the immense range of materials out there. There are many more writings to be found, in libraries and archives, in memoirs and journals, in magazines and newspapers, and all the writings in theatre and performance art, accounts of history, and critical essays, which deserve further study and public circulation. And neither does this collection account for all the traditional forms of writing in Saskatchewan. "Writing," of course, is not limited to the alphabetic-phonetic system we use in English, but extends to any form of graphic sign system. In this sense, methods of signification have been used in the lands of present-day Saskatchewan for thousands of years. They are found in the ancient rock formations and petroforms, such as the Moose Mountain Medicine wheel, or in the petroglyphs and rock paintings, such as those found on the side of the cliffs near Mantiou Powstik. There are the pictographic narratives on animal hides and parchments, like the remarkable representation of the Treaty 4 negotiations by Chief Pasqua, the only known document depicting treaty negotiations from an Indigenous perspective. Then there are the patterns of beadwork that convey narratives in their graphics on clothing and other materials, allowing individuals to wear their stories as they walk. And, of course, there are the syllabic writing systems, first developed for the Cree language, but which all the Indigenous languages in Saskatchewan now have. These syllabic writing systems allow for oral traditions to be recorded in their own writing systems, as well as for new works today to be written originally in their Indigenous languages. Honouring all of this work would require several more anthologies and collections, and I encourage readers to learn more about these traditional forms of writing.

For now, this anthology is a collection of Saskatchewan Indigenous writings in English, a language once used to negate Indigenous cultures, but which is now a language of empowerment and resistance, a language that our writers have skillfully adapted to articulate their experiences in powerful ways, embedding a sense of tradition with new understandings of the world and expressions of the imagination. They help define the strength of Indigenous writers today, and also help to enrich and develop the relationships among all of the Indigenous and settler communities in the province, as we continue to move forward and create new stories of Saskatchewan.

I often think of the story Thunderchild told to Ahenakew, about the extreme hardships his people endured that winter, and about the store of buffalo meat he discovered. I also think about the publication history behind Ahenakew's collection, and how it was almost lost to history. Ahenakew did not publish Thunderchild's or his own Old Keyam stories during his lifetime. It wasn't until some time after his death that his niece found the manuscript buried away in a drawer in his cabin. They were eventually edited by Ruth M. Buck and published as *Voices of the Plains Cree*, first by McLelland & Stewart in 1973 and then by the Canadian Plains Research Center, now the University of Regina Press, in 1995. There are many other examples like this, of stories that were kept from publication for one reason or another for decades—but what is undeniably clear is that the voices of Saskatchewan Indigenous peoples have always been here.

The writings in this anthology echo these countless voices that speak to us from across history, mixing with the new voices of our writers, and storytellers, and community members, active and present and alive. They are like the stores of buffalo meat buried under the snow, left there by people before us, to be uncovered by us today. They are everywhere on the land, as in the pages of this book, to give us sustenance for survival.

Saukamappee (Young Man)

Cree · c. 1700–1793 · Pasquiaw River

We begin this anthology with Saukamappee, or Young Man. Though born Cree, or "Nahathaway," in his youth he fought notably with the Peigan against the Shoshone. After the war, he remained with the Peigan in the western plains and foothills. When explorer David Thompson wintered with the Peigan in 1787, Saukamappee was by that time an elder storyteller and chief. Thompson describes meeting Saukamappee in his journal:

After a few days [staying together] the old man spoke to me in the Nahathaway language and asked me if I understood it, and how long since I had left my own country. I answered 'this is my fourth winter and the Nahathaways are the people we trade with, and I speak their tongue sufficient for common purposes,' upon which, with a smile, he said, 'I am not a Peeagan of these plains I am a Nahathaway of the Pasquiaw River' (a River that joins the Kisiskatchewan about fifty miles below Cumberland House). He said 'it is many winters since I last saw the ground where my parents lie. I came here a young man, and my name is still the same I then received.' [...] He remained silent for some time, and then said, 'What a stranger I now find myself in the land of my father's.'

Saukamappee's story "Life among the Peigans" was translated by Thompson and included in his *Travels*. It offers a glimpse of life before European arrival, the Peigan-Shoshone war in the 1730s, and the arrival of smallpox in 1781. Hudson's Bay Company trader Peter Fidler, who was wintering with the Peigan in 1792–93, reported that Saukamappee died in June 1793, from an infection after his leg was bitten by a beaver.

Life Among the Peigans

The Peeagans were always the frontier Tribe, and upon whom the Snake Indians made their attacks, these latter were very numerous, even without their allies; and the Pee a gans had to send messengers among us to procure help. Two of them came to the camp of my father, and I was then about his age, (pointing to a Lad of about sixteen years) he promised to come and bring some of his people, the Nahathaways with him, for I am myself of that people, and not of these with whom I am. My father brought about twenty warriors with him. There were a few guns amongst us, but very little ammunition and they were left to hunt for the families; Our weapons was a Lance, mostly pointed with iron, some few of stone A Bow and a quiver of Arrows; the Bows were of Larch, the length came to the chin, the quiver had about fifty arrows, of which ten had iron points, the others were headed with stone. He carried his knife on his breast and his axe in his belt. Such was my fathers weapons, and those with him had much the same weapons. I had a Bow and Arrows, and a knife, of which I was very proud.

We came to the Pee a gans and their allies, they were camped in the Plains on the left bank of the River (the north side) and were a great many. We were feasted, a great War Tent was made, and a few days passed in speeches, feasting and dances. A war chief was elected by the chiefs, and we got ready to march. Our spies had been out and seen a large camp of the Snake Indians on the Plains of the Eagle Hill, and we had to cross the River in canoes, and on rafts, which we carefully secured for our retreat. When we had crossed and numbered our men, we were about 350 Warriors (this he showed by counting every finger to be ten, and holding up both hands three times and then one hand) they had their scouts out, and came to meet us, both parties made a great show of their numbers, and I thought that they were more numerous than ourselves. After some singing and dancing, they sat down on the ground, and placed their large shields before them, which covered them: We did the same, but our shields were not so many, and some of our shields had to shelter two men, in [....] Theirs were all placed touching each other, their Bows were not so long as ours, but of better wood, and the back covered with the sinews of the Bisons which made them very elastic and their arrows went a long way and whizzed about us as balls do from guns, they were all headed with a sharp, smooth, black stone (flint) which broke when it struck any thing. Our iron headed, arrows did not go thro' the shields, but stuck in them; On both sides several were wounded, but none lay on the ground; and night put an end to the battle, without a scalp being taken on either side, and in those days such was the results, unless one party was more numerous than the other. The great mischief of war then, was as now, by attacking and destroying small camps of ten to thirty tents, which are obliged to separate for hunting.

I grew to be a man, became a skilfull and fortunate hunter, and my relations procured me a Wife she was young and handsome and we were fond of each other. We had passed a winter together, when Messengers came from our allies to claim assistance. By this time the affairs of both parties had much changed; we had more guns and iron headed arrows than before; but our enemies the Snake Indians and their allies had Mis stut im (Big Dogs, that is Horses) on which they rode, swift as the Deer, on which they dashed at the Pee a gans and with their stone Puk a mog gan knocked them on the head, and they had thus lost several of their best men. This news we did not well comprehend and it alarmed us, for we had no idea of Horses and could not make out what they were. Only three of us went and I should not have gone, had not my wife's relations frequently intimated, that her father's medicine bag would be much honored by the scalp of a Snake Indian.

When we came to our allies, the great War Tent with speeches, feasting and dances as before; and when the War Chief had viewed us all it was found between us and the Stone Indians we had ten guns and each of us about thirty balls and powder for the war, and we were considered the strength of the battle. After a few days march, our Scouts brought us word that the enemy was near in a large war party, but had no Horses with them for at that time they had very few of them. When we came to meet each other, as usual, each displayed their numbers, weapons and Shiel[d]s, in all which they were superior to us, except our guns which were not shown, but kept in their leathern cases, and if we had shown they, would have taken them for long clubs. For a long time they held us in suspense; a tall Chief was forming a strong party to make an attack on our centre, and the others to enter into combat with those opposite to them; We prepared for the battle the best we could, those of us who had guns stood in the front line, and each of us two balls in his mouth, and a load of powder in his left hand to reload.

We noticed they had a great many short stone clubs for close combat, which is a dangerous weapon, and had they made a bold attack on us, we must have been defeated as they were more numerous and better armed than we were, for we could have fired our guns no more than twice; and we were at a loss what to do on the wide plain, and each Chief encouraged his men to stand firm. Our eyes were all on the tall Chief and his motions, which appeared to be contrary to the advice of several old Chiefs, all this time we were about the strong flight of an arrow from each other. At length the tall Chief retired, and they formed their long usual line by placing their shields on the ground to touch each other, the shield having a breadth of full three feet or more. We sat down opposite to them, and most of us waited for the night to make a hasty retreat. The War Chief was close to us anxious to see the effect of our guns. The lines were too far asunder for us to make a sure shot, and we requested him to close the line to about sixty yards, which was gradually done, and lying flat on the ground behind the shields we watched our opportunity when they drew their Bows to shoot at us, their bodies were then exposed and each of us, as opportunity offered, fired with deadly aim, and either killed, or severely wounded, everyone we aimed at.

The War Chief was highly pleased, and the Snake Indians finding so many killed and wounded kept themselves behind their shields; the War Chief then desired we would spread ourselves by two's throughout the line, which we did, and our shots caused consternation and dismay along their whole line. The battle had begun about noon, and the Sun was not yet half down, when we perceived some of them had crawled away from their shields and were taking to flight. The War Chief seeing this went along the line and spoke to every Chief to keep his Men ready for a charge of the whole line of the enemy, of which he would give the signal; this was done by himself stepping in front with his Spear, and calling on them to follow him as he rushed on their line, and in an instant the whole of us followed him, the greater part of the enemy took to flight, but some fought bravely and we lost more than ten killed, and many wounded; Part of us pursued, and killed a few, but the chase had soon to be given over, for at the body of every Snake Indian killed, there were five or six of us trying to get his scalp, or part of his clothing, his weapons, or something as a trophy of the battle, as there were only three of us, and seven of our friends, the Stone Indians, we did not interfere, and got nothing.

The next morning the War Chief made a speech, praising their bravery, and telling them to make a large War Tent to commemorate their victory, to which they directly set to work and by noon it was finished.

The War Chief now called on all the other Chiefs to assemble their men and come to the Tent. In a short time they came, all those who had lost relations had their faces blackened; those who killed an enemy, or wished to be thought so, had their faces blackened with red streaks on the face, and those who had no pretensions to the one, or the other, had their faces red with ochre. We did not paint our faces until the War Chief told us to paint our foreheads and eyes black, and the rest of the face of dark red ochree, as having carried guns, and to distinguish us from all the rest. Those who had scalps now came forward with the scalps neatly streched on a round willow with a handle to the frame; they appeared to be more than fifty, and excited loud shouts and the war whoop of victory. When this was over, the War Chief told them that if anyone had a right to the scalp of an enemy as a war trophy, it ought to be us, who, with our guns had gained the victory, when from the numbers of our enemies we were anxious to leave the field of battle; and that ten scalps must be given to us; this was soon collected, and he gave to each of us a Scalp.

All those whose faces were blackened for the loss of relations, or friends, now came forward to claim the other scalps to be held in their hands for the benefit of their departed relations and friends; this occasioned a long conversation with those who had the scalps; at length they came forward to the War Chief, those who had taken the trophy from the head of the enemy they had killed, said the Souls of the enemy that each of us has slain, belong to us, and we have given them to our relations which are in the other world to be their slaves, and we are contented, Those who held scalps taken from the enemy that were found dead under the shields were at a loss what to say, as not one could declare he had actually slain the enemy whose scalp he held, and yet wanted to send their Souls to be the slaves of their departed relations. This caused much discussion; and the old Chiefs decided it could not be done, and that no one could send the soul of an enemy to be a slave in the other world, except the Warrior who actually killed him; the scalps you hold are trophies of the Battle, but they give you no right to the soul of the enemy from whom it is taken, he alone who kills an enemy has a right to the soul, and to give it to be a slave to whom he pleases. This decision did not please them, but they were obliged to abide by it.

The old Chiefs then turned to us, and praising our conduct in the battle said, each of you have slain two enemies in battle, if not more, you will return to your own people, and as you are young men, consult with the old men to whom you shall give the souls of those you have slain; until which let them wander about the other world. The Chiefs wished us to stay, and promised to each of us a handsome young wife, and [to] adopt us as their sons, but we told them we were anxious to see our relations and people, after which, perhaps we might come back. After all the War ceremonies were over, we pitched away in large camps with the women and children on the frontier of the Snake Indian country, hunting the Bisons and Red Deer, which were numerous, and we were anxious to see a Horse of which we had heard so much. At last, as the leaves were falling, we heard that one was killed by an arrow shot into his belly, but the Snake Indian that rode him, got away; numbers of us went to see him, and we all admired him, he put us in mind of a Stag that had lost his horns, and we did not know what name to give him, but as he was a slave to Man, like the dog, which carried our things; he was named the Big Dog.

We set off for our people, and on the fourth day came to a camp of Stone Indians, the relations of our companions, who received us well and we staid a few day[s]. The Scalps were placed on poles, and the Men and Women danced round them, singing to the sound of Rattles, Tambours and flutes. When night came, one of our party, in a low voice, repeated to the Chief the narrative of the battle, which he in a loud voice, walking about the tents, repeated to the whole camp, after which, the Chiefs called those who followed them to a feast, and the battle was always the subject of the conversation and driving the Snake Indians to a great distance. There were now only three of us to proceed, and upon enquiry, [we] learned a camp of our people, the Nahathaways were a days journey's from us, and in the evening we came to them, and all our news had to be told, with the usual songs and dances, but my mind was wholly bent on making a grand appearance before my Wife and her Parents, and present-ing to her father the scalp I had to ornament his Medicine Bag; and before we came to the camp, we had dressed ourselves, and painted each other's faces to appear to the best advantage, and were proud of ourselves.

On seeing some of my friends I got away and went to them, and by enquiries, learned that my parents had gone to the low countries of the Lakes, and that before I was three Moons away my wife had given herself to another man, and that her father could not prevent her, and they were all far to the northward there to pass the winter. At this unlooked for news I was quite disheartened; I said nothing, but my heart was swollen with anger and revenge, and I passed the night scheming mischief. In the morning my friends reasoned with me upon my vexation about a worthless woman, and that it was beneath a warrior anger, there were no want of women to replace her and a better wife could be got. Others said, that if I had staid with my wife, instead of running away to kill Snake Indians, nothing of this would have happened. My anger moderated, I gave my Scalp to one of my friends to give to my father, and renouncing my people, I left them, and came to the Pee a gans who gave me a hearty welcome; and upon my informing them of my intention to remain with them, the great Chief gave me his eldest daughter to be my wife, she is the sister of the present Chief, and as you see, now an old woman.

The terror of that battle and of our guns has prevented any more general battles, and our wars have since been carried by ambuscade and surprize, of small camps, in which we have greatly the advantage, from the Guns, arrows shod of iron, long knives, flat bayonets and axes from the Traders. While we have these weapons, the Snake Indians have none, but what few they sometimes take from one of our small camps which they have destroyed, and they have no Traders among them. We thus continued to advance through the fine plains to the Stag River when death came over us all, and swept away more than one half of us by the small pox, of which we knew nothing until it brought death among us. We caught it from the Snake Indians. Our Scouts were out for our security, when some returned and informed us of a considerable camp which was too large to attack and something very suspicious about it; from a high knowl they had a good view of the camp, but saw none of the men hunting, or going about, there were a few Horses, but no one came to them, and a herd of Bisons feeding close to the camp, with other herds near. This somewhat alarmed us as a stratagem of War; and our Warriors thought this camp had a larger not far off; so that if this camp was attacked which was strong enough to offer a desperate resistance, the other would come to their assistance and overpower us as had been once done by them, and in which we lost many of our men.

The council ordered the Scouts to return and go beyond this camp, and be sure there was no other, In the mean time we advanced our camp. The Scouts returned and said no other tents were near, and the camp appeared in the same state as before. Our Scouts had been going too much about their camp and were seen; they expected what would follow, and all those that could walk, as soon as night came on, went away. Next morning at the dawn of day, we attacked the Tents, and with our sharp flat daggers and knives, cut through the tents and entered for the fight; but our war whoop instantly stopt, our eyes were appalled with terror, there was no one to fight with but the dead and the dying, each a mass of curruption. We did not touch them, but left the tents, and held a council on what was to be done. We all thought the Bad Spirit had made himself master of the camp and destroyed them. It was agreed to take some of the best of the tents, and any other plunder that was clean and good, which we did, and also took away the few Horses they had, and returned to our camp.

The second day after this dreadful disease broke out in our camp, and spread from one tent to another as if the Bad Spirit carried it. We had no belief that one Man could give it to another, any more than a wounded Man could give his wound to another. We did not suffer so much as those that were near the river, into which they rushed and died. We had only a little brook, and about one third of us died, but in some of the other camps, there were tents in which everyone died. When at length it left us, and we moved about to find our people, it was no longer with the song and the dance; but with tears, shrieks, and howlings of despair for those who would never return to us. War was no longer thought of, and we had enough to do to hunt and make provisions for our families, for in our sickness we had consumed all our dried provisions; but the Bisons and Red Deer were also gone, we did not see one half of what was before, whither they had gone to we could not tell, we believed the Good Spirit had forsaken us, and allowed the Bad Spirit to become our Master, what little we could spare we offered to the Bad Spirit to let us alone and go to our enemies. To the Good Spirit we offered feathers, branches of trees, flowers and sweet smelling grass. Our hearts were low, and dejected and we shall never be again the same people.

To hunt for our families was our sole occupation and kill Beavers, Wolves, and Foxes to trade our necessaries; and we thought of War no more, and perhaps would have made peace with them, for they had suffered dreadfully as well as us; and had left all this fine country of the Bow River to us. We were quiet for about two or three winters, and although we several times saw their young men on the scout we took no notice of them, as we all require young men to look about the country that our families may sleep in safety and that we may know where to hunt. But the Snake Indians are a bad people, even their allies the Saleesh and Koo ta naes cannot trust them, and do not camp with them, no one believes what they say, and are very treachourous; every one says they are rightly named Snake People, for their tongue is forked like that of a Rattle Snake, from which they have their name.

I think it was about the third falling of the leaves of the trees, that five of our tents pitched away to the valleys in the Rocky Mountains, up a branch of this River (the Bow) to hunt the Big Horn Deer (Mountain Sheep) as their horns make fine large bowls, and are easily cleaned; they were to return on the first snow. All was quiet and we waited for them until the snow lay on the ground, when we got alarmed for their safety; and about thirty Warriors set off to seek them, it was only two days march, and in the evening they came to the camp, it had been destroyed by a large party of Snake Indians, who left their marks, of snakes heads painted black on sticks they had set up. The bodies were all there with the Women and Children but scalped, and partly devoured by the Wolves and Dogs.

The party on their return related the fate of our people; and other camps on hearing the news came and joined us. A War Tent was made and the Chiefs and Warriors assembled; the red pipes were filled with Tobacco, but before being lighted an old Chief arose, and beckoning to the Man who had the fire to keep back, addressed us, saying, 'I am an old man, my hair is white and have seen much: formerly we were healthy and strong and many of us, now we are few to what we were, and the great sickness may come again. We were fond of War, even our Women flattered us to war, and nothing was thought of but Scalps for singing and dancing. Now think of what has happened to us all, by destroying each other and doing the work of the bad spirit; the Great Spirit became angry at our making the ground red with blood; he called to the Bad Spirit to punish and destroy us; but in doing so, not to let one spot of the ground, to be red with blood, and the bad Spirit did it as we all know. Now we must revenge the death of our people and make the Snake Indians feel the effects of our guns, and other weapons; but the young women must all be saved, and if any has a babe at the breast, it must not be taken from her, nor hurt; all the Boys and Lads that have no weapons must not be killed; but brought to our camps, and be adopted amongst us, to be of our people, and make us more numerous and stronger than we are. Thus the Great Spirit will see that when we make war we kill only those who are dangerous to us, and make no more ground red with blood than we can help, and the Bad Spirit will have no more power on us.' Every one signified his assent to the old Chief, and since that time, it has sometimes been acted on, but more with the Women than the Boys, and while it weakens our enemies makes us stronger.

A red pipe was now lighted and the same old Chief taking it, gave three whiffs to the Great Spirit praying him to be kind to them and not forsake them, then three whiffs to the Sun, the same to the Sky, the Earth and the four Winds; the Pipe was passed round, and other pipes lighted. The War Chief then arose, and said 'Remember my friends that while we are smoking the bodies of our relations and friends, are being devoured by wolves and Dogs, and their Souls are sent by the Snake Indians to be the slaves of their relations in the other world. We have made no war on them for more than three summers, and we had hoped to live quietly until our young men had grown up, for we are not many as we used to be; but the Snake Indians, that race of liars, whose tongues are like rattle snakes, have already made war on us, and we can no longer be quiet. The country where they now are is but little known to us, and if they did not feel themselves strong they would not have dared to have come so far to destroy our people. We must be courageous and active, but also cautious; and my advice is, that three scout parties, each of about ten warriors with a Chief at their head, take three different directions, and cautiously view the country, and not go too far, for enough of our people are already devoured by wolves and our business is revenge, without losing our people.'

After five days, the scout parties returned without seeing the camp of an enemy, or any fresh traces of them. Our War Chief Koo tanae Appe was now distressed, he had expected some camp would have been seen, and he concluded, the Snake Indians had gone to the southward to their allies, to show the scalps they had taken and make their songs and dances for the victory, and in his speech denounced constant war on them until they were exterminated. [Affairs were in this state when we arrived, and the narrative old man having given us the above information, lighted his pipe; and smoking it out said,] the Snake Indians are no match for us; they have no guns, and are no match for us, but they have the power to vex us and make us afraid for the small hunting parties that hunt the small deer for dresses and the Big Horn for the same and for Bowls. They keep us always on our guard.

—1787

James Settee
Swampy Cree · c. 1809–1902 · Split Lake, Manitoba

James Settee was born near Split Lake, in what is now Manitoba, of Swampy Cree and English descent. He arrived at the Anglican school in Red River in 1823, and after years of school and missionary work was ordained an Anglican minister in 1853. As a missionary, he spent considerable time moving throughout what is now Saskatchewan, including the Moose Mountain area, Lac La Ronge, Stanley Mission, the Qu'Appelle Valley, and Prince Albert. He was fluent in Cree, Ojibway, and English, and he recorded many detailed descriptions of Aboriginal life at the time. It is this extensive experience that gives him a strong presence in the history of Saskatchewan Indigenous literature.

The first selection, "An Indian Camp at the Mouth of Nelson River Hudsons Bay," was written sometime in the late 1880s when Settee was in his seventies. In it,

Settee recalls the story of Wahpus, the Rabbit, which he heard at a feast as a young boy in 1823. This remarkable story remained unpublished during Settee's lifetime, and did not find publication until 1977, when anthropologist Jennifer Brown submitted it to the proceedings of the Eighth Algonquin Conference. (The presentation here follows that of the first publication; in the introduction to the text, the editor notes that the text as presented "conforms as closely as possible to the original Settee manuscript with all its idiosyncracies; and bracketed insertions for clarity…have been kept to a minimum. Questionable readings are indicated.") The second selection, "Wars between the Sioux and Saulteaux," was written in April 1891 and is also a recollection of a story he heard in his youth. Despite the Christian influence in his work, he preserves a strong sense of Cree tradition in his writing.

An Indian Camp at the Mouth of the Nelson River Hudsons Bay. 1823.

On the latter end of September, my grand Father wished [to go] to the spot where he was born at the mouth of Nelson River. We was at Split Lake where my grand Father had settled and made a home [for] his old age[.] He was provided [for] by the H B company. His Father Captain Smith had placed a sum of money into the hands of the Company and this was to support [him] so much annually. My father got leave to take grand father down to the sea. We embarked in a Bark Canoe & followed the stream, saw plenty deer, geese, bears &c. but did not mind them, [as] we had enough of provision. We saw

A large Camp

The whole plantation of the mouth of Nelson River was full lodges of deer skins tents as white [as] white cloth. Hundred of Indians had assembled from Churchill, Severen and moose Factory from James' Bay York Factory. All the Head men came & greeted my grand Father and took him to a large Tent prepared for us. My grand Father had been elected as the Chief of all tribes living on the seacoast. he was called the Little Englishman The Union Jack floated in the breeze alongside the big tent. The Indians or the young men had a pow-wow, the same night.

The Feast began

A long tent had been made I cannot say how long and size the tent was but it was admit some thousand of people for in those days every large rivers in the Country was full of Indians. In the middle tent there were three rotation of Kettles of all sizes full of the best meat moose deer beaver the bear geese wavey, grease a large quantity.

An Invitation given.

Ever man had to bring his dish with him, a place assigned for the head men. inside the tent a whole piece of print of different colours was all hanging on the tent poles & hankercheifs gartering The old men with the skins of all of all sorts on their shoulders. deer skin robes lead for carpets, bear skin beaver wolves skins and the polar bear skins the faces of the young men & women all painted with vermillion in the time the stewards loading the dishes by waggon loads. My grand Father was called to invoke the gods of the aire[?] to come and take a part of the food prepared by their children. Oh, oh, a mile long. the old mills began it was no fun to [see] a mountain demolished as an old friend would say, I saw greater eating up a couple of geese and drink pure oil from the seal or a chunk of blubber. They believe a greater has an evil beast in the stomack; I took notice what was going, there was a young by the name Tomtit, he had his low, one fellow sitting next to him looked up and looked at man and said to him, "why are you cry for? the fellow then said because I cannot eat up all that is before. the other fellow, told him, "if you eat what is before you to put it aside and eat it tomorrow. I think the fellow eat up all at meat that was before him before he went to bed that night. An old woman who was called a glut[ton], ate till fell asleep with her hands on each Kettle that was near. so ones came and eat up all that [was] in kettles when she awoke she called out like a night Owl, "who ate all the meat that was in two kettles alongside of me." one good thing there was no fire water. The Feast continued for some days perhaps a week. at the Tom, tom, tom, dancing all nights. There being good supply of Blubber they pots of iron, they filled the iron pot put cotton and raised them and put torch & the flame rose up very high one could see the Camp miles from the sea some Sloops and Whale Boat ran in to see the great doings at the Camps and see how the Indians were amusing themselves some nights they had conjuring tents to converse with their gods as they called. I never saw my grand Father to go see them, in those conjuring every thing had a voice the wind spoke the beasts and the birds spoke the stone the tree the different animals in the waters also, the departed dead they also spoke, the Indians living far away also spoke. An Englishman also enters into the Conjuring lodge and say to the Conjurer "nekanes, nekanes, I am god-like too, I can turn stone into Iron and make the fire and water to obey me and do my service and do justice to me;" But the great Manito does not speak only through his representatives as the wind & thunders & the earthquake. A woman never attempts to enter the Conjuring, if she does she must die through the displeasure of the gods.

The end of the Feast

A general meeting is called The head men now calls for some one to relate an old tradition to be remembered by all the Band till they meet again, at last one of oldest man told the Band that he had heard an old story when [he] was a lad about 14 or 15 winters old, he would relate the particulars of the Story [When] A very [great] crowd gathered at the big tent The old man began. I was among the [boys] but I did know what the old men was speaking about, but my father related the whole story to me. I remember when the old man said.

There was a time when their was a man and wife living alongside of a river enjoying peace and plenty of deer and beaver to eat, the daily occupation of the man was to preparation his bow and arrows to hunt the large animal, out all day after a chace of Moose or a deer, but never absent from his tent at night time he would tell his wife of his success he had and kill a moose or a deer, sometimes a Beaver. He had run one day and quite fatigued he would retire to bed earlier than usual. the woman sat up dress the skin of the moose or deer or other animal. She retired to bed too on one side, when morning came the mas was fast asleep the woman prepared breakfast and her husband clothes. at last the man opened his eyes the sun was high up. The man put on his clothes and breakfast laid before him he tooks a bit of meat and set his dish aside and did not speak, the woman thought that he was sick, at the last the woman said, "Dear husband are you unwell, the man said, I am well and in perfect health. the woman relieved in her mind. the man told his wife, he had a dream that troubled him, he did not understand it: the dream was about her his wife. He dreamed of a person like himself, a man, did not know where he came from, the man spoke to him, and said that he came to tell him to caution his wife when she was at her work, when she stooped to take any thing from the ground, never to stoop with her back to the west, where the sun set, she could stoop to the north east or south. now my wife the man said, be very Careful that remember that injunction from that god man, dont break it in any wise, the man follow his occupation as usual; the woman never forgot what her husband had strongly advised to be careful. One morning the man asked his wife to build her tent in a new place the tent was taking down and a clean spot selected the woman raised the poles, arranging them in a perfect order, she saw that there was more poles on one side and one pole moving to fall she instantly laid hold on another pole that lay on the ground and she stooped down with her back to the west, just immediately after she remembered she had broken the injunction laid upon her, but she held her peace never to told her husband one morning the man said I have found out the secret. You have broken the injunction that was given to thee by that god man whom I saw in my night vision. "yes, my husband the wife said "In erecting our tent in a new spot of ground one pole went wrong if it fell on the ground all the framework of the tent would fallen to the ground so to keep up I snatched the pole that was moving and to hold on another the pole the frame and stooped down with my back to the west, the man said that settles your case. The woman began to grow very stout at last could scarcely raise herself from the ground the man remained more closely at home the woman could not attend to her tent. at last the woman could not walk she got so big and she told her husband pains was coming upon her the man prepared every thing against the great event that coming upon his wife.

The woman's full time

The man said a new change is to take place in the world & a man is to do duties which he never knew before, must do for the best. the woman called out invoking the gods to help her. she gave birth the first a son, she still felt another a second a son the third a son the fourth a son the fifth a son the sixth a son, six sons born at one time The mother had her hands full to nurse these six babies the man had now work, but he did not care he put a mark on each child so that he might know the eldest to the youngest. The man made more snares and traps gather a large store of provision, the woman did not see the necessity so much food, but the man had a meaning in so doing.

The naming of the six boys

The man had roasted lots of meat the Beaver & Bear's meat the fowls of all sort that is eaten there being only man and the mother of her children she could eat very little the man was satisfied that his tasted the food. he made a speech asking the great Being to come partake a little of the food he made for all the guests who dwelling now known and now gods to gave names to his sons, the eldest the first born the gods called Kewatin, the north wind, the second, wahpun or East day light, the third Shawan south the fourth Nekwahpahun west, the fifth Pewahnuk, the flint, the sixth wahpus, Rabbit, youngest. In a short the boys was very useful to father and mother in process of time all grew to be men. the man began to find out the disposition of his sons

The man assembles all his sons

He tells them that he could [not] keep all in one place every one of them was [to] selected where he would made it his home and arrange every thing for his comfort

Kewatin took the north quarter the wahpun took the East the Nekwahpahan took the west Shawan took his stand on the south, Pewahnuk flint he would remain with the parents wahpus would never leave his father and mothers but would [remain] them while the world lasted. And now sons return to your place of abode so that after time you may meet again to inform to each of you what you have done or intended what you wish to do. another meeting again a time.

Kewatin engaged about conquest and have all power over his brethren and to rule all brutal & flying creation Shawan studying to raise a large family of animals Birds of all kinds, fruit food both man and beast. he feel happy that he can make all creation to rejoice wahpun he is engaged in takin a survey at the moon and stars but his pride is full to bring up the Sun without the shadow of a cloud. to see every creature enjoy the sun light and work for their good—and now Kekabahun West. He watches how is his brothers are getting along. he prepares his artellery some fire arms. he means to oppose the wahpun who knows what he will do in the latter days.

Pewahnuk and wahpus they never trouble themselves about any thing they live happily near the tent of their parents—the man see them every day.

The meeting of the Brothers

It had been proposed before they would meeting & relate what he had and how he arranged his affairs to carry on their works.

Kewatin the eldest

First speakers he said the first thing that had occupied his attention was, how to support his superiority and establish drastic mean to keep order the whole world to keep his brethren under subjection, that he had artillery to drive the heavenly elements from the skies and subdue the whole face of creation, the brothers did not approve the speech. the Rabbit would leap up and callout, hear, hear, & have a hearty laugh, the rest of the brothers was rather amused with him but being a pet & harmless never minded what he did. The rabbet, shouted "I will rule & subdue" humbug, that cannot take place I will have own way, Kewatin was very much offended to be interrupped in his speech. but he threatened to punish the Rabbit for his insolence the rest of the brothers smiled Kewatin he would bind the raging of the sea like an infant is bound in a cradle. the tree would reel at his pleasure & the highest mountain would quake, the stone would break with terror, Wahpus said "such nonsense" and then, a hearty laugh. here Kewatin stops

Shawan South

He he said, you have heard the speech of brother Kewatin, what he said is quite foreign to my ideas I am [engaged] too much in arranging plans for the comfort and happiness of those who are to dwell on the face of the earth, there must be provision to sustain both man and other living creature to provide for the big animal & for the fowl and to bring warmth on the waters, to produce life in the waters vegetation to rise in the earth so that all living animals that moves on the earth may have food to live upon. Rabbit cried out, excellent, excellent; I mean to unbind every thing that has been bound, so that there may be communication even in the waters among men I want all nature to rejoice and to sing aloud with joy our brothers and sisters who will take their stand in the world with have a large family and they will require all the necessaries of life the small animals will need all the help they can get the flying fowl will need support to, all, all, will require help, but I mean to maintain my part granted to me by our Father and by the gods. All the brother said, well spoken, the end of Shawan's address, he did not allude to what Kewatin said.

The wahpun the east

Wahpun, Brethren I do not altogether [forget?] the injunction lade by our Father the last moment we parted with him and our brother Father said to be Kind and live peaceably among yourselves that is true happiness help one another. My plans is how to act to please all the moving creature on the face. well, I thought best to produce a bright object to shine through the world to make your face bright and beautiful and at the same to enable all creation to do their work of whatever they may be. I may make many mistakes, I hope it may not effect your concerns, I may name will be in mouth of our brethren who may inhabit our Coutry more than your names all of you, but I will not pretend to lord over you, man will acknowledge that I am a great benefactor and great help in raising large families in the world, I do not admire at broth-ers [Kewatin] speeches, but Shawan I do endorse word he said, he means to raise families what is better than to see the world moving with human beings "There it is, There it is the Rabbit shouted. one brother told him, to be quiet and not disturb the speaker he had low laugh, but said no more Wahpun was much displeased with the Rabbit, but he thought in his heart he would give a good beating some day." I know who to succeed me he is no mark, he hides my work every moment. he meant when the sun sets.

Nekwapahan West

Nekwapahan, Brothers I have sat without contradicting your various subjects which you have uttered, I have been very much interested with your remarks on various, particularly with regard to our short lives that is the principal subject for all beings who breathe the are as father used to say. to talk about power and might that cannot lodge with us, we see the world is moving with life creature they must pass away, where do they go? we cannot see, the gods say they live in different places. I did not agree with brother Kewatin with all his boast everyone of us might make a pretence and say we are gods, we beg for life for might and power. If we had, we might ruin all creation, passion goes from one man to another, it always do bad things we want great things, if we had them we would abuse them perhaps or[?] smile to our brother. I ask what is the use of all the artillery I heard mention and the threatening language being employed, I might say the same myself – But one thing I must really gainsay, when it is said that I conceal and shut the eyes of the world. I do so I acknowl-edge because the man who is on the chace of a moose or deer is fainting and will not rest till he accomplishes his object, when he kills the animal then he can rest comfortably because he loves his tentmates he has food for them. rest is good and when the great light comes into my quarter, I tell to rest so that all beings might have sleep, good good all the brothers shouted, Nekapahan continued I work at that time when all are at rest. I attend to plants to provide for themselves.

Pewahnuck Flint

He said not one word to the Brother who had made long speeches. he saw there was different opinion, indeed, he formed his own thoughts of Wahpus

Rabbit the youngest brother, for why no one could conceive, but because he intended to remain in the land of his nativity and would try and assist his father, as matter of maintaining heat. He found out that Steel & flint could produce fire, and it was necessary to prepare what it would be when the storm would burst which he forsaw it take plain in the work. He knew perfectly that Kewatin & the Shawan would never agree, indeed all the brothers knew this. Pewahnuck, anticipated that much trouble would arise among the inhabitance in the world. Rabbit shouts, "poh, poh, nobody care about that, and as for your fire no one will care for it." Pewahnuck, dispise his young brother by saying to him, he did not see how Wahpus could live and it useless to take notice of him. Wahpus held his peace, he was prepared to meet him at any moment. There was discord. but Pewahnuck would trouble Wahpus.

Wahpus

The Rabbit time came when he would address his brothers He said, I am the youngest and the weakest among you all, but I mean to stand before the most powerful element that can rise up against what I have prepared and mean to carry it out, is to make abode alongside my parents lodge to look after them and provide substance such as food and warm clothing which none of you will ever done, "Shawan "bravo" P'shaw—says Pewanuck, You will starve and freeze to death"—Wahpus, did not listen to Pewanuck he thought mean of him, Wahpus he took a small dance shouting out he should walk through the whole world and enter in the Palace of the great ones & be feed by the sons of the gods & by their Queens. The brothers was very amused at their young brother, but the youngest, Shawan, south, thought that he might do something great work yet. Wahpus, told his brothers that he was entirely independant of them. and never be under control no ruler no master but his own will. Kewatin shut his ears would not listen such folly here end the brothers speeches.

The general opinion of the Speeches among the Brethren.

Kewatin I am the oldest and must be leader, Shawan I cannot submit to such prosistion[?], Nekapahun west say I disagree with Wahpun East. Pewanuck says I differ from Wahpus. All agreed that there was no concord.

A Proclamation of war.

Kewaten threatened Shawan, the South. Shawan said he was prepared to meet any time.

All the Brothers were troubled and afraid that war was to arise which they never heard such thing. A cry is made, that a might host was visible just arising from the north. One shouted that Kewatin was to be seen riding on a storm and everyone warned to prepare and put every thing in order that an aprehension of danger was about to take place in The The whole sky was in darkness the

wind carrying mountains of snow & hurling it to the earth & tearing & breaking the rocks & overturning the deep & laying up the water in heaps marking
the water as hard as a flintstone The wild animal fleeing to shelter on rocky
mountains to every den and in the thickets.

All the large animals gathered into the piles of trees where the wind had
carried them to other small animal had prepared a place for themselves the
animals that live partly in water were well provided they had gathered food
during summer. the wolf & the Fox and the Rabbit they were enjoying the fun.
But Kewaten was mad to see the rabbit making a sport of him he determination
was to freeze Rabbit to death. One coldest night the world ever knew. there was
the Rabbit sitting in the highest peak in the world with his face near the mouth
of Kewaten taking his morning lunch and having a reel. shouting, "Come on
come on you wicked curse wetegoo, do your worst, Kewatin could [not] touch
or hurt wahpus Shawan was watching and ready to fly if it was necessary to save
his young brother, the other brothers was astonished to see the rabbit so strong
to resist against such awful storm and the cold. Kewaten could go further than
he went half across the world Shawun would allow him. Kewatin did what he
could conquer the whole world but he failed Shawun highly displeased what
done. Shawun said I will pay him for this which he will not like it

Shawan

Shawan is quite prepared to attack Kewatin These two brothers never
agreed together in any thing though Shawun always want matters to run well,
but Kewatin wanted every thing to run in different direction, however matters had begun. every thing was now in a most deploration condition every
ruin that could be made the vegetable creation was Killed even the earth was
a perfect wreck, the skelitons the bones of beast birds of all sorts who could
fly from the wild of Kewatin. Shawun threatened he punished Kewaten and
drive out of the Country.

Shawun

He peeped out to see the earth, he looks again. he put out his head, there
was sparks to be seen. All the brothers saw the sparks, Kewaten, asks "what is
that sparks." all the brothers said, that is Shawun. Kewaten smiles The sparks
rose up higher and higher, till it rose a yard from the earth Shawan had covered
himself with cloud untill it was perfect darkness. the lightening was playing in
the heaven, Kewaten wonders and in a moment a Thunder utters a loud voice
and lighting at the same time, Kewaten is quite bewildered. At another moment
twenty thunders uttered their voice this is the artillery of Shawun. he retires a
certain distance, Wahpus advised Kewaten to go back further back Kewaten
says, not one inch more, Wahpus calls "step back step back" Nekapahun west,
"Tell them brother to withdraw" Kewaten would not. the next moment, Ten

thunders uttered their voices it sooke Kewatn, he stared around & now Twenty thousand thunders uttered forth their voices Kewatin to a certain distance and said he would move one step move. Wahpus having his fun all the time and now an hundered thousand thunders uttered their voice Kewatin now fliess with all might and Shawun pouring out hot thunder blots after him, and graving him to have pity upon and to retire in peace. Shawun now now after driving Kewatin far he returns to this earth and began to raise plants of all sorts the fruit trees the birds of the air returned to this land and thanked Shawun in driving the great enemy the beast of the earth looked on Shawun as the great King of all living. It was proposed by all Creation both man & beast and fowl of the air that a concert would be made for him annually when a dance to fol- low in a short time the earth began to be decked with beautiful flowers & the trees waving in the air new dresses, the young birds singing beautiful songs, all nature rejoying to see the face of Creation look so pretty. (this is only one half what the old man said)

Wahpun East

Wahpun said that he dint intend to hold them long but merely to tell them that he had done what he could for the good of the world in general, he saw that the living on this earth, they would require light to guide them through life. All most endorse this. All the brothers agreed on this. Nekwapahun West, said to some extent that the light would very much benifit the Shawan's fam- ily. Wahpun would introduce may foreign wares from abroad to support life. food, tools & raiment. Oh! called out the Rabbit yes you will introduce many useful things such as you mention, but you will introduce the Weedigoo who will cross the Atlandic and consume humns flesh." the Indians in this Country believe that Weentigoo come other Country and that Wahpun brings them in this Country Wahpun said that Kewaten had better show then Shawun the brothers all disagreed against him.

Nekawpahun West

Nekawpahun I approve all that brother Shawan did. he would not mention Kewaten north or Wahpun east but he approved one thing that Wahpun did, that is the light and the great Lights sun moon & Stars. these are very useful, but that he had prepared and to use them, he thought it would be no use, he allude to Wahpun for he would command the Weetigoos and men eaters to come into this land, but he said, that he would resist them and drive them into the deep—He would play his artillery some time to drive away the plagues that Wahpun would send in this land. "It a belief among the Indians in this Country that the devil brings diseace & death into the world, but the west would stand against it" How that can be done"

Nekapahun says no more.

Pewahnuck Flint

Flint, Pewahnuck speaks he said I do not intend to speak outside this earth where on I was born but confine myself to what I had laid up in my mind, and it is to befriend to the inhabitants of the being that will dwell and live, I mean to devote whole body to them you will understand this hereafter. I contritic none who spoke for they will never will have any thing to do with, but I will establish my seat among fastnesses of the highest rocks in the world and request me to supply them of arms for the disputes that may arise among the brethren at large None of the brethren can touch one hair of my head, or can speak one words me, but I can only say that he who will suceed me is the weakest that the world has produced the small insects that crawls or fly in the air will put him to flight. so he will be no use in the world, the wahpus sitting listening all that is said against him. Shawun south he pities his young brother, but he always to stand by him if any trouble arose against him. Pewahnuck, said no more.

Wahpus, Rabbit

Wahups rose up. all eyes up him. He shouted out and said now give me a song that I may dance a livily reel before I begin with my speech. The earth began with the sung. Calling upon the world to join him with. All the heavens the cloud the lightings the snow—the beast of the earth the fowls that fly above the earth, all the grass of the earth the flowers the trees the herbs the worms and every thing that breadth, wind & storms cold and heat. the water element the whale and the fishes the hills and mountains leaping and dancing with Wahpus. The whale and the Polar Bear the wolf-tribe all shouting loud, Hurrah, hurra, for wahpus." The brothers looking on thing that Wahpus was mad out of his senses, Shawun had his fun he could not understand his young brother, Wahpus was so independant, but he loved him. Wahpus now gave an address. 'he said, I mean to live in the home where father and mother lived, I will live in the tent. I will provide food and raiment to keep the young families warm. my service will be welcomed by the whole human. I will sit with the great ones in the earth the great tents and the strong & big men. I will not trouble with the blood thirsty characters my hands will be clean from the blood of any creature my babies will feed with young birds and with the youn moose Deer and with lambs no quarrelling or jealousy among them. Every hand will rest on my shoulders because I mean to be good and kind to all. it will so follow I will have enemies but they will never conquer me I will stand to the end of time.

The Wahpus went through the earth and piled up peebles in heaps ever where and having done that, a battle is to take place between Pewahnuck— and Wahpus. A large number assembled to see fight. The Wahpus pelted the

Pewahnuck on the side with the peebles every blow the sides of Pewahnuck would from blow after blow with the peebles. Pewahnuck all sides was getting for every blow the Flint fly like glass before stone. the brothers saw that Pewahnuck was no match for Wahpus.

Pewahnucks now tooks his heels and ran but wahpus was after through hills & through mountains the whole a world, and Wahpus stopped and said well. I have done one good thing for those who will inhabit the world whever a man plants his tent he will find a flint to make him a fire to warm and his children. Thus end The Tradition

Now the old men said There is a moral lesson to be drawn from this tradition and who can tell?

One old man almost the oldest in the Band said, I can only say what think of this story.

There is to be a great revolution in the world. great differenc is to arise in the world an army will first arise from the north there will be no peace with Kewaten, he will use every means to subdue everyone and take all under his power yes he will do so. but he will not succeed for the Shawun will also oppose but he will defeat him, the others will contend too and at last join Kewaten except the Small One. The Rabbit Kingdom, he will join with Shawun the great man. Shawun & Wahpus will be united together and defeat all before them. The whole camp shook with the cheers of the Indians. A well informed person would make a pleasant subject of this subject. I Mr Ross you make it interest as possible to relate it in the Cree tongue it is very delightful there is mistakes. but as you will add a sentence here and there I am satisfied the tradition will be written nicely by you who understand the Cree tongue in all its ramifigations

J Settee

—*late 1880s*

Wars between the Sioux and Saulteaux

Some years before the year 1784 a bad disease had depopulated the Country. Thousands upon thousands of the Indians died by the small pox, that ended the wars for a long time. The Sioux Indians threatened the Ojebways that if they attempt to come up and rob them of their Horses and buffalo they would scalp them. The Ojebways & Crees sent their compliments in return that if they came to Red River or its neighbourhood they would shoot them down—but murders was committed between the two partys—the Sioux, Black Feet & the Ojebway & the Cree on the autumn of 1822. One Ojebway Chief name Black Duck sent his Tobacco to all the tribes living in Lake Superior and up Country but would not ask the Crees to asist him. Pegwys was asked to join them. He had received tobacco but did not understand that he was asked to go to war.

He was sorry he had taken the stem the pipe stem. When once a man takes the pipe stem and draws a little, he consents to the war. The reason that Pegwys was sorry in taking the stem, was the Cree chief was not invited; the greatest warrior in the Great Plains. Invitation to all the Saulteauxs living in the Rainy River and neighbourhood and north of that Country towards Albany, James Bay—Great many Saulteauxs around the Shores of the Lake Winnipeg and from Manitoba Lake & Wannipagoos.

In the Spring of 1823 report reached Red River as it was then called in those day, that the war party on its way, and would pass through our Settlement to ask for war implements and provision. The warriors began to make their appearance. The high road was litterally full with Indians—they passed through the road for one whole week travelling up to Pembina where the whole body of them was to meet. I remember the Indians had passed day after day and nights—

When on Sunday morning which was now the seventh day since the Indians had begun the warpath when four Indian Chiefs called to see our minister the Revd. David Thos. Jones to speak to him and to ask him to pray for their success. Mr Jones told them, that it would be wrong to him to pray for the destruction of his fellow men. He told them he would ask God to convert their hearts and change them by his good Spirit, that they might forgive their enemies and love them as their brethren. The Chief Black Duck stared at the Minister. Mr Jones said to the chiefs 'You hear the Bell at the Church I am calling for my children to come and hear the Great Book, God words that they might be made wise unto salvation through faith which is in Christ Jesus, and thus secure the salvation of their souls.' Black Duck answered that he never heard such a Lecture so foolish, to hear a book and to listen to it, when Keche Manito spoke to him almost every night. Mr Jones advised him to recall his followers & select a nice spot of land & plant a Church and a school and teach his people to read the word of God and to make farms. The old Chiefs laughed at Mr Jones advice. Old Pegwys came he was the last. he only took out his body-guard about one hundred men. Away they went about 50 canoes going up stream they were to go no further than Pembina about sixty-nine above our mission station. At Pembina a Large Camp was made waiting for warriors who was to join. They had to come from all parts. The Cree Indians was not invited. The Saulteauxs thought they were able to cope with Plain tribes alone.

Chief Pegwys joined them, he had been detained by the Officers of the Hudson Bay Company, not to join, but Pegwys had accept the Pipe of peace with the Chiefs, so he was bound to follow, but promised he would only go about fifty miles south of Pembina—which is now called Dakota. When Chief's Flagg made its appearance the very place ringed with the shouts of hundreds of Indians, during their stay at Pembina for the rest of their party, the days were employed in feasting and dancing and all night at their conjurations two weeks was spent in this way. Black Duck assured the Indians that the warfare about to take place would result to the favour of the Saulteauxs & destruction to Dakotas or the Sioux tribes.

A number of women & children who had followed so far was to remained at Pembina about one hundred women with their children hundreds of wives with the children had been left at different parts from whence the warriors came. Three or four men were left behind to watch over the children & their mothers.

The warriors moved out a large body of Indians they kept together in one body. The first camp, the General Black Duck made his prophecies by telling the Indians that at a place called gods Lake. the enemy had made their camp there and that the whole camp was given to him by the gods—very few of his band would fall, and that the whole plains was one flame of fire, nothing escaped the fire. The second evening the night was employed to ask the conjurers how the warfare would end, success, success, was the reply by many. Chief Pegwys told the conjurers that he did not see the enemies' camps in his conjurations nothing whatever. The third day they came to the gods Lake, no sign of the Sioux to have visited the place. Black Duck was greatly put out at the non fulfillment of his prophecy.

Chief Pegwys saw that the old Black Duck was labouring under a false delusion, and would assuredly lead many fellow Indians to destruction. On the fourth day old Pegwys assembled all the Chiefs and Captains. He told them he wanted to tell them, that did not intend breaking his word or the promise he made to the Officers of the Hudsons Bay Company and to the Minister at St. John's, now Winnipeg, but would return from the gods Lake. The rest of the Chiefs, that it was cowardice that made him return, but Pegwys never broke his word he was most conspicuous for this. Pegwys ordered his Band to return. The young fellows was sorry they wanted to see the fun.

The following evening Black Duck's followers discovered a camp of the Siouxs to the number of 300 lodges an attack was to be made on fifth day. The warriors examined the situation of the ground and how the camp was laid out. at mid-night they approached the camp and laid wait until at dawn as soon as they could see distinctly an hundred yards the signal was given every man rushed for the tents. in twenty minutes every man women was scalped two young men escaped and ran to a large camp that was near and told the fate of their friends. In less than an hour had passed while they were gathering the spoil. The saw thousand of horse men coming flying like the birds of the air. A young man son of Black. He raised his hands & pointed his weapon to the Sun and he said, 'Sun you told me last night that you would allow me to accompany you to mid-day.' 'Comrades, now is the day that you have longed stand firm, led world know that you are the Ojebways that never turned your backs from the enemy.'

The Ojebways took their position into square The Sioux tried to break their rank, but it was impossible. The Ojebway pouring in volley after volley among the Sioux and shooting them down by hundreds every shot. The young man the Black Duck's son got of the ranks with three companions. Those four made lively times among the Sioux. They felled every man that came in their way and they kept near together. The young warrior calling out—'Sun stay a little' and the Siouxs sometimes rushing for him and at times fleeing by hundreds before him. while thousands of Siouxs was adding every minute and still thousand of the Sioux rushing to the war. at the very commencement of the second attack, Black Duck was disabled by a bullet that fell on his knee and broke his leg. but he still fought of his knee, He was a splendid shot. he shot down more twenty Sioux. he called for his son at times, he was told four of them where playing a beautiful game with the Siouxs. about eleven o'clock Black Duck fell over a stray bullet fell on his head. The Ojebways was furious. They swore by the god of the Sun and the god of Thunder, they would avenge the death of their leader and lay their bones besides Black Duck. The young man heard Black Duck's son that his father had fallen. He said, Thanks to the gods that the father shall not weep for the son, nor the son for the father. I will join to you.' He spoke as if speaking to his father. The Ojebways looking at the sun Young Duck would fall there was twenty Indians at him constantly, but he brought down so many every minute at last he fought with the butt of his gun breaking the skulls of Sioux, shouting, 'Hurrah Ojebways play the men. The rest of the Ojebways scattered among the Siouxs fighting hand to hand but the Ojebways killing them. At 12 o'clock the Young Duck fell the whole battle ground was filled with shouts by the Sioux the other three men an hour after. The Siouxs continued pouring in to the battle but the Ojibways had no reservation to fall upon. but they did not care. it is the glory of the Indian to die in the battle field. Towards evening the Oiebways rank was dwindling down a small body, but they still shouted, the battle raging as fierce as ever. Gunpowder was exhausted the Ojebways fought with the butt end of their guns—the Siouxs with their bows—the weight of a bow is light, but a blow from a gun is no joke, the Siouxs skulls felt the weight of the gun, in that way the Ojebway maintained their ground obstinately.

Before sun-down six Ojebways and one woman made up their minds to escape from the battle field. The Siouxs determined not to allow one Ojebway to get away, but these six men and one woman declared publickly that they would have their power to escape. These seven persons broke through a large body of the Siouxs while hundred arrows was flying after them, and horse-men with their spears. No, the men fought and now began to load their guns & shooting at the enemy by that means—they kept off the Siouxs when night came upon them the Ojebways got off and one woman. The Sioux Indians told their people, that the six men and the woman could run opposite any horse in the plains. Out of that multitude of Ojebways only six men and one woman escaped to relate the destruction of that tribe.

On the latter part of August we heard voices above the river, we thought some people were singing but it was the cries of the widows and orphans who had waited for their people at Pembina. They related that only one man had come to relate the state account of Black Duck and his warriors. the others who had made their escape had gone respectively their hunting lands where their friends would remain. It was most distressing scene to see so many widows and orphans and not able to give them help, except something to eat.

One could hear cries through the settlement for many families were con-nected with the Ojebways by marriage. Pegwys made a great lamentation for his tribe. Mechat kee-yew-up was extremely sorry that he had not been invited. Pegwys knew the mistake it had been made when the Crees were excluded. but it showed afterwards to the Saulteauxs that the Cree was able to cope with any tribe in the land. A decree then went forth that a Battle was prohibited that is on such large number without the consent of the White man unless another tribe invades another to take his land from him. This battle was fought in the summer 1824—the largest Indian war in my day. If the Ojibways had invited the Half-breeds, they would have prevail against them. But our missionary the Rev Mr Jones would never have given consent to it.

—*April 1891*

Charles Pratt
Cree-Assiniboine · 1816–1888

Charles Pratt, or Askenootow (Worker of the Earth), was a *nehiyaw-pwat*—Cree-Assiniboine, or Cree-Nakoda—born in 1816 in the Qu'Appelle Valley. At six years old, he was sent to the Church Missionary Society (CMS) in Red River, where he received a formal education. Pratt left the mission school in 1830 and joined the Hudson's Bay Company as a boatman in the Swan River District. In 1848 he returned to the CMS and worked as a catechist for the next thirty-three years throughout the lands of present-day Saskatchewan. He established five missions and served as an interpreter for Treaty Four negotiations in 1874. In 1884, Pratt suffered a stroke and remained bedridden in his home on the George Gordon First Nation until his death in 1888.

The selection below is from his mission journals, written between 1851 and 1884, which contain hundreds of pages of unpublished materials. They are mostly of the genre of missionary literature, or, more specifically, Indigenous missionary literature.

CMS catechist meets Cha-wa-cis, Saulteaux Medicine Man, Fort Pelly, July 1851

12th Tuesday morning. Getting home our house wood. At even[ing] Indians from the plain arrived here—a principal man, by named Cha-wa-cis, with a few Indians with him, but no sermon they came, they received rum from the master of the fort & made them all drunk all night both men and women. The said old man came to my tent at night encompanied by his young man with his great conjuring articles in his hand, quite displeased with me forbided me to build home. He told me the following words—"Who told you to come here. I never told you to come & build on my lands, go back go back, from whence you came, & do not pressure further to build, & if you still build you shall find the dread of me so long as I here. you shall not be safe go back & build on you own land." I told him, "there was but little wood on my land to build but if you wish me to build on my own country I shall build in the middle of your territories." he sat studying a while & then asked me "do you pray." I replied "yes my friend I do pray to the almighty God our heavenly father who made heaven & earth & all things that are there." He answered with a high tone "I dont pray. God tells me all the praying go to the devil & as for me & my children we will not pray." I told him "let me speak my turn, my friend. The God that told you to hate prayer, is the devil, who even how means to destroy men souls to everlasting fire. & now I will tell you god tells me, who is the God of gods & a Lord of Lords— who created the heaven & the earth by his words & in whose hands Our life & breath depends. God tells me that you & me & every body must pray to him through his son Jesus Christ with all our hearts" I told him further. "The Great God said that the wickt'd shall be turned to hell with all the nations that forget God! Think around my friend, how much all our country-men are passing their lives living without God & without hope in the world." He still…threatened me closely, when an indian came in & siezed him by the right arm & led him out. I scarce had my sleep this night for he came a second time & began to me again, but some other indian came in & led him out, so he did not come again.

13th Wednesday morning, I paid a visit to the old man, with a piece of tobacco, & had a long discourse with them, he seemed very sorry for what he had said to me last night, not knowing that I was one of his country-men, at even[ing] he came with another indian to my tent, after supper ended I took the Great Bible, the Old & New Testaments, the present I received from Mr. Coleman, holding the two volumes in my hand I told them to look at these great books of wisdom & knowledge in thence their lies the unreachable riches of Christ the Everlasting father offered to all man-kind of every tribe through the whole world around. they made deep sighs. I told them "I Suppose you wonder to see such books you have seen the outside of them & now I will tell you something of the inside." I began to read the 1st Chap of Gen[esis] Telling them In the beginning God created all things in heaven & in earth. by the wand of his almighty power in six days & all very good. & on the seventh day to be keept holy unto God through-out all generations telling them how God had formed man out of the dust of the ground & breathing into his nostrils the breath of life & man became a living soul. I told them repeating the prophets & good men of old spoke as they moved by the holy ghost fore telling of things to come, & for all this people still went on sinning the sting of death prevailing amongst mankind till they filled the measure of the unequity. God could not bear longer with their sort a great flood of waters up on the face of the earth to destroy them. save one good man [h]is wife & three sons & daughter in law these that were righteous & obeyed God commands were saved & of clean beast by seven, of unclean beasts by two kept alive in the ark remained their, till God removed the waters from the face of the earth, & so these came forth of the ark with all their creatures. from these three sons of Noah. Shem. Ham. & Japheth, was the ... of the nation to their present time. I showed them of the distinguishing characteristics of the three sons of Noah, The one of them was a man & his descendents after him, the second did not think so much of God or his souls as much as making instruments of music. *The third son thought less of God & of his soul wandered from God land & was left to himself & was lost to the present time & we are his offspring I here we are still lost. Thanks be to God for his unspeakable gift. Who has found out away to redeem us back into himself, through the offering up of his son to die for us that he might deliver us from the curse of the law* [emphasis added]. The wrath of God that was upon us, Jesus Christ hath taken away upon himself by his dying for us. but he did not die long death could not confine him in his grave nolonger than a part of three days & three nights, he burst the tomb layed his grave-clothes aside & rose from the dead like a triumphant conquerer. He was of a great people after his resurrection, Instruction to his people telling them "Go ye therefore & teach all nations baptizing them in the name of the father & of the son & of the holy ghost, teaching them to observe all things whatever I have command you, & lo I am with you always even unto the end of the world. Amen." Then he ascended up into heaven where he was before, he now this present moment he siteth on the right hand of God—making continuall intercession for us. He is ever holding out his hands unto us telling us to come unto him that we might have life. O let us not delay or neglect his offers of mercy we are the people for whom he came to seek & to save, we cannot get to God without him, for his word says NO man can come to the father but by me. Even if we come to God it must be through his son no other way. For there is no other name under heaven given amongst men whereby we can be saved but through Jesus Christ, he is the way the truth & the life. We must served God in spirit & truth for such he seeketh to be worshipped, O let us then with one heart & voice cry mightly [sic] unto God that [we] may obtain mercy & find grace to help in time of need. I proceeded further that all that are in the graves shall rise again at the last day to appear before this Great God, that we have so long neglected & will everyone according as is work have has ... those that have obeyed God laws to the ressurection of life. & those that have done evil & disobeyed the commands of the most high shall be thrust out from the presence of God & from his holy angels. To dwell with the devil & all bad spirits. Were the soul dieth not & the fire shall never be quenched. My dear friends do not let these words sound in your ears as an idle tale, they are the words of the everlasting God, who continually watches over people what heed they to his word you must understand that God gave his word to us as well as to the whiteman. otherwise we should have never it. Thanks be to God we now hear it. we indeed ought to be truly thankful seeing & hearing the things that Kings prophets, & wise men of old have denied to see the things that we see & have not seen them & hearing things, that we hear & have not heard Them. We then see that God has mercy upon us. O let us not cast his word behind our back to trample under foot what the good men of old have wished for. They saw it but afar off & counted themselves pilgrims & strangers in the earth. If we do not take heed to the word of the living God, it will ... unto us Instead of a blessing.

14th Thursday. At our usual occupation. the plains Indians their returning back to the plains the old man went off quite pleased. he told me to build on & try to get the house up. Do not be afraid there will be no danger.

—July 1851

kā-kišīwē (Loud Voice)
Plains Cree · c. 1796–1884 · Qu'Appelle River Cree

kā-kišīwē, or Loud Voice, was a longstanding chief of the Qu'Appelle River Cree, respected as a medicine man and brave warrior. During the negotiations for Treaty 4, Chief *kā-kišīwē* was the recognized leader of the Cree people, although he chose to let *atakawinin*, or The Gambler, speak for the most part, specifically to address the grievances the Cree had with the Hudson's Bay Company (HBC) and the transfer of land between the HBC and the Canadian Government, without consulting the Cree. The first quote below addresses these issues, while the second quote is historically significant, as it expresses *kā-kišīwē*'s assent (although clearly dissatisfied with the terms) to join together and make treaty. When *kā-kišīwē* died in 1884, he was succeeded by his son, *ochapowace*, whose name was given to his reserve.

Speeches at Treaty Four (Morris)

I do not wish to tell a lie. I cannot say who will speak for us; it will only be known after consultation.

—September 8, 1874. Qu'Appelle Lakes

If I could speak, if I could manage to utter my feelings there is reason why I should answer you back; but there is something in my way, and that is all I can tell you. This man (the Gambler) will tell you.

—September 12, 1874. Qu'Appelle Lakes

I would not be at a loss, but I am, because we are not united—the Crees and the Saulteaux—this is troubling me. I am trying to bring all together in one mind, and this is delaying us. If we could put that in order, if we were all joined together and everything was right I would like it. I would like to part well satisified and pleased. I hear that His Excellency is unwell, and I wish that everything would be easy in his mind. It is this that annoys me, that things do not come together. I wish for one day more, and after that there would not be much in my way.

—September 14, 1874. Qu'Appelle Lakes

I am very much pleased with that, to listen to my friends, for certainly it is good to report to each other what is for the benefit of each other. We see the good you wish to show us. If you like what we lay before you we will like it too. Let us join together and make the Treaty; when both join together it is very good.

—September 15, 1874. Qu'Appelle Lakes

atakawinin (The Gambler)
Saulteaux · c. 1842–1916

---

atakawinin, or The Gambler, was a Saulteaux headman for Chief *waywayseecappo*. During Treaty 4 negotiations, he spoke by far the most of all the chiefs, as both Chief *kā-kišīwē*, who represented the Cree, and Chief Cote, who represented the Saulteaux, deferred to *atakawinin* to speak for them, specifically to address the grievances they had with the Hudson's Bay Company (HBC). Essentially, *atakawinin* explains that they cannot start treaty negotiations until the Crown acknowledges the problem "in the way"—namely that the HBC had sold their land to the Crown. *atakawinin* was not asking that the HBC leave—indeed he wished for them to remain at their posts. Rather, he was trying to reach clarity on the point that the land was not the HBC's to sell to the Crown. Lieutenant-Governor Morris failed to fully understand *atakawinin*'s grievance, which led to a contentious atmosphere during the treaty negotiations. The quotes below include primarily *atakawinin*'s words: in the original treaty text, Morris responds to each of *atakawinin*'s points, explaining that the Crown "had nothing to do with the Company," much to *atakawinin*'s incredulity. *atakawinin* did not sign the Treaty at Qu'Appelle, though his chief, *waywayseecappo*, signed the adherence at Fort Ellice the following week.

Speeches at Treaty Four (Morris)

This morning I saw the chief of the soldiers, who asked me what is in your way that you cannot come and meet the Queen's messengers; then I told him what was in the way. And now that I am come in, what do I see? You were rather slow in giving your hand. You said that the Queen spoke through you and spoke very plainly, but I cannot speak about what you said at present; the thing that is in the way that is what I am working at.

[...]

I told the soldier master you did not set your camp in order, you came and staid beyond over there, that is the reason I did not run in over there. Now when you have come here, you see sitting out there a mixture of Half-breeds, Crees, Saulteaux and Stonies, all are one, and you were slow in taking the hand of a Half-breed. All these things are many things that are in my way. I cannot speak about them.

[...]

I have understood plainly before what he (the Hudson Bay Company) told me about the Queen. This country that he (H. B. Co.) bought from the Indians let him complete that. It is that which is in the way. I cannot manage to speak upon anything else, when the land was staked off it was all the Company's work. That is the reason I cannot speak of other things.

[...]

It is very plain who speaks; the Crees are not speaking, and the Saulteaux is speaking, if the Queen's men came here to survey the land. I am telling you plainly. I cannot speak any other thing till this is cleared up. Look at these children that are sitting around here and also at the tents, who are just the image of my kindness. There are different kinds of grass growing here that is just like those sitting around here. There is no difference. Even from the American land they are here, but we love them all the same, and when the white skin comes here from far away I love him all the same. I am telling you what our love and kindness is. This is what I did when the white man came, but when he came back he paid no regard to me how he carried on.

[...]

The Company have stolen our land. I heard that at first. I hear it is true. The Queen's messengers never came here, and now I see the soldiers and the settlers and the policemen. I know it is not the Queen's work, only the Company has come and they are the head, they are the foremost; I do not hold it back. Let this be put to rights; when this is righted I will answer the other.

[...]

When one Indian takes anything from another we call it stealing, and when we see the present we say pay us. It is the Company I mean.

[Lieut.-Gov. Morris—"What did the Company steal from you?"]

The earth, trees, grass, stones, all that which I see with my eyes.

—*September 12, 1874. Qu'Appelle Lakes*

kamooses
Plains Cree · 18??–??

Chief *kamooses* tried to improve the terms of the Treaty during negotiations. The second selection is haunting in terms of the outcome of Canadian history and the residential schools system. The third selection is significant, as it shows that the Treaty chiefs were concerned about the rights of the Métis peoples.

Speeches at Treaty Four (Morris)

Is is true you are bringing the Queen's kindness? Is it true you are bringing the Queen's messenger's kindness? Is it true you are going to give my child what he may use? Is it true you are going to give the different bands the Queen's kindness? Is it true that you bring the Queen's hand? Is it true you are bringing the Queen's power?

[...]

Is it true that my child will not be troubled for what you are bringing him?

[...]

Yes, we want each Chief to have a copy of the treaty, we ask that the Half-breeds may have the right of hunting.

—*September 15, 1874. Qu'Appelle Lakes*

mistawāsis (Big Child)
Plains Cree · c. 1813–c. 1903

mistawāsis, or Big Child, was born around 1813. His father was Métis and his mother was Cree. He was a leader of the House People, referring to the groups of Plains Cree living near Fort Carlton, where he often worked with the Hudson's Bay Company.

mistawāsis was one of the two main chiefs, with *atāhkakohp*, who supported the Treaty Six negotiations at Fort Carlton, and he was the first chief to sign the treaty. He settled his people on a reserve at Snake Plains, near present-day Prince Albert. Later, when treaty promises failed to be fulfilled, he took part in the Council at Duck Lake in August of 1884, which included twelve prominent chiefs who drew together a petition of grievances of the treaties.

The two speeches below were recorded at the Treaty Six negotiations at Fort Carlton. The first was recorded by A.G. Jackes, for Morris's official government publication. The second was recorded by Peter Erasmus, and accounts for events not included in the Morris version.

Speech at Treaty Six (Morris)

It is well known that if we had plenty to live on from our gardens we would not still insist on getting more provision, but it is in case of any extremity, and from the ignorance of the Indian in commencing to settle that we thus speak; we are as yet in the dark; this is not a trivial matter for us.

We were glad to hear what the Governor was saying to us and we understood it, but we are not understood, we do not mean to ask for food for every day but only when we commence and in case of famine or calamity. What we speak of and do now will last as long as the sun shines and the river runs, we are looking forward to our children's children, for we are old and have but few days to live.

—*August 22, 1876. Fort Carlton*

Speech at Treaty Six (Erasmus)

I have heard my brothers speak, complaining of the hardships endured by our people. Some have bewailed the poverty and suffering that has come to Indians because of the destruction of the buffalo as the chief source of our living, the loss of the ancient glory of our forefathers; and with all that I agree, in the silence of my teepee and on the broad prairies where once our fathers could not pass for the great number of those animals that blocked their way; and even in our day, we have had to choose carefully our campground for fear of being trampled in our teepees. With all these things, I think and feel intensely the sorrow my brothers express.

I speak directly to Poundmaker and The Badger and those others who object to signing this treaty. Have you anything better to offer our people? I ask, again, can you suggest anything that will bring these things back for tomorrow and all the tomorrows that face our people?

I for one think that the Great White Queen Mother has offered us a way of life when the buffalo are no more. Gone they will be before many snows have come to cover our heads or graves if such should be. (There were loud groans and exclamations of despair at the latter statement from many places among the group. Mista-wa-sis continued after waiting for the murmur to die down.)

I speak the tongue of the Blackfoot. I have been in their lodges. I have seen with my eyes and listened with my ears to the sorrows of that once-proud nation; people whom we have known as our enemies, the Peigan and the Bloods who are their brothers. Pay attention, listen hard to what I am about to say. The Big Knives of the south came into Blackfoot territory as traders; though few in number they have conquered these nations, and that, all the Crees in the days of our fathers and their fathers before them failed to do. How did they do it? Listen closely, my brothers, and you will understand. What was done to them can be done to us if we throw away the hand that is extended to us by this treaty.

These traders, who were not of our land, with smooth talk and cheap goods persuaded the southern tribes it would be a good thing to have a place to trade products of the hunt, the hides and tanned goods. The traders came and built strong forts, and with their long rifles that can kill at twice the distance of our own and the short guns that can spout death six times quicker than you can tell about it, they had the people at their mercy. The Blackfoot soon found out the traders had nothing but whisky to exchange for their skins. Oh, yes! They were generous at first with their rotten whisky, but not for long. The traders demanded pay and got Blackfoot horses, buffalo robes, and all other things they had to offer.

Those traders laughed at them for fools, and so they were, to sell their heritage for ruin and debauchery. Some of the bravest of the Blackfoot tried to get revenge for the losses but they were shot down like dogs and dragged to the open plains on horses to rot or be eaten by wolves.

The Great Queen Mother, hearing of the sorrows of her children, sent out the Red Coats. Though these were only of a number you could count on your fingers and toes, yet the cutthroats and criminals who recognized no authority but their guns, who killed each other on the slightest pretence and murdered Indians without fear of reprisal, immediately abandoned their forts, strong as they were, and fled back to their own side of the line. I ask you why those few men could put to flight those bad men who for years have defied the whole of the southern Indian nations?

Surely these Red Coats are men of flesh and blood as ourselves and a bullet is just as effective on them as on any Blackfoot. Why of course, they are of flesh and blood. They could be killed as easily as any Blackfoot, but ask yourselves why the traders fled in fear from so few men. The southern tribes outnumbered this small Police Force one hundred to one, but they were helpless in spite of their numbers.

Let me tell you why these things were so. It was the power that stands behind those few Red Coats that those men feared and wasted no time in getting out when they could; the power that is represented in all the Queen's people, and we the children are counted as important as even the Governor who is her personal speaker.

The Police are the Queen Mother's agents and have the same laws for whites as they have for the Indians. I have seen these things done and now the Blackfoot welcome these servants of the Queen Mother and invite her Governor for a treaty with them next year.

I, for one, look to the Queen's law and her Red Coat servants to protect our people against the evils of white man's firewater and to stop the senseless wars among our people, against the Blackfoot, Peigans, and Bloods. We have been in darkness; the Blackfoot and the others are people as we are. They will starve as we will starve when the buffalo are gone. We will be brothers in misery when we could have been brothers in plenty in times when there was no need for any man, woman, or child to be hungry.

We speak of glory and our memories are all that is left to feed the widows and orphans of those who have died in its attainment. We are few in numbers compared to former times, by wars and the terrible ravages of smallpox. Our people have vanished too. Even if it were possible to gather all the tribes together, to throw away the hand that is offered to help us, we would be too weak to make our demands heard.

Look to the great Indian nations in the Long Knives' country who have been fighting since the memory of their oldest men. They are being vanquished and swept into the most useless parts of their country. Their days are numbered like those of the buffalo. There is no law or justice for the Indians in Long Knives' country. The Police followed two murderers to Montana and caught them but when they were brought to the Montana court they were turned free because it was not murder to kill an Indian.

The prairies have not been darkened by the blood of our white brothers in our time. Let this always be so. I for one will take the hand that is offered. For my band I have spoken.

—*August 22, 1876. Fort Carlton*

atāhkakohp (Star Blanket)
Plains Cree · c. 1816–1896

atāhkakohp, or Star Blanket, was born around 1816 near the Saskatchewan River. Along with his cousin mistawāsis, he was a leader among the House People and traded with the Hudson's Bay Company. He was the second chief to sign Treaty Six in 1876, after mistawāsis, and settled his people at Sandy Lake, northwest of present-day Prince Albert. During the 1885 Resistance, atāhkakohp remained neutral, to maintain treaty relations with the government. atāhkakohp died December 4, 1896, and was buried on his reserve.

The three speeches below were recorded at the Treaty Six negotiations at Fort Carlton. The first two were recorded by A.G. Jackes for Morris, and the third speech was recorded by Peter Erasmus.

Speeches at Treaty Six (Morris)

The things we have been talking about in our councils I believe are for our good. I think of the good Councillors of the Queen and of her Commissioners; I was told the Governor was a good man, and now that I see him I believe he is; in coming to see us, and what he has spoken, he has removed almost all obstacles and misunderstandings, and I hope he may remove them all. I have heard the good things you promise us, you have told us of the white man's way of living and mentioned some of the animals by which he gets his living, others you did not. We want food in the spring when we commence to farm; according as the Indian settles down on his reserves, and in proportion as he advances, his wants will increase.

—*August 22, 1876. Fort Carlton*

I never sent a letter to the Governor; I was waiting to meet him and what we have asked we considered would be for the benefit of our children. I am not like some of my friends who have sent their messages down, even stretched out their hands to the Queen asking her to come; I have always said to my people that I would wait to see the Governor arrive, then he would ask what would benefit his children; now I ask my people, those that are in favour of the offer, to say so. (They all assented by holding up their hands and shouting.)

—*August 23, 1876. Fort Carlton*

Speech at Treaty Six (Erasmus)

Yes, I have carried the dripping scalps of the Blackfoot on my belt and thought it was a great deed of bravery. I thought it was part of the glory of war but I now agree with Mista-wa-sis. *[Raising his voice with conviction:]* It is no longer a good thing. If we had been friends we might now be a host of people of all nations and together have power to demand the things some of you foolishly think you can get and insist on now demanding.

No, that is not the road we took, but killed each other in continuous wars and in horse stealing, all for the glory we all speak of so freely. The great sickness took half our lodges and the dreaded disease fell as heavily on our enemies. We are weak and my brother Mista-wa-sis I think is right that the buffalo will be gone forever before many snows. What then will be left us with which to bargain? With the buffalo gone we will have only the vacant prairie which none of us have learned to use.

Can we stop the power of the white man from spreading over the land like the grasshoppers that cloud the sky and then fall to consume every blade of grass and every leaf on the trees in their path? I think not. Before this happens let us ponder carefully our choice of roads.

There are men among you who are trying to blind our eyes, and refuse to see the things that have brought us to this pass. Let us not think of ourselves but of our children's children. We hold our place among the tribes as chiefs and councillors because our people think we have wisdom above others amongst us. Then let us show our wisdom. Let us show our wisdom by choosing the right path now while we yet have a choice.

We have always lived and received our needs in clothing, shelter, and food from the countless multitudes of buffalo that have been with us since the earliest memory of our people. No one with open eyes and open minds can doubt that the buffalo will soon be a thing of the past. Will our people live as before when this comes to pass? No! They will die and become just a memory unless we find another way.

For my part, I think that the Queen Mother has offered us a new way and I have faith in the things my brother Mista-wa-sis has told you. The mother earth has always given us plenty with the grass that fed the buffalo. Surely we Indians can learn the ways of living that made the white man strong and able to vanquish all the great tribes of the southern nations. The white men never had the buffalo but I am told they have cattle in the thousands that are covering the prairie for miles and will replace the buffalo in the Long Knives' country and may even spread over our lands. The white men number their lodges by the thousands, not like us who can only count our teepees by tens. I will accept the Queen's hand for my people. I have spoken.

—*August 22, 1876. Fort Carlton*

payipwāt
Plains Cree (Sioux) · c. 1816–1908

payipwāt, or Payepot or Piapot, was born around 1816 near the southern border of present-day Saskatchewan. He was originally named *kisikawawasan*, or Flash in the Sky. As a child, he was taken captive by a Sioux war party, and lived among the Dakota. Around 1830, he was reunited with his people when a Cree war party found him, and he returned to the area around the Qu'Appelle River. He later acquired the nickname *payipwāt*, which means "A Hole in the Sioux." "Payepot" or "Piapot," the names by which he is most widely known, are spelling variants of *payipwāt*.

payipwāt initially refused to sign Treaty, but eventually settled his people in the Qu'Appelle Valley near the Fishing Lakes in 1884. He was pivotal in maintaining the continuity of Cree traditions under the prohibitions of ceremony in the Indian Act. Throughout his life, he continued to hold ceremonies and was arrested twice for practicing "Indian worship," once in 1895 and again in 1901. When the government removed *payipwāt* as chief, his people refused in protest to elect another chief until after his death in 1908. The selections here reflect his high wit in defending the Rain Dance and Cree traditions.

To the Superior-General of the Oblate Order

In order to become sole masters of our land they relegated us to small reservations as big as my hand and make us long promises, as long as my arm; but the next year the promises were shorter and got shorter every year until now they are the length of my finger, and they keep only half of that.

—*1895. Lebret*

Defending the Sundance to Indian Commissioner A.E. Forget

Very well, I will agree not to pray to my God in my way, if you will promise not to pray to your God … in your way.

Getchie Ogimow (the commissioner) arises in the morning. He has various dishes placed before him. He takes an iron implement and conveys something from a dish to his mouth, and if he doesn't like it, he takes the contents of another dish. He does not know what it means to be hungry. The poor Indians often know what it is to have an empty belly, and they just tighten their belts and pray to Getchie Manitou (the Good Spirit) to give them food. Their way of praying is to make a Sun Dance. That is all I have to say.

—*1895. Regina Jail*

Response to Father Hugonard's Offer of Baptism

Oh! No … I am only going to accept half of your religion. I will belong half to the Christian Religion and half to the Indian, because you may turn out to be wrong after all, and the Indian Religion might happen to be right and then I would have nothing to fall back upon.

—c. 1905

wīhkasko-kisēyin (Sweet Grass)
Plains Cree · 18??–1877

wīhkasko-kisēyin, or Sweet Grass, was born in a Cree camp sometime in the early 1800s. His mother was a Crow woman who had been captured by the Cree. He was given the name wīhkasko-kisēyin later in life, after giving an elder his horse and a Blackfoot scalp that was stuffed with sweet grass. wīhkasko-kisēyin became chief in 1870. He died in 1877, when he was accidentally shot by his brother-in-law, who was handling the revolver that wīhkasko-kisēyin had received as a gift from Commissioner Morris at the Treaty Six negotiations.

A precursor to the Treaty Six negotiations, the first selection below is a petition sent to Fort Garry in 1871. After learning that the Hudson's Bay Company territories had been sold, and concerned about the Canadian government's treatment of the land, wīhkasko-kisēyin led a group of Cree chiefs to Fort Edmonton to send their petition through W. J. Christie, the Chief Factor of the Saskatchewan District. In his letter to Governor Archibald, Christie emphasized that dismissing the chiefs' demands could lead to "acts of violence" and "the beginning of an Indian war." Including the chiefs' petition, Christie urged the "establishment of law and order" and "the making of some treaty or settlement with the Indians who inhabit the Saskatchewan District." wīhkasko-kisēyin maintained his support of treaty, and the second selection is from Jackes' record of the Treaty Six negotiations.

Messages from the Cree Chiefs of the Plains, Saskatchewan, to His Excellency Governor Archibald, our Great Mother's representative at Fort Garry, Red River Settlement

1. The Chief Sweet Grass, The Chief of the country.
GREAT FATHER,—I shake hands with you, and bid you welcome. We heard our lands were sold and we did not like it; we don't want to sell our lands; it is our property, and no one has a right to sell them.

Our country is getting ruined of fur-bearing animals, hitherto our sole support, and now we are poor and want help—we want you to pity us. We want cattle, tools, agricultural implements, and assistance in everything when we come to settle—our country is no longer able to support us.

Make provision for us against years of starvation. We have had great starvation the past winter, and the small-pox took away many of our people, the old, young, and children.

We want you to stop the Americans from coming to trade on our lands, and giving firewater, ammunition and arms to our enemies the Blackfeet.

We made a peace this winter with the Blackfeet. Our young men are foolish, it may not last long.

We invite you to come and see us and to speak with us. If you can't come yourself, send some one in your place.

We send these words by our Master, Mr. Christie, in whom we have every confidence.—That is all.

2. Ki-he-win, The Eagle.

GREAT FATHER,—Let us be friendly. We never shed any white man's blood, and have always been friendly with the whites, and want workmen, carpenters and farmers to assist us when we settle. I want all my brother, Sweet Grass, asks. That is all.

3. The Little Hunter.

You, my brother, the Great Chief in Red River, treat me as a brother, that is, as a Great Chief.

4. Kis-ki-on, or Short Tail.

My brother, that is coming close, I look upon you, as if I saw you; I want you to pity me, and I want help to cultivate the ground for myself and descendants. Come and see us.

—*April 13, 1871. Edmonton House*

Speech at Treaty Six (Morris)

I thank you for this day, and also I thank you for what I have seen and heard, I also thank the Queen for sending you to act for our good. I am glad to have a brother and friend in you, which undoubtedly will raise us above our present condition. I am glad for your offers, and thank you from my heart. I speak this in the presence of the Divine Being. It is all for our good, I see nothing to be afraid of, I therefore accept of it gladly and take your hand to my heart, may this continue as long as this earth stands and the river flows. The Great King, our Father, is now looking upon us this day, He regards all the people equal with one another; He has mercy on the whole earth; He has opened a new world to us. I have pity on all those who have to live by the buffalo. If I am spared until this time next year I want this my brother to commence to act for me, thinking thereby that the buffalo may be protected. It is for that reason I give you my hand. If spared, I shall commence at once to clear a small piece of land for myself, and others of my kinsmen will do the same. We will commence hand in hand to protect the buffalo. When I hold your hand I feel as if the Great Father were looking on us both as brothers. I am thankful. May this earth here never see the white man's blood spilt on it. I thank God that we stand together, that you all see us; I am thankful that I can raise up my head, and the white man and red man can stand together as long as the sun shines. When I hold your hands and touch your heart, as I do now (suiting his action to the words), let us be as one. Use your utmost to help me and help my children, so that they may prosper. (The Chief's remarks were assented to by the Indians by loud ejaculations.)

—*September 9, 1876. Fort Pitt*

mistahi-maskwa (Big Bear)
Plains Cree · c. 1825–1888

mistahi-maskwa, or Big Bear, was born in 1825 on the shores of Jackfish Lake near the North Saskatchewan River. His father was Black Powder, chief of a mixed band of Cree and Ojibwa. His mother was Cree or Ojibwa.

mistahi-maskwa arrived at the Treaty Six negotiations in Fort Pitt as they were closing. He is notable as the first major chief not to sign the treaty, calling for more protections of the buffalo and traditional way of life. He was the last chief to accept Treaty Six, signing an adhesion in 1882. However, the government did not grant his choice of reserve. He played a minimal role in the North-West Resistance, though his main concern was always for a better treaty. In 1885, his band was involved in the Frog Lake Massacre, and although he was not present and many attested to his innocence, he was charged and convicted of treason-felony and sentenced to three years in Stony Mountain Penitentiary. Released after two years and ailing in health, he died on the Poundmaker Reserve on January 17, 1888. As he never acquired a reserve, his band remained scattered on other reserves.

To Rev. George McDougall

We want none of the Queen's presents! When we set a fox trap we scatter pieces of meat all around but when the fox gets into the trap we knock him on the head. We want no baits! Let your Chiefs come like men and talk to us.

—*1875. Cree Territory*

Speeches at Treaty Six (Morris)

After the signing ceremony of Treaty Six at Fort Pitt
I find it difficult to express myself, because some of the bands are not represented. I have come off to speak for the different bands that are out on the plains. It is

no small matter we were to consult about. I expected the Chiefs here would
have waited until I arrived. The different bands that are out on the plains told
me that I should speak in their stead; the Stony Indians as well. The people
who have not come, stand as a barrier before what I would have had to say; my
mode of living is hard.

Stop, stop, my friends, I have never seen the Governor before; I have seen
Mr. Christie many times. I heard the Governor was to come and I said I shall see
him; when I see him I will make a request that he will save me from what I most
dread, that is: the rope to be about my neck (hanging), it was not given to us by
the Great Spirit that the red man or white man should shed each other's blood.

To Governor Morris

What we want is that we should hear what will make our hearts glad, and all
good peoples' hearts glad. There were plenty things left undone, and it does
not look well to leave them so.

Parting Words to Commissioner Morris

I am glad to meet you, I am alone; but if I had known the time, I would have
been here with all my people. I am not an undutiful child, I do not throw back
your hand; but as my people are not here, I do not sign. I will tell them what I
have heard, and next year I will come.

—*September 13, 1876. Fort Pitt*

Speech at the Council of Duck Lake

Yes, I am willing to speak. Since the leaves have begun to come it is why I have
been walking, walking, trying to make myself understood. It is why I have
come to Duck Lake. To show you why I have been so anxious, it is because I
have been trying to seize the promises which they made to me, I have been
grasping but I cannot find them. What they have promised me straightway I
have not yet seen the half of it.

We have all been deceived in the same way. It is the cause of our meeting at
Duck Lake. They offered me a spot as a reserve. As I see that they are not going
to be honest I am afraid to take a reserve. They have given me to choose between
several small reserves but I feel sad to abandon the liberty of my own land when
they come to me and offer me small plots to stay there and in return not to get
half of what they have promised me. When will you have a big meeting. It has
come to me as through the bushes that you are not yet all united, take time and
become united, and I will speak. The Government sent to us those who think
themselves men. They bring everything crooked. They take our lands, they sell

them and they buy themselves fine clothes. Then they clap their hands on their hips and call themselves men. They are not men. They have no honesty. They are an unsightly beast. Their faces are twisted from the appearance of honest men.

—*July 31, 1884. Duck Lake*

Letter to Sergeant Martin, N.W.M.P.

My Dear Friend,

Since I have met you long ago we have always been good friends, and you have from time to time given me things, and that is the reason that I want to speak kindly to you; so please try and get off from Pitt as soon as you can. And tell your Captain that I remember him well, for since the Canadian Government had left me to starve in this country, he sometimes gave me food, and I don't forget the blankets he gave me, and that is the reason I want you all to get off without bloodshed.

We had a talk, I and my men, before we left our camp, and we thought the way we are doing now the best—that is, to let you off if you would go. So try and get away before the afternoon, as the young men are wild and hard to keep in hand.   —Big Bear

P.S. you asked me to keep the men in camp last night and I did, so I want you to get off today.   —Big Bear

—*April 15, 1885. Fort Pitt*

Address to the Court

I think I should have something to say about the occurences which brought me here in chains.

I knew little of the killing at Frog Lake beyond hearing the shots fired. When any wrong was brewing I did my best to stop it in the beginning. The turbulent ones of the band got beyond my control and shed the blood of those I would have protected. I was away from Frog Lake a part of the winter, hunting and fishing, and the rebellion had commenced before I got back. When white men were few in the country I gave then the hand of brotherhood. I am sorry so few are here who can witness for my friendly acts.

Can anyone stand out and say that I ordered the death of a priest or an agent? You think I encouraged my people to take part in the trouble. I did not. I advised them against it. I felt sorry when they killed those men at Frog Lake, but the truth is when news of the fight at Duck Lake reached us my band ignored my authority and despised me because I did not side with the halfbreeds. I did not so much as take a white man's horse. I always believed that by being the friend of the white man, I and my people would be helped by those of them who had wealth. I always thought it paid to do all the good I could. Now my heart is on the ground.

I look around me in this room and see it crowded with handsome faces—faces far handsomer than my own. I have ruled my country for a long time. Now I am in chains and will be sent to prison, but I have no doubt the handsome faces I admire about me will be competent to govern the land. At present I am dead to my people. Many of my band are hiding in the woods, paralyzed with terror. Cannot this court send them a pardon? My own children!—perhaps they are starving and outcast, too, afraid to appear in the light of day. If the government does not come to them with help before the winter sets in, my band will surely perish.

But I have too much confidence in the Great Grandmother to fear that starvation will be allowed to overtake my people. The time will come when the Indians of the North-West will be of much service to the Great Grandmother. I plead again, to you, the chiefs of the white men's laws, for pity and help to the outcasts of my band!

I have only a few words more to say. Sometimes in the past I have spoken stiffly to the Indian Agents, but when I did it was only in order to obtain my rights. The NorthWest belonged to me, but I perhaps will not live to see it again, I ask the court to publish my speech and to scatter it among the white people. It is my defence.

I am old and ugly, but I have tried to do good. Pity the children of my tribe! Pity the old and helpless of my people! I speak with a single tongue; and because Big Bear has always been the friend of the white man, send out and pardon and give them help!

How! Aquisanee—I have spoken!

(With no further ado, Richardson sentenced Big Bear to three years in prison for treason-felony.)

—*September 25, 1885. Regina Courthouse*

kā-miyēstawēsit (Beardy)

Willow Cree · c. 1828–1889

kā-miyēstawēsit, or Beardy, was born around 1828 near Duck Lake. He received his name because of his beard, which was uncommon for Cree men at the time. He was said to possess great medicine power, and he became chief of the Willow Cree around 1870. He welcomed the prospect of treaties with the government, but he did not attend the main negotiations, in protest that they weren't held at Duck Lake in accordance with a vision he had received. Commissioner Morris instead held a special meeting with *kā-miyēstawēsit* at Duck Lake on August 28, after negotiations were completed at Fort Carlton. Although he considered the treaty promises to be inadequate, *kā-miyēstawēsit* signed and chose land for himself and Chief *okemasis* west of Duck Lake. The selections here are from this meeting.

After 1876, *kā-miyēstawēsit* continued to call for more protections for the buffalo, and he criticized the government for their poor implementation of the treaties. On August 6, 1884, Beardy convened the Council at Duck Lake, which was attended by twelve prominent chiefs, including Big Bear, Lucky Man, and Poundmaker, as well as *mistawāsis* and *atāhkakohp*; Riel made a brief appearance. This council was the first major event of Indigenous activism in Canada regarding the treaties. However, any momentum gathered at the meeting was soon interrupted by the outbreak of the 1885 Resistance. Although *kā-miyēstawēsit* himself remained neutral during the conflicts, a number of his warriors fought with the Métis, prompting the government to suspend his band from treaty. He died on April 16, 1889, on his home reserve.

Speeches at Treaty Six Special Meeting (Morris)

I feel grateful for this day, and I hope we will be blessed. I am glad that I see something that will be of use; I wish that we all as a people may be benefitted by this. I want that all these things should be preserved in a manner that they might be useful to us all; it is in the power of men to help each other. We should not act foolishly with the things that are given us to live by. I think some things are too little, they will not be sufficient for our wants. I do not want very much more than what has been promised, only a little thing. I will be glad if you will help me by writing my request down; on account of the buffalo I am getting anxious. I wish that each one should have an equal share, if that could be managed; in this I think we would be doing good. Perhaps this is not the only time that we shall see each other. Now I suppose another can say what he wishes.

[...]

Those things which the Almighty has provided for the sustenance of his children may be given us as well; where our Father has placed the truth we wish the same to be carried out here, I do not set up a barrier to any road that my children may live by: I want the payment to exist as long as the sun shines and the river runs: if we exercise all our good, this surely will happen: all of our words upon which we agree, I wish to have a copy written on skin as promised; I want my brother to tell me where I can get this. He has said, 'what I have done with the others I will do with you:' I accept the terms, no doubt it will run further according to our number. When I am utterly unable to help myself I want to receive assistance. I will render all the assistance I can to my brother in taking care of the country. I want from my brother a suit of clothing in color resembling the sky so that he may be able when he sees me to know me; I want these two (sitting by him) to be Chiefs in our place with me and to have six Councillors (two each) in all.

—*August 28, 1876. Camp near Fort Carlton*

wāwikanihk kā-otāmahoht (Strikes Him On The Back)

Cree · 1830–1884 · Sweet Grass

wāwikanihk kā-otāmahoht, or Strikes Him On The Back, was born in 1830. He signed Treaty Six at Fort Carlton in 1876. He became chief of *wīhkasko-kisēyin*'s people after *wīhkasko-kisēyin* (Sweet Grass) was killed, and remained chief until 1883, when he was deposed by Young Sweet Grass. The first selection is from his speeches at the Treaty Six negotiations in Fort Carlton. The second selection is of a speech he gave in May 1882, recorded in the *Saskatchewan Herald*. Likely prompted by the Indian Agent, he encourages his band to become farmers.

Speech at Treaty Six Negotiations

Pity the voice of the Indian, if you grant what we request the sound will echo through the land; open the way; I speak for the children that they may be glad; the land is wide, there is plenty of room. My mouth is full of milk, I am only as a sucking child; I am glad; have compassion on the manner in which I was brought up; let our children be clothed; let us now stand in the light of day to see our way on this earth; long ago it was good when we first were made, I wish the same were back again. But now the law has come, and in that I wish to walk. What God has said, and our mother here (the earth), and these our brethren, let it be so.

—*August 23, 1876. Fort Carlton*

Become Farmers

[Strike-Him-On-The-Back, May of 1882, made a lengthy speech, likely prompted by the Indian Agent, to his band encouraging them to become farmers.]

My people, I have, while paying a visit to the town, learned much about ourselves and what is expected of us at this time. I am now old and cannot do much myself. When I was young I did not expect my old father to do much because I thought it my duty to help him; and it is the duty of you young men, and all that are at all able, to work and support the old and the sick, and the very young.

We cannot look much longer for help from the big Governor.... I am quite sure that the agent will help us; but if we do not work we cannot expect to get help.… We must not think we can gain a good living without work; that time had passed away, and now we must obey our instructor.… I have promised half my obedience to our agent and the other half to our instructor, and I want you all to do the same, and then we will all live well and have plenty.

…The agent and our instructors have done much, but we did not seem to understand them, or our own position. Now I see it. My friends have told me many things for our good, and we must try to do better for ourselves and our children.

—*May 1882*

tatanka iyotake (Sitting Bull)
Lakota · c. 1831–1890

tatanka iyotake, or Sitting Bull, was born around 1831 in Dakota Territory. He was a Hunkpapa Lakota Chief and led the resistance against U.S. army advancement, culminating in the defeat of Lt. Col. George Custer and the 7th Cavalry at the Battle of Little Big Horn in 1876. Months after the battle, *tatanka iyotake* and his group sought protection on the Canadian side of the medicine line, settling at Wood Mountain in the North-West Territories, present-day southwestern Saskatchewan, and remaining there in exile for four years.

The first selections below are from records of *tatanka iyotake*'s first meeting with Major Walsh and Colonel Irvine upon entering Canadian territory. The second selections are taken from Mounted Police records of the famous meeting between *tatanka iyotake*, N.W.M.P. Commissioner Macleod, Major Walsh, and U.S. General Terry, who visited Fort Walsh to deliver a message from the President for *tatanka iyotake* to return to the United States, with full pardon in exchange for full surrender.

tatanka iyotake returned to the U.S. in 1881, under safe custody with General Hammond, and was taken to Fort Buford. In the years following, he toured briefly with Buffalo Bill's Wild West Show, eventually returning to Standing Rock Agency in South Dakota. He died from gunshot in a scuffle during an attempted arrest on December 15, 1890.

Arriving at Wood Mountain

Meeting Major Walsh
Yesterday, I was fleeing from them [the white men] and cursing them as I moved. Today they plant their lodge by the side of mine and defy me. Have I fallen? Is my reign at an end?

To Colonel Irvine
O God, remember this is the land I was brought up on, me and a woman. This is the reason I came back. I was brought up here.… Why do Americans want to drive me? Because they want only Americans here.… I have only two friends—the English and Spaniards.

To the Priest

I don't believe the Americans ever saw God and that is the reason they don't listen to me.... You know, as the messenger of God, that they tried to kill me. Why did you wait until half of my people were killed before you came? ... Do you think it's the will of God to have some of His people under your arms, so you can laugh at them? You are waiting for my people to come to your land so that the Long Knives may rush at them and kill them.... Are you here to ask me if I am going to throw my land away? I never thought of giving my land to the American people.... If I go back to the Americans, are they going to take all my stock away? God raised me on horseback to make my living. Did God tell you to come and make me poor?

What would I return for? To have my horses and arms taken away. Once I was rich, plenty of money, but the Americans stole it all in the Black Hills.

—*June 1877. Wood Mountain*

To the American Commissioners

For 64 years, you have kept and treated my people bad; what have we done that caused us to depart from our country? We could go nowhere, so we have taken refuge here. On this side of the line I first learned to shoot; for that reason I come again; I kept going round and was compelled to leave and come here. I was raised with the Red River Half-breeds, and for that reason I shake hands with these people [Colonel Macleod and Major Walsh]. In this way I was raised. We did not give you our country; you took it from us; see how I live with these people [the Police]; look at these eyes and ears; you think me a fool; but you are a greater fool than I am; this is a Medicine House; you come to tell us stories, and we do not want to hear them; I will not say any more. I shake hands with these people; that part of the country we came from belonged to us, now we live here.

—*October 17, 1877. Fort Walsh*

To Major Walsh

I will remain what I am until I die, a hunter. And when there is no buffalo or other game, I will send my children to hunt prairie mice, for when an Indian is shut up in one place his body becomes weak.

[...]

I want to tell you why I came to see you. It is to contradict a report carried by one of our men, the Black Wolf, to the Americans. I request you to let the Americans know that the man—a rascal—was not sent by this Council to make such a statement.... What I wish to say to the White Mother is that I have but one heart and it is the same today as when I first shook your hand … I went at your request to the White Mother's Fort to meet the Americans [the Terry Commission] but I will never meet them again. I have forbidden my people to use my name to the Americans. I have always said to my people in Council: 'if any of you want to go back, tell me.' None has done so yet. I am looking to the North for my life and I hope the White Mother will never ask me to look to the country I left although it is'mine and not even the dust of it did I sell, but the Americans can have it…. I am never going to leave the White Mother's country.

[…]

I will die a hunter. For many months, you have been advising us to think of getting our living from the ground. Will you tell me where we will get the ground?

[…]

Those who wish to return to the Americans can go, and those who wish to remain here if the White Mother will give them a piece of land, can farm. But I will remain what I am until I die, a hunter.

—*March 20, 1879*

peopeo kiskiok hihih (White Bird)
Nez Percé · 18??–1892

peopeo kiskiok hihih, or White Bird, was a chief of the Lamatta band of the Nez Percé. Under Chief Joseph's leadership, the Nez Percé enjoyed a peaceful existence in the United States until the government ordered their removal from their traditional lands in 1877, events which led to the Nez Percé War. Refusing to surrender, the Nez Percé fled over 1,100 miles from Oregon to Montana, under constant pursuit and attack by the U.S. Army under General Nelson Miles. After a five-day battle in the Bear Paw Mountains, Chief Joseph surrendered to Miles. However, *peopeo kiskiok hihih* escaped to Canada, arriving at Sitting Bull's camp in Wood Mountain with "98 men, 50 women, about as many children and 300 horses." He was welcomed by Sitting Bull and his warriors, and was met by Major James Walsh, who reported in his journal: "We found White Bird—while not much of a speaker—a very intelligent man of fine and good judgment, less diplomatic than Bull but more clear in perception and quicker in decision—a greater General than Bull." In this selection, *peopeo kiskiok hihih* tells his story to Walsh through an interpreter. His story is significant in the historical context of Saskatchewan as a place of refuge, for a time, from the aggressive removal policies in the United States.

The Nez Percé War

Our home was in Oregon Territory, located in a beautiful valley; our herds, horses, cattle and sheep, covered every hill. We lived in houses. had churches

and schools. We were becoming acquainted with agriculture, had given up
the chase as a means of livelihood. Our children were being educated and our
people Christianized and no period of our nation's life was more prosperous
than the year that Howard came to move us from our homes. The hereditary
Chief of our nation was Joseph. He succeeded his father, also named Joseph.
Old Joseph, as he was called, like his son, was an exceedingly good man and
very fond of the whites and anxious to have them settle around him. In this
respect, he differed from most of his people. I remember the first white man
who came to our country and asked to remain among us. Joseph was pleased
with the idea and consented to give him horses, cattle and land. I was then a
young man and loved Joseph. I had a sort of suspicion of white men and that
their association would be of no advantage to us and expressed my feeling
to Joseph. He said I was wrong, that we should encourage the white men to
come to us. There was much we could learn from them in growing grain and
vegetables and cultivating the soil. He wanted his people to improve and they
must have instruction.

Only a short time elapsed when another white came and Joseph held out
his hand as he did to the first. I again protested against whites joining us and
told Joseph the day would come when we could regret the course he was now
pursuing, that white men would deceive him and bring misery upon his people.
He dismissed me saying I was blinded by prejudice and the inborn feeling
of my race towards the whites. I could not quarrel with Joseph.... Year after
year, white men came to locate in our country. Poor old Joseph was happy and
always their friend. Joseph knew the presence of white men did not suit me....
Joseph died and his son became Chief and continued the policies of his father.
Our people were at this time rich in herds, horses and cattle. We were happy
and prosperous. More white men came but could find no room. Our hills and
valleys were all occupied with herds of the Indians and their white friends. But
the white men saw our good grass, our thousands of animals and their hearts
grew hungry. They asked the Great Chief at Washington to give them Joseph's
country and remove the Nez Percé to some other locality. It is a beautiful country and should be opened to white settlement, let the Indians be moved over
the other side of the gravel range. The country there is good enough for them.

The white Chiefs in Washington said 'Yes, move Joseph.' Our people were
notified of this decision. Consternation filled every heart. Were we to be driven
from the homes our fathers gave us and, if so, why? Joseph's head was bowed.
Upon him the blow fell the hardest. 'Oh my Father,' he asked, 'what have we
done that this misfortune comes upon us?'

Joseph called a council of all the head men of his tribe. The question was
placed before them and discussed. Joseph was crushed in spirit. I objected to

the decision from Washington and advised a protest immediately. He made it but a reply came that it was settled; the Nez Percé must move. Another Council was called. Joseph, always peaceable and obedient, recommended that the Government command be complied with. I could not agree with him and asked if he fully realized what such a move meant. Were the hills not covered with our stock? Was not our fortune in these herds? Were we, after years of toil by our fathers and by ourselves, going to throw this property away? Who were richer than Joseph and his people? ... We shall not give away our country, handed down from our fathers whose graves mark a period of possession of 200 years. We will not surrender.... If I have to leave this home, I shall never accept another south of the British line.

Joseph considered and begged that we, on account of our families, should accept the change and move across the mountain to the new territory selected by the Government for us.

... Joseph meets Howard and places the matter before him. Howard's ears are dumb and he replied you must move and your departure must not be delayed longer than one week.... Joseph was so oppressed he knew not what to do. To go to the new reservation meant paralyzing of his people; to resist the order meant war and killing of his people. At this juncture I felt I should speak and act and I said: 'Joseph, I shall never submit to this.'

Which direction do you go, my friend?' Joseph said. 'North,' I replied, 'to the red coats' country....' Looking Glass said: 'You shall not go alone. I will accompany you.' 'And I and I,' was resounded from a hundred voices and Joseph, the last to speak, said: 'And I'.

The following day, with women's hearts breaking, children weeping and men silent, we moved over the divide that closed our eyes upon our once happy homes, forever, and made us wanderers on the prairie and for what? White man's avarice. He wanted the wealth our nation had accumulated and he got it. We who yesterday were rich are today beggars, made so by the orders of Christian White Chief of Justice at Washington.

—*October 1877. Sitting Bull's Camp, Wood Mountain*

Gabriel Dumont

Métis · 1837–1906 · Red River

Gabriel Dumont is most widely known as the Métis war general for Louis Riel during the 1885 Resistance. The selections below are from Dumont's first-person account of the events leading up to and during the 1885 Resistance. Dumont dictated his memoirs in 1903 to a group of friends, one of whom wrote them down. These writings remained

unpublished in the Manitoba Provincial
Archives until discovered by accident in
1971 by Michael Barnholden. Subsequently,

Barnholden translated them into English
from the French transcription of Dumont's
spoken Michif dialect.

Batoche

The English were camped at my homestead. They burned my house and tore down my stables to reinforce the *Northcote* and protect it from gunfire. The Métis scouts saw them and we knew that the *Northcote* was going to come downriver to surround us.

On Saturday they arrived at Batoche before noon. I had placed some Métis on the right side of the river, below the cemetery where the river channel passed a long beach. I thought the *Northcote* would pass close to the side of the river and almost touch the shore. I had also placed, on the other side of the river, some Métis who could fire on the *Northcote*, right after it had been fired on from the left. It would be very difficult to get past these two.

I had also given the order to lower the ferry cable, but the men thought it was low enough and didn't move it.

The cable barely touched the steamboat. It drifted by. The steamboat anchored a little below Fagnan's.

While this was happening, the English had arrived at Caron's. They were trying to turn by Belle Prairie.

I sent Michel Dumas and his men to stop the English from fixing the steamboat's chimney, but they were stopped on the height of the bank and their mission was useless.

During the first push, the English tried to sweep through Belle Prairie. They established a machine gun just this side. Once they fired on me and my horse, from about one mile, but the bullets fell in front of me.

They pulled back at night.

We dug holes near the riverbank, the cemetery and Emmanuel Champagne's. They were about seventy-five yards apart, two or three men in each hole. There were about fifty men in these pits. The other men were hiding among the bush. There were about 150 men on this side of the river, and one hundred on the other side.

At night we fired at the English, as they ate, from the ridge in front of the old forge.

During the night we watched the troops, and the Indians liked to fire on them.

The second day, Middleton worked to establish his fortifications all around his camp so he could sleep easily.

The English started firing right after breakfast. They controlled the church and the cemetery. They moved the machine gun to the small prairie at the top of the trail that ran down into Batoche. It was to the left of the old abandoned trail and to the right of the new trail.

I moved up with my men, crawling along in the small aspens. I told my men, "Let me go ahead. I have already been close enough to take a shot in the head—this time they might not miss. When I start shooting, we must take the machine gun, and get down the trail as quickly as possible." I was almost at the place where I could get a good shot away, when my men began to fire. The artillery hadn't started firing yet and reinforcements were arriving, so I withdrew.

During the first three days, the English could not break our lines of defence. They sat and didn't move much. One report said that Middleton planned to make us use up our bullets, no doubt on the advice of Father Vegreville.

During the last two days, a Sioux named Joli Corbeau broke his leg at the cemetery. J.B. Boucher, the father, was wounded in the buttock.

Armiel Gariepy's wrist was broken and his chest was pierced by the same bullet.

Each night the police returned to their camp, and often there were bullets left on the ground, usually at the foot of a tree, where they had stopped to reload. Often we found machine gun belts which held forty bullets each. These were the same calibre as many of the Métis twelveshot hunting rifles.

We also took the guns of the dead. We had sixty or seventy at the end.

We also came across something very serious—I was amazed when I was shown the exploding balls. We thought it was understood between nations that only mortars could be explosive, as their debris was very destructive. But for a man in combat to be exposed to exploding bullets was to cause a terrible wound and certain death, which was against the basic principles of war. You wanted to score a direct hit, and temporarily disable, but not necessarily kill, the enemy soldiers. A simple bullet wound would disable a man and his wound would get better, while the wound of an exploding ball caused internal wounds and broke bones, and was always deadly. The government troops committed a huge crime against humanity and against the rights of the men of the Métis nation.

—1903

The Fourth Day

Around three o'clock, the English still hadn't moved past where they had been the day before. The sun was already low when they took Batoche's house. They were pushing in on all sides at once, when they stormed through our front-line, they advanced right to the house without stopping.

I was against digging the pits because I knew what was coming. In them the men could stay completely secure and hold on right to the end, and then they couldn't leave without being killed.

This is how it happened. The English advanced in large battalions, without stopping. They rained bullets on the foxholes: the Métis could not raise their heads to fire. When the English got so close that there was no hope, the Métis tried to fire but were killed instantly.

After the English had entered Batoche's house, which was no longer occupied by the Métis, I continued to resist around there for another half hour. With me were the elder Joseph Vandal, and his nephew Joseph Vandal, the elder Ouellette, Pierre Sansregret, David Tourond and a young Sioux.

We were under Batoche's house. Daniel Ross was wounded in Batoche's house: he yelled to me and the others to come and drag him off the field of battle.

"Are you dead or alive?" I yelled to him.

"I won't last much longer," answered Ross.

"I'll be killed if I try. There'll be two deaths instead of one." Daniel Ross was between Batoche's house and Fisher's store.

The English occupied Batoche's house. There was a red curtain in the upstairs window—we couldn't see them. I kept firing at the curtain to frighten the English, so they would not have time to shoot.

This is when Captain French was shot in the bedroom I had used. He wasn't killed point-blank, but was hit in the bedroom just off the passage, and rolled down the stairs, leaving blood stains. He was found at the bottom of the stairs.

Joseph Vandal, the elder, was also wounded at this point. He had both arms broken, one in two places. He was limping, lost his balance, and fell forward. He tried to get up but failed, so I helped him and said, "Get out of here. Leave now."

"No," said Vandal. "I prefer to die now that I have two broken arms."

"Go! Go!" I told him, but he wouldn't go, and I wouldn't leave him. So I forced him to leave. He went across the trail that went down to the crossing, and I went back to fight from below Batoche's.

A little later we also crossed the trail. The English had already occupied Fisher's store. We fought them from the hill between Fisher's store and his home. It was here that old Ouellette was killed. We were above the women's tents, which had been abandoned. I found Joseph Vandal in Tourond's tent and made him run on alone now. We found him a quarter mile further on, towards Emmanuel Champagne's house, dead and bayonetted.

There was a young wounded Sioux in a wagon near mother Tourond's tent. There was a bullet lodged in his chest: he could not go on. I had to leave him: he was too close to death, bleeding from the mouth. He was the son of Joli Corbeau, who had already been wounded.

After old Ouellette was killed, we returned to the women's tents to wait for the English to come. "It is over," I said. "But only now that we have held up the English long enough for everyone to escape." I was with Joseph Vandal, Pierre Sansregret and David Tourond. We met Phillippe Gariepy, John Ross, Carbatte—the son of John Ross, a young English Métis who was the son of Tom Anderson—Hilaire Paternotre and Henry Smith.

Most wanted to leave, but I wanted us to take our last shots. We followed the English in the half-light, and found many bullets as we went.

We followed the river almost to Emmanuel Champagne's. When we got there, I asked Hilaire Paternotre what he had done with the halfbarrel of powder he had found. It was nearby. I wanted him to go and get it, but he wouldn't. So I said to Henry Smith, "You are not afraid, you go and get it. There is no danger. The English aren't there now."

Henry Smith took off his shoes so he could run better. His shoes were hard to run in. He also gave his rifle to John Ross. I waited with his shoes, and the others left. John Ross took his rifle it was gone when Henry returned.

It was night and we needed to eat. I remembered a Sioux lodge nearby that had had a lot of meat in the last few days. I went and got a leg of dried meat.

I came up just this side of Edouard Dumont's where the women had gathered. I gave the calf leg to my wife and told her to share it with the others. Riel's wife was there and so was Riel. It was the last time that I saw him. I heard him say to Madame Riel, "I believe God wants me to live." Everyone was telling them to flee. I wanted to get him a horse so he could get away, if he wanted to. I said to my wife, "Wait for me here." I went to Emmanuel Champagne's stable where I knew there were always horses, but the police had already occupied it. I left without firing on them. I wanted to, but I also wanted to return to my wife and the others.

When I returned she was alone, so I hid her on an island in the river. I went and found a stallion of Batoche's, but he roared and reared so much that I had to tie him in a bluff and go and find another. I met Henry Smith and John Ross' son, who was looking for his father, and Smith wanted his gun back. They told me that Pierriche Parenteau's horses were nearby, so we went to find them.

I found a kettle and carried it with me. Henry Smith had the stallion that had gotten loose. We went to Daniel Gariepy's house, where Maxime Lepine had been living. His closest neighbour was Edouard Dumont. We lit a lamp, and I brought out two plates, two pots and two knives and forks. Then left to get my wife.

I found a young tan mare that had been taken from the police.

When I got near my wife's hiding place, I tied the stallion and the mare in a bluff nearby. While I was tying the stallion, Pierriche Parenteau's horses galloped by. I thought it was the police. It was now the middle of the night. I went to hide near the bluff with my rifle so I could get the jump on the police when they passed. First I realized these were free horses; then I realized they were Parenteau's, so I caught another mare and let the stallion go.

I put my wife on one of the mares but she had never ridden bareback, so I had to lead her horse with a rope. On the other mare I put a half-bag of flour that I had been carrying when I was leading the two horses. The stallion followed the two mares and wouldn't leave them. Finally I had to hit him hard with a stick to stop him.

We camped at the northeast edge of Belle Prairie. We spent the morning in the woods where we ate breakfast. I left my wife hidden there and went on foot to find Riel.

I climbed the bluffs, going from side to side, hiding in the smaller bluffs as I went. I saw a man hiding near the top of the bluff. It was a Sioux, so I snuck up on him and spoke to him in Sioux. He was very surprised.

I kept looking for Riel. But I couldn't find where he was hiding, so I started calling him very loudly. Jim Short answered me from off to the side but he wouldn't come up to the prairie, so I went to him. Jim Short told me he had been trying to hide with his horse, but he was going to abandon it because he couldn't hide with it.

"I'll take it myself," I said.

"Take it," he said, and he untied the rope he had around his body and gave it to me. I went to get the horse and started calling for Riel again. This time, the three young Trottiers answered. They were looking for their mother. There were many Métis horses on the trail so I told them to take them, or the police would.

I returned to my wife with Jim Short's horse. The rest of the Métis were passing through there as they fled, so we followed them. When we arrived at Calixte Lafontaine's, we found Emmanuel Champagne's wife in a wagon. She told us that many people who had fled had passed by there. We went on and found the wife of Baptiste Parenteau, Riel's sister. We followed their tracks and caught up with them near Montour Butte, about ten miles away. There were ten women with Elie Dumont, Pierre Laverdure, and the son of Pierre Sansregret.

We camped with them, and the next day I left one of the mares with the women and gave the other to Alexandre Fageron, my adopted son. I was going to my father's, when I saw three policemen on the trail being escorted by some Indians. I had my rifle, as always. They were about three hundred yards away when the Indians saw me and told the police. The police knew my reputation for taking advantage of small enemy patrols, so they sent one of the Indians to talk to me. When he was close enough to speak, I ordered him to stop.

"Are you afraid of me?" asked the Indian.

"Certainly," I said. "How is it that yesterday you fought against the police, and today you help them look for me?"

"You have no reason to fear me."

"Don't come any closer or I will have to shoot you."

The policemen stayed at a distance. They wouldn't come any closer because they knew I wouldn't let them take me alive. I said to the Indian, "I will not lay down my arms—I will fight forever. And the first who comes for me, I will kill." The Indian went back to the police and they left, no doubt to return with reinforcements. But they could not find me.

I went on to my father's and met J. B. Parenteau, who I gave my best horse, so he could save himself.

Moise Ouellette was at my father's. He had a letter for Riel and the others. He gave me the warrant, and I asked if he knew what was in it: "Give it to me and tell me what it says."

"Yes: they promise you justice, if you give yourself up with Riel," answered Moise.

"I will not surrender, but I will keep searching for Riel—not to make him surrender, but escape. If I find him before the law does, I won't let him surrender. I will find him first, Moise."

I did not see Riel again.

—*1903*

pīhtikwahānapiwiyin (Poundmaker)
Plains Cree (Stoney-Métis) · c. 1842–1886

pīhtikwahānapiwiyin, or Poundmaker, was born around 1842 near present-day Battleford, and became an influential Plains Cree chief. His father was Stoney and his mother was mixed Cree and European. He was a maternal nephew of *mastawāsis*, and was renowned for his great skill in hunting buffalo, particularly by drawing them into pounds. He had a close relationship with the Blackfoot Chief Crowfoot, who adopted him in 1873.

In 1876 at Fort Carlton, though not yet a chief, he had an important presence during the Treaty Six negotiations, demonstrating his oratorical skills with the powerful metaphor, recorded by Peter Erasmus: "This is our land! It isn't a piece of pemmican to be cut off and given in little pieces back to us. It is ours and we will take what we want." He resisted signing Treaty Six for several years, but eventually signed, and in 1879 settled on reserve lands near Battleford.

The first selections are from the Morris records of the Treaty Six negotiations. The second and third selections are from the events of the Battle of Cut Knife Creek and the 1885 Resistance. The fourth selection is from *pīhtikwahānapiwiyin*'s address to the court during his trial for treason-felony. After the verdict, he asked to be hanged rather than imprisoned, but the judge sentenced him, along with *mistahi-maskwa*, to three years at Stony Mountain Penitentiary.

pīhtikwahānapiwiyin was released early, but died four months later in 1886.

Speeches at Treaty Six (Morris)

We have heard your words that you had to say to us as the representative of the Queen. We were glad to hear what you had to say, and have gathered together in council and thought the words over amongst us, we were glad to hear you tell us how we might live by our own work. When I commence to settle on the lands to make a living for myself and my children, I beg of you to assist me in every way possible—when I am at a loss how to proceed I want the advice and assistance of the Government; the children yet unborn, I wish you to treat them in the like manner as they advance in civilization like the white man. This is all I have been told to say now, if I have not said anything in a right manner I wish to be excused; this is the voice of the people.

—*August 22, 1876. Fort Carlton*

I do not differ from my people, but I want more explanation. I heard what you said yesterday, and I thought that when the law was established in this country it would be for our good. From what I can hear and see now, I cannot understand that I shall be able to clothe my children and feed them as long as sun shines and water runs. With regard to the different Chiefs who are to occupy the reserves, I expected they would receive sufficient for their support, this is why I speak. In the presence of God and the Queen's representative I say this, because I do not know how to build a house for myself, you see how naked I am, and if I tried to do it my naked body would suffer; again, I do not know how to cultivate the ground for myself, at the same time I quite understand what you have offered to assist us in this.

—*August 23, 1876. Fort Carlton*

Letter to Riel

A letter was sent from the rebel camp near Cut Knife Hill to Riel and his council which was delivered by Alex Parenteau and three other couriers. This letter was later used against Poundmaker at his trial.

To Mr. Louis Riel, I want to hear news of God's work. If any event has occurred since your messengers came away, let me know of it. Tell me the date when the Americans will reach the Canadian Pacific Railway; tell me all the news that you have heard from all places where your work is in progress. Big Bear has finished his work; he has taken Fort Pitt. 'If you want me to come to you, let me know at once', he said; and I sent for him at once. I will be four days on the road. Those who have gone to see him will sleep twice on the road. They took twenty prisoners, including the master of Fort Pitt. They killed eleven men, including the agent, two priests and six white men. We are camped on the creek just below Cut Knife Hill, waiting for Big Bear. The Blackfoot have killed sixty police at the Elbow. A half-breed, who interpreted for the police, having survived the fight, though wounded, brought this news. Here we have killed six white men. We have not taken the barracks yet, but that is the only entire building in Battleford. All the cattle and horses in the vicinity we have taken. We have lost one man, a Nez Perce killed, he being alone, and one wounded. Some soldiers have come from Swift Current, but I do not know their number. We have here guns and rifles of all sorts, but ammunition for them is short. If it be possible we want you to send us ammunition of various kinds. We are weak only for the want of that. You sent word that you would come to Battleford when you had finished your work at Duck Lake. We wait still for you, as we are unable to take that fort without help. If you send us news send only one messenger. We are impatient to reach you. It would encourage us much to see you, and make us work more heartily. Up to the present everything has gone well with us, but we are constantly expecting the soldiers to visit us here. We trust that God will be as kind to us in the future as he has in the past. We, the undersigned, send greeting to you all.

Poundmaker
Oo-Pin-Ou-Way-Win [Poundmaker's Band]
Mus-Sin-Ass [Strike-Him-On-The-Back Band]
Mee-Tay-Way-Is [Strike-Him-On-The-Back Band]
Pee-Yay-Cheew [Red Pheasant Band]

When this reaches you send us news immediately, as we are anxious to hear the news. If you send us news, send as many men as possible.
—*April 29, 1885. Cut Knife Hill*

Letter to Middleton

(Poundmaker, upon learning of Riel's capture, sent three couriers to Middleton with the following letter written by Robert Jefferson)

Sir—I am camped with my people at the east end of the Eagle Hills, where I am met by the news of the surrender of Riel. No letter came with the news, so that I cannot tell how far it may be true. I send some of my men to you to learn the truth and the terms of peace, and hope you will deal kindly with them. I and my people wish you to send us the terms of peace in writing, so that we may be under no misunderstanding, from which so much trouble arises. We have 21 prisoners, whom we have tried to treat well in every respect. With greetings.

Signed POUNDMAKER   His
                           X
                           Mark
                               —*May 19, 1885. Eagle Hills*

Address to the Court

I am not guilty. A lot has been said against me that is untrue. I am glad of what I have done in the Queen's country. What I did was for the Great Mother. When my people and the whites met in battle, I saved the Queen's men. I took the firearms from my following and gave them up at Battleford. Everything I could do was to prevent bloodshed. Had I wanted war, I would not be here but on the prairie. You did not catch me. I gave myself up. You have me because I wanted peace. I cannot help myself, but I am still a man. You may do as you like with me. I am done.

—*August 18, 1885. Regina Courthouse*

Louis Riel
Métis · 1844–1885 · Saint-Boniface, Red River

Louis Riel was born in 1844 in Saint-Boniface, Red River Settlement. By the 1860s, he had become the political and spiritual leader of the Métis. He led the 1869 Resistance at Red River and was instrumental in the creation of Manitoba as a province, though he was banished from Canada for five years due to the events at Fort Garry. After several years living in exile in the United States, he returned to Canada, at the request of Gabriel Dumont and the Métis, to lead the 1885 Resistance in present-day Saskatchewan. After the Métis defeat at Batoche, Riel surrendered and was imprisoned in Regina to await trial. He was charged and convicted of treason, and was executed on November 16, 1885, in Regina.

The first selection is representative of Riel's call for support in mobilizing forces for resistance, and is reflective of his deep religious convictions. The second selection is the Revolutionary Bill of Rights, written to establish a new provisional government in Saskatchewan. The remaining selections are poems that Riel wrote in jail while awaiting his trial and execution.

Message to the Métis of Battleford

God Almighty has always taken care of the Half-breeds. He has fed them for a long while in the wilderness. It was Divine Providence that increased the herds of buffaloes grazing on our prairies and the abundance which our forefathers have enjoyed, was as marvellous as the manna falling from heaven. But we have failed in gratefulness towards God our Almighty Father, and it is on account of that that we have fallen into the hands of a government whose sole aim was to plunder us. Oh, if we had understood what God was doing in our favor before Confederation, we would have adopted measures in consequence, and the Half-breeds in the North-West would have exacted the necessary conditions to secure for our children that freedom, that possession of the land which are indispensable to one's happiness. But fifteen years of suffering, of poverty and underhand and malicious persecution, have opened our eyes, and the sight of the abyss of demoralization into which the Dominion plunges us deeper and deeper every day has, through the mercy of God, struck us with terror, and frightened us more of this hell where the mounted police and the Government are trying to drive us openly than we are of their fire arms, which after all can but destroy our bodies. In our alarm, we have heard from the bottom of our hearts a voice which said: 'Justice commands you to take up arms.' Dear relatives and friends, we advise you to be on your guard. Be ready to face all events. Take with you all the Indians, gather them from all sides. Seize all the munitions that you can, in every store wherever it is. Grumble, growl and threaten, raise the Indians. Proclaim that the police at Fort Pitt and Fort Bataille is powerless. We beg of God to open the route for us, and once we have entered it, we shall help you to take Fort Bataille and Fort Pitt. Trust in Jesus-Christ. Trust in and put yourselves under the keeping of the Holy Virgin. Pray to St. Joseph for he is all powerful with God. Implore the powerful intercession of St. Jean-Baptiste, the glorious patron saint of the Canadians and of the Half-breeds. Make your peace with God. Obey his commandments. We ask Him to be amongst you and to make you succeed.

Try to communicate as soon as possible to the Half-breeds and Indians at Fort Pitt, the news we send you. And tell them to be on their guard, to be ready to face all events.

—March 22, 1885

Revolutionary Bill of Rights

1. That the half-breeds of the Northwest Territories be given grants similar to those accorded to the half-breeds of Manitoba by the Act of 1870.
2. That patents be issued to all half-breed and white settlers who have fairly earned the right of possession on their farms.

3. That the provinces of Alberta and Saskatchewan be forthwith organized with legislatures of their own, so that the people may be no longer subjected to the despotism of Mr. Dewdney.

4. That in these new provincial legislatures, while representation according to population shall be the supreme principle, the Métis shall have a fair and reasonable share of representation.

5. That the offices of trust throughout these provinces be given to the residents of the country, as far as practicable, and that we denounce the appointment of disreputable outsiders and repudiate their authority.

6. That this region be administered for the benefit of the actual settler, and not for the advantage of the alien speculator.

7. That better provision be made for the Indians, the parliamentary grant to be increased and lands set apart as an endowment for the establishment of hospitals and schools for the use of whites, half-breeds, and Indians, at such places as the provincial legislatures may determine.

8. That all lawful customs and usages which obtain among the Métis be respected.

9. That the Land Department of the Dominion Government be administered as far as practicable from Winnipeg, so that the settlers may not be compelled as heretofore to go to Ottawa for the settlement of questions in dispute between them and the land commissioner.

10. That the timber regulations be made more liberal, and that the settler be treated as having rights in this country.

—*March 8, 1885. St. Laurent*

Palpite! ô mon esprit!

Palpite! ô mon esprit! ô mon âme! tressaille!
La paix vous ouvre un champ et plus libre et plus beau
Que la champagne ouverte ou le champ de bataille.
La paix et ses fruits font reculer le tombeau!

L'heureuse paix du Coeur dans les plus grandes luttes
Toute seule vaut mieux que tous les autres biens.
Les revers, avec Elle, ont l'air d'être des chutes
D'abord; pour devenir ensuite des moyens.

O mes amis! La paix que Jésus-christ nous donne
Produit sous tout rapport d'admirables effets.
La paix qui vient du monde est précieuse et bonne

Mais tous ses résultats sont bornés, imparfaits.
Ayons la paix de l'âme! Et l'Infini nous ouvre
Des apperçus nouveaux, gais à chaque moment.
Avec la paix de Dieu, le bonheur se découvre
     A nos yeux Merveilleusement.

Faire la volonté de Dieu nous rend plus calmes
En face du danger, plus paisibles que l'eau
Sans aucun courant d'air. Ouvrons bien les deux palmes
Des nos mains vers le ciel. Renaissons de nouveau!

Sainte Vierge, obtenez qu'un torrent de lumières
     Vienne éclairer le genre humain.
Saint Joseph! priez Dieu qu'un fleuve de prières
En Jésus-christ nous sauve aujourd'hui pour demain.
                 —*August 1885. Regina Jail*

Shudder, My Spirit
[translation by Warren Cariou]

Shudder, my spirit! Quiver, my soul!
Peace opens a vista more free and lovely
Than open countryside or battlefield.
Peace and its fruits will repel even death!

A peaceful heart in the greatest battles
is better than anything in this world.
Our trials might seem like failings at first
but with time they show us the way.

O my friends! The peace of Jesus Christ
Creates such beauty under everything.
The peace infusing the world is precious and good
But its earthly appearance is shrunken, imperfect.

Let us have peaceful hearts! And the Infinite will open
For us new visions, joyful in each moment.
With the peace of God, that goodness unfolds
     Brilliantly before our eyes.

Giving our thoughts over to God calms us
In the face of danger, more peaceful than water
Without a breath of wind. Let us open our palms
Toward the sky. Let us be reborn anew!

Blessed Virgin, create a torrent of light
        Come illuminate humanity.
Saint Joseph! Pray to God for a flood of prayers
For Jesus Christ to save us, today for tomorrow.

Margaret: be fair and good

Margaret: be fair and good.
Consider the sacred wood
On which the perfect Jesus
Died willingly to save us.

Truly Christ will save us all
Believe it: and hear his call.
His spirit always teaches you
What your dear soul has to do.

He remembers as son of god
That our flesh is nothing but mud.
In him you find the merciful.
His love indeed is beautiful.

And is he not the Son of man
To cherish all what is human?
If we follow well his commands
He will grant our dearest demands.

The holy ghost mild as a dove
Makes you hear the voice of his love.
His voice resounds during your sleep.
        Deep.

Awake! art thou not his daughter?
Revive: don't wait any later.

Obey the words of his scripture.
He will strengthen your weak nature.

What is volupty? What is gold?
For our god, why did we grow cold?
Let us change, before we perish
And fall in the place of anguish.

The body dies: but not the soul.
Perhaps to night death on its roll
Will in a sudden call our names
To stand before God with our shames.

Begin the work which is thine own.
Amongst your friends you are alone
If you miss god, by doing wrong.
This life is short: the next is long.

Margaret! will we be the prey
Of bad spirits? no, let us pray…
Be sweet to my words: and listen
When I write you with a golden
     Pen.

—August 1885. Regina Jail

Robert Gordon!

    Robert Gordon!
    I beg your pardon
     For so having
     Kept you waiting
After some poor verses of mine.
You know, my english is not fine.
    I speak it; but only
      Very imperfectly.

———————

    The snow,
Which renders the ground all white,

From heaven, comes here below:
In pine frozen drops invite
     us all
To white—keep our thoughts and our acts,
So that when our bodies do fall,
Our merits, before God, be facts.

How many who, with good desires,
Have died and lost their souls to fires?
Good desires kept unpractic'd
Stand, before God, unnotic'd

O, Robert, Let us be fond
Of virtue! Virtues abound

In every sort of good,
Let virtue be our soul's food.

Louis "David" Riel.

October 27th, 1885,
     Regina Jail.

kā-papāmahcahkwēw (Wandering Spirit)
Plains Cree · 1845–1885

kā-papāmahcahkwēw, or Wandering Spirit, was born in 1845. He was a war chief of mistahi-maskwa's, or Big Bear's, band. During the events of the 1885 Resistance, kā-papāmahcahkwēw superseded mistahi-maskwa's authority, and was a main instigator of the violence at Frog Lake in 1885. According to Garry Radison, kā-papāmahcahkwēw "was the first war chief to declare war" against the Canadian government. He was charged and convicted of treason, and was executed with seven others on November 27, 1885, at Battleford.

The first selection was interpreted by Pritchard during a meeting between W. J. McLean, mistahi-maskwa, and kā-papāmahcahkwēw, in regards to the Métis during the 1885 Resistance. The second selection was paraphrased by William Bleasdell Cameron, who was present.

Council Speech

You have spoken enough. We believe what you have said about the Hudson's Bay Company and of yourself[;] we know you through our ears long since, but you have said too much about the government[;] we do not want to hear anything about him. We are tired of him and all his people and we are going to drive them out of the country. Why do you want us to believe that the government has plenty of soldiers? Look at the few Red Coats that you are keeping at the fort[.] Is that plenty? Is that all the government can send? He has been trying to send more for two years to frighten us. We are not afraid of them. We are going to finish them off before the sun goes down, and we would have killed them long ago were it not for you and your wife and children. We do not know why you keep the Red Coats in your fort. That is the only thing we have against you. The fort was built for us many years ago, not for the Red Coats. They will not be there long. We will make short work of them and kill them like young ducks, but we want you to get your wife and children out of the way of danger.

[When McLean tried to respond, kā-papāmahcahkwēw put his hand on McLean's shoulder and said,]

Do not speak too much. That is why I killed the agent. I am going to tell you now that we have already taken your old place (Fort Qu'Appelle), Calgary and Edmonton. We have torn up the iron road and cut down the poles with the speaking iron (telegraph).

—*April 1885*

Speech to Warriors

Fourteen years ago when we fought the Blackfoot, the River Men (Plains Cree) were afraid of nothing. When we heard the enemy was near we rushed to meet him, and you all know Kahpaypamahchakwayo. He was never behind. I look around me today and what do I see? None of the faces I saw about me then—instead, the faces of young men. How will it be now? It is because you asked me, you young fellows, that ashes is all that is left of Frog Lake—that I did what I did. I hope we see the Queen's soldiers soon. When they come you will hear me shout the war cry of the River Men—and if any does not follow me, he shall die as the white men died at Frog Lake!

—*May 1885*

acāhkosa kā-otakohpit (Star Blanket)
Plains Cree · c. 1845–1917

acāhkosa kā-otakohpit, or Has a Star for a Blanket (Star Blanket), was born around 1845, the son of *wahpiimoosetoosis*, or White Buffalo Calf, one of the chiefs who signed Treaty Four at Fort Qu'Appelle in 1874. *acāhkosa kā-otakohpit* was present at the signing of Treaty Four. When his father passed away in 1875, *acāhkosa kā-otakohpit* became chief. He worked for the implementation of the treaty promises, and the selection below is an historic letter he sent to the Governor General, HRH The Duke of Connaught, in 1912.

Letter to Governor General

Star Blanket Chief of a Cree band of Indians at File Hills, son of White Calf a Chief who signed a Treaty with the Great white mothers speaks to the Great White Chief who has come such a long way to visit us. A distance so great that we have no way of speaking to you only when a time such as this comes. We have waited patiently for many years for a chance to speak to some one who would carry a message to the Government and to our white brothers in the east. The first part of our message Great Chief is one of Good wishes and peace to yourself first and then to the Government. For as I was both with two legs and as these two legs have not yet quarreled, so I wish to live in peace with the white people. When I was in middle life the Government of the Great White Mother sent some wise men to ask us to give them much land. A large camp of Indians was made near Qu'Appelle and there the Government and Indians after much talking signed a treaty, on paper and much was promised as well. One of these papers has been carefully kept by us, and by it we Indians gave to the Government a large piece of land and held back for ourselves some small pieces as Reserves. In the treaty we made then the Government promised to make a School for every band of Indians on their own Reserve, but instead little children are torn from their mothers' arms or homes by the police or Government Agents and taken sometimes hundreds of miles to large Schools perhaps to take sick and die when their family cannot see them. The little Ants which live in the earth love their young ones and wish to have them in their homes. Surely us red men are not smaller than these Ants. For many years I have not been paid all my treaty money, it was not much only Twenty-five dollars a year. I need it much as I am now nearly eighty years old and not able to work. I do not care so much for myself as I am nearly finished with life, but for many years I have had a sore heart watching my old people nearly starving. The buffalo and deer are gone and our people will soon be hard to find but while we are still here I would ask that the Government not to forget their treaty, to send out some honest men to enquire into our troubles and let us explain them. And then as the Great Spirit lives I trust justice will be done.

—*1912*

kā-miyo-kīsikwēw (Fine Day)
Plains Cree · c. 1847–1941

kā-miyo-kīsikwēw, or Fine Day, became a war chief of the River People branch of Plains Cree. He participated in events surrounding the 1885 Resistance, including *mistahi-maskwa*'s (Big Bear's) Thirst Dance on *pīhtikwahānapiwiyin*'s (Poundmaker's) reserve and the Battle of Cut Knife Hill. Later in life he became a successful reserve farmer and notable storyteller.

The first selection is of a traditional war song. It was first sung by kā-miyo-kīsikwēw's Grandmother to chastise her brother, after dishonour in a conflict with the Gros Ventre, but, according to Garry Radison, "the song became important and was often sung by women when warriors returned from a successful raid." The second selection is taken from an interview of kā-miyo-kīsikwēw recorded by Campbell Innes and translated by Robert Jefferson, and first published in *The Cree Rebellion of '84*, in June 1926. The third selection is from a collection of stories told by kā-miyo-kīsikwēw and recorded in the University of Regina's Indian History archives.

Song for Returning Warriors

When I asked you to go you refused me,
When I told you that I was poor
But I tried to go.
I got to the Sweet Grass Hills when it was good.
When I told you this you were sitting here at home.
You are still sitting here.
At last I got to the Sweet Grass Hills
And you are still sitting here at home.

Big Bear's Last Thirst Dance

I was there and took part in the preparations and dance. The day before the dance all gathered around Big Bear, who naked, except for the clay which covered his body, prayed that the dance might be successful, and that all prayers would be answered, especially the prayer for water. Big Bear did not eat or sleep that night. Early in the morning he sent messengers to call for trailers (men on horseback with ropes) to come. When these came they were asked to search for a proper stick for the tent. When this was found it must stand to honour the god who was to give all. All dressed in their best accompanied the searcher for the stick. When this was found Big Bear prayed, facing east, north, west, south, in turn. The tree was chopped down, falling to the south. The moment it fell the guns were fired and then all rushed to get a branch as a trophy from the battlefield. The young warriors dragged the tree to the spot. A nest was prepared at the top which contained some precious article from the Indian to please the Great Spirit. Big Bear offered prayers and then a hole was dug for the stick. It was put in an upright position while Big Bear chanted prayers. Rafters were next secured and placed from the upright stick to poles placed upright in the ground. Branches were piled on this skeleton roof.

A square hole was dug opposite the main entrance to be 16 inches deep. A stick was placed in each corner and one in the centre. Big Bear then filled the pipe and pointed to each stick in turn, then to the east, north, west, south, then above, praying, "To you who have given what we have to-day." He lit the pipe and pointed to each point of the compass, east, north, west, south, and prayed the same prayer. The pipe was passed from warrior to warrior gathered round the square. When it had gone round the bowl of the pipe was placed over the centre hole and the stem was thrown away. Incense was made with sweet grass. Big Bear uttered another prayer before the drum commenced, which was the signal for the dance. These men and women dancers thirsted in proportion as their prayers demanded more or less sacrifice (half a day to a day). The great deeds of each were recounted as he danced and made his promise.

—1926

The First Person

The first person the Creator made was *askiwiyiu* "Earth Person," the first woman was *ota-watas* "Carrier." He told them that he was going to stay with them for a long, long time. He made the man and woman after he had made everything else. He stayed with them a long, long time. They raised a big family. When there got to be a lot of people the next thing he gave to the Indians was the Thirst Dance. He said that it was to be done in two days. But he then saw that there would be too much to do for two days so he split it up into other dances. They are *pihtwauwika-mik*—Smoking Tipi; *manipanikamuwikamik*—Night Singing Tipi or also called *wasakamecimuwikamik*—Round Dancing or *nayahtcigau*; *Wihtigohkanikamik*—Cannibal Tipi; *muskwacimuikamik*—Bear Dance Tipi. Next comes the Bundle Ceremony just as we had it, *kami-tchkwiskwe-pita-guu*, "Giving a Bundle."

The Creator showed these things and they are worth a lot. When he showed them he called up the *atayohkan* so that the people would know which ones to talk to and which would talk hard to the *manito* for them.

The Creator made the *atayohkan* and told the people that they would appear to the old men, and would tell them what names to give to the children.

He said, "Where I go now you will never see me, but I will always be with you. You will see the *atayohkan* only at night, not during the day. Young children will see them often—while they are clean—and to them the *atayohkan* will give power. I give you everything you need to live…. I put all those things handy for you. But I also leave something for you to be afraid of. Some things whereby you will be hurt. It will be thus forever."

He also said, "The Thirst Dance—the one that will be honest and do it correctly will deserve a part of my name and will be called *kiceimu*, 'Eternal.' When you are afraid of your life ending, you can promise one of the things I showed you and I will be right there listening. But you must first name that which you are promising. You will see these *atayohkan* from the time you are small—night after night. Once in a great while a person will meet one in the daytime when he is all alone."

Then he turned around to the whole bunch of *atayohkan* and told them, "There will be an extra tipi made for you when somebody wants to know something. And when you are called, you must all go."

When *manito* does not want the Indians to know anything, he will take away the atayohkan. But as long as they are there we will always have them.

In my kindness to *manito* I am telling you this…. [W]hen you make any history of this, please, it would be best to put it first.

—*1935. Sweetgrass Reserve*

piyēsiw-awāsis (Thunderchild)
Plains Cree · 1849–1927

piyēsiw-awāsis, or Thunderchild, was born in 1849 near the South Saskatchewan River. He initially refused to sign Treaty Six, allying himself with *mistahi-maskwa* in demanding better negotiations. However, with the loss of the buffalo, he accepted an adhesion to treaty in 1879, eventually settling his people on their own reserve west of Battleford in 1883; the band subsequently moved reserve to Brightsand Lake. In later life, *piyēsiw-awāsis* became a strong advocate for treaty rights and opposed the prohibitions against traditional ceremony. He passed away on his home reserve in 1927.

The selections below are from a group of stories recorded during the time *piyēsiw-awāsis* spent visiting Edward Ahenakew, when the ailing Ahenakew was convalescing on *piyēsiw-awāsis*'s reserve in 1923. Realizing the importance of the stories, Ahenakew transcribed and translated them. Set in the times just before the treaties, these stories are, as Ahenakew describes, "tales of struggles almost super-human, of endurance, of perilous adventure, of long hazardous excursions into enemy country, of love, of anything indeed that was ever of any consequence in the Indian life." However, although Ahenakew recorded these stories in the 1920s, they remained unpublished in his lifetime, found buried in a drawer by his niece several years after Ahenakew's death. They were published in 1973 in *Voices of the Plains Cree*.

A Winter of Hardship

When I was still young and my father was alive, we came through a winter of great hardship. My brother took me with him on many long hunts, but the buffalo were scarce that year, and there was hardly any food. Everyone looked for old bones to make grease, but it was rancid.

At first there were plenty of foxes. We caught many in deadfall traps, and traded their skins for tobacco, shot, tea, and sugar, when traders came to our camps; but when we tried to buy pemmican, they would not sell us any.

We had travelled far out onto the plains, and there were no more trees to make traps. We were told that there was food at Fort Pitt, and we started in hope towards that post. We still had five horses and many dogs, but wolves followed us, and when we camped our dogs would chase them. Sometimes the dogs killed a wolf, but every day wolves killed some of our dogs. We had to kill dogs too, for we had nothing else to eat; then, we had to kill our horses for food.

One day *Na-pa-ke-kun* (Night Scout) came to our camp. He told us that the people we had left at the encampment had also tried to reach Fort Pitt when they learned that there was food there, and they had died along the way. He and his wives were the only ones left. They had five horses, and they killed one for food, but would give us none. We took the skin, and we boiled that and ate it, but we were too weak to follow *Na-pa-ke-kun* north when he went on with his wives and the other horses. We could go no farther.

The winter was ending. Our women seemed to be stronger than the men. Though they were not eating, they kept moving, if it was only to make fires to keep us warm. The three little children with us were only skin and bones, and their mothers cried over them. We found it hard even to breathe.

One night I dreamed that someone came to me and said, "You can save yourself. Look to the south!" And looking south, I saw that the country was green, but to the north there was only darkness. I tried to flee to the south. The dream was vivid, and when I awoke it was almost morning. I lay thinking about the dream, and then I told it to my father. "Maybe it is only hunger that made me dream," I said. But my father told me, "Dreams count, my son. Try to go south, all of you; and if I cannot follow, leave me. I will do my best."

The thaw had begun. The women went ahead of us, carrying all they could. I had a gun and I tried to hunt, but I had to rest often. Gophers were appearing, and we killed some and made fires with buffalo chips to cook them. We camped four times before we came to any bush. Then early one morning, my aunt suddenly cried out that she had seen an "old man buffalo." We thought that she had gone crazy but we looked where she pointed and there stood a buffalo, about two hundred yards away. "*A-a-hay-a-ay*. It is going to be hard. Who can go?"

My brother took his loaded gun and moved slowly down the valley, resting often, for he was very weak. We stayed and watched. Sometimes he was out of sight, and then we would see him again, crawling towards where the buffalo had been, but it had moved on and we could not see it.

After a long time, we heard the sound of my brother's gun, and I went to meet him. He told me that he had hit the buffalo, and it would surely die, but we would have to move our camp and follow its trail. It took us a long time to pull down the tent and move slowly after the buffalo. It was not far, but we were weak. My aunt took the gun. "I will follow the trail," she said, "and I will kill the buffalo if it is still alive." The other women went with her, all except my mother.

Night came, and it was bright moonlight when we heard the women returning, dragging great loads of meat. They were able to bring most of it back to where we had camped. The buffalo was old and its meat was tough. The women boiled it to make soup, and that was easier for us to eat, but after long hunger my mother and my brother almost died. *A-a-hay*, we were poor, but now we could fatten ourselves a bit, and we began to feel life in our bones once more.

When I was stronger, I wandered through the bushes where we had pitched our tent, and I saw an old camp, with the tracks of foxes and wolves around it. There was a mound of melting snow, and when I kicked it I saw a corpse, a man dead from hunger. I went back to our camp and we moved to the river, hoping that we might meet some Stoneys, my aunt's people.

Each day, we were able to walk a little more, and the snow was almost gone when we reached the river. Away to the west, we could see people moving in single file. We knew they might be Blackfoot and so we loaded our guns in readiness, but when they saw us they turned towards us, moving slowly, for they had no horses and were carrying heavy loads. They were Stoneys, and they greeted my aunt affectionately as a daughter.

There were eleven families, and everything they had was in the loads on their backs, for they had killed and eaten their horses. But they had buffalo meat, and they fed us grease and dried meat. When we had eaten they wanted to go on, though my father asked them to camp with us by the river, at the old Sun Dance place. We gave them tobacco and tea, and they gave us meat; but the next day they crossed the river. We were sorry to see them go.

We camped at the old Sun Dance place, where there was plenty of wood. The women found a buffalo head and neck in the snow, and they made a fire to boil it. I climbed the bank of the river, and as I sat there I saw something that moved and disappeared again with the wind. I went to find out what it was, and I came to a big snowdrift with a pole at the top, from which a bit of cloth blew in the wind. It marked a cache.

I took off my coat and began to dig through the hard crust of snow. Down inside the drift I found hides that covered the meat of two buffalo, cut in pieces. I had to sit down then, for I remembered my dream and was overcome with feeling and with thankfulness to the spirits who had guided us.

I tied the meat into one of the hides and pulled it down the bank as far as I could, and then I left it and went on to our camp. I found the others eating the head that the women had boiled, and my sister-in-law called to me to come and eat. I ate, and when I was finished I said to my father, "We will have another meal, a good one," and I told him what I had found. "Dreams count, my son," he said to me. "The spirits have pitied us and guided us."

The women hurried to bring the meat to our camp, and we stayed at the Sun Dance place until they had dried much of it and made pemmican, and had scraped and tanned the hides. When all that was done, we moved on. It was spring, and we went to where there were maple trees, and made sugar. Truly a change had come, for now we had sugar; and the hunting was good, with a kill every day. It was pleasant in that valley, just to be alive and well, all of us; and yet we felt ashamed to be so poor, without any horses. It was lonely too.

I had begun to feel that I must have things of my own, and I was restless. I said that I would go to see if I could find some of our people, and I had not gone far when I saw a rider, a Stoney whose name was *Cho-ka-se*. I told him all that had happened to us, and he said, "Come with me and I will lend you horses and carts." He came back to our camp with me. My father was surprised that I had come back so soon, and he was pleased that *Cho-ka-se* would lend us horses and carts; but that is the Indian way.

Then *Cho-ka-se* took us to his camp and he gave us what we needed to travel. Scouts who had gone ahead had found the women who had been with *Na-pa-ke-kun*. He had died of starvation and yet they still had the horses that they had refused to share with us. The scouts came on Big Bear's band too, those with horses helping to carry the others. All through the country north of the Saskatchewan River there had been many deaths from starvation, and the Crees were moving west along the river, hoping to make a truce with the Blackfoot. The scouts said that the Blackfoot had not starved, for they had many horses and could follow the buffalo herds.

We travelled west until we came to a Blackfoot camp. They knew of the hardship we had suffered and we were invited into a big tent. At first we could use only signs, and then one of the Crees came who could interpret. My brother made the Blackfoot his namesake; the old man gave him a fine horse and cart. He gave me a two-year-old to ride, but I made up my mind after all the troubles of that winter that I would never again be dependent upon others.

A Fight with the Sarcee

Sweet Grass and two others were hunting early one morning when they saw a man looking over the country from the top of a hill. They were certain that he must be a scout for the Sarcees, and two of the Crees went back to the camp to tell the others, while Sweet Grass stayed to watch. But the scout had seen them, and he warned the others of his party, who began to shoot at Sweet Grass and to dig pits for the attack that they knew must come.

It was not long before the Crees came, racing their horses and firing their guns as they rode. Many of the Sarcees were killed in the first attack. Then *Pe-ya-pa-se-se-mo* said, "Let me go down to the creek. I may see them from there." He found a big Sarcee creeping through the bush, and he jumped out and grabbed him; but to keep from being dragged away by the big man, he had to hold on to a tree, and he lost his knife. Still, he would not yell, for fear of ridicule. Then another of the Crees, *Cha-cha-mo-kan*, saw the struggle and threw his spear, killing the Sarcee; he and *Pe-ya-pa-se-se-mo* went back to the fight again, calling out, "Let us rush them before they kill too many."

Pay-chak, a short stocky man, very dark, sang what was in his thoughts, "Ready, ready. Trouble lasts for only a day." Waving his spear, he leaped forward and others followed him in hand-to-hand fighting until the Sarcees fled, leaving twenty-two of their number dead.

Many Crees died in that fight too; when the women were mourning for their dead, one of them cried out, "Whoever avenges my husband's death, I will live with him and be his woman." Redwing heard her. He was too old to have taken part in the fight but he went then and scalped one of the Sarcees, and he brought the scalp to her, and she became his woman. That was the grandmother of *Moo-so-min*. The hair on the scalp that was given to her was four feet long, and the Sarcee was Cut Knife. That is how the creek got its name.

The Sun Dance

The lodge for the Sun Dance must be built reverently, and always at that time of the spring or early summer when the trees are coming into leaf and the first blossoms appear.

In all the activities of the tribe or the band, scouts had a real responsibility. They were chosen as loyal and truthful men, able to report what they observed. Their part in the building of the Sun Dance lodge represented this trust. Scouts who go to search for the tree that will be the centre pole of the lodge follow the rules of their training faithfully and reverently.

The lodge is built with its entrance to the south. At the north end, a buffalo skull is placed to show the trust of the people in the Great Spirit who provided the buffalo. The men who take part in the dance sit at the west side of the lodge, the women at the east.

The Sun Dance is a sacred institution. Through it, prayer is made for all people; and in the camp there is reverence, with fasting for two days and nights, and abstinence from sex, as proof that it is with pure hearts that the people dance, or watch the dancing. Many sit in the lodge without dancing, but they fast. They sing four times, and those who are sick or in trouble make a vow to dance later, to give thanks for the help they will receive. In the dance, those who have made their vows to the Great Spirit during the winter, in any of the four pipe ceremonies, fulfill their vows.

The lodge is open to all who come in reverence, not only to Chiefs and headmen. Each person may have his own reason for taking part. When there is sickness in the family, a father or a mother may pray, "Save my child, Giver of all things." A dancer may remember his own needs, or express his own thankfulness for personal blessing, but the dance itself is a prayer for all people.

Offerings of food and clothing are made, and these are distributed to the lame and the blind, to the widows and orphans, to the old. Those who receive these offerings go in their turn to the centre of the lodge and there pray for blessing, not only upon the givers, but for the whole band or tribe.

When a man gives of himself to those who are unfortunate, when his heart says, "I thank thee, Great Spirit," can one believe that nothing comes of it? White people have not understood and they condemn the dance. I see only blessing from it; and when it ends, when all that can be done is finished, there is everywhere a spirit of deep reverence and contentment that lasts for days....

Today, the dance is forbidden; those who have made their vows cannot fulfill them, and it is heart-rending. *Ka-mi-yo-ki-si-kwew* (Fine Day) is one who is not permitted to make the Sun Dance that he vowed, and the shock has stunned his wife, as though she had been shot.

Can things go well in a land where freedom of worship is a lie, a hollow boast? To each nation is given the light by which it knows God, and each finds its own way to express the longing to serve Him. It is astounding to me that a man should be stopped from trying in his own way to express his need or his thankfulness to God. If a nation does not do what is right according to its own understanding, its power is worthless.

I have listened to the talk of the white men's clergy, and it is the same in principle as the talk of our Old Men, whose wisdom came not from books but from life and from God's earth. Why has the white man no respect for the religion that was given to us, when we respect the faith of other nations?

—*1923. Thunderchild Reserve*

Sacred Stories of the Sweet Grass Cree
Sweet Grass Cree Storytellers

In the summer of 1925, Leonard Bloomfield, a linguistics professor from Yale, spent five weeks on the Sweet Grass Reserve. He recorded and translated stories dictated to him in Cree by *kā-kīsikāw-pīhtukāw* (Coming-Day), Adam Sakewew, *kā-wīhkaskusahk*

(Maggie Achenam), and *nāh-namiskwākāpaw* (Louis Moosomin). From this visit, Bloomfield published two collections of stories, *Sacred Stories of the Sweet Grass Cree* (1930) and *Plains Cree Texts* (1934). The *Sweet Grass* collection includes specifically ātaýōhkēwin, or traditional stories, set in primordial times before the present world when *wīsahkēcāhk* was still on the earth. The selections below provide a small sample of the entire collection.

nāh-namiskwākāpaw (Louis Moosomin)

nāh-namiskwākāpaw (Louis Moosomin) was blind from childhood. At the time of his visit in 1925, Bloomfield describes him as "a man of middle age." This would place his birth at sometime in the 1880s. The two stories below tell of the trickster figures of *wīsahkēcāhk* (Wisahketchahk) and *wīhtikow* (Windigo). Notably, one can already see the presence of Christian narrative elements integrated into the Cree oral tradition, though the basis of Cree culture still remains most prominent.

The Birth of Wisahketchahk and the Origin of Mankind

Once upon a time, long ago—I am now telling a sacred story—once upon a time, of old, a certain man dwelt in a lone lodge with his wife and his two children. Then presently, whenever he went away, his wife put on her finery. He did not know why his wife put on her finery. So then at one time he merely pretended to go away to hunt; he hid himself, thinking of her, "Let me see what she will do." And then he saw her beating a tree, and a serpent came out, and he saw that his wife had it for a lover, at once he was very angry. When his wife struck the tree, she said, "My husband, now I have come!" He was very angry. He was jealous; for the serpent was loved more than he. Those of whom I mean to tell the sacred story were Wisahketchahk's mother and father. So now that man was very angry; he could not sleep.

He said to his wife: "I am going far away to hunt."

He really went very far away to hunt. He stayed over one night.

"Why did you stay out over night?" his wife asked him.

"I have been far off to hunt," he told her; "But you, you are to fetch the meat," he told his wife.

"Very well," said she.

As soon as his wife had gone, he took her skirt and put it on. He went to where that serpent was inside the tree.

"My husband, I have come!" he said to the serpent.

Really, it came out. He cut through its neck with a knife; he took the serpent home; he made broth. Then he hid his children.

One must keep in mind that before the earth existed they had many kinds of power. He plunged his two children into the ground. And that woman, too, had great power for all things, and could talk even to every kind of thing and accordingly receive answer from it. And then the man forbade every object that was in their dwelling to tell her anything.

Then his wife arrived. He gave her the serpent to eat which he had cooked into broth.

"Oh, what is this," asked the woman, "which tastes so good?"

"The blood of your husband, the serpent; from it I have made this for you," he told her.

The woman was angry.

"It is not true, is it, that you have done even this?" she asked him.

She went to where she was in the habit of visiting the serpent. Then she struck the tree. The serpent did not come out. She was very angry, as she came back, loudly bewailing it. When she entered the dwelling, her husband cut off her head. Then he rose into the air, to flee.

"I shall needs go dwell there in the sky. Let me be a star!" he said, as he rose higher and higher.

And that woman, that severed head presently opened its eyes. Then presently that head spoke.

"Come, my dish, where are they?"

Without delay, she asked all her utensils. She spoke to every single one in turn, questioning it. At last a stone told her that her husband had sunk them into the earth. Four things that man had given his children, at the time when he started them off; that they might make a river, fire, a mountain of stone, and a forest; a forest of thorn-trees.

Then that head began to call. "My children, wait for me! You are making me wretched by leaving me!" it cried.

That woman called all the time. And that little boy who was fleeing under ground, from afar he saw that severed speaking head, as he was being carried on his elder brother's back.

He said to him, "Big brother, our mother is not there. It is only a talking head," he said.

He took that which his father had given him, that from which the Cree make fire; he threw it behind him.

"Let there be fire here!" he said.

And really that being was entirely brought to a stop, when far and wide the fire blazed. For it was but a severed head which went along. Because he, at any rate, who is called Indian was helped by evil beings, was why that severed head could roll along. Finally it passed the fire. Then it again pursued its children. All its hair was aflame.

Then presently when again that child looked about, who was being borne by the other, "It is not our mother, big brother! Let us flee with all our might!" he told him.

Again he took that which his father had given him that he might make a hill of thornberry-trees. He threw it behind him. That Rolling Skull was really blocked. Then it bade a Great Serpent to bite through the thorn-trees and make a passage through for it, that it might go unchecked. And so it managed to go on, unchecked.

Then, when again they had fled a long ways, again that child who was being carried saw the Skull come rolling. And again, he threw behind them that which he had been given by his father that he might make a mountain of rock. Vastly that rocky crag extended. That Skull-Being could not manage to go across it. At once it employed a beaver with iron teeth to bite that rock to pieces. Then it was able again to go on. Again it pursued its children.

Again that child who was being borne by his elder brother saw it coming. Then that which his father had given him that he might make a river, he threw it, by mistake, on ahead. The child kept crying its cry. Then they wept in terror that the rolling Skull would kill them, their mother's skull.

Then, as they wept, "Do not weep! I will take you to safety!" a Great Serpent said to them.

Then he carried them across the water. When he had brought them to the far shore, he crossed back, who had taken those children across.

When the Rolling Skull saw him, it said, "Take me across, too!" it said to him.

"But do not be impatient" he told it.

So he carried it across. It rode on his back.

Just when they were in the middle of the stream, "Great Serpent, you are going altogether too slowly!" said that woman.

Then he threw her into the water.

"'Sturgeon' will be your name!" he told that Rolling Head.

Then those boys wandered about, suffering many hardships. That boy was Wisahketchahk in his childhood.

Then they departed from there, he with his little brother. He made a ball for him to play with.

Then at one time, as they were walking by the river, the elder boy was told, "Come here!" by an old man in a canoe. When he stepped into the canoe, this person carried him off. They left the smaller boy behind.

Then as he began to weep, "Big brother, now I shall have to turn into a wolf!" cried that little boy, the younger one.

Thus only Wisahketchahk was taken, and the old man brought him over yonder to his dwelling. He put him under his canoe as he tipped it on the beach; he did not even care to take him home. The old man went to his abode, to his two daughters.

"My children, I have brought someone for you to marry," he said; "Go look at him," he said.

The older girl went out of the tent and looked at him. Why, he was very ugly!

"I cannot marry a child!" she said of him.

"Oh, he is handsome enough. Perhaps it is only because he has been weeping too much," he said.

Then the younger sister went there. This young woman brought the lad home, after washing his face. She took care of him; she really took him for her husband. The elder sister disliked him, and all the more so as the child wantonly played tricks,................

On the fourth night, however, he said to them, "Do you build a lodge for the steam-bath; I shall make my body," he said.

Accordingly a sweat-lodge was built for him, and he made his body. Then he was very handsome, when he had made himself over. Then she who had disliked him conceived a passion for him. But even though she plied him with speech, he did not care to have her so much as speak to him. Then the old man was urged by that elder daughter of his to try and kill him.

And really, "Yes, I shall try to kill him," said the old man.

"I wonder where I can get good little arrow-sticks?" said the youth.

Then, "I shall take my son-in-law to such a place," said the old man. And so he took him to an island.

Thus spoke the old man: "My dream guardian, I feed you this man!" he said.

Hardly had the youth gone into the brush, when out came a bear at him, one of those who are white.

"'I shall kill him,' is that what you are thinking?" said he; "You cannot kill me," he said; "For I, too, have you as my dream spirit," he said.

The youth really slew it. He took its head. He took it home with him. He outdistanced the old man; he walked along on the surface of the water. When the old man went home, there he saw the bear's head hanging over the doorway; the old man bewailed his dream guardian who had been slain.

Presently, as they dwelt there, the youth spoke thus: "I wonder where I can get pretty feathers to make my arrows?"

"Over yonder amid the rocky cliffs, there the feathers are very fine. I shall take him there," said the old man.

Really, he led him off, to go there. And so he brought him there where the Thunderers had their nests.

"Come, my dream guardians, I feed you this man!" he said to them. With that he turned to go home. Again, he killed all those Thunderers.

Once more, "I wonder where I can get a good osier to make my bow?"

Then again, the old man: "I shall take him where the willows are good."

Really, he took him there.

Again, "Come, my dream guardian, this one I feed to you!" he said to a Great Serpent.

And again, the youth slew the Great Serpent to whom he was being fed. He took home its head. Again the old man was the second to arrive. He grieved over this dream spirit, too.

"Great Serpent, my dream guardian!" he cried.

Then he did not know how he could freeze him to death, to kill him, but by freezing him.

So he said, "Let us hunt, my nephew!" he said to him.

Accordingly, they went hunting. At nightfall, no sooner, they killed a moose.

"Pshaw! We shall have to sleep out! We are soaked through to the bone!"

It was a warm-weather snowstorm.

"Let us dry our clothes," he said to him.

So they dried them, feeding up a huge fire in a cedar-grove. As soon as he knew that his son-in-law slept, he took the latter's clothes from where he had hung them. He burned them all.

"What is that burning? Your clothes have burned up!"

"Hah, of course, for you are trying to kill me!—So then I shall turn into a moose!" said the youth.

As the old man went away, he called the Cold. And really, it grew very cold. For he had called it. Then that youth went home. He out-distanced his uncle; he was in the form of a moose, as he went home.

Then, "Why thus?" his wife asked him.

"Because your father is trying to kill me, he burned up all my clothes."

When the old man arrived, his son-in-law sat there. His daughter upbraided him.

"Why now did you burn up your nephew's clothes?" his daughter asked him.

"Oh dear, because I was walking in my sleep," said the old man.

"Let me try once more!" thought the old man. "My son-in-law, let us hunt!" he said to him.

Accordingly, they went hunting.

"We shall not be able to go home!" he said to him, again.

Not before nightfall they killed a moose.

"Let us camp," said the old man; "We shall dry our clothes," for, "In spite of all, I shall try to kill him this way," thought the old man.

Then, after feeding up a fire, they hung up their clothes. As soon as the other slept, the youth took down all of his own garments. He put them down where he slept. Then the old man got up. He squinted from under his eyelids, pretending to walk in his sleep. The old man himself burned up all his own clothes.

"What is that burning?" he asked him.

"Here are my clothes, lying here," said the youth; "I daresay it is your own clothes you have put in the fire," he said to the old man; "But seeing that you did it to me, I too shall now leave you, as you left me."

"Very well! I suppose I shall then turn into a moose!" said the old man.

But he did not succeed in turning into a moose. Wisahketchahk called the Cold. He killed the old man.

Of course the old woman now was very angry, when her husband had been killed.

"We shall fight!" she said to her son-in-law; "With this pounding-stone four times I shall threaten you; then I shall strike you!" said the old woman.

When for the fourth time she held it over Napiw as if to strike, he took it; he smashed her head with it. He killed her too.

Thereupon that other young woman, her, too, he killed. So he killed them all. Of course Wisahketchahk and the other stayed there.

Then he set out, for he heard that his little brother who had turned into a wolf had been slain by the various Great Panthers and Great Serpents that dwell under water. He was very angry.

"I wonder what I shall do to go under the water!"

When he saw, as he always looked into the waters, his little brother, where he had been slain by them all, hanging over the doorway of the Chief Fish, he was filled with grief and hate. Presently he went there; he went and shot with an arrow that Chief Fish. Then he wandered about. Presently he saw a frog.

"What is your errand?" he asked it.

"Why, I am going to doctor by breathing," said the frog.

"What do you do, when you are breath-doctoring?" asked Wisahketchahk.

When it told him, he killed it. He turned himself into its form; he made himself to be a frog. He went to where they kept the Red Wolfskin.

As soon as he entered, "Make way for this person! This is the one who has come to cure him whom Wisahketchahk has shot with an arrow," was said of him.

Accordingly, they made way for him. When he was treating him whom he had come to tend, then, truly, with a vim he thrust in that arrow.

"What is that about a frog would be breathing on wounds! Rather, you have angered me much by killing my little brother!" cried Wisahketchahk.

Then he fled.

"You have enraged the evil beasts!" the Lord told him; "The earth will be flooded. Take one each of every beast, and of all those who fly. Build a great canoe," He told him.

At that time, we are told, before this earth was flooded, all kinds of animals ate each other. Even the buffalo ate men, no matter where they were. That is the way things were. Wisahketehahk took one of every kind, in pairs, one male and one female. Of all who fly and of all who walk about this earth, of each he took two. Then he built a great canoe. Then deep darkness came. All the stars ceased to be. Everywhere the earth was flooded, when he had finished the great canoe. Then, when the flood was everywhere, and all the mountains of rock were submerged, then they drifted about. At last he nearly starved to death. His wife starved to death. Then, when all the creatures that dwell in the water, the evil beings, tried to kill him, when in vain they came there, and he slew them, then at last all creatures feared him. Presently God descended to him.

Thus He spoke to him: "If you cannot scrape up some earth, then never will these waters recede," He told him.

It was forty cubits to the bottom; the flood had covered all. "Now how am I to do?" he thought, none the less.

But he had all the beasts on his ship. Presently he bade the loon try to take up some soil. It turned out quite unable. Then presently he employed the otter. It was entirely unable to do it. Although he employed all, as many as are good divers, they could not at all scrape up any earth. Then in time he sent the muskrat. It was a long time coming back. A little earth was sticking to it. Again he bade it go. Again it brought some. Four times he sent it off to fetch earth.

"It is enough!" the Spirit told him.

Thus it was that the Indians were given this by the spirit powers, that first they had an earth here. For then all the water ceased to be.

Then Wisahketchahk went away from here. Then the Spirit decreed that he was to have man as a companion, and decided to create man. He made two human beings of earth. Then before He brought the men to life, from each of them He took the lowest rib, and then He brought them to life.

When man first spoke, after being created, we are told that he said, "Water!"

When he spoke again, we are told that he said "My food!"

They were feared by all creatures, for no cause. Then the man was named. "Dug-out-Canoe" the first man was named. Then the woman. Four of them dwelt there, being in different wise related, so as to make a family.

Then from there the raven was first sent out to make the circuit of the earth. In the outcome he was needs rejected. Then the eagle was sent out.

In the time that began then, people never died. They lived quietly and undisturbed, until at last they came to be many. They found how to keep themselves alive. From that time to this in successive generations has come the Cree, the Indian.

Of all the different peoples I understand this story which is desired. Of how the Cree lived, as the Cree have come down through the generations to this time, all of this I know. And the Christian worship which the white man has brought here with him of this, too, I know all, of how it has been announced to this time. I have chosen to tell the sacred story of how the first man was created, the Indian. Because I have thought that doubtless this is what is desired, that doubtless people wish to know of the life of the Indian, that is why I tell this sacred story.

When twice a hundred years had gone by, at that time, this first man was killed by a bear, and so he died. Then, we are told, he was assigned by the Spirit to care for the souls of the dead of us who are Indians. I question if it is still so; I cannot say. For too greatly are we destroying ourselves. The Indian was forbidden to practise the Christian religion; that is what I mean.

"I say this only to him who is called Indian: thou shalt not worship in Christian wise! Not to thee do I give this. I give my Son to the white man, that he may suffer for having slain my Son," said the Lord.

So much for this discourse.

Burnt-Stick

Once upon a time, long ago, a Windigo carried on his work of extermination. Ten youths took flight. That Windigo, with a face on either side of his head, no matter how many tents there were, always killed off all the people.

Then those youths, who were ten, said, "Let us flee! We alone shall not be killed," they said.

So they made ready; far off on a mountain they went to build their tipi. Then, after a time, they went back; they fetched their little brother. They had their tent off there alone. Then, at one time, as they continued to dwell off there, and the little boy always stayed to keep the house, then presently, as he was feeding the fire, he ran a splinter into himself. He pulled out the sliver of wood. When he threw out of the door that sliver of wood which he had run into his foot, there came crawling in a little girl.

He lifted her up, thinking, "It is no use, I should not be able to bring her up."

When she came into the tent, after he had twice thrown her out, again he threw her out.

Then, when again she came in, she called to him, "Big brother!"

"Ho, I had better do it again! I should not be surprised if she were to turn into a young woman, if I threw her out again!" he thought. Then he spoke thus: "Let her be a young woman, since it seems that I am being aided by the Powers!" he said.

Then, when there entered a young woman, "Be seated, my big sister!" said the boy.

"Burnt-Stick" it seems that he called the young woman. And now he was glad to have a big sister; and he was glad that all his elder brothers would have this young woman to do their household work for them.

And now it appears that in his usual way Wisahketchahk was staying with these young men; it was because they knew in which direction that Windigo would take flight. For Wisahketchahk was badly frightened; that was why he had asked hospitality of these young men.

"You will see, little brother!" he must have said.

Wisahketchahk was always the first to come into the tipi.

"What would you think," asked the boy, "of our having a young woman?"

And Wisahketchahk, for his part, said, "We shall have her as our younger sister!" for it seems that Wisahketchahk had every manner of creature for his younger brother or sister.

Then this younger sister of theirs was very diligent, sewing for them, and doing their household work. It seems that she kept them very well, so that they, in turn, became very fond of her. When they did their hunting, without delay, it seems, she always tanned the hides and made clothes for them, taking in every way excellent care of them.

Presently Wisahketchahk spoke as follows: "Oh, by this time the Windigo with a face on either side of his head knows that we are here," he said; "But we shall go visiting," he told her; "And then, if you hear anything, never listen to it, when you are gathering wood," he must have told the young woman who was called Burnt-Stick; and, "Never, when you see anything, take it up," he told her; Never take it up. Then we shall be off visiting again. If then again you hear anything, when we are not at home, great manitou power has that two-faced Windigo. So great that even I, Wisahketchahk, fear him," Wisahketchahk must have said; "Then, again, you will hear exactly, as it will seem, the sound of our voices," he said; "Really, for four nights we shall be off visiting. And it will be very cold weather. Then you will hear our voices; do not open the door," he must have told the young woman.

Accordingly, when the young woman had been instructed, she started to gather firewood, as soon as all her brothers had gone away. And she split all the wood, so that it should be quite ready for use; and she brought it all indoors ready for use; and she cut a big poplar tree besides. Then she closed up their tipi solidly. It was very cold weather.

Presently she heard someone call, "Little sister, here we are!" seemed to be spoken for her to hear.

But, after all, she had been warned; she did not stir from the spot. At last all round the lodge there was the sound of them dying of cold. In the morning she arose; when she went outside, she found not even a footprint. She wondered.

"So it really is thus!" thought the young woman.

When four nights had passed, the young men arrived. Then, when the young woman always gathered wood all day, she never picked up anything, although she saw all manner of things. But then at one time she saw a most beautiful feather.

She picked it up, when, "Of course I could not get the better of you!" said the two-faced Windigo, suddenly rising from the feather.

Thus spoke the Windigo: "Truly, I shall have good eating, when I eat Burnt-Stick! Now, Burnt-Stick, first I shall take you home with me; I shall make you fat."

With that the Windigo took the young woman on his back and carried her. He took her home with him, to where he had an old woman whom he led a dreadful life; every day this old woman had his stew ready for him, cooking it done before he got home, for every day he ate two men, his habit being, as soon as he got home, first to eat their entrails.

So now, "Grandmother," he said; "have you boiled the entrails ready for me to eat? Now very pretty is the young woman I have brought home to eat. Do not spare your pains to fatten her," he said.

Then, "Very well," said the old woman.

The old woman became very fond of the maid, Burnt-Stick.

Then, it seems, "Grandchild, surely I hate the very thought of killing you," she said; "Do try to deceive him; do you, instead, kill me," the old woman said; "And then you will set me to boil," said the old woman.

Truly, the maid was pleased at what the old woman told her. "But how must I do to kill you?" asked the young woman.

Thus spoke the old woman: "You will take an ax; you will strike a blow on my head," said the old woman; "Yonder, in the direction where there is no sun, are four hills, the first and nearest of which you will climb. From there you will see the second hill. When you have crossed four hills, there try to reach in your flight an iron house. The one who dwells there will overcome him. If you manage to get there in your flight, then you will live," she told her; "When you reach the place in your flight, speak thus: 'Big brother, the both-side-faced Windigo wants to kill me!' you will say. Then they will open the door for you."

Accordingly, even as the old woman had directed Burnt-Stick, she struck her on the head. Then she skinned her and cut her up, whom she had slain. She put her in the kettle to boil. When she had cooked her done, she ran away as fast as she could. She ran with all her might. Presently she saw a hill, and all night long she ran. Then she saw another hill; she crossed it, too. She saw another hill; this, too, she crossed. When she climbed the next hill, already she heard the Windigo shouting to her.

"It is no use! The earth will not be large enough to give you refuge!" he shouted to her.

It appears that the Windigo was very angry at having eaten his grandmother. Now she was running down-hill; as she climbed the next rise, there down below was the iron house. When she looked behind her, already she saw the Windigo coming; then really she fled with all her might. When she reached it, she forgot the instruction she had been given by the old woman whom she had killed.

"Open the door for me! Both-Side-Eyes wants to kill me, big brother!" she cried.

Although she called in all manner of ways, he was even about to seize her, when she remembered what the old woman had told her.

"Big brother," she cried again, "open the door for me!" she cried; "Both-Side-Face wants to kill me!" she cried.

The door of the iron house swung open. She went in. She saw those who had their dwelling inside there, a young woman and a young man.

Then the young woman said to her, "Sister-in-law, sit down!" Soon with noise the Windigo arrived outside.

"Open for me, Iron-House-Dweller!" he cried.

Then the young man opened the door and chopped off the Windigo's head.

Then the young woman stayed there. For that young woman and that man were very good to her. Then in time, they gave her something to keep in the bosom-fold of her garment, to give her manitou power. And really, she had great strength; she too had now manitou power. Then they made men's clothes, which she put on, * * * * * * * * * * Then really, she went about hunting.

Then at one time they said to her, "Your brothers miss you very much. They are suffering greatly; you ought to try to see them," they told her; "Now, not far from here you will come to a hill. There you will see a very large tipi. He who lives there is intent on tormenting people; he builds a nest from which he jumps on people. That place is full of people who suffer from all kinds of injuries, since that evil person who lives there breaks different parts of their bodies as he comes down on them," they told her; "This is the only difficulty, but, after all, he takes only young women; he pays no attention to men. As soon as he sees you, he will say to you, "* * * * * * * * * * * * * * * * * *" they told her; "That is what he will say to you."

When the young woman had been instructed, she went out of the house, taking provision for the journey. She set out. Presently, just as the day had reached noon, she saw the place. Although she walked far round to avoid it, she must have been seen by that evil man who all day jumped down on young women, taking pleasure in tormenting them.

When he had come and met her, he said to her, "* * * * *"

So it seemed he was her cousin. * * * * * * * * * * * *

"'My male cousin,' I have been calling her; why it is Burnt-Stick!"

Thereupon she secretly took up a stick of saskatoon wood; she used it as a cane. He led her home by the hand and took her into his tipi. And there she saw nothing but young women whose bodies were broken in every way from having been jumped upon.

These young women said, "Only to think that we, too, were as beautiful as this young woman!" Thus spoke those crippled ones.

Then, when he had placed a seat, and had climbed up on a tree which stood there, she took that stick which she had picked up.

"Let it turn into iron!" she said; "When he comes leaping, let him impale himself!" she said.

And truly, as he jumped, he impaled himself, that evil man who used to kill the young women. So Burnt-Stick killed him; she killed that evil man.

She went to where she had left her brothers when she departed.

What did she see, they were weeping, mourning for her, and all the while saying, "Our little sister was eaten by the Windigo!" Thus spoke her brothers as she listened to them.

"Enough; cease weeping, brothers! I have come!" she said.

Those young men were very glad. She had picked out ten of the women she had restored to life, and taken them for her brothers. Then those men were very glad to have wives.

Then at one time, "I am not really a human being," said the young woman; "And now my father wants me. So I shall turn into a deer. I have completed my benefaction to all of you, in giving you young women."

—1925. Sweet Grass Reserve

kā-kīsikāw-pīhtukāw (Coming-Day)

Bloomfield describes *kā-kīsikāw-pīhtukāw*, or Coming-Day, as "a blind old man" when he met him in 1925, which would date his birth to sometime in the mid-1800s. According to Bloomfield, *kā-kīsikāw-pīhtukāw* was considered to know "more traditional stories than any other member of the band."

The selection below is an example of a teaching story, where *wīsahkēcāhk* (Wisahketchahk) teaches an aspect of survival, usually by inflicting damage on himself or by misadventure. See John Cote's "Nēnapohš and the Shut-eye Dancing Ducks" and "Nēnapohš Makes Red Willows" for a Saulteaux version of this story, and also Bertha O'Watch's "Ịktómi and Fox" for a Nakoda version of another aspect of the story. Together, these versions exemplify the interconnectedness of Plains oral traditions.

The Shut-Eye Dancers

Once upon a time, as Wisahketchahk was tramping along—as usual he was hungry—as he was tramping along, he saw some ducks and many geese and ducks.

Then this was what he thought: "How shall I kill them?" he thought.

Presently he saw a little lake, and by the water's edge some weeds. He took them and rolled them up. He tied up a great bundle of them, took it on his back, and went off. When he came walking close to where the ducks were, they caught sight of him.

The ducks said, "Ho, our big brother! What is that he's carrying on his back?" they said.

"Suppose I ask him," said one duck.

"Yes, do," they said.

"Big brother, what is that you're carrying on your back?"

He kept right on walking; just as if he had not heard, he kept on walking.

Again the duck asked him, "Big brother, what is it you're carrying on your back?"

Only then did Wisahketchahk stand still. "Say," it said, "what is it you're carrying?"

"Why, Shut-Eye Dances!" said Wisahketchahk.

"What is a Shut-Eye Dance?" said the duck.

Wisahketchahk spoke thus: "A saltatory rite," he told the other.

"Do you give us a dance," said the duck; "Let us dance the Shut-Eye Dance!"

"Splendid!" cried Wisahketchahk; "Oh, it is fine that you have taken pity on me, little brothers! No one has given heed to me until now, and danced, when long ago I had pledged myself to give a ritual dance," said Wisahketchahk; "So then, come ashore."

Off went the ducks and geese. All of them came.

Thus spoke Wisahketchahk: "Hopeless ninnies, I've been starving! I shall have a big meal!" thought Wisahketchahk.

They came to where he sat.

"Ha, come here, little brothers!" said Wisahketchahk.

Setting out and making for a clump of trees, he came to where there was plenty of wood for a fire.

"Ha, little brothers, take up some faggots," he said.

Accordingly they took up a plenty and built themselves a lodge, which they thatched with those weeds. The little doorway was very small.

"Ha, now, little brothers, come inside," he said; "First the geese and the big ducks will come in," he said; "Especially those who are chiefs," he said.

Accordingly these, the geese, sat like this, at the far end, facing the door. Over at the other end, by the door sat the little fellows. Then that Wisahketchahk blocked up the doorway, thinking "So that they can't get out." Then Wisahketchahk wept.

"Little brothers, I thank you for having built this lodge. When no one took pity on me, it was you who pitied me," he spoke, weeping.

Then he ceased weeping.

Thus spoke Wisahketchahk: "Now, little brothers, here in the centre I shall stand; I shall sing. When I sing, you will dance; you will close your eyes. Not until I cease singing will you open your eyes. When I summon the spirit-power, I shall say, 'Hwe, hwe, hwe!' Then you will dance with all your might, when you hear me call thus."

"Very well," they answered.

Then Wisahketchahk took hold of a branch that had old leaves on it which rustled when he swung it, like this, just like a bell, those leaves. Thereupon he began singing.

These were his words:

"Shut-Eye Dances

I bring here!"

were the words of his song.

Then, when they all had closed their eyes and were dancing, presently, "Hwe, hwe!" went Wisahketchahk, taking hold of a big goose and wringing its neck. In this way he kept on circling round, singing all the while, and, as he went, wringing the necks of the geese and of the big ducks. Over yonder by the door danced Hell-Diver, and when he heard something or other, and opened one eye as he danced, there he saw Wisahketchahk killing one after another.

"Yah!" he cried, "It's the same old story, Wisahketchahk is killing us off!"

When the others opened their eyes, Wisahketchahk said, "What sort of a dance would I be bringing you blockheads? I was hungry, that's all!" he said to those ducks.

They fled out of doors, the others, trying to get away.

Thereupon Wisahketchahk went out of the lodge, laughing and rejoicing, thinking, "I shall eat a plenty." So then he tore up that lodge of his, taking the faggots and building a fire to roast those summer creatures. He roasted them whole. Having made too big a fire, he began to feel hot.

He went off, thinking, "First I shall get over feeling hot; by that time my geese will be done."

And so when he had walked a little ways, there he saw Fox, who had a pain in his leg, and was limping and could not walk properly, as he tried to run away from him.

"Wait a moment, little brother!" he called to him.

"Dear me, no!" the other answered; "You are only going to play me some new trick," he said to him.

"No!" he told him; "It is only that I want to tell you some news. Do you see all the smoke rising over here?"

"Yes," said the other to him.

"Over there I have killed a lot of geese and ducks, and there I am roasting them," he told him; "We shall have plenty to eat," he told him; "But first let us race. Let us run around that hill not far from here."

"Oh dear, no! You see I can't walk, with my sore leg," said Fox.

Wisahketchahk spoke thus: "I shall tie stones to my leg," he said.

"Very well," said Fox.

Wisahketchahk took some stones and tied them to his leg.

"There, little brother, come on!"

So they set off at a run. Wisahketchahk left Fox behind.

"Hey, I thought this Fox was a runner, this poor little brother of mine, whom I am leaving so far behind! I shall give the poor fellow a few of them when he arrives from his run," said Wisahketchahk.

As soon as Wisahketchahk was out of sight behind the hill, that Fox turned back, and his leg was not sore at all, as he made for the rising smoke. When he got there, there he saw the geese and ducks a-roasting. He took them and ate, robbing Wisahketchahk of his roasts. He ate them all up. Only the feet of those geese and ducks, only those did he put into the embers, thinking, "Let Wisahketchahk see them." Then he made for safety, thinking of Wisahketchahk, "He will be angry at me."

Then, when Wisahketchahk arrived, he was very hot; for he had had quite a run.

"Hah, when I am no longer hot, I shall eat," he thought; "I shall give my little brother a few, too," he said of Fox, "when he gets here," he thought.

He did not know that the other had already eaten his geese. So now he took one of those feet. There was not any goose.

"Oho, I have overcooked him!" he said.

At last he took them all out; every one was gone; only the feet were there.

"Oho, it's surely Fox has been fooling me again, eating up my geese! And so I am to stay hungry!" he cried; "Ho, you have got me angry, Fox! The earth will not be big enough for you to escape. It was I created the earth; I will find you; and when I find you, who ate up my geese!" cried Wisahketchahk, as he went off to look for Fox.

He had not gone far, when he saw him taking a nap, his belly all big; for he had eaten a hearty fill. He took up a stone, to strike him.

"Yah!" he said; "I shall ruin his hide," he said; "I might as well have a cap of his fox-pelt!" he said; "I had better make a fire round him so that he chokes in the smoke," he said.

The other was listening to what he said about him. So then he made a fire, setting fire to the grass round about. When the blaze came, Fox got up. The smoke was getting too thick for him.

"Ha," said Wisahketchahk; "Haha, just you eat up my geese again!" he said to him.

Fox dashed about in a circle, this way and that, as the smoke grew denser. At last Wisahketchahk could see him no more. Up leaped Fox, jumping across the flame, and making for safety. Wisahketchahk did not see how he ran away. At last there was a big fire, and Wisahketchahk kept walking round it.

"I have surely put an end to Fox; burning him to death," said Wisahketchahk; and when he saw the ashes lying, where there had been buffalo-dung, "Surely I have burned him to a sorry end!" said he; "I shall eat what is left of him, if there is any of him left from the fire," he thought; and he was going to take up the ashes there, thinking, "And this must be Fox, burned up in this fire," as he deceived himself.

Even now he did not know that the other had got away.

And so this is the end of this sacred story.

When he kicked Hell-Diver, "Now then, ahead in future time mortal man will grow up; he will see here on you where I have kicked your rump crooked. 'Hell-Diver,' they will call you. You will not be handsome; too much have you angered me by telling this and by opening your eyes," he told him.

So much for this.

—*1925. Sweet Grass Reserve*

kā-wīhkaskusahk (Maggie Achenam)

In 1925, Bloomfield describes *kā-wīhkaskusahk* (Maggie Achenam) as "a middle-aged woman." This would date her birth at sometime in the 1880s. Bloomfield also patronizingly describes her as "something of a sorceress." The stories below all have a girl as the central hero in adventures with the Thunderers, the Hell-Diver, and the *wīhtikow* (Windigo).

Thunderbird and Winter

Now another story.

Once upon a time an old woman dwelt with her daughter. They were Cree. They suffered hunger, for the woman's daughter merely gathered thornberries, which she boiled, and that was all they had to eat; they were almost dead of hunger.

Then at one time the young woman went off to go about gathering thornberries, when she saw someone who had killed game. She went near. That person would not even look at her. Quickly he prepared all the meat. Then he went away. But she, the other, picked up the clots of blood to eat. She went home. Then she made a broth of the poor thornberries, and this broth they ate, only this.

On the next day she went out again. Again that man killed a buffalo. It was very cold. The young woman, as she went about, picking thornberries here and there, went to where that man was.

"You have come just in time to where game has been killed," the man said to her; "Cut off for yourself as much as you please."

The young woman was pleased.

"Now my mother will eat much meat!" she thought.

At once he gave her one buffalo. She went home; she took home the meat entire. When she arrived at her home, they had a big meal. The old woman was glad.

"Go out again; perhaps you will see him again making a killing."

She went. She saw him killing a buffalo. Again he gave her the entire carcass. She was pleased.

And then, "Are you married?" "No," she answered him. "Then let me marry you."

"Only wait," she told him; "Let me first tell my mother. If she is content, I will marry you. Tomorrow I will tell you."

"Very well," said the man; "I am very glad."

Then she departed. On the next day the old woman's daughter asked her.

"Let me marry this man," she asked her. "Yes," said the old woman.

Then the young woman went; she saw the man.

"Now I shall tell you: 'Yes,' says my mother; I may marry you."

She brought the man home with her. They arrived at the lodge. She had him as her husband. Every day he killed game. But when the weather was hot, the young woman became listless.

"Why are you so listless?" he asked his wife.

"Because this is the time, always, when my husband is about to come," said the young woman.

"And so you mean to say you have a husband, this man!" he said to her; "If I had known that, I should not have married you. How looks the sky when your husband is about to come?" he asked the young woman.

"When he is about to come, there is white sky; and yellow clouds are in the sky. That is when my husband has come near on his hither way. And close now, close has he come. Flee; he will kill you."

Then the man, "No; here I shall stay."

Presently the man hid indoors. There came a great thunderstorm.

"That is my husband," said the young woman.

Close by the other came to earth; he came into the lodge. "Get up, my fellow-husband!" he said to that man.

Then he got up.

"We shall have a contest," the other said to him.

"Very well; you first. What sort of contest shall we have? You first," the Thunderer was told.

Then he roared. There came a great rainstorm; it hailed. Then that man changed his form. A snowshoe lay there during the great storm of rain and hail. Presently he ceased; he came inside the lodge.

"Your turn now, my fellow-husband; shoot your arrow," he told his fellow-husband.

"Very well," said he; "Now let there be intense cold!" he spoke; "Let there be very clear sky; let there be a clear cold sky!"

It grew very cold. And there was a great flurry of snow; there was a strong wind, until the branches snapped and crackled in the cold. The Snowshoe's rival husband froze almost to death.

"Enough, my fellow-husband! Keep you our wife, as you please," he told him.

Thereupon the weather again grew very hot.

"Keep you our wife, as you please; you have defeated me," he said.

And so now I have finished this story too.

Hell-Diver

Now another story.

Hell-Diver wanted to be a man. Once upon a time he made some breeches for himself out of cedar bark. Also he made himself a bow and arrows. Then he went to this Cree country here. He saw people; he went there.

"What are you after here?"

He did not understand when they spoke to him. "Maybe he is a Stony Sioux," they said.

But when they spoke Sioux to him, he did not understand.

"Shay chah," he said.

"Why, it's the diver-duck!" they said of him. He fled, waddling off in no particular direction.

Now, once there were ten people, men, who spent their time hunting, and one woman took care of all these men, who were her elder brothers. Then, at one time—while she gathered firewood every day, her brothers went on their daily hunt. Then, at one time, some women came to where she was tanning. These women asked her to go away with them. She did not listen to them. The others took something away from her; they went off with it. Then she pursued them; when they had gone a long ways, the others gave it back to her. Then they went from there; she accompanied the others. Then they came to a river.

"It's a husband we're going after," the others told her, "the Bead-Man."

There by the river they stayed. Presently a little man came in a canoe. He beached his canoe where they were. Those two women got into the canoe. The other one was left behind as they paddled off; she wept and wept. And the others paddled along.

"Kill some game," they told him.

They saw some buffaloes. Then that hell-diver beached his canoe. He killed one.

"First let me eat the belly-fat!"

"Oh dear, no! I should say not! I am going to use it when religious rites are performed."

Then that one woman said, "He is the diver-duck."

The other, "No! The Bead-Man."

Then they got into the canoe again. In due time he beached it.

"Stay here," he told his wives.

So they stayed.

"Your sister-in-law will come call you," he told them.

Then he went. In due time someone came: two young women.

"Come, sister-in-law!"

.... Then they went there. They arrived over there.

Then that other woman who had been left by the canoers arrived there; she found another man for herself. Then, when night came they danced.

Then, "Don't peep in where the dance is going on," that hell-diver told his wives.

But those women peeped in just the same. There was the hell-diver being trampled on, their husband, the hell-diver. Then that one woman hated having the hell-diver as her husband. They went away; they went to take another husband. They took a crumbly old log that had many bugs on it; they placed it like someone lying down in their bed. Then they went away.

When the dance was over, the hell-diver came home.

....

The other one, also, kept pinching him.

"Now both of you pinch me, even though there has been a dance," he said to them.

Something there spoke: "Long ago by this time they have gone to find a husband; it's bugs are biting you there; ....

Then the hell-diver wept. Then he looked for them. He found them staying with another man. He cut the other man's throat; he killed him. Suddenly the women woke up; that man had been killed. They went away from there.

The Foolish Maiden

Another woman set out. She came to a river, and there she saw a man approaching in a canoe.

"Get in," he said to her.

She stepped aboard. There, when she looked at him, he had a face at either side of his head. Then she wept.

"Is it 'Do let me live!' you are thinking?" he asked her; "My intention is to eat you," he told her.

She wept.

"Sit still! It is no use; I mean to eat you."

They reached an island. He disembarked.

"Grandmother," cried that Windigo, "Come fetch her; prepare to boil this person I am bringing."

A little old woman came and fetched her. She brought her over yonder to her lodge. The young woman gazed at her.

"You don't stop staring at me," said the little old woman; "What matter, since I am bound to boil you?" she said to her.

Then the young woman answered her: "It is because I recognize you, because 'My grandmother,' is what I am saying to myself."

"And so it is my grandchild! I had almost been her undoing! Kill me, my grandchild. Then set the whole string of my entrails into water. That is what the Windigo will eat first. Also you will cut off my arm; 'Chop wood, grandmother!' you will say; 'You are to split wood!' Then I shall really split wood. And as for you, you will be running away. Run with all your might!"

Then she ran away. Her grandmother chopped firewood. Soon the Windigo arrived.

"Grandmother, come home! I want to eat!" he cried.

"Wait a bit! I am gathering wood," she said.

"Be quick, now!"

"Do you eat meanwhile. I shall be back soon," said the old woman, while her arm all by itself cut wood.

The Windigo began to eat. He ate his grandmother. He was impatient because his grandmother was not coming promptly. Then he began to search. When he came there, behold, there his grandmother's arm fell to the ground.

"Whither can you flee, you who have bereft me by killing my grandmother! She cooked for me. I will chase you," he called to her.

Then that Windigo started in pursuit. The young woman fled. Soon he came close with noise. She was in great distress.

"Now he will kill me," she thought.

She came to a man who had a house.

"Open! A Windigo is trying to kill me," she called to him.

He paid no heed to her.

"Quickly, big brother! Take pity on me! A Windigo is trying to kill me," she called to him.

At last he opened the door. She went in. The other had already got there on the run.

"Open the door for me! I come in pursuit of my wife," he cried.

His words went unheeded.

"Quick, open! I want to see my wife."

Then the woman, "Don't! Do not open! He is a Windigo, not my husband."

And the man, "Open! I have come to fetch my wife."

"No!" she cried.

Then at one time the man opened the door. When the other man had got half-way in, he flung it shut; he killed him. Then the woman went out. She took a great amount of firewood. Then she made a fire. She threw that man into it; she burned him up.

Then her big brother, "Do not take anything!"

All kinds of things were lying around; bowls, spoons, kettles, forks, all kinds of good things which had fallen out when the Windigo was burned. She picked up a bowl; she could not let go of it. It began to sink into the earth.

"Brother, brother!" she cried.

Out came her brother; he took the thing. "Do not take anything more!"

He smashed all the things. Then she went inside. The man made some garments. Then she put on those man's clothes. Then she went away.

Presently, as she walked along, she saw a buffalo-lane and a man sitting up aloft on it. He came down and headed her off.

"Let us try our strength," he said to her.

"No," she answered him; "I am on my way home," she said to him.

But at last he talked her into it.

"You first," he said to her; "Show your power," he said to her.

Then they contended. The woman was defeated. That man took her home with him; he took her to the buffalo-lane. There she saw a great crowd of none but women whose knees had been broken.

Then she asked them, "What has he been doing to you?"

"This person climbs trees; he comes leaping down; he falls on our knees; as he lands he always breaks our bones."

"Now, he shall not treat *me* this way!"

She came inside. The man climbed up.

"Sit there!" he told the woman.

Then the woman sat there. He leaped into the air. The woman held out an iron bar. She impaled him and killed him. Then she rose to her feet. Those woman rejoiced, for they had been miserably dealt with.

"Go, all of you, to whatever place you came from!"

They did not know from where they had come. At last that woman took some of them away with her towards her home. They arrived at yonder place. She had ten women with her. Her brothers were glad when she arrived. Ten was the number of her brothers. And likewise ten were they whom she brought. Now her brothers fared well. They stayed there. Her brothers now had wives.

After a time she set out again. A stag took her away with him. He did not like it when in turn other animals took her away. But the woman herself liked it. The stag was her husband. Then he made a nest for her and left her there. Then when the stag bellowed as he ran about, whenever he ran by below there, the woman taunted him as he went by. For he had no way of climbing up there to beat her. Then at one time, hither came that husband of hers and bellowed. He was all covered with scars here on his body where he had been attacked, and he was lean to the point of starvation.

Then he told her: "Your brothers are starving to death. Now I shall go feed my body to them. Afterwards I shall come back to life," he told her.

"Very well!"

Then she went to her brothers.

"But they are not to crack my bones as they eat. They are to wrap them in a fresh hide; they are to put them away somewhere. When four nights have passed, I shall come running back."

So then she slew him. When four nights had passed, her brothers arrived.

"So it is you who have come!" she said to her brothers.

She wept; she grieved for her husband.

So much of this.

—*1925. Sweet Grass Reserve*

Plains Cree Texts
Sweet Grass Cree Storytellers

Published in 1934, the collection of *Plains Cree Texts* comprises the second volume of stories that Leonard Bloomfield recorded and translated when visiting the Sweet Grass and Star Blanket Reserves in 1925. While the *Sweet Grass* collection contains ātaýōhkēwin, or sacred stories, the *Plains Cree Texts* contain ācimowin, or discourses and narratives of everyday life, worship, the past, and the powers around us. The stories in this section are a brief example of the entire collection.

nāh-namiskwākāpaw (Louis Moosomin)

Ancient Life. The Sun-Dance

The people of old were in a piteous state, when first they lived here on earth. The Higher Powers had put them down here with nothing at all. They went naked.

They had no clothes, no knives. All they had for a knife was a bone. From the beginning they had no fire. With merely an arrow they killed animals, fastening bones to their arrows. They had nothing; they were in a piteous state. Presently they made fire for themselves, doing it like this; when it was hot, they got fire from it. Also they pounded a stone, and when it sent out sparks, from this, too, the people got fire. Their pots and kettles were of earth. Also, they would dig a hole and put in a hide, and heat some stones; in this way they cooked meat. Then in time they began to have beaver-pelts for their clothes.

Then at one time a certain man dreamt that the Canadian, the White Man, would land here. He told when they would land. Truly, he was not given credence; only some believed him. Then they moved their camp out there to the east, close to the great sea.

"Now the time is close at hand when they will land !" he said; "Surely very soon," he told the people.

Every morning he would go and look out upon the water. Then at one time he saw boats coming.

When the others arrived there, they shook each other by the hand and greeted each other. For, indeed, thus it was that the Indian first saw the Whiteskin. They gave him everything to live by: the knife and the gun and all kinds of ammunition for his use. So then he began to be taught how to take care of a gun. From that time on the Indians were well off. At a certain time after this they began to have horses to pull their loads. And, strangely enough, it was only the people in the south who had horses; the Indian who dwells in the north from that time to this has never had horses.

Presently, because they had no way of worship, presently a certain man whose children had suffered to the point of death from thirst—for it seems that of old nothing ever grew from the earth; only grass ripened,—then a certain man who was very good, was told by the dwellers in the sky, "Now, I will take you whence you will have your source of life."

Then truly he was taken to the place of the noonday sky, even as he slept; dreaming of that place, he was told by the Higher Powers of the Sun-Dance Lodge. The people were given the annual performance of this rite. And at the same time he was taught how to perform it; by the dwellers in the sky he was taught. Surely it would be well, if it were always permitted to the Indian; so we think. Crops would always grow well. The Sun-Dance Lodge is not an evil thing. To be sure, "The Cree perform all kinds of evil things for the Evil Spirit," say the missionaries. On the contrary: the Cree was not put down here on earth with these things; the Cree has never known and does not know an Evil Spirit or a Son of God; and the Cree does not know him who is called the Evil One. But rather, well may the Cree believe that the Spirit looks with kindlier pity on him, since he is never killed by winds. Never is a Cree killed by wind. Never is a Cree killed by the Thunderers. Never is a Cree killed by fire. That is why we think that the Cree is favored by the Higher Powers. Perhaps it is because he has angered the Spirit by putting a stop to the Sun-Dance Lodge, that in such numbers they break up the Canadian's towns; so we think; and that every day fire destroys the wooden houses; every day we learn that everywhere houses have caught fire, every time we go to town. And every summer we hear that in many places towns have been destroyed by windstorms. It is not an evil thing which the Spirit has given to us, but ways of worship, only that good things may be prayed for. Thus did the Spirit set us down here on earth, us who are Cree. Strange, that some dances which arose much later are not stopped by the White Man, dances in which various things are used up, while the Sun-Dance involves no waste. It was given to the Cree, every year, for two days to go without eating, and to pray that all things might grow well, and to pray for rain. It was thus that the poor Indian was set down here on earth.

I too shall be glad to have my speech go far abroad, I who am blind. For from the time I was born, I have been blind. Never have I seen the earth. Yet when from time to time I mean to go anywhere, I go there; I never get lost.

So much for this, for this one story.

—*1925. Sweet Grass Reserve*

kā-kīsikāw-pīhtukāw (Coming-Day)

How Sweet-Grass Became Chief

In the time of the men of long ago he was chief. Here at Sweet-Grass they dwelt. One morning, he took a horse; he saddled it and mounted; he set out to roam. As he went along he saw someone climbing a hill, a man. He observed him, watching through a spyglass, this man who was looking for people. He knew him for a Blackfoot. He loaded his gun and attacked him as he lay on the ground. When the Blackfoot perceived that a Cree was attacking him, he fled; he hid in the bushes. The Cree tried to shoot him, but the gun did not go off. From the place where he had fled into the woods, twelve Blackfoot came out upon the trail. The lone Cree attacked them, wanting to do battle and shoot them. The Blackfoot fled, fearing the one Cree who was shooting at them. They fled into another wood. Again they came forth in their course. But the Cree on his horse was driving them to where the Cree were many in their tents. The Blackfoot meanwhile, thinking, "In this direction I shall escape," did not know that there were many people, many Cree in the place to which they were going. When they saw the Cree, they turned, at the sight of the many Cree.

Then, as the one was pursuing the twelve Blackfoot, in a wooded place they made for a creek. They went into the water to cross. There one of the Blackfoot ducked under water to hide, thinking, "The Cree will not see me." The other eleven fled; they went into another wood. There the Cree surrounded them, the Blackfoot making a kind of trench as they fought. When the Cree went near to where the Blackfoot were, then he who had pursued them, he went in the lead, like an officer, and the Blackfoot saw the Cree come near the trench where they were. And the Cree stood there close to the pit. Then one Cree—holding it like this stick here—with his knife began to stab the Blackfoot; one Cree did this. Thereupon all the Cree began to enter the trench, knife in hand, stabbing one Blackfoot after another. They slew them; not one of those eleven Blackfoot was left alive. Then with their knives they scalped them; the Cree cut the scalps from their heads. Then they ceased. They had finished them all; that was why they ceased. For this exploit he who had gone alone, and had first seen those Blackfoot, he became a great chief for this exploit. His name was Sweet-Grass. He was chief among the men of old.

This is a story of long ago. In his land I heard this story of him; even here where I sit, in this his land I learned this story. That is all.

A Great Herd

The old-time buffalos, for a distance of some ten miles the earth was not visible, as the buffalos covered it. This story is not old, perhaps fifty years ago it was, when the buffalos were so many. Five men they were who told of it, having seen it when they were out for a walk, these Cree. They shook their blankets like this, to drive the buffalos apart, and behind them the herd closed in again. And for a distance of ten miles there were buffalos so numerous that there was no opening where they walked. Ten miles in length was the herd of buffalos which these Cree saw of old, some fifty years ago. That is a story; that is all there is to it.

One man was called Powamekan; he saw these buffalos. And one man was called Tampesin. And one was called Bird-Tail. They saw the herd of buffalos that was so great. That is all.

A Buffalo in Human Form

A certain old man whom I am old enough to have known, used to tell this story. "I shall tell of what I have seen," he would say.

At one time a certain man was going to set out to look for Blackfoot. He told me of his purpose (said this old man). So he set out. I went along; eight was the number of us young men who went on the war-path. Presently as we marched along, after we had gone a great distance, then once, as we sat smoking, a young man left camp to reach the crest of a hill, to look out for Blackfoot, and when this scout reconnoitred, as he looked yon way, he saw four buffalo. He signaled to his companions. Accordingly they rose to their feet and went to where that young man was.

When they reached him, "How is it?" the leader asked him.

"Oh, merely that there are some buffalo here."

"Very well, try to kill them," said that old man.

A young man set out to shoot them. Then, when he crept up to them and was crouching now quite near, he saw a bear stealing up to these buffalo. Thereupon the young man came back, afraid of the bear, and told his companions the story.

"A bear is stealing up to these buffalo," he told his companions.

"Let us go see how this bear will do," they said.

So they arose and seated themselves on a small eminence of the ground to watch the animals. By this time the bear had got close to the bull buffalos. Suddenly one bull arose, left the others, and went up to the bear. When the bull came near, the bear also rose. They fought. Not long did they fight. The bull was killed. As soon as it had been killed, another rose and went to where the first one had been killed. This one, too, fought with the bear. Soon it, also, was killed by the bear. Then another still rose up and encountered the bear and fought with it. They fought; this one, too, the bear killed. Then the remaining one rose up, angry. It, too, went up to the bear. It, too, fought; the bear killed it. The bear killed all four of the bulls. Then from that place where those four bulls had been there arose a young buffalo. It ran along angrily toward the bear, to attack it. When it got up, it had the form of a man holding a lance. The bear was afraid of this one. When it tried to escape, the man attacked it. He stabbed the bear and killed it. Then he flung himself on the ground; when he arose, there was again that young buffalo. So the young buffalo ran away; it made for the open prairie.

Thereupon the young men went to the place to look at the buffalos that had been killed. When they got there and examined them, it appeared that the bear had broken the necks of them all, and in the bear's back they could see the place where the buffalo-calf had stabbed it, exactly as though a man had made the wound. Then the young men skinned them and cut them up.

"We shall eat," they said.

Accordingly they built fires to prepare parched meat and to eat.

Then the old man spoke as follows: "Youths, I am an old man; never have I seen anything like this. Perhaps we shall not fare well; perhaps the Blackfoot will slay us. We had better go back. It will be better if we go home," said the old man.

"Very well," said the young men.

They stayed there one night. In the morning they set out for home. At last they reached their camp. They told their story.

"That is why we have come home, 'Perhaps we shall not fare well,' was our thought, so it seemed to me; that is why I turned back."

So much for this story. Twin-Buffalo, he is the one who had this experience; my mother's brother was this old man.

—*1925. Sweet Grass Reserve*

kā-wīhkaskusahk (Maggie Achenam)

How Women Were Treated

Another thing which used to happen, was when some Blackfoot became suspicious about another man.

"You are consorting with that young man," he would tell her.

"Oh dear, no!"

"Yes, you are, just the same! Tomorrow you will go to the great sand-hill."

Then, the next morning, when he had made ready, "Put on your best clothes." Accordingly she dressed up.

"Go outside now and for the last time look upon the holy sun."

Then the woman went outside. She looked upon the sun; then she came in.

"Which will you take?" he asked his wife; "To die, or that I cut off your nose."

Then the woman answered him, "Cut off my nose."

He cut off her nose.

This is another example of how the Blackfoot of old, when they were jealous, treated their wives, before there was law, when they did what they pleased to their wives. But now this no longer happens; now the women live in peace. Then they were tormented; but now they are delivered from it. These Cree, too, mutilated their wives when they were angry at them, but they never went as far as killing them; they only cut them up, did these Cree. That was what these Cree did, but now it has ceased. The women are glad that it has stopped, for they are delivered from great suffering.

How the Blackfoot Killed Their Wives

Now another story.

A man's wives gathered berries. He had two wives. When they met a youth or even a boy, he became jealous of him.

"I can tell that youth is your man!" he said to her.

"No," she answered him; "I only met him by chance."

"Oh no! You say that just because he is your man," he told her.

That Blackfoot took some arrows. When he encountered his wife and a boy who was with her, first he shot arrow after arrow into his wife. Then the boy, too, him too he shot; he killed him. Then he looked for the young man; he rode about in the woods. He could not find him.

Then, "No one is to take up the bodies of those I have killed," he said.

His wife and the boy he had slain with her would lie there then, because if anyone were going to take them up, he would kill him.

This too was a custom of the Blackfoot; before there was any law was when this took place; when the people were still living on buffalo-flesh,—the Blackfoot and the Assiniboine, the Sarsi, the Snakes, the Earth-Lodge People, the Salteaux,—that was when this took place.

—*1925; Sweet Grass Reserve*

Abel Watetch
Cree · c. 1878–1964 · Piapot First Nation

Abel Watetch was born around 1878, in *payipwāt*'s camp, during the band's move from the Cypress Hills to their new reserve lands in the Qu'Appelle valley. Born Herald in the Sky, he was given the name Abel Watetch when he attended residential school. A nephew of *payipwāt*, he was close to the chief, learning *payipwāt*'s stories and teachings until his death. In 1908, while a young carpenter, he built the coffin that Payepot was laid to rest in. Watetch was a veteran of the First World War, and he spent much of his later life gathering stories of Chief *payipwāt* and his people's history.

Watetch's *Payepot and His People* is an oral history, tape recorded by Blowden Davis, Acting Secretary of the Saskatchewan Arts Board in 1957, then transcribed and published serially in *The Western Producer*, and then as the first publication by the Saskatchewan History and Folklore Society in 1959. It was reissued by Canadian Plains Research Center (now University of Regina Press) in 2007. The selection here is from this work, and focuses on the history of the Rain Dance and on *payipwāt*'s defiance of the prohibitions in the Indian Act against holding traditional ceremony. Often misunderstood by non-Indians to be an "uncivilized" practice by a "savage" people, the Rain Dance, as described by Watetch, was a way to communicate with the Creator as the source of all life.

The Meaning of the Rain Dance

The Cree Rain Dance is based on reverence for life. The Indians have never named the source of that all-pervading energy of life which they recognize in every kingdom of nature, and they refer to the source only as the Great Spirit. The manifestations of that Spirit take many forms, the greatest of which is the sun. The stars, the winds, and many such things are, as one Cree put it, "the hired men of the Almighty." These lesser entities may be experienced in such a form as that of the Thunder Bird.

Communication between the individual and such a manifestation as the Thunder Bird involves precise forms of discipline handed down by Medicine Men from great ages of antiquity. There are, in fact, many factors in the surviving ceremonies, disciplines and experiences of the Rain Dance, even as it is carried out today, to relate it to other forms of similar approaches to a universal Spirit in use in many other parts of the world, including some Masonic ceremonies.

The first step in the preparation for a Rain Dance begins with the individual. It involves a series of meditations. Traditionally, the right to sponsor a Rain Dance is considered a great honour. To work towards this point of achievement the Indian youth begins his disciplines while he is still virgin. Failing this he has no hope of rising to this place of honour in the tribe. But making the required approach, he is set on the road to become eventually a Medicine Man. No man could become a chief who was not also wise in the ways of the tribal medicine.

During any Rain Dance the youth of the band are given preliminary training, tasks and responsibilities so that they can associate with the elders and Medicine Men and so learn the outer forms of the ceremonies. This will, of course, whet their desire to know more about the mysteries and to prepare themselves to participate in them.

When the young men come to the age where they have deep and irresistible aspirations to become sponsors of a Rain Dance, they begin by lonely meditations which take place on the peak of some hill or in some secluded wooded spot where they will not be disturbed for days at a time. Each man must choose his own seclusion and go alone and fasting to his vigil. He neither eats nor drinks but spends his time in concentrated appeal to the Great Spirit for revelation and guidance. Usually on the third day he will hear a voice or see a vision. If not, he may persist for four or five days.

On his return to the camp he asks for the advice of four elders or Medicine Men. To them he explains all that has happened to him. It may be they will find the experience insufficient and he is advised to make a new attempt. But if he is an unusually sensitive young man his experience may win the approval of the elders. Even so, this is merely preliminary. No one wins a place of honour on one experience.

He may repeat his meditation in a month or two, or a year or two, or five or ten years, all depending on "human nature." "Human beings, being what they are," said one of the elders, "some are anxious, some reluctant, some eager, some cautious."

The aspirant must have the same experience repeated at least three times, sometime in his life, before he makes the grade as a sponsor of a Rain Dance. If he persists and is finally approved, the process is called The Great Meditation. When he actually gives the Rain Dance depends on many things. The Indian is never in a hurry.

When the elders eventually agree to allow a certain man, already eligible, to undertake the great responsibility, actual preparations begin in the autumn when the leaves are beginning to turn colour. The ceremony itself takes place the following year when the leaves are full in the late summer.

The council of elders meets again with the sponsor to make it clear just why the Rain Dance is to be performed and the sponsor must explain his motives, his objectives and his plans. A Rain Dance may be given for many different reasons. If a man has a loved one who is ill or handicapped he may want to give the Dance to petition for aid. If he has been the recipient of good fortune, he may want to express his gratitude in this way. It may be that the band is facing difficulties which he feels can be helped to a solution through this means; or it may be for a wider brotherhood, all humanity, that he is making an appeal. But the motive must be well-defined.

Once all this has been cleared away, it is then open to anyone else to participate in the Rain Dance on the basis of some personal and secret vow. Such a person takes part in all the preparations and makes the appropriate invocation for aid or gratefully pays a spiritual debt. One day a white man came to Payepot reserve and asked if he would be allowed to participate. He had a very sick son and no one seemed able to help him. "I believe in your attitude to the Great Spirit," he said. He was accepted, taught the rituals and followed the preparations. In due time his son was restored to health. In gratitude he returned to the Rain Dance for many years.

With plans and motives clarified, the preparations begin to move. First there must be a symbolic Thunder Bird created. Wise old women of the band are entrusted with this work. In secrecy they take twists of tobacco and fasten them together to make the figure of the bird. They then take 40 braids of sweet grass, such as the women make in every home, and wrap them securely around the Thunder Bird. These braids made by the women are kept for use all the year round. They are burned in thunder storms to invoke the protection of the Thunder Bird. They are used as incense in some rituals.

Next comes another wrapping provided by the sponsor. In the old days this would have been some fine fur, perhaps some white skin. But since the Hudson's Bay Company moved down into the Prairies to trade with the Indians, they have imported what the Crees call sacrificial cloth. It is called stroud in trade and has always been a rare and expensive fabric, in blue, white or red. The

Crees never hesitate to give what is best to the Great Spirit. Stroud came to be the most precious fabric known to the Indians and two yards were required for the wrapping. Outside this sacrificial cloth came other wrappings until a considerable bundle resulted, securely tied into a great medicine bag.

The sponsor selects one man to be his chief acolyte and he is put in charge of the symbolic Thunder Bird. From that day until the day of the Rain Dance, the medicine bag never leaves him. He will not take it into a house which is not clean.

Another man is nominated to take charge of the four ceremonial pipes. One of these pipes, belonging to the sponsor, must be a new one. It takes priority over all the other pipes when used ceremonially. The acolyte takes great care of the pipes, he cleans them, he purifies them with the smoke of sweet grass and he sees to it they are always available when needed. When the pipes are passed around in a ritual, they always move with the sun.

Finally four elders, Medicine Men, are selected by the sponsor to act with him in the long and complicated rituals entailed in the Rain Dance. If during the year of preparation the sponsor dies, these men will carry out his obligations in the short form of the dance which can take place in one day.

There are four song services leading up to the Rain Dance. The first is in the autumn, the second in midwinter, the third in the spring and the fourth just before the dance itself. The medicine bundle containing the symbolic Thunder Bird must be at every song service. These gatherings last all night and are intended to generate spiritual enthusiasm. The traditional songs are sung with great dedication and fervor and the drums beat out the mesmeric rhythms that accompany all the tribal ceremonies.

Fasting from food and drink plays a considerable part in all the Cree religious functions. But when an Indian for any reason, a single day's fast, or a preparation for the Rain Dance, determines to drink no water for a specified time, he precedes the fast by addressing the spirit in water by explaining that he is not repudiating the use of this good manifestation of the Great Spirit, but that he is making a sacrifice in refraining from its use. If he fasts from food he also explains the sacrifice he is making. To him, food and water are conscious of him and it is courtesy to explain his actions.

It is difficult to explain why the Cree approaches the Great Spirit as he does. It is not merely that he seeks protection or even some good to be applied to some others. It is indefinable, a sort of fusion of the particular with the universal, of the lonely and separated man with the Great Spirit from which he emanated—perhaps a kind of demonstration of the essential unity underlying the visible and tangible world and all humanity. Words but confuse the real meaning of his religious impulses.

The Rain Dance is a true community enterprise. As Payepot told the Indians in Montana: "Making rain is something that is not in my power. It is in your power: Not one or two can do this. Only the whole community joining together can call upon the Great Spirit to act in pity for us." So after the four song services, after all those who have made vows, and have taken whistles to the services to be blessed, after all the acolytes have been appointed to their various responsibilities, the days appointed for the Rain Dance have come and the entire band is in action.

The rites performed in Montana, that came down from antiquity, are performed yearly on Payepot reserve. The old Medicine Man seeks the tree in a vision, he finds the tree, invokes its blessing, and marks it with the sacrificial cloth. The sponsor and his acolytes perform the ceremonial cutting, and it is dragged to the site of the new lodge with rejoicing and dramatic pantomime. Then, where the hole has been dug, the top of the tree is marked with the symbol of the sun, and it is then raised with four forked poles. The ceremonial nest of the Thunder Bird is placed in the crotch of the limbs, left for that purpose. Around the lodgepole the lodge itself is built.

As the first day of the Rain Dance dawns, the people of the reserve and visitors from reserves at distances from Payepot arrive with their teepees and set them up in a great circle. In the lodge the sponsor and his acolytes and the singers and drummers are assembled, all fasting.

When the sponsor has raised his ceremonial rattle to give the signal for the dance to begin, the singers and drummers and dancers set the ceremonies in motion. For three days they will neither eat nor drink.

One by one those who have made vows approach the lodgepole and signify their participation by knotting a sacrificial cloth around the pole. From time to time they will join the dancers, feeling in every nerve and muscle the ceremonial rhythms through which their devotion is expressed. The singers will try to distract them from their deep concentration as a test of their sincerity, for these dancers are hoping that at some point before the Rain Dance ends they will have achieved an experience, an insight, a revelation, as an answer to their avowed intention. So earnest are these dancers that they are prepared to go on dancing and fasting for the three days in order to earn a spiritual revelation.

The dancers can come and go at will, returning to their teepees to rest or visit with their friends. The sponsor and his acolytes never leave the lodge, but when they are exhausted merely lie down on the earth to snatch a little sleep.

The Indians never try to convert anyone to their religion. They never quarrel about religion. It is an intensely personal matter and indeed its community efficacy depends upon the individual's sincerity. The chief aim of their religion is to express the individual's gratitude for what he receives in this life. Life itself and its chief end is the unity of the Indian group, expressed in the reiterated injunction "love one another." "The first thing a parent teaches a child, the last thing a dying Indian says to those around him is 'love one another'," said one of the elders.

The Indian loves the land, the sky, the birds and animals about him because they are all expressions of the one life. One of the things that strangers to the Prairies will notice is an Indian or a group of Indians sitting quietly in some high spot, the side of a coulee perhaps, for hours at a time, just looking at a familiar landscape.

Difficult as it may be for the organizing and competitive mind of the white man to understand this phase of Indian life, it is necessary to understand it in order to evaluate the Indian. The Rain Dance has survived in spite of all the changes that have come to the Indian in the last century. None but an Indian can go to a Rain Dance without an invitation. The non-Indians who are invited are only those who will, perhaps, try to understand. When the guests make their way over the long, twisting trails to a remote part of the reserve on the floor of the valley, they can have little doubt of the solemnity of the three-day ceremony in which they are welcome to share for a few hours. There they find the circle of teepees reminiscent of the great buffalo-hunting encampments of old. In the great open space even the drumming and singing and dancing in the leafy lodge is muted, and there is an atmosphere of peace and quiet. There is also an air of mystery as participants in tribal costumes come and go. Sometimes the music lapses and there are spells of silence until the dancing begins again and the drums throb. There is a small sacrificial fire within the lodge and there are mysterious comings and goings by the men who have charge of the ceremonial objects.

At the end of the three-day ceremony, all who participate officially retreat to a sweat house. This is large enough to hold eight men. It is built of 40 willows, bent and bound together with willow bark. In the centre of the sweat house is a hole into which eight white-hot stones are dropped. Blue stones are used for this purpose, for they can be heated without cracking. Sticks fashioned in a way used since antiquity are made to carry the hot stones to the pit. When the men in breech cloths are in the sweat house, water is thrown on the stones by sweetgrass braids which are also burned as incense. There are songs and invocations used in the sweat house as the sponsor and acolytes purify them- selves in the final act of the Rain Dance.

There is a great deal of gift-giving in relation to the Rain Dance, and when the dance is complete the sacred medicine bundle is opened. The tobacco and the sweetgrass braids are distributed, in small pieces, to be carried away as talismans, in a kind of communion service. They are symbols of Life.

The Rain Dance has always been a thorn in the side to the government which was trying to adjust the Indians to the white man's way of life, and to the Royal Canadian Mounted Police who carried out the instructions of the Indian department. The three reasons given for the efforts to suppress the Rain Dance, or the Sun Dance as it was originally known, were, first that it kept the Indians away from their farms; second, that they gave away too many of their possessions in connection with the dance; and thirdly, the white man's dislike of the ceremony of piercing the flesh in the making of braves.

The last Rain Dance in which the piercing of the flesh was carried out was about 1899. It was the cause of 20 years of unhappiness for the Crees of Payepot reserve. It came about in this way.

By that time a whole generation of young Indians had grown up who knew nothing about the buffalo-hunting days except what they heard from the elders as storytellers. Perhaps the youths began to think the old men were telling tall tales.

A Rain Dance was about to take place when one evening a group of about 20 Cree youths sought out Chief Payepot. They were of the age at which, even 50 years earlier, they would have been initiated into the status of young warriors. Their spokesman told the old chief that they wanted to be pierced and allowed to perform the dance of which they had been told so much. In a spirit of bravado, they asked the chief to make warriors of them. They wanted to ape the old braves.

Payepot looked at the band of young men and silently thought the matter over. Then he answered them:

"This is not a laughing matter. But since you have asked for this experience, and the Great Spirit has heard you and knows what you ask, you must carry it through. Come back tomorrow morning before dawn and you will be pierced."

Sobered by the old man's words the youths went away to talk it over. Their chief's reaction was a challenge and they suddenly realized they could not back out now without becoming the laughing stock of the tribe, and the whole countryside.

In the cold dawn the young Indians turned up at Payepot's home in breech cloths only. Payepot had brought another Medicine Man to carry out the function of piercing. The old men were doubtless silently enjoying the discomfiture of the young men who were looking at each other and at the elders with questions in their eyes. The old men were making the most of the opportunity. The man who was to officiate carried in his hand a great bear claw which was traditionally used for the piercing. He went from one young man to the other pinching the flesh on his breast, pulling it from the bone, thoughtfully feeling and measuring it. "Ah! so you want to be pierced, eh?" he asked from time to time, prolonging the anxiety of each of the boys. Slowly and impressively he completed his preparations.

The ritual was to open two slots on each side of the young man's breast and cut the flesh free, so that a length of *shaganapi*, or buffalo hide, could be inserted. In the dance the ends of these thongs would be fastened to the lodge pole. In the dancing the youth, singing with all his force, danced slowly farther and farther from the pole, loosening the flesh and wearing it down until finally it broke. The young man would have proved his ability to endure pain courageously and would be left with two big scars on his breast to testify to his initiation.

All the young men were pierced, and took part in the Rain Dance. It was the last time the rite was carried out on the Prairies.

One of the elders recalling the incident says that the ritual made "good men" of some of them. In their ritual dances they cried aloud to the Great Spirit for strength and courage. Some of them eventually became Medicine Men.

But word must have got about on what had happened on the Payepot reserve. Not long afterwards, Chief Payepot was arrested by the Mounted Police and taken to the prison of the force in Regina.

At that time Harry Ball, who later became Chief Sitting Eagle Changing Position, was a boy at school in Regina, in a Presbyterian industrial college. One of the staff came to him one day and said, "Your chief is in prison in Regina. Do you want to visit him?" The boy went immediately. As he came to the cell where the old man was held, he saw beside the door a paper with his name and his indictment.

During his visit Chief Payepot said: "What am I in here for?" "It says on the paper outside that you were arrested for being drunk."

"But I never drink," protested the old man. Then after a pause he went on: "I know why I am here. It is because of the Rain Dance and the piercing of the boys."

The Indian department deposed Chief Payepot and invited the band to elect another chief. Twenty-five years after he had signed away to the Crown his rights to his native land, 15 years after he had prevented the southern Indians from joining the Métis in rebellion, he was imprisoned on a false charge of drunkenness and deprived of the chieftainship he had held for half a century.

It broke the old man's spirit. He returned to the reserve, humiliated and sad. On the reserve there was one silent, unbroken determination to have no other chief as long as Payepot lived. On the books of the Indian department the band had no chief. In the hearts of the Crees on Payepot reserve, most of whom by now had known no other leader, he remained the chief, the great Medicine Man, the old warrior, the wise and durable leader.

The years went by and they refused to elect a chief. The old man had told them to love one another as a protection against the hostile world into which time had driven them. To this day Chief Payepot dominates the reserve as a symbol and his medicine is still potent.

Year after year the pressure of government and police was aimed at ending the Rain Dance. One of the elders said smilingly, "The Rain Dance was a short form of the Sun Dance. Like low mass and high mass. We performed the Rain Dance in one day instead of three days we had to dance the Sun Dance. The white man never knew that it was the same ceremony."

The piercing of the flesh had been abandoned. Symbolically, the same dance was performed with the dancers fastening ribbons to their clothing and tying the ends to the lodge pole.

But for all the efforts made to stamp out the Sun Dance or its new form of Rain Dance, it persisted. The white men who now dominated the country were determined to make stay-at-home farmers of the Indians, thrifty, cautious and hard-working. Never in the thousands of years of Indian culture lying behind them had the Indians ever had the need to be stay-at-home, thrifty and cautious. They were nomadic, non-agricultural, adventurous. Their survival depended on pursuit, speed, skill, recklessness. Nothing in their religious or social history held a clue to the property-owning, competitive way of life. They had no fear of death, and their religion had no hell. Life was abundant and inexhaustible, and on the other side of death was a world like this world, only with less of its difficulties.

Then came the First World War. Under the Indian treaties no Indian could be conscripted for service in the armed forces. But about 85 percent of young Indians of military age volunteered to serve in the Canadian Army. Many young men on Payepot reserve went to serve Canada in Europe.

At the close of the war when some of these young men came back, the band wanted to express its gratitude by an old-time Sun Dance, or Rain Dance, as they now called it. They sent one of the returned soldiers to Regina to ask permission of The Big Boss, Indian Commissioner W.P.R. Graham. He explained the situation and asked that the band be allowed to revive its ancient ceremonial for the event. Graham refused. "Look," he said, "you have been forbidden to hold the Sun Dance. It's part of the Indian religion and it's no damn good."

The young soldier spoke quietly:

"I went to the war. I fought for you and I fought for all those who sat in this office during the war. I have a right to ask you to give us back our Sun Dance."

There was silence in the office and the commissioner found it difficult to make an answer. Then he said:

"On one condition. You can have it for yourselves. You cannot invite the Indians from any other reserve."

"We will give no invitation," said the soldier, "but I cannot say the Indians will not come."

"If they come," said the commissioner, "the mounties will put a stop to it."

"We will not prevent them from coming," said the soldier. The preparations for the Sun Dance began. In due time the days of the dance arrived. Indians from nearby reserves had heard about the preparations and came to join it. When everything was about to begin, the mounties arrived.

"These people don't belong here," they said pointing to the visitors. "They should be on their land working." They threatened to break up the festival.

At this point the Indians of Payepot had to compromise with the short form of the dance. But they did not give up the struggle. "We got a lawyer to back us up." From that day to this Payepot reserve has the ancient right to perform its Rain Dance in conformity with tradition.

They try to maintain the old spirit. There is much gift-giving at the dance. The Indian is generous, the white man might say foolish, in his gifts, but he makes his gifts as sacrifices to the Great Spirit.

The history of the Sun Dance, even in its modern form of the Rain Dance, is almost over. There are few left to carry on the tradition. The youths who once learned the ethics of the Crees in various steps of participation are no longer in training in sufficient numbers to maintain the tradition. It is almost impossible to find young men of the necessary quality. They are contaminated by their contacts with the worst side of the white man's culture before they are of an age to begin their training. The Indian, even when he is corrupted by his contacts outside the reserve, has a great respect for tradition. He will not try to carry on an empty form if he has not the true qualifications for attempting his communion with the Great Spirit. The Crees will not feed on the husks of ancient rituals. No man will attempt to sponsor a Rain Dance if he knows he lacks the spiritual capacity. Moreover, the Rain Dance demands powers of endurance and self-discipline which few will possess when the present elders are gone.

—1957

Edward Ahenakew
Cree · 1885–1961 · Sandy Lake, Ahtahkakoop First Nation

Rev. Edward Ahenakew was born in 1885 and grew up on Sandy Lake, Ahtahkakoop First Nation. He was a grandnephew of pīhtikwahānapiwiyin (Poundmaker). In the early 1900s, he attended Emmanuel College, an Anglican theological school in Saskatoon. After graduating in 1910, he did missionary work throughout northern Saskatchewan.

By the 1920s, he realized the loss of language that was happening among his people. In response, he started a newsletter called the Cree Monthly Guide, and he published it until he passed away in 1961. Significantly, the Guide was written in Cree syllabics with translations.

In 1922, when Ahenakew became ill, he traveled to piyēsiw-awāsis's (Thunderchild's) reserve to convalesce. *piyēsiw-awāsis* would visit him at his cabin, and they would tell stories to pass the time. Ahenakew realized the importance of preserving these stories, and so began to write them down. At this time, Ahenakew also wrote his own stories of Old Keyam, a fictional persona that served as a voice for Ahenakew's own concerns about the changing world of the Cree and the social conditions of First Nations communities in the 1920s. Significantly, none of these stories were published at the time, and it wasn't until several years after Ahenakew's death in 1961 that his niece found the hand-written manuscript buried away in a drawer in his cabin. The stories were eventually edited by Ruth M. Buck, with the help of several translators, and published by McLelland & Stewart as *Voices of the Plains Cree* in 1973, and then by the Canadian Plains Research Center, now the University of Regina Press, in 1995.

The selection is story No. 5 from the Old Keyam section of *Voices of the Plains Cree*.

That Fatal Day at Frog Lake (Old Keyam No. 5)

After such a night of story-telling, Old Keyam was assured an attentive audience when he spoke again, about a week later.

"When I last talked to you, I scared you," he began. "That was my intent, for sometimes you deserve it, and you know that. I talked to you of our old superstitions, and of the terrors that wait in all primitive life. I showed you as well that the Indian responded to the majesty and wonder of nature. It is through knowing our past, that we can come to know ourselves; if a man understands himself, his heart is strong to meet the difficulties of life.

"I was born just before the Plains Cree began their life on reservations, and I was still a child when the Rebellion broke out. Our band took no part in that. When it was over, I went away to school; I tried to fit myself to the white man's way of life—and I failed. In my failure, however, I still kept to what I believed was the best in Indian life; I have seen the degradation and shame of others who did not hold to that. You call me 'Old Keyam' because you think that I am both old and indifferent; I am neither. It is discouragement and failure that have aged me; it is heart-break, both for myself and for others, that has made me 'Old Keyam.'

"When I talk to you, it is to make you know yourselves and your people; and sometimes I hope that my words may reach out to others in this country. Indians have been too long without a voice in the affairs of Canada, sitting as silent as women in a council of headmen. Some of the fault has been our own lack of education, so that we sit as though we were dumb, permitting others to form opinions and to shape policies that concern us, and that are often wrong, quite wrong.

"Sometimes I feel that I must shout to make these others hear; words burst from me as though I were speaking directly to them, and not to you only. It may be that way tonight, and you will wonder to whom I am speaking, for I am going to try to present the Indians' side of the story of the Frog Lake massacre of 1885. That is long ago, I know, but its scars remain in our relationship with the white man; and sometimes, for us, the wounds bleed afresh, which only adds to our self-pity and the harm that that does to us.

"I am one who has tried to observe what affects our lives, and it makes me sad, my children, when I hear anything that reflects wrongly upon us. It is our responsibility to correct that, however limited we may be. White men's accounts of that fearful day at Frog Lake make it appear that it was our thirst for blood that brought about the massacre. I have been told of many private incidents in the days and months before that bloodshed, and I am not surprised that ill-feeling against some of the men who were killed should have come to a head with the news from Duck Lake.

"The accounts of the massacre vary, and that is natural, for the events happened rapidly and not all at the same place. Excitement was intense. The story is becoming almost legendary, yet it is not yet so far removed in the past as to have made it impossible for me to have heard accounts from men who were eye-witnesses. Some of these men may have done more than simply look on, but that need not be pried into now, for the Government made a careful investigation, and all who had taken an active part were supposedly brought to justice.

"When I talked to men who were there, they said, 'It was the fault of Indians from the plains who had refused Treaty, and who came to our camp as desperate men.' But these desperate men, these last resisters of the white man's power, represented Indians who had lived and roamed over these great plains, who had breathed that freedom, whose will had never been called into question, and whose only restraint had been through the persuasion of the Old Men of the tribe. They knew the ways of their country, they had mastered its hard conditions, and from that life had drawn the manhood that surged within them. Their freedom was intense and vital to them; they could only resist whatever threatened to restrict it, as unnatural and wholly wrong.

"Now the first white men who came amongst us experienced all that too, and understood it and the Indians. Many of them took our women as their wives. There was mutual respect between them and the Indians, for they knew us as individuals, and they judged us as men, and not simply according to our race. It was undoubtedly to the interest of the fur-trading companies to maintain this respect and friendship. Even to this day, it is generally true of the Hudson's Bay Company, but it was most evident when the Company, through its charter, felt responsibility to maintain law and order in the land.

"Then the Government of Canada assumed that responsibility with all the others; and settlers, who had come at first only in small groups, came by the hundreds and thousands when the railroad was built. These people regarded the Indians, sometimes with fear, sometimes with derision. Only a few came to know us, or could possibly do so, for we were living then on reserves.

"We were to become farmers, it was decreed. That seemed logical and proper in a society where agriculture was the primary industry and endless work was highly regarded. But the Indians had been nomadic through countless centuries, through all our history; to settle down as farmers meant the complete reversal of habits bred into us by our previous way of life.

"Farming in those first days of settlement was indeed hard labour, under conditions that could drive even the white settler to desperation. But it was possible for him to escape to another way of life. We were hobbled like horses, limited to our reserves, and quite unfitted for any life outside. It was natural for the Indian to become discontented, to look back to the days when everything that he needed came with more readiness to his hand; and that feeling of discontent and resentment waited only to be brought to a head by any provocative action.

"There were many who could not agree to the signing of the Treaty, though they were over-ruled in the decision. Some said that it was the liberal distribution of money and the easy purchase of many things in the Hudson's Bay Company posts at that time that made an impression on the people, so that even the dissenters wavered. I am not discussing the justice or the injustice of the Treaty. I am simply speaking of things as they appeared to the untrained mind of the Indians at that time. They could not realize what the signing over of their land meant.

"Only in this present age is it understood that abrupt change can bring serious shock, with harsh effects upon a human being. The Indian could not know that he was totally unfitted by previous training for settled agricultural life. He could not realize that it meant continuous application of mind and body to one end, if he was to succeed; nor that such steady application was the very reverse of his previous life. No more did he recognize that he would have to live within a definite code of laws that would fence his spirit utterly, and that this ever-tightening hold of the law would come to rouse his deepest resentment.

"Government agents were no wiser in their turn, for many of them were small men who owed their position to political patronage alone, who used the law to become despots in their own areas. It seemed to the Indian that the Government was pulling the reins of control even tighter, that the white man's customs were steadily asserted, the Indian ways shoved aside, and that finally he would be ignored altogether in the making of policy.

"The times were very hard, for the buffalo had disappeared from the plains, and the Indian quite rightly associated this with the advent of the white man. He recognized that he had taken his own part in that indiscriminate slaughter, but it had been encouraged in the Canadian west, and it had been a deliberate policy, he knew, south of the international border, to subdue other war-like tribes through starvation.

"What people, unless totally devoid of spirit, unless slavish for a thousand years, would not have felt bitter resentment, would not have blamed the white man for it all, for all the misery, and all the degradation?

"The Treaty had been made in due and proper form. There had been justice apparently, and kindliness too on the part of those who represented the Crown. Yet at the signing there were men, both white and Indian, who were sick at heart because they knew the almost certain outcome, yet could see no alternative.

"Looking back now, we can recognize that the massacre at Frog Lake was the last effort of the Indian to register in letters of blood his opposition to the ever-increasing and irresistible power of another race in the land that had been his."

Keyam had risen to his feet, his clenched fist emphasizing his words, his actual audience forgotten while his voice called to ears that would not hear: "You Anglo-Saxon people, who never called any man or nation master, who since the days of the Norman kings have never had the manners and the customs of others forced upon you—how can you understand?

"We too loved our ways, humble though they seemed; we too preferred to run our own affairs however poorly it may have been; we too loved our freedom. In all conscience, how can you blame the resentment of uneducated Indians, primitive and wild?

"If it has been for our ultimate benefit that you took over our land, and if in gratitude we should go down upon our knees to thank you for doing so, then might it not have been to your benefit that the Normans came to England? And did the Anglo-Saxon drop upon his knees in gratitude?

"You would not have been the race you are today, if you had been capable of that. It is right that you should be conscious of your worth, and of the greatness of your nation, but has that left you unable to see why other peoples do not readily forsake their own way of life in order to take yours, under coercion? The love of freedom that has flowered so splendidly in your national life can be found in the breasts of humbler people.

"'But the Indians have freedom!' perhaps you say. Then ask yourself: In 1885, was the Indian—or is he now—in a position to recognize a freedom based on a highly complex system of laws? Would that freedom, to ignorant eyes, not seem something quite the opposite?"

Keyam's own eyes fell upon his actual audience, intent, seeming to believe that all those others were listening too. With a shrug of his shoulders, he brought himself back to reality, denying the fantasy. "*Na-moitch!* Never mind!" His voice was calm and resigned. "They will not hear! But I've shown that I know some other history than our own. Let us talk about ours.

"In those days before the Rebellion, the reserve at Frog Lake seemed to be developing. The Indian Agency was there, and an outpost of the Hudson's Bay Company from Fort Pitt. There was a mill too, run by water-power. Everything is gone now, only the cellars remaining, and a heavy wheel from the mill.

"The Chief of the reserve was *Chas-cha-ki-s-kwas* (Head-upright), and he and his band were Bush Cree, a quiet and peaceable group. But there were five bands in all encamped at Frog Lake, each under its own Chief. The Plains Cree under Big Bear were long used to bloodshed, brought up from childhood to regard battle as the highest test of their manhood, ever at war with the Blackfoot and the Bloods in a feud that meant killing at sight, in the quickest and most practical manner. The other bands were Indians who had lived in closer proximity to the Hudson's Bay Company posts, somewhat in that protection, yet familiar with warfare, and living by the chase.

"The winter had been severe, and with so large an encampment the hunting was difficult. The presence of Big Bear's band fostered discontent and resentment, and envoys from Batoche did all they could to enlist Indian sympathy for a possible uprising, even before news came of the incident at Duck Lake. The immediate cause of the massacre, however, was the dislike that some of the Indians had for certain of the white men at Frog Lake.

"They had kept this to themselves, because a personal quarrel was always a dangerous thing in Indian life, usually meaning death to one or the other involved; and, with no evidence of open strife, the white men may have thought that all was well and that the Indians were friendly. I am not going to speak of the reasons for that bad feeling. They have existed always and are with us still today. What is past is past, and paid for in lives. The feeling did exist, however, and there were grounds for it, though nothing might have come of it all, had that spirit of unrest not prevailed throughout the North-West. Insults become unbearable in times of great stress and excitement.

"Immediately after word came of the fight at Duck Lake, the Indians held a council. Wandering Spirit was present, as one of Big Bear's headmen, and I have been told by those who knew him well that he was utterly wild and reckless, 'a no-good man' were the words used of him. The Indians listened with more confidence to those who, like *A-yi-mi-ses*, Big Bear's son, urged a council meeting with the Chiefs of Onion Lake and Long Lake, who were moderate men.

"The day before the outbreak of violence was quiet except for the business of preparing for a feast and dance, yet a feeling of foreboding hung over the camps, even the dogs howling now and again as though they could sense trouble. Then the dancing began, and though it was not a war dance there was bound to be recklessness where so many young men were gathered. Everyone who has told me of the tragic happening has said how the excitement and restlessness mounted steadily, until by midnight it was truly alarming.

"The first real act of hostility came in the early morning when a young Indian took a horse that belonged to one of the white men. Then the young men began to race at full speed about the encampment, yelling as they rode, more and more out of control. The white men were gathered together, and the Agent was the first of nine to be killed.

"Big Bear is often blamed because he was Chief of the band to which the leaders in the massacre belonged. I believe that he was no more responsible than any of his headmen, and much less responsible than some who only incited the killing. That he was Chief gave him no power to command without question. It was possible for any reckless spirits to go against his advice in a time of great excitement. When the first shot was fired, he yelled at his men to stop, but it was too late. They were past obeying any orders.

"The scars of that day are with us still, for the bitterness that led to the massacre infects the wound and must first be healed. That fatal day at Frog Lake is like a curse upon us all and upon our relationship with the white man."

His words lapsed into silence, and Keyam looked old and tired. His head drooped for a moment before he raised it to say simply, "I have spoken. Let my words be heard."

—*1923. Thunderchild Reserve*

Michel Benjamin
Dene · c. 1888–19?? · La Loche

Michel Benjamin was born in 1888 or 1889. The following story is from an interview in the *Dene Elders Project*. In it, Benjamin recounts the historical figure of Thanadelthur, the first Dene person to meet a European fur trader. "The story of Thanadelthur has been told and re-told in Dene communities throughout the north for almost 300 years. It varies little in the telling, although sometimes she is called Slave Woman or the Women in Red." Benjamin told the following story in Dene; the translator is unknown.

The Story of Thanadelthur

The Cree came from the south and had a long association with trading furs at the post at Hudson Bay. They had everything—guns, powder, shot, caps—and they would use their guns to intimidate the Dene people. Sometimes a fight would break out and they would kill the Dene, but they told the white traders that the people they killed were very ugly people. They said they didn't even look like humans. Sometimes the Cree would take Dene women to live with them as their wives.

When the Cree were out of powder and shot, and had furs to trade, they would return to the fort on Hudson Bay. They would camp a few miles away and tell their women to stay behind. One of these women, a Dene who had been taken as a slave, became curious and followed the Cree. As she got close to the fort she saw some white men. They didn't notice her right away but when they did she became frightened. "Don't do anything to me," she said to them. The white men took her to the fort and it was there that she met the Chief Factor, James Knight.

James Knight asked her many questions. He wanted to know how her people lived. He found out the Cree were not telling the truth about the Dene people. "You are a pretty lady. The Cree said your people were ugly," he said. She told him that the Cree had killed all of her people with the powder and guns he had given them.

The Chief Factor sent her out with supplies to find her people and bring them back to the fort. She left the fort on snowshoes with two other people, dragging a toboggan behind them filled with food, guns, medicine and other supplies.

Two Dene hunters were out looking for moose when they came across the snowshoe tracks. They thought they were the tracks of the Cree because of the kind of snowshoes, the same kind of snowshoes that white people use. They followed them and saw the two white men walking ahead of a woman dressed in Cree clothing. They tried to kill her and had her down on the snow ready to stab her with a spear. "Don't kill me," she said, and then told them the story of what happened. "The Cree Indians killed all of our friends. Only me, I'm alive. We've brought things for you on the toboggan behind us."

When they had seen the food and guns, the woman said, "How far do you stay?" "We live too far," one of the men replied. They decided that one of the Dene men would go alone to the camp and tell the woman's story. That same night he came to where the Dene stayed and told all of the story that he knew from the woman. The Dene came the next day to where the woman and the white men were.

When she saw them, the woman waved at the people, her relatives. The Dene did not trust her. At first she said little, then she told them that she was there to help them. "I am Dene too, and I have brought you things you need," she said.

So she gave her people the food, guns and medicine. They didn't know how to use the guns so the white men showed them how, and they practiced by shooting at targets. The woman told her people that they would be returning to the trading post, and if they would come with her they could get more supplies in trade for their fur.

As they returned to the fort, her people walked beside her. She would use an axe to chop down trees as she walked, and she would tell them stories.

When they arrived at the stone house—as the fort was called—the Cree were gone. Only the traders were there. They showed the Dene how to trap. The white men killed the beaver by breaking open the beaver house. The Dene followed along to learn how to get the fur and prepare it for trade. And so the Dene were brought into the fur trade.

This did not end the fighting between the Dene and the Cree. Five years later the Cree killed five more Dene and took their guns. These six Cree hid out for some time until they finally ran out of supplies and went to town. The son of one of the Cree told on his dad by saying, "Dad, you told me that you shot that man in the head." The six Cree were captured and put in jail for these killings. After that things were quiet for awhile.

—19??

Charlie Janvier
Dene · 1889–1984 · La Loche and West La Loche

Charlie Janvier was born in 1889 in La Loche, but lived most of his life in West La Loche. He married Helen Herman in 1912. A skilled trapper and hunter, he hauled freight for the Hudson's Bay Company from Big River to La Loche, and through the Methye Portage to Fort McMurray. The following story is from an interview in the *Dene Elders Project*.

A Man and a Wolf

One time there was a man who lived with a wolf. In the springtime when it was time for the wolves to mate, the wolf went someplace. Then came late summer. The wolf came back to the man. The man was still waiting for him. The man had killed a moose so they lived on that. Then they went walking around. Finally the wolf had six cubs.

The man and the wolf raised them, and in the fall time when it was freezing up they went up north to the barrenlands. The man, the wolf and the six cubs all went together. They came to a big lake. As they were going along the shore two of the wolf cubs were far ahead because they were to hunt for food for the others. As the little group was following the wolf cubs, they saw something like smoke or dust in front of them. A little later it happened again. They didn't know a man was hunting and had shot the two little wolves.

The man who shot the wolves went on the lake and the other wolves went after him. They killed the man and tore him to pieces. They continued on to the barrenlands. On the way they came to a lake again. They saw someone walking along the shore. So the man told the wolves that it was another hunter. They went after the hunter and tore him to pieces and killed him.

The man went to where they had killed the hunter. He told the wolves, "In the future, don't ever kill a human being like that again." Ever since that time no wolf has ever killed a human again. That's the way I heard about it.

When they were in the barrenlands they had nothing to eat so they moved on. The man and the female wolf headed south, and they didn't know what to do because they were so hungry. There were no caribou, and no moose either. They were getting weaker and weaker until finally they met a wolverine so they told him, "We are very hungry."

The wolverine said, "I have left some food not far from here. Let's go there."

When they came to that place the wolverine started digging in the ground. The wolverine had killed two beaver and hid them there so he took them out for them. But the man and the wolf said, "It is too bad but we don't eat beaver because its castors are too strong."

So the wolverine once again said, "I have stored something not far from here." They left for the place, and when they got there the wolverine started digging again and this time he took out some old dry ribs and they ate them.

After they finished eating, the wolverine left them so the man and the wolf went up a mountain. There they found moose tracks. Although they could hardly see the tracks, they could still smell them. So the wolf said, "My grandson, stay here for me. I'll try my luck."

So the female wolf crawled under the snow towards the moose. As she was crawling under the snow she was hardening the snow with her paws. It was not long when the wolf saw the moose. She jumped to attack but the snow gave way under her so the moose got away. Again she ran after the moose.

The man went and followed her. Not far from there the man said, "I found my grandmother lying on the snow. She had fainted because she was so hungry. She was just shaking." The man passed her and followed the moose because he could smell the scent and knew it was not far away.

The man said, "I came to a little lake and already the moose was in the middle of the lake so I went around to where there were big drifts of snow but the moose got over them before I could get there." But the man chased after it until there was another little lake and the moose was not far from him.

"I went to where the big drifts of snow were. When the moose got to the big drifts, I jumped on it and bit the moose's hind leg. Already my grandmother was on the moose's throat and we killed the moose."

The wolf said, "Let's sing before we eat." So they sang and they ate the best meat with the fat on it first. They stayed there for awhile till they got their strength back. Then they went back to the barrenlands, still using the moose meat.

That's how much I know about the man and the wolf.

—19??

Charles Ryder
Nakoda · 1889–19?? · Carry-the-Kettle

Charles Ryder was born in 1889 at the Fort Qu'Appelle Agency. According to Valerie Drummond, Ryder "traces his family back to the Fort Belknap Reservation in Montana. His father was one of the *chuwiknaka eyaku* (Man Who Took the Coat) band, who moved from Cypress Hills to Indian Head in 1882." When Chief *chuwiknaka eyaku* passed away in 1891, he was succeeded by his brother, Carry the Kettle. The selections below were recorded by Drummond in her 1976 linguistic study of the Carry-the-Kettle dialect of Assiniboine, *Carry-the-Kettle Assiniboine Texts*.

Notably, "The Pipe of Peace" makes reference to the Gruvons—this is a spelling variant of the Gros Ventre peoples, who lived in the Saskatchewan area prior to the arrival of the Blackfoot and Cree.

The Pipe of Peace

Long ago an old old man told me this story.

At one time the Gruvons and the Assiniboines were enemies and fought many battles. This once the Assiniboines had gone off to war against the Gruvons, and while the two tribes were face to face in battle, an Assiniboine man took a pipe from the Gruvon camp. This pipe was what we would call a *chanupa wakha*. The stem was decorated with feathers and porcupine work and the Gruvons considered it holy. They smoked it and held it for the special religious prayers before meetings. This pipe, then, was taken in battle.

The Assiniboine man got home with it and kept it for some time. Winter came on. (He had taken it during the summer.) That winter he had an unexpected dream. In it the pipe wanted to be returned home, "If you don't take me back to my people, something terrible will befall you." He paid no attention to the dream and didn't mention it to anyone.

Within a few days there was a big blizzard which prevented them from going out to their hunting grounds and caused a famine.

Some time later this man had another dream. Again the pipe said, "If you don't take me home, another terrible disaster will befall you all." He still paid no attention and didn't discuss it. And an epidemic struck them. Many of his people died.

Once again as spring was approaching, he had another dream. Again he dreamt about the pipe. The pipe said, "If you don't take me home, disasters will continue to befall you all."

He still ignored it. This time the epidemic struck the children and many of them perished. The man was troubled by this—he was frightened. He gathered the Assiniboine people together for a meeting where he told them everything. In the dreams about the pipe he had foreseen that all of this would happen.

First he spoke about the terrible blizzard. He also spoke about the epidemics that had struck them, "Even this last one when all of the children died—all of this I have brought upon us because of the pipe," he said. "What should we do about it? Should we take the pipe back?" he asked.

"Yes," his people agreed. They were willing.

"Then we will give the pipe back to the enemy," he said.

By now summer was coming on.

"When the grass is green, we'll leave," he said. Once it was summer, they got ready and started out travelling.

About this time the Gruvon man who had the pipe before, also had a dream. He dreamt that the pipe was returning home.

He told the people about this—the Gruvon people. They were very pleased.

The Gruvons set off. The Assiniboines were approaching and the Gruvons went out to meet them. In a big flat on a hill they made camp opposite each other. The next morning the Assiniboines carried the pipe towards the Gruvon tents. The Gruvons came forward as well. In the middle of the flat they sat down together in a group.

Then the Assiniboines untied the pipe roll. Inside the roll with the pipe were some sweetgrass, tobacco of some kind and kniknik. Someone unrolled all of this. Then the pipe was filled and lit.

An Assiniboine man took the pipe to pray with. They all prayed for peace as he held the pipe. From that time forward they were to be friends and relatives. They spoke together. Both tribes spoke and talked with each other.

The Gruvons were all in agreement. They lit the pipe and smoked it. Then they passed it around. When the Gruvon man who formerly had the pipe took the pipe, he too held it and prayed. He, too, said, "From now on there will be peace and we will be friends and relatives together. This will be carried on into the future."

He placed the pipe, first over his heart and then over the right side of his chest. Then again the filled pipe was passed around for everyone to smoke.

From that day forward the two enemy tribes—the Assiniboines and the Gruvons—were at peace. From then on they were united. Now that they were one people, there were intermarriages. Assiniboine women married Gruvon men. Gruvon men married Assiniboine women. Now they are all related and live together.

This, then, is the story of the pipe of peace. It is a story that was told to me long ago by an old old man. And now I have told it here.

—1976

A Bear Story

I'm going to tell you a story about a bear.

Long ago there was a war being fought. And during the battle a certain man was wounded by the enemy. He was shot through the leg so that he couldn't walk. He was wounded above the knee. His people tried to carry him towards home, but he suffered too much from the movement. So they laid him down and made him a small tent and a lean-to to sit in. They put out both wood for a fire and sliced meat where he would be able to reach them. They hung up the meat in such a way that the animals couldn't reach it. They brought him a stick of a certain length and placed it ready for him. And they also sharpened a stick and gave it to him so that he could reach for the meat.

The man sat there for some time. Night fell when suddenly a wolf appeared. This wolf sat for awhile at the door of the man's tent. The man took down some of the meat and fed the wolf. He did this because he feared the wolf. The wolf ate and went away.

The following night a bear appeared. He, too, sat at the door. Again the man took down some meat and fed him. The bear ate it up and continued to lay there. Then he, too, went away.

The next night the bear arrived once again. The wolf stayed away. The man fed the bear again. That done, again the bear went away.

As before, the bear returned the next night and the same thing happened.

The third night the bear came inside the tent and pushed his nose against the man's leg. The man wondered why the bear was doing this. The bear was pressing his nose against the bound wound. Then the man understood. He unbound the wound, wondering exactly what the bear was going to do to the wound. The bear licked the wound and the man was pleased by this.

The following night the bear came again. He entered the tent and the man immediately unbound his wound. Again the bear licked it. He continued this day after day and gradually the wound healed. The man was pleased at his recovery and was soon able to crawl about. The bear kept this up for several more days.

Then one day he came into the tent and laid down beside the man, then moved up against the man. "It seems that the bear wants to carry me on his back," the man thought.

He prepared everything remaining, including the meat, for departure. Carrying everything that he had, he got on the bear's back. The bear stood up and set off carrying him. He carried him quite a distance and then towards daybreak he lay down. The man got off and the bear went away. The man sat there throughout the day and that night the bear returned. Again the man climbed on his back. This continued until the bear brought the man to the top of a hill near the man's home, where the bear lay down again, the man got off, and the bear went off somewhere.

At daybreak the man was sitting on this hill. It was then he noticed that they had reached his own camp below. "The bear has brought me home," he thought.

He could easily be seen sitting on the hill, and two boys who happened to be out walking noticed him as they walked towards him. They thought he was someone else, perhaps an enemy. They weren't going to pay attention to him when suddenly the man signaled to them. Then they went over to him and discovered who it was—the wounded man.

When he had been wounded in battle and they had left him behind, they had told him they would return to get him, if they managed to reach home. They hadn't done that yet and he was back—the bear brought him back home.

The boys went back to camp and told about this, "The man who was wounded is sitting over there on the hill. He has come home. We don't know how he got back," they said. Some went over and saw that it was indeed him—the man who had been wounded.

They brought him down into camp and he told them his story. He told them everything about the bear bringing him home, actually carrying him home on his back.

After this experience with the bear, this man was always able to handle bears well. Once, inside a certain bear's den there sat a bear. This man went inside and brought that bear out with him.

And also, after this experience he didn't want anyone to kill bears. Whenever anyone was going to do such a thing, he would go elsewhere. He didn't want to witness it.

Because of the bear who did all of this and brought him home, this man respected all bears.

—*1976*

Peter Vandall
Cree · 1899–1985 · Ahtahkakoop

Peter Vandall was from the Ahtahkakoop First Nation at Sandy Lake. He was a member of the House People, the branch of Plains Cree who lived near Carlton House. The selection below is from *wâskahikaniwiyiniw-âcimowina: Stories of the House People*, edited by Freda Ahenakew.

It is a collection of stories recorded at the Saskatchewan Indian Cultural College in Saskatoon on February 16, 1982. The stories were told in Cree and then transcribed and translated into English. The selection below is a *kakeskihkemowina*, or "counselling text."

Social Control

This, for instance, is how the Crees raised their children long ago, and also how they taught their young people. Long ago there were a great many Crees, they were travelling around and the people lived only on buffalo then.

And there were great numbers of people, the elders used to tell, across the camp-circle, for instance, one could barely distinguish a horse even if it was white, so big was the circle of these tipis, there were so many Crees long ago.

And it was rare for the Crees to commit any crimes against one another at that time, even though there were so many people of different tribes, they did not very often commit violent crimes against one another, they lived together peacefully.

There were, of course, people who were responsible for this, just like the police when they say something today, and our elders long ago called it a 'Dance-Lodge'—where the circle of poles stood, the braves decided how one should travel and how one should live, even when to move camp, they made the decisions—and now the elders, once the decisions had been made, there were men who went around and announced them to all the people. They walked around the entire camp-circle, announcing what they would do, what was to be done, what they were to do; and this they followed.

And in the morning, when they arose, I used to hear the elders; just as the singing of birds sounds beautiful in the morning, at day-break, so it was with the elders who could be heard all over as they sang—they would even sing in response with their wives—they took such pride in themselves, and their journey through life was very beautiful.

And there were also elders, just as in preaching, who sometimes walked one behind the other in procession. As they went along, they preached to the young people not to commit any crimes, not to do any harm to one another—they preached to them just as the priests today try to preach to the people, that was their purpose.

And the Crees led a really clean life, very clean. They never did anything very bad, even though it looked as if they were not subject to any formal law when they did do something wrong. But the Crees, too, had their own rules, always to treat one another with respect and for the young people to pay heed to the elders.

That is it for now.

— *February 16, 1982. Saskatchewan Indian Cultural Centre, Saskatoon*

Marie Merasty
Woods Cree · c. 1900s–1983 · Peter Ballantyne

Marie Merasty was Woods Cree from the Peter Ballantyne First Nation and lived in Prince Albert. Her traditional stories of the wīhtikow (Wetiko) were collected in *The World of Wetiko: Tales from the Woodland*

Cree, translated by Bill Merasty and edited by Candace Savage, with illustrations by Sarain Stump. These stories have become renowned and the subject of much research.

The Wetiko Mother

Although human in form and origin, the Wetiko was both less and more than an ordinary person. Becoming a Wetiko involved a change of appetite: once a person had eaten human flesh, he found other foods distasteful. His appearance changed, until one glimpse could terrify a victim into helplessness. In the first place, a Wetiko lost the instinct to keep clean: its hair was long, shaggy, matted and full of dirt or whatever else would stick to it; its body went unwashed; its teeth discolored; its finger- and toe-nails grew long and broke off. Its clothes were dirty, smelly and sometimes so tattered the Wetiko roamed almost naked through the wilderness.

And then there was its toothy, lipless grin. In its hunger, the Wetiko literally ate its own lips. The patch of ice on its back made it even more frightening. There is no good explanation for this condition which lasted right through the heat of summer, but many stories, especially those about the death of a Wetiko, mention ice which seemed to have replaced living tissue. Apparently, it was a curse which marked one as a true Wetiko. Almost always, a Wetiko was burned as soon as it had been killed. In such cases, the fire had to be tended because the melting ice from its back put out the flames.

Once there was a family of several people living together in a camp. And it happened that they fell upon hungry times, although they tried hard to obtain food. They hunted and fished but were unable to kill game of any kind. One day the young man of the family went fishing. He carried with him something sharp, perhaps a bone fastened to a stone or piece of wood. As the young man was returning, coming into view, the mother went to meet him in hope of killing him. The youth must have sensed the danger because he threw his dagger at his mother. His aim was close but he missed.

The mother seized her son and killed him. Dragging the body to the house, she said to her daughter, "Now we will be able to feast quite heartily. I have killed the young of a moose." She had mistaken her son for a calf.

One by one, the mother killed her children for food until only the eldest and the youngest daughters remained alive. Because she could overpower her mother, the older girl was able to prevent her own death. When she went to chop wood, she always took her little sister along. Before one of these trips the old lady told the daughter, "You shouldn't have to take your sister along. She will only be in your way. I'll look after her."

The daughter thought that perhaps the mother had recovered because she had spoken in a clear, concise manner for a change. So she left the little girl with the mother and tried to hurry with the task of gathering firewood but she had quite a distance to haul it. As she approached the house with the firewood her mother called, "Come and eat this new-born moose that I have cooked." She had already cooked the young girl. She must have bludgeoned the youngster the minute the older daughter departed and then roasted her child over the fire. Now only one daughter remained.

"I almost killed her then and there," the older daughter was to remark later because her mother had made her so angry.

This had all happened while the father was away hunting. He had been gone for quite a while but now he could be heard approaching. "My children, we now have much to eat. I have killed something," he called from outside the house. He was struggling to carry a sack which contained a variety of organs taken from a moose—the heart, the liver and other things.

The behaviour of the young lady which followed is unbelievable...

Knowing that her father was approaching and that the mother was waiting for him by the door with an axe in hand, she should have shouted out to warn him of the danger. She should have helped him. She had been counting on him to take them to a relative's camp where perhaps the mother would have recovered.

As the husband stepped in, the woman swung the axe and killed him. Taking the sack in hand she said, "It stinks!" So the young lady took the sack and cooked the contents for herself. She had not been eating human flesh; she had been living on rabbit meat instead.

"Let's go to my sister's," the young woman suggested. "Where are they living?"

"Okay, we'll go there," the mother said. The husband was her last food, for she had eaten all the children save the one. So the two women left for yet another daughter's place, and upon their arrival, the hostess sensed an air of uneasiness and asked the mother what they had been doing.

"We have died off one by one," the mother lied. "We have gone through lean times." Unsatisfied, the hostess questioned her sister in private, after they had stepped out.

"It was mother who killed off our kin," her sister explained. "We were very short of food but we were not starving outright. Our father was the last one she killed."

The hostess now went to a group of men and passed this judgment: "My mother and sister are going to go fishing. You are to go and kill them. When they come around the point, you should be there ahead of them, waiting in ambush. Kill them both. My sister has angered me for letting mother kill our family when she could have overpowered her. My mother has particularly angered me by killing my father. Don't let them escape. Kill them."

When they sat down to eat, the hostess knew something was wrong when she noticed that her mother was slipping the food under her clothing and refusing to eat. The visiting daughter, on the other hand, ate heartily because there was nothing wrong with her.

After the men had killed the two women as planned, they threw the bodies into the fire. The daughter's body burned away without incident but the old woman's body burned a long time before it was reduced to ashes. Ice had formed on her back and the melting of this ice put out the fire several times.

A Race for Life

In general, the ability of the Wetiko was below that of a normal person. Because it could not build a canoe, it could be stopped by a lake. Because it could not make a shelter, it had to find one ready-made. The Wetiko was an animal that was less keen and fit for survival than the other residents of the forest in which it roamed.
One time, after the ice had cleared enough to allow canoe travel, a man called WETSOONESEW went to visit a nearby camp. "I'll be back shortly," he told his wife. "I am going to check on that camp. There were several people living there."

He arrived at the site to find the tipis in disorder. "I saw bones scattered in a display of white," he related later. "I spied a small tipi with smoke rising from it, so I looked in. A human foot was being boiled!" He had the feeling that someone was heading for him so he ran back to where his wife was. He knew what it meant and he ran swiftly.

His wife greeted him with, "The dog is lying in the sun in the brush."

"Quickly then!" he urged her. "Throw him into the canoe and get in yourself. I am going to make a fire and then jump into the canoe last. A Wetiko is nearby."

The woman put the little dog in the canoe, got in herself and began edging along the shore. As soon as the man had made a fire, he jumped into the canoe too and started off across the lake. Just then a Wetiko charged into view! It managed to scratch the canoe, but failed to catch a proper hold of its bow. The couple were on a lake and, thus, in a position to leave the Wetiko stranded on shore.

"Go and eat the foot you had boiling," the man taunted. "Don't bother us."

The Wetiko watched them leave and, since it was daylight, he could see them heading far out into the lake. There, on an island, the man built a huge bonfire. He knew that a long portage and a winding creek were the last barriers between them and a major lake. That the Wetiko might catch them in the creek was the man's main concern. So he built the bonfire in the hope of fooling the Wetiko into thinking they were camping out on the lake.

Now they ran over the portage, the woman helping to carry their belongings. Now they wound their way through the creek, paddling furiously. They had almost reached the mouth of the creek.

"Oh no, here he is!" the man shouted.

It was as if the things along the path of the Wetiko were being tossed, it was rushing so fast. The couple were just gliding onto the lake, the canoe swaying with the effort, when the Wetiko launched itself at the canoe and into the water. But it was unable to grab ahold of the canoe.

"Go on, go on," the man taunted. "Go and eat that foot you had boiling." Once on the big lake they had no trouble escaping because the Wetiko had no canoe in which to chase them.

The Last Laugh

The best—or only—defence against an aggressor employing medicine power was one's own power. Someone with powers could usually defend himself and perhaps launch a counterattack of his own.

An old woman once made an attempt on Whitebear Chief's life. She threatened him after he neglected to offer her a drink at KETSIWASKAIKAN (York Factory). The old lady had such power that she had two young men to transport her from place to place in a canoe. She wanted Whitebear to give her a drink at her command, having heard that he too possessed powers. But Whitebear refused and she became angry.

"Just wait," she threatened. "You beware of me when winter comes!"

"Okay, but you beware of me, too," he replied. And as winter set in Whitebear went about his work, leading a nomadic life, perhaps hunting, but whatever else he did he always prepared his bed high in a lofty tree. One night, as he was sleeping, he awoke to find himself staring into the open jaws of a huge animal somewhat like a horse. It was going to kill him!

"What do you think you're doing?" he asked innocently. "In a dream I had about you earlier, you took pity on me. It's me!" he said in a soothing tone. Whitebear Chief was stalling for time.

Now, the helping spirit of Whitebear Chief chopped off the head of the beast. Chief had been sleeping with an axe by his side, but it was his helper, at Whitebear's bidding, not Whitebear himself, who chopped off the beast's head. Whitebear climbed down from the tree and skinned the head. He peeled and dried the ears. When summer returned and the people made the trip down to York Factory, Chief pinned the ears to his hat in the hope of making sport of someone.

Again the old lady was being transported down the river. Whitebear Chief overheard her saying, "Do you see that person decorating his hat with those things? They happen to be my animal's ears." She wasn't even embarrassed to admit it!

And so the old lady was not able to bully Whitebear Chief; she could not outdo him.

Experience as a Medium

One year towards spring, we were to travel to WETIKO SAKAIKAN (Wintego Lake) so I went to pay a visit to an old lady, the wife of Alexander Daylight, for whom I used to feel affection. She was happy that I had called on her. Then we travelled towards our destination. We remained at our camp for quite a while. The conditions were still good for travelling so your grandfather said, "I'll go and get some things. We might run short of something, sugar, for instance, and flour. That way we will have extra supplies. It will be a long wait during breakup." And away he went.

Most of the snow had disappeared from around the house we were living in; a large house it was. I was living with my daughter, Angelique. No one else had lived there that spring but us, it seemed. We shut the windows—the place had windows.

There were some dogs with us that day; your grandfather had taken some others with him. Angelique was sleeping and I was sitting up; there was still some daylight remaining. By and by, the sound of approaching footsteps. The dogs growled. They ran to the back of the house where you could hear the sound of heads banging. Growling, bunching together at intervals, slamming against the house with thuds.

I thought to myself, "For certain, they have seen a porcupine. I'll take a look out the window." Nothing in sight. I sat down.

Maybe you don't remember that place on Wintego Lake, the path leading up from the shore. The ground is like a mound. Walking on it produces a particular sound, a sucking sound, and very audible. I heard the sound of someone walking up the hill with deliberation, towards the house.

And the dogs! They were growling with such savageness, yet with such fear. They would not come out from behind the house.

"I wonder what manner of appearance 'this someone' will reveal when it steps into the house."

I decided to remain seated; I didn't move; I sat. I didn't want to wake up Angelique because she was so easily frightened and perhaps she would be adversely affected. It approached the doorway, the way a human steps, exactly—I am not lying. I never used to become frightened over minor incidents or for no apparent reason because I had often stayed alone at different places. I was never easily spooked. It approached the doorway. Just as it would have reached for the doorlatch, the footsteps ceased.

Only then I stood up, and going to the window which would serve the purpose, I drew back a corner of the shades and looked out. There was no one at the doorway.

I slept now. No, I mean, I lay down, not sleeping. I thought I might as well get up; Angelique was sleeping. The dogs were coming out from behind the house by this time. And now I looked around to see if it had been a porcupine.

Another time, dogs had barked at one which had lurked about for I don't know how many nights. My late sister Charlotte had been there then, the dogs barking, barking, in the direction of the woods. One day, she came to me saying, "Remember how the dogs had been barking so. I have killed the one who came to us from without, the one who would never let us sleep nights."

"Who?" I asked her.

"The porcupine!" she said. "It was lurking about the shed and that was why the dogs had been barking so much."

Now I woke up Angelique. "Wake up," I told her, "I believe we are going to receive news of some kind. This animal they call the dog has powers. It is as if nothing stands in its way."

I went on to relate what had just happened and added, "Maybe we are going to be hearing about something. Those dogs didn't act up for nothing."

Later your grandfather arrived. He greeted me with the news, "Your aunt has died, the one to whom you paid a farewell visit."

See, that was whose presence I had felt! She used to feel much affection for me. At times, I used to think that maybe she had wanted me to pray for her.

—1974

Eleanor Brass
Cree-Saulteaux · 1905–1992 · Peepeekisis

Eleanor Brass (nee Dieter) was born in 1905 and grew up on the File Hills Colony farming settlement at the Peepeekisis Reserve. Her father, who was Cree, and her mother, who was Saulteaux, met at the Indian Industrial School in Regina. She married Hector Brass in 1925, and they farmed on the reserve before she embarked on a career as a storyteller, becoming active in Native education and in improving social conditions for First Nations. In 1944, she became the first woman executive to serve as the secretary-treasurer of the Association of Indians of Saskatchewan. In 1949, her piece "Breaking the Barriers" was published in the *Regina Leader Post*, which led to a regular column. She continued to tell Cree legends and write newspaper articles, and she published two books: *Medicine Boy and Other Cree Tales* (1979) and her autobiography, *I Walk in Two Worlds* (1987). She passed away on May 20, 1992, in Regina.

The first two selections, from *Medicine Boy*, are examples of her adaptation of traditional storytelling to a contemporary context. The third selection, from her autobiography, provides an example of her social criticism.

Medicine Boy

The Old Woman, *Pimosais*, or Little Flyer, was sitting in front of her tepee by a campfire sewing a garment, when her granddaughter came to join her. The young girl was always fascinated with her grandmother, for there seemed to be something mysterious about her. She had the finest painted tepee in the camp and the figures on it were unique. Her clothes were well made and decorated with the same kind of unusual figures.

The girl had heard that her grandmother once had a strange experience and she wanted to know what it was. One day she decided she would ask her.

As she sat down and made herself comfortable, the young girl said, "*Kokoom*, I know you had an adventure in your life that you won't speak to anyone about. But being your grandchild, and being old enough to understand, would you tell the story to me?"

"*Tapway, nosesim*, Yes, my grandchild. I believe you're old enough to understand and I know that you'll respect what I tell you and only pass it on to your grandchildren.

"A long time ago, when I was a young girl like you, I was small for my age and moved around quickly, so they called me Little Flyer. I was promised to a handsome young man, *Ka-ki-she-wait*, Loud Voice, to marry. But I didn't want to get married right away, so I used to go to the forest to think about it. One day I was sitting on a log deep in thought when I heard a branch snap. Looking behind me, I saw the handsomest young man I'd ever seen. He wasn't very big, about my size. He was so straight and strong looking that I just stared at him speechless.

"He said, 'Don't be afraid. I've been watching you for days and I've noticed that you have something weighing heavily on your mind.'

"I was so surprised I couldn't say a thing.

"Then he said, 'I think you're a very beautiful maiden, and I'd like to see you often. Could you come out here again?'

"I just nodded my head in assent and ran back to camp.

"Mother was always busy sewing garments, for she had several sons and daughters, and I helped her. I used to hurry with my work in order to finish early so I could go to the forest to meet my handsome friend. Every day he was there waiting for me. We'd talk about the birds, animals and the mysterious ways of nature. He knew so much about them. He always carried a small leather bag with herbs in it. I was curious about him. His attractiveness was even deeper than just his appearance. He'd never speak about himself except that he was Medicine Boy, gathering herbs for his tribe. But I felt that he didn't belong to any Indian camp.

"One day when Loud Voice saw me coming out of the forest he said, 'What were you doing in there? You look so happy, I believe you're meeting someone, and I'm going to find out.' I was afraid to go out for a few days, as I knew that Loud Voice would be watching my movements. I made certain that he was out hunting for the day before I went back to the forest.

"Medicine Boy was waiting for me as usual and said, 'I've been worried about you, Little Flyer. Have you been sick?'

"'No,' I answered, 'I was only being cautious, as Loud Voice is suspicious. He says that he's going to catch and harm you, and I don't want you hurt.'

"He said, 'Don't worry about me, he'll never catch me.'

"Loud Voice had been noted for his skill in hunting, but it seemed that his luck had changed for he could not kill any game to bring back to camp. One day, he came over to see me and said that he was going to bring back a lot of meat. So he went out hunting and saw a deer. He started creeping up close to try and get a good shot, when a small man ran out of the bluff and frightened the deer. It happened again and again all day. Every time he had a good chance to kill something, it was frightened away. He suspected the little man was following him just to keep him from killing anything.

"Then Loud Voice decided to try fishing. Just as his net was full of fish, he upset his canoe and fell into the water and all the fish got away. Then he saw the same little man swim from under the canoe. Then he knew it was a trick of one of the *May-may-quay-she-wuk*, the little people.

"During this period, every time I saw Medicine Boy, he'd ask me about Loud Voice and his hunting; I'd tell him what happened and he'd laugh. It seemed strange that he always knew when and where Loud Voice was going to hunt and fish. However, I loved him and I didn't want anything to spoil my companionship with Medicine Boy, so I just laughed along with him.

"I used to ask, 'Medicine Boy, where do you come from?' He'd answer, 'Quite a long way from here.' 'What tribe do you belong to?' 'It is a tribe that you have never heard about.'

"This only made me more curious so I decided that I'd follow him and see for myself. I waited every day for a chance when I wouldn't be missed from the camp. My opportunity came one time during the berry season when all the women and children were going out to pick berries while the men were out hunting. I pretended to be sick, so they left me and told me to prepare the evening meal if I was feeling better by then. As soon as they were gone I went out into the forest and Medicine Boy was there waiting for me.

"He said, 'How are you, Little Flyer? I have a funny feeling about you this morning; it seems you have something weighing heavily on your mind. Could I help you?'

"'No, I'm fine,' I answered. 'Only I worry about us; perhaps some day we'll be caught. Do you think we should change our meeting place?'

"'I've thought of that myself. I know of another place that isn't far from your camp, only it's in another direction. Come and follow me.'

"We skirted the forest and came to a high place of ground where there was a large buffalo dugout with a low growth of brush all around it. We could peer through the brush and see for quite a distance around us. The place was well beaten down inside as Medicine Boy had used it for a hideout.

"We sat down on some boulders close to the entrance and talked for awhile, then he went away. I waited until he was nearly out of sight, then I got up and followed him.

"He would stop to pick some leaves off the foliage and kept looking back. I guess he felt that someone was following him. I kept on, but it seemed as though it was taking him a long time to arrive at his destination. I watched closely until finally I saw some tiny men and women come out to meet him. He resembled them only that he was a little bigger in stature. They were dressed in buckskin clothes and the women had the most beautiful designs on their dresses. I had never seen such work before. They used porcupine quills for embroidering and the colours glowed. I looked hard at the designs, thinking perhaps I could remember and use them on my own dresses.

"All this was a surprising sight to me, but it was dulled by the shocking truth that my beloved was a *May-may-quaish*. I went home feeling sad, for I knew that I could never marry my handsome Medicine Boy.

"When I got back to camp I tried to remember the designs on the tiny women's gowns. I got out the material and tried to copy them but my hand kept getting cramps. I tried and tried but it was of no use.

"The next time I went to see my handsome friend, he was waiting as usual. He said, 'You know who I am, don't you?' 'Yes, I saw your people and the women who have such beautiful dresses. I tried to copy the work on them for a dress for myself, but my hands kept getting cramps.'

"'My beautiful Little Flyer, you can't copy their designs, but you'll always be a fine design worker and your dresses and tepees will always have fascinating figures. Because I happen to be an extra big *May-may-quaish*, I was appointed to go out and gather herbs for my people for they thought I wouldn't arouse much attention. But from now on I'll always avoid coming near your camp. Go and marry Loud Voice. I'm sorry I played tricks on him, to belittle him before your eyes, for he's a good man and a good hunter. You'll be happy with him. I knew you had followed me and I let you do it, as I knew that we would have to end our friendship sometime. This is good-bye, my Little Flyer.'"

Legend of Qu'Appelle

Blue Cloud was a guide for the white traders in the early days. He was a handsome and robust young man who travelled across the prairies, to the Great Lakes, and north to the Arctic regions.

On one of his trips to the Qu'Appelle Valley, he met a lovely Indian maiden by the name of Evening Bird. Her skin was smooth as a flower petal and her hair was glossy like the sheen of a raven's wing. They talked and he told her of his travels around the country and the strange ways of the newcomers. She listened intently, fascinated by his tales and admiring him for his bravery.

When it came time for him to leave again she was very sad and wondered how she would endure the waiting till his next return. While he was away she dreamed of his coming back and was always first to hear the swish of his paddle coming down the lake towards her.

At the same time Blue Cloud's thoughts were always of Evening Bird and the time that she would be his forever. Finally, on one trip back he decided she was old enough so that he could ask for her hand in marriage.

Evening Bird met him as usual at the lakeshore and both were overjoyed to see each other. They sat down by the canoe and talked, Blue Cloud telling all about his travels.

At last he said: "Evening Bird, I've something important to ask you and I think you're old enough to consider this. I would like you to be my wife and if you will consent, then I'll go to your father and ask him for your hand in marriage."

"Oh, Blue Cloud, you know that there isn't another man in this world that I would consider marrying but you, and I know that we'll be very happy."

"Then all there is left to do is go and ask your parents."

"Blue Cloud approached the tepee of Evening Bird's parents and found them sitting outside by the campfire. Her mother arose and went into the tepee when she saw him coming, for it was the custom that a mother-in-law should not speak to her son-in-law, and she expected that the visitor soon would be her daughter's husband.

The father welcomed Blue Cloud to his camp and offered to share a smoke with him. "My son," he said, "I know you have something on your mind and I'll be glad to listen to you."

"Yes," said Blue Cloud, "you've probably noticed that I've been interested in your daughter, Evening Bird, for a number of years. Now that she is old enough to know her own mind, we've talked this over and have agreed to marry. I'm asking for your consent."

"My son, I've observed you for some time and I know that your trips are hazardous and that you are a brave man to carry on this work. I would be glad to give you my daughter in marriage and I know that you'll take good care of her. We'll prepare for the marriage on your next trip back."

Blue Cloud went away very happy but on his next trip the time seemed to pass slowly. He made his rounds back and forth across the country, up north and back until at last it was time to return to the Qu'Appelle Valley. He travelled quickly, making it in double time by paddling day and night. When he was drawing near the valley, he suddenly heard his name being spoken and he cried out, "*Awayna-cahtay-pwayt*? Who calls? Who calls?" There was no answer. He paddled even faster, and twice again he heard the voice, the last time more distinct. He recognized it as the voice of Evening Bird and he thought perhaps she had come to meet him. Again he cried, "*Awayna-cahtay-pwayt*? Who calls? Who calls?"

When he finally arrived at his destination he went right into the camp; it was strangely quiet and suddenly he felt frightened. Finally one of the women came to meet him and said "Evening Bird has just left. She called your name three times, and passed away at the first gleam of dawn."

Blue Cloud turned sadly away and left heartbroken. He knew that every time he came to the Qu'Appelle Valley, he would hear her voice calling his name. When his white friends heard the story, they repeated it in French, "Qu'Appelle? Who calls? Who calls?"

—*1979*

Excerpt from *I Walk in Two Worlds*

My sister used to say that I came with the frogs and my mother said I came with the flowers. It was a typical day in spring on the first day of May, 1905; the buds on the trees were bursting forth, the frogs were singing lustily, and the birds were joyously chirping as if to welcome my entrance in to the world.

I was born in a log cabin on the Peepeekisis Indian Reserve near Balcarres, Saskatchewan. Our home was cosy and comfortable, with lovely curtains at the windows and colourful patchwork quilts on the beds. Mother was an excellent homemaker. My grandmother, who was the midwife at my birth, travelled two hundred miles especially for the occasion. There were no hospitals nearby and the doctor lived quite a distance away.

My sister Janet was fifteen months old at the time and still an infant. Mother was still breastfeeding her; she thought it was the proper thing to do. Because my sister was always the delicate child, she got all the attention. I didn't have any clothes at birth, so dad wrapped me up in one of his shirts, saying, "Poor little darling." Later on a lady who was a principal of the nearby Indian school brought me a layette so at least I had some clothes.

I was put on the bottle and received only passing notice. There was a small hammock suspended from the ceiling in the upstairs bedroom where I spent most of my infant days. They said that I was a very good baby; no wonder, I had no chance to know what it was like to be pampered. But I had a happy childhood; our parents were proud of us and gave us the best care. We were fortunate...

Our childhood days were interesting. Our parents took us to Indian feasts and sometimes to funerals. We liked the feasts but the funerals used to scare us. We didn't understand the rituals where the women seemed to do a lot of wailing. After attending them I would get nightmares, so my parents stopped taking us.

Instead, they would leave us with some elderly Indian woman to babysit us. They were our *kokooms* (grandmothers). They were so kind to us and would lovingly say, "*Nosisim, mitoni, kitamakasit nosisim.*" ("My poor grandchild.") This was their way of petting and caressing us. We didn't speak Cree in our house as our parents spoke two different languages—mother was Saulteaux while father was Cree. Our parents thought we would be held back in school if they spoke nothing but Indian languages to us. I am sorry about this. When we went to school we learned some Cree from our schoolmates but we often found that what we learned wasn't in good taste when we repeated it to our parents. They told us never to say those words again and not to learn any more Cree from our schoolmates.

As we grew older we often accompanied our parents to town. While they were doing their shopping we would sometimes wait for them outside on the street and watch the people go by. Some of them would stop and speak to us while others would just smile. Once some boys came by and called us "little squaws" but we didn't realize then that we were Indians. We called back to them "little squaws yourselves." This marked the first of many episodes both good and bad that were to influence and affect my life.

It has never ceased to be interesting to be an Indian and to walk in two worlds, watching, learning and trying to understand the many cultures and the thinking of the various races of people. While I know that my Indian culture is one of the noblest in the world, I feel that other cultures have affected my life in various ways.

I remember in the early days, the farmers on the colony had to haul their grain quite a distance away to Indian Head. It meant having to stay over a night or two since they used horses and wagons. The women were left to do the chores and look after the stock. One day while father was away on one of these trips mother couldn't find me. I was about four years old and as usual had been snooping around where I shouldn't have been. Somehow I got into a manger in front of a team of colts that were being stable broke. I was terrified and crying while the frightened colts were stamping and snorting. Mother heard the racket and came down to see what was going on. When she saw me in the manger in front of the colts, she stood there for a minute not knowing what to do. Then she quietly spoke to me, telling me to come towards her slowly till she could get hold of me and drag me over to the other stall. Somehow she got me out without anyone being hurt. She was so frightened and relieved that she forgot to punish me. I think the experience itself was enough punishment for both of us.

I also remember when a great cyclone struck in 1914. We watched the black cloud coming towards us, looking like a huge snake dragging on the ground. Quickly father put us all down in the dirt cellar while he watched from the upstairs window. He saw our neighbour's house being lifted off the ground and blown to pieces. Father immediately went out to the barn, hooked up a team to a democrat and drove over to their place. He found Henry McLeod badly hurt and trying to crawl over to our place for help. Dad loaded him on the democrat then looked for his wife, Eliza; he found her lying under a portion of roof. He thought she was dead as she was pale and covered with blood but she eventually recovered.

Then dad looked for the baby, Jaky, who was about a year and a half old. He searched around the wreckage but couldn't find him until the dog came running out of the barn, barking as if trying to get dad's attention; he went over and found the baby in the stable. He thought the dog must have dragged him there for safety, as the mother said the last thing she remembered was hanging onto him. The baby wasn't hurt except for a small bruise on his forehead but he was soaking wet and cold. The dog should have been decorated for it must have been responsible for Jaky's safety.

This was a horrible experience for the McLeods. They were just recently married and Jaky was their first child. After the cyclone they stayed at our place for a while. Mother put up beds for them in our front room and the doctor came to treat them. Henry had a broken back and multiple bruises while Eliza had a broken leg and bruises.

My sister and I had the job of looking after Jaky. We changed him and fed him and babysat him. The neighbours also came over, taking turns to assist in any way they could. Then the grandparents came and took Jaky to look after him. As soon as the parents were in a condition to be moved, they were taken to Lebret and put in the hospital wing of the school where they were nursed back to health. They built another house almost on the same spot as their old one and never had the same experience again.

Meanwhile, our family was growing. I had a little brother by the name of Charles but when he was fifteen months old he developed pneumonia and passed away. We were all so sad and for a long time mother hardly ever smiled. About two years later I had another brother, Harold. We girls were so happy and always wanted to hold him but we weren't allowed to do that for very long.

In the early years there were no churches on our reserve. The Presbyterians sent out a minister—or as they called them at that time, a missionary—to look after our spiritual needs. He boarded in the different homes in turn. When he lived in our home, it was extra work for mother and a certain amount of worry.

I was always a lively, curious and outspoken child, which kept mother on edge wondering what I was going to say next when the minister was around. Apparently I embarrassed her a few times in spite of her constant cautioning me not to speak, especially at mealtimes.

The minister had his sleeping quarters in our living room and we had to go through it to reach the dining and kitchen areas. Once when I was passing through I caught the minister just getting up and as he pulled on his trousers, they fell to his ankles. I was shocked and in my childish way I ran into the kitchen to describe the incident to mother.

"Momma, Momma," I shouted, "I saw the minister's bum." "Shh! Shh!" she said. "Don't ever say that to anyone and don't you say one word at the breakfast table."

That morning at the table, every time I was going to speak, mother would give such a look that I kept my mouth shut.

Church services were held in the various homes until a church was built. These services were always an ordeal for me. When I sat with mother, she pinched me if I didn't sit quietly and when I sat with dad, he only stood so much from me, then took me outside and gave me a spanking. When he brought me back into the building, I sat quietly even afraid to breath too loudly. There were no Sunday school classes for us and we were expected to sit with the grownups all during the service. I wondered why the minister had to talk so long and sometimes yell at the people.

While I was small, I noticed that mother had a large book that she guarded carefully from us children. This made me very curious and once when she forgot it on the table, I immediately grabbed it, put it on a chair, and started turning the pages. It was full of coloured pictures of the human body. As I slowly turned each page. I tried to figure out what the pictures were. My aunt was visiting at the time and they wondered why I was so quiet, so they began to watch me from the doorway. I was chattering away to myself, wondering what this was and that was. When I came to a picture of a naked man, I turned the book upside down and looked at it from every angle; some parts of the body were obviously different from a girl's. I kept saying to myself, "What's that? What's that?" Then I finally turned the page over and said, "A mouse, I guess."

Later, the twins, Edna and Edward, were born. Mother had her hands full but the neighbours were always ready to go over and do what they could for her. From there on the family grew to twelve children—nine boys and three girls. Wilfred, the last one, was born the year I was married and always thought that my husband was his real brother.

—1987

nêhiyaw (Glecia Bear)
Cree · 1912–1998 · Green Lake

nêhiyaw, or Glecia Bear (nee Laliberte), was born in 1912, and is Plains Cree from Green Lake, the site of North West Company and Hudson's Bay Company posts since 1781. The mother of eleven children, and another fifteen adopted, she became a respected Cree storyteller and the first woman chief of Flying Dust First Nation. In 1988, *nêhiyaw* took part in a series of Cree story dictations recorded by her niece Freda Ahenakew. *nêhiyaw*'s stories, along with ones by Janet Feitz, Irene Calliou, and Minnie Fraser, were published in *kôhkominawak otâcimowiniwâwa: Our Grandmothers' Lives As Told In Their Own Words*, edited and translated by Freda Ahenakew and H. C. Wolfart, published by Fifth House in 1992, and reissued by Canadian Plains Research Center, now the University of Regina Press, in 1998. The selection "Lost and Found" is an autobiographical story that can be dated to 1924 or 1925. Of note is how the story reveals some of the changes that Christianity and farming had made on traditional communities in the decades since the signing of the Treaties. Despite these influences, *nêhiyaw*'s original Cree telling reveals many aspects of Cree social structure, and the translation and transcription clearly retain the characteristics of the Cree oral storytelling tradition. The wave-hyphen (-~) indicates that the speaker has interrupted herself, resulting in a fragmentary sentence or word. Manual and facial gestures are indicated in brackets, as are explanatory insertions, designated by *sc.*

Lost and Found

My little sister is called *Gigi*, we lived at *kwâkopîwi-sâkahikanihk*, she was eight years old, and I, I was eleven years old. And I had been to church early that morning to take communion. I had gone with my mom to take communion. On our way home, my dad—he had told us, telling us the previous evening already, that one cow would be calving somewhere in the bush over here; so he had said, "Watch out for her at the smudge!" (they used to make smudges long ago, with the cows standing about there), "Look out for that female!" he had said, "'When she goes into the bush, then you all follow her!' my dad had said to me; "you follow her, but you should not follow her too closely, for when she stops now and then [sc. during contractions], she will know that you are following her, you have to follow her from afar -~ from a little distance, so that she will not see you," he had said.

And then, just as we were getting home, my mom and I, as we were arriving home from church, at that moment the cow, the very one for which my dad had told us to look out, was going off, wow, hey, she had lots of milk; she was heading into the bush. So I straight away ran inside over there and asked my little sister along. "Come with me," I said to her, "to follow that cow!" I said to her—I rushed her, she was barefoot but came like that, for we did not think it would be far. She was barefoot but I, I still wore the clothes in which I had gone to communion. But I had not eaten—for in the old days you had to fast before you went to confession and communion, not like today. You used to kneel in church when you were given communion, whereas today you stand and the host is put in your hand and you put it in your mouth yourself; also, it is not the priest but an ordinary person who is giving you communion; things are done very differently in church today. I do not know what one should believe, the Catholic Church or the White-Man's religions and what is going on today; in the old days, the Catholic Church was highly thought of. In fact, I myself still follow it all the way; what my parents had taught me, I would never let that go, and I will die with what my parents have left to me.

And so we took off, with my little sister following me, exactly as my dad had said, "Follow her from a distance!" he had said. As soon as the cow was about to come to a halt, we would duck down and stay there; so long as we continued to keep her in view to see where she was going.

Oh my, as we arrived over there, all at once there she stood sideways [sc. at a right angle to the path] (but we had walked a long way, it must have been far off where she had her calf), there she stood sideways, suckling her calf. Oh my, and now we went over there, oh, we were excited; oh my, the little calf was sucking. When I had tied it fast with my belt, from my sweater, around its neck, then my little sister held it [sc. the calf]; and then I, I milked the cow, she had so much milk: we just kept laughing, then, as we played with the milk, with me squirting it on my little sister's face. When we had drained the milk from her teats, I drove the cow forward. And, indeed, she started walking, with us following behind the calf as it followed her, the calf was quite weak.

Oh my, after a while there ran a creek, and there now the cow refused to cross. Then I whipped her and we chased her into the water (as it turned out, in fact, into a bog), and then the cow began sinking into it, and as she moved she began to sink in deeper and deeper. So now, as she [sc. my little sister) had tied the calf around the neck with my belt—with that [sc. belt] I tied the calf up, I tied it up there in the bush. So now we were about to go and tell about the cow sinking in; from the distance, half of her could still be seen when we left.

And with that, as it turned out, we were lost. It was already early fall, when it begins to get cold. Oh my oh my, and now we walked and walked, and my little sister was crying, and I myself was yelling and yelling so that we might be heard. Hey, we were crawling under fallen spruce-trees, we would crawl through underneath, where there was a little opening, as we went along.

At last it was night, oh, and now it rained. So then I sat under a spruce-tree, our clothes were already quite torn by the branches; sitting under a spruce-tree, it was a big spruce-tree where I sat, there I held my little sister, huddled over her and covering her with my sweater so as to keep her warm, so that she, at least, would be warm. All night we were there like that, and she did indeed sleep, and I slept too. As we were waking up, oh, my little sister had badly swollen feet since she had cut herself. And in the old days, of course, all you had to wear was flour-sacking—slips made from that kind, and the brassiere for your breasts was also made from that kind, from flour-sacks, that kind was all you had to wear. Then I said to my little sister, "I will take off my slip and bind your feet with it," I said to her. And so I took off my slip and tore it in half and then wrapped her feet up with it.

So now we left again, walking all day, and again we walked so much. We had nothing to eat, and the first night we felt hungry, towards evening; as my sister wanted to drink, I dug a hole when we reached a muskeg until I found water, and then gave her water to drink with my cupped hands. And so we would travel on some more.

Well, at last she simply wore out the rags on her feet, as I kept moving them around, the little slip with which I had bound her feet, she wore it out completely. And now I used my brassiere (the cloth from my breasts, it was much like a bra), now I also used that to bandage her again, tearing it in half and wrapping it around her little feet, barely covering the tips. Well, it was not long before, being in the bush, she had none of that left, also having lost one by getting it caught. "Now I am not going to walk any further," she said to me. And with that she cried so much that, finally, she could not even be heard any more, so much had she been crying.

I carried her on my back now; but I, too, was tired; and she was quite big, she was eight and she used to be fat. I carried her on my back now, walking and walking and carrying her on my back. Well, and again it was night, and again I looked for a spruce-tree for us to stay underneath there. There we stayed, underneath, oh my God, there was lightning now, it was such a bad storm that night. But we did not get wet for we were beneath a spruce-tree, but our clothes got wet when we were walking, eh? And again I sat underneath there, the same thing again, holding my little sister, well, with that little sweater, oh my God, she was torn ragged. And again I used that one, I had nothing to use for myself, but I wrapped her up with that, and again she fell asleep for she was tired. I slept too; towards dawn, suddenly I heard an owl hooting there, on that spruce-tree above. My little sister woke up, the owl woke her up, too, and she started crying right away, "It is going to attack us," she said about it, as the owl would flap its wings like that [*gesture*]. I thought so, too, as it looked at us where we sat.

Well, "We will leave," I said to my little sister; and again we left. But I was again carrying her on my back, as we left again. Her feet were so swollen and I, too, had cuts all over my legs but I wore oxfords that day. And now, indeed, as soon as we left, straight away the owl also flew off; landing on a tree over there, quite a distance ahead of us. It turned to face us, in the same way [*sc.* as before], moving its wings like that [*gesture*] and, on top of it all, making [*sc.* strange] noises at the same time and flapping its wings as if it were going to attack us. When we got close, again it flew off, again landing on a spruce-tree over there. In the same manner, it looked towards where we were, doing the same thing, making [*sc.* strange] noises. "Oh my," I said to my little sister, "we will follow it," I said to her, "maybe it is going to show us the way when it does that," I said to her. "No!" she said, "it is going to attack us when it does that," said my little sister, "we will not follow it," she said. "No," I said to her, "we will follow it and see," I said to her.

And indeed we again followed the owl, in the same way. It must have changed its perch about four times, and we followed it. *Boy*, all at once it seemed as if I heard someone yelling. I yelled out but, of course, my voice was weak, I was not loud enough. But they heard it, Alec Bishop was his name, and Louis Morin, Salamon Morin and Johnny Sinclair. It appears they had planned teams of four, these men would go in fours; they had been given guns, shells and rubber overshoes by the Hudson's Bay store to search for us; they had been searching for us all the time since first we had got lost, since that first day. First of all they had gone around everywhere on horseback, looking for us in all the houses, eh? and then they knew that we were lost.

If we had not left that cow where she got stuck in the bog, where she was sinking in,

> (*David Merasty, a hunter, had been hired to track us, eh? but lost our tracks, look! because it had rained so much, well, finally our tracks were no longer visible, I guess, but he had tracked us—as a*

*matter of fact, he had gone and found the cow. She had already sunk
in up to her neck but she was still alive, he went back over there to
kwâkopîwi-sâkahikanihk to tell that he had found the cow; he came
back to tell my dad about it. So my dad gave the cow up to be shot;
and they came and killed that cow, and also the calf.)*

we would have been found the same night, they were given lanterns, all the men
were provided with lanterns from the Hudson's Bay store to use, eh?—there were
no flashlights in the old days. And those whom we now heard, the one who was
yelling now, I knew right away that now it was a man [*sc.* not an animal], yes.

And *wâpikwayâs*, Louis *wâpikwayâs* had said, "They may even run away," he
had said, "let the men go around that way [*gesture*], over here where we think
we have heard them, just in case they run away if they get scared and think it
might be some strange person," he had said. And so one man had come straight
across towards us to come and fetch us, towards where they had heard us. He
could be heard yelling, well, and now I knew for certain that it was a human
being, "We have been found," I said to my little sister. I yelled but, of course,
my throat [*sc.* was weak], then Alec Bishop came into view there. Straight
away he came and grabbed both of us and cried, he kissed both of us, this old
man—no, he was young then, he was not an old man.

And so, with the gun which he carried, he straight away shot three times. So
it was not long before the others, who had gone around, came running there.
Each of them had also been given a horse to ride, they carried food, shells and
everything, eh? for themselves to eat and to cook for us when we would be
found. So then Louis *wâpikwayâs* right away made a fire so that we could try
to eat. Oh, and it was not long before shots were fired all over, when he had
fired his shots, shooting was now heard just everywhere, so that it would be
known to these people, too, that we had been found, they were firing shots all
over. So then they were going to give us tea to drink there, so that we might
eat, hey, everything, for the food had simply been given out by the Hudson's
Bay. We were not even able to swallow the tea, we certainly could not eat at all!

So then Louis *wâpikwayâs* said that we would ride on horseback, and we
rode as they led the horse and we were taken home. Then, as we arrived over
there at our house (—I forgot, this owl truly just flew away, that owl, once we
had been found by these men, it was that owl that showed us the way home). As
we arrived over there at our house and came into view, oh my God the horses,
simply everybody in *kwâkopîwi-sâkahikanihk* was there, there simply were
horses everywhere, and also wagons. They had apparently been praying all the
while, with the priest there, that we might be found, the priest and everyone
else had simply been praying there that we might be found.

As we came into view now, over there, I of course was a young girl already, "I am not going to go over there," I told Alec Bishop, "with my clothes so torn up," I said to him. "Hey, do not think about it, my girl," Alec Bishop said to me, "there will be such joy that you have been found," he said, "since there was a lot of misery," he said, "do not let modesty get in the way!" he said, "We have brought you back." Hey, *boy*, and as we arrived over there, all kinds of people were just kissing us. Frank Seguin was the name of the Hudson's Bay store manager, a Frenchman, he came and just hugged us amid tears; and then he said, "As for clothes," he said, "let someone come and fetch something at the store over there for them to wear," he said. And, indeed, my late grandmother went over there and fetched things, Hudson's Bay clothes, he simply gave them to us and fitted us out with clothes.

So then again now they were going to—they had cooked already and we were going to be fed, but we still would not eat anything, we could not eat as our throats still hurt. And as soon as my little sister had been put to bed, she fell asleep straight away even as they tucked her in for warmth; her feet were so cut up, and they pulled the thorns out with a needle; so cut up were her feet.

And so -~, and my mom, although she had just recently had a baby, had nevertheless gone out, together with Alice Derocher, the two of them together, and had searched for us; my mom crying as they went about.

And now, of course, that we had been found, now the people went home after they had finished praying again, and then I was again given communion, but my little sister had not yet had her first communion at that time; I, on the other hand, was given communion. And I, too, when I lay down, must have fallen asleep immediately; it was morning before I woke up.

We really had had a terrible time; I saw how hard it is when a person is lost. And we never were afraid, we were not even afraid of bears or anything else, and with the thunder, in the dark of the night, I marvel that I did not think of anything, anything at all, of which to be scared. If I were to be lost some place today, I would be scared to death! We were lost for two days, and were found exactly at noon on the following [*sc.* the third] day.

And over there [*sc.* in the bush] I had seen one place, like that [*gesture*] (for my grandfather *nâcowêw* used to do much snaring), with the willows cut like that [*gesture*], they were cut like that [*gesture*], we had arrived at a little lake over there. When I saw the willows like this, and the grass piled up like that [*gesture*], as if someone had sat there, I had said to my little sister, "Look!" I had said to her, "we are nearly at home," that was the first night, towards evening, "we are nearly at home," I had said to her, "our grandfather must have done some snaring around here," I had said to her; "he must even have sat here and smoked, by the way it looks," I said to her.

But it had not been that, it appears it must have been hunters on the lookout [*sc.* for game], it must have been for that, according to what my grandfather said, that the willow-bushes had been cut and the grass piled up over there, for the hunters watching for game; it was that kind of a place which we had reached. I had walked around there, looking around for something, thinking, "Perhaps they had something left over and have thrown it away," as I had looked around for something for us to eat.

That is all, I guess.

—*November 15, 1988. Flying Dust Reserve*

John F. Cote
Saulteaux · 1912–1999 · Cote First Nation

John Cote was born in 1912 and was from the Cote First Nation. In 1933, he married Madelaine Stevenson, and they had four children. Cote worked as a farmer and as a trapper in the winter, and served as a spiritual elder at many ceremonies and dances. He was also a notable storyteller and keeper of the Saulteaux oral tradition.

These two stories below are take from *Nēnapohš āhtahsōkēwinan*, or *Nēnapohš Legends*, a collection of Saulteaux language texts, narrated by Saulteaux Elders and transcribed and translated by Margaret Cote, John Cote's daughter. They tell of *nēnapohš*, the Saulteaux Trickster, and are classic examples of traditional teaching stories. The collection was published by the University of Regina Press, in coordination with First Nations University of Canada, as part of the ongoing First Nations Language Readers series.

Nēnapohš and the Shut-eye Dancing Ducks

One day Nēnapohš was out walking around in the woods, this is what he often did. This day he had been unsuccessful at hunting. As he was walking along the shore of the lake he heard some ducks. The sound of the ducks made his mouth water, and his stomach began to growl. As he got closer to the ducks he was thinking of how he could trick them. He started picking up some roots and moss and put them into a bag that he always carried around with him everywhere he went.

He proceeded to walk along the shore and pretended to be deaf even though a duck was calling to him. "Hey Nēnapohš, what is that you are carrying on your back?" Nēnapohš just kept on walking. He was whistling to himself and pretended he did not hear that duck. The duck yells out to him loudly, "Nēnapohš, what is that you are carrying on your back?" This time Nēnapohš turned toward the ducks and answered them: "Oh, it's you, my little brothers, you want to know what I have in this bag, these are my songs. I always carry around these songs of mine."

By this time the little ducks were really curious to know what it was; and one little diver asks, "Oh Nēnapohš, please may we hear your songs?" Nēnapohš replied, "Oh no, I only sing my songs inside a lodge but I don't have a lodge."

The ducks talk among themselves and decide that they will help Nēnapohš build a lodge. There was a loon in the group and this is what he told Nēnapohš: "We will help you build a lodge because we all want to hear your songs." Nēnapohš agreed and they all began building the lodge. Nēnapohš sat around and gave orders telling the little ducks what to do; they did all the work. Every now and then Nēnapohš just about burst out laughing.

When they completed the lodge, Nēnapohš sat in the middle of the lodge, he then took out his little drum from the bag and began to sing. He was making up songs, and he then told the ducks; "Whatever I sing, you must do." Loon did not really trust Nēnapohš, so he danced by the doorway. Nēnapohš was singing: "*Pišankwāpišimonan, pišankwāpišimonan*; Shut-eye Dances, Shut-eye Dances." So all the little ducks danced; they danced with their eyes shut.

One by one Nēnapohš grabbed them and broke their little necks and put them in a pile behind him. Loon, who was dancing by the door, snuck a peek. When he saw what Nēnapohš was doing to them, he yelled loudly, "Nēnapohš is killing us, let's take off." The remaining ducks all ran out the door, the loon waited until all the ducks were out. The loon was the last one out and as he was running out, Nēnapohš kicked him on the backside. That is why, even to this day, loons can't walk on land because this one was kicked on the backside by Nēnapohš.

—1985

Nēnapohš Makes Red Willows

Nēnapohš now has plenty of ducks, and he thinks to himself as he makes a fire, "I sure tricked those ducks, I could have had more of them had it not been for that darn loon." Nēnapohš put his ducks into some hot ashes to roast, with only the feet sticking out. "I'll sleep for a while," thought Nēnapohš, so he told his rear-end to watch out for his ducks. "You make good and sure to wake me up and warn me if anyone comes near my ducks." While he was sleeping some wolves came by. Immediately his rear-end let out a loud fart to wake him up. When he looked around he did not hear or see anyone. He thought that his rear-end was playing tricks on him. He checked one of his ducks, but it was not quite ready. So once again he told his rear-end, "Don't you dare wake me up again for nothing, if you do that I shall punish you severely." He went back to sleep. Soon a couple of hunters came by and they began quietly eating his ducks. This time his rear-end was afraid to warn him because he did not want to get punished if Nēnapohš woke up and the hunters would be gone.

When Nēnapohš woke up, he thought about his ducks and his mouth began to water. One by one he pulled out the duck legs, but all he pulled out were bones. There were no ducks. He immediately asked his rear-end; "Where are my ducks, why didn't you warn me? I am really going to punish you now!" Nēnapohš is really mad now. He makes the fire bigger and puts a big rock on it. When the rock was red hot, he told his rear-end; "I'm going to teach you a lesson you'll never forget." He sat down on the red-hot rock to punish his rear-end. "Shhhhh, shhhhh!" was the only sound that came from his rear-end.

He was in such a daze from the pain he began to wander around, and as he was walking around stepping over shrubs some of the blood from his rear-end changed their color to red. Nēnapohš told the shrubs, "For as long as there is an earth the Anihšināpēk will call you 'red willows' and they will use you for medicine and for a smoking mixture in their kinnikinnick." That is why there are red willows today, this is what Nēnapohš had done.

[Note: the inner bark of the red willow, *miskwāpīmakōn*, is used as a tobacco mixture, and also when red willows are boiled it is used as a pain-relieving medicine.]

—*1985*

Alice Ahenakew

Plains Cree · 1912–2007 · Sturgeon Lake and Sandy Lake

Alice Ahenakew (nee Mary Alice Bush) grew up in Sturgeon Lake with her adoptive grandparents after she lost her mother to the influenza epidemic of 1918. She married Andrew Ahenakew, who became an Anglican priest and a Cree healer, known for having great medicine power, and moved with him to Sandy Lake. In the late 1990s, Freda Ahenakew recorded several stories that Alice dictated in Cree. These were transcribed and translated in *âh-âyîtaw isi ê-kî-kiskêyihtahkik maskihkiy: They Knew Both Sides of Medicine: Cree Tales of Curing and Cursing*. These stories include reminiscences of childhood, courtship and marriage, as well as an account of the 1918 influenza epidemic, and encounters with a *wîhtikow* (windigo). The selection "The Priest's Bear Medicine" is a fascinating and complex account of her husband's bear vision, from which he acquired his healing powers. As told by Alice Ahenakew, the story is a clear example of oral storytelling techniques of narration at a remove and story through quotation. The wave-hyphen (-~) indicates that the speaker has interrupted herself, resulting in a fragmentary sentence or word. Manual and facial gestures are indicated in brackets, as are explanatory insertions.

The Priest's Bear Medicine

And my late husband, for a long time, oh my, he had so many visions, he must have been a good person, he was gifted in so many different ways. But once when he went over there to the Pas, Manitoba for a meeting, I did not go with him, he was gone for one week, he went for a meeting.

At one time, while he was there (and at that time my one brother-in-law, his name was Walter, had been sick, he had cancer); he [my husband] was getting ready to go to bed over there when he knelt down to pray, praying for his brother who was causing him such worry by his sickness. And then he said, "And so I went to bed" (he had taken a motel room where he was going to stay). And so, "All of a sudden," he said, "'It seemed as though I was sitting outside,' I thought," he said (he did not tell me right away, either, about his vision over there, it must have been about a week after he had come back), "All of a sudden it seemed as though I was sitting outside," he said, "all of a sudden an animal could be seen approaching; he seemed to come running in mid-air, but as though in mid-air; approaching, he came to a stop here where I was sitting and simply looked at me," he said. "'It is from the holy place over there,' as he looked up above, 'it is from the holy place that I have been sent hither, and I have come to give you my body,' is what he had come to say to me," he said; that animal had come to give up his body. "'I have come to give you my body, for since God made the earth, when He made the animals, we, we are still as God has made us in the very beginning, we have no sickness in our bodies,' he said," he said, "the one who had come and stopped here," he said. "'Thus He has sent me hither that I might give you my body, for you to use, for you to make medicine there from my body and to doctor people who are sick,' he said to me," he said.

"I simply looked at him," he said, "for now I remembered the collar [I wore], the clerical collar—and he knew it right away—'That is what you are thinking,' he said to me," he said, "'but, in any case, you will do it nevertheless, that which I have come to tell you,' he said to me," he said. "He even went so far as to show it to me, what it looked like, 'It will look like that when you make the medicine,' he said to me," he said, "then, 'This is what you are to use on them (the people are all sick, with various kinds of sickness), on your people,' he said to me," he said. "When I remembered my younger brother in his sickness," he said, "then I was going to doubt him," he said; "'You are doubting me, but you will nevertheless do what I have told you! For I have been sent hither from the holy place, that I might come to give you my body for you to use in healing people,' he said to me," he said. "And so, oh my, I was confused," he said, "I was exceedingly surprised at what he had come to say to me," he said.

And then (of course I forgot some of it, he was indeed told many and various things, he was told, about them, but I forgot some). But then, "All of a sudden now, when he had finished speaking to me," he said, "he proceeded to turn around," he said. (Oh yes, this he also told him, this is what I forgot: "'You think, «How will I get hold of you, as you are from so far away in the north,» you think of me,' he said; 'We exist everywhere, four, there are four of us but we are all the same,' he said to me," he said—"Any one of the four of us," he was told by him. "But they are all the same, I who live over there far in the north [the polar-bear]; some [the grizzlies] live in the Rocky Mountains, some [the black-bears] live everywhere, they are the same as I," that one also said to him;—"'they are the same, for you to be able to make use of them for that,' he said to me," he said—"Because you think, 'How will I get hold of you, as you live so far away in the north,' you think of me," he had also said to him.) "And so, with that he proceeded to turn around," he said, "and he was gone, proceeding to run off in mid-air, gone back to the north," he said.

"It was as though I was not asleep," he said, this—, the fact that that one had come to him; "and then, as I awoke, I thought about it," he said, "'What, moreover, will the Bishop say to me about this, for it is like Cree medicine; after all, I am a priest, I would definitely have to see him first,' I thought," he said.

And then, as he came back here after the meeting was finished, he had forgotten about his dream. It must have been a week later when suddenly he said to me, "Look, oh yes, I had a dream," and then he told me the story. "Wow," I said to him, "you have been given a gift by the powers, you must do as you dreamt, that is not for nothing," I said to him. "No," he said, "it cannot be; go on, no," he kept saying to me. "No!" I said to him, "You must do it," I said to him; "truly," I said to him, "you have been given something sacred, this has been given to you by the powers," I said to him. I kept at him for a long time before I convinced him of it; and then, too, his younger brother was sick. And so, of course you cannot get hold of these animals just any time (it had been a polar-bear, it was that kind which had come to him); you cannot get hold of that kind just any time, for they hibernate over the winter. Oh my, then at last, at last, at last; at last it had been a long time, and we could not get hold of these things. And then at last my brother-in-law died, and then also he [Andrew] became very discouraged, he was discouraged, my brother-in-law had died. So then already another of my brothers-in-law became sick, and he also had cancer, the name of that brother-in-law of mine was Austin Ahenakew. So then at one time we heard that over there, it is called Cochin, close to Battleford over there, it was told of a certain man that he had killed one of that kind, and we drove there and tried to get hold of the parts of that kind—there's three parts, and they are certain parts. And we did indeed get hold of them and then we came home to our house here [at Sandy Lake], "Well, make it!" he said to me; "No," I said to him, "it is not I to whom it has been given by the powers, it is you," I said to him, "you, you make it! But if, if you are not able to make it, I will take over for you," I said to him, "I, I will take over," I said to him, "if you can't make it," I said to him.

And so (and of course that one [the bear] had also told him, "When it is completely quiet, late at night, when everything is quiet," that is when that medicine is to be made; and also, it's not supposed to touch any kind of metal, eh; it has to be enamel or something like that). And so he made it then way in the night, and I, I had gone to bed; and then he poured it [into a jar] when he had finished making it. "Oh my," he said, "what that one had shown me did not look like this," he said, "not at all," he said, "I cannot do it," he said. "Well, then I will, then tonight I will do it, I'll try," I said to him, "see it let's see if I might be able to," I said to him. And so he went to bed the next night, and then I made it. And so, when I thought I had finished making it, then. I poured it in a -~, I poured it into a little bottle. Then, in the morning, I went to show it to him. "This is the way!" he said, "You, you have succeeded," he said, "you, you have been able to make it," he said to me, "this is exactly how it looked," he said. So from that time on I always used to make that medicine myself.

And it was so -~ we did not want to tell anybody about it, eh? It was more or less as though we were sort of doubtful about it, we had, so then, "Let's test it, let's, ah, see if it's any good," we said [laughter]. Then we each drank a little bit of it, oh my, what was this, gone were the times when we used to be barely able to climb the stairs there, it did us a great deal of good. So then, my other brother-in-law [Austin] who was in the hospital, he was over there at *kistap-inânihk*. And my sister-in-law was still alive, her name was Mrs Minnie Fraser, my late husband's older sister, and had come to visit. He told her the story of his dream, and he also told her the story of that medicine and that we had already finished the task of getting hold of it, at first we had not said anything at all there, not telling anybody about it. Then he told her the story of it, and then my sister-in-law must have gone there right away to see her younger brother in hospital. She told him the story of this medicine, "Do tell my older brother to come and bring that medicine here right away!" he said. And so my sister-in-law came back over here [to Sandy Lake] and told him [my husband], "Our brother wants you to go and doctor him."—"Look! That will be the day, the doctors will give me trouble," he said, "oh my, I am afraid," he said; "they will give me trouble if they find out about it," he said. And then my brother-in-law indeed had cancer; then he [my husband] went, and he took this medicine with him in a little bottle;—and a plastic spoon also had to be used; he also took along that kind, a plastic spoon. "When I went in there," he said, "as soon as he saw me, 'Oh my, my older brother,' he said to me, 'I hear you have this medicine, if you do not doctor me, then I'm a goner,' he said to me," he said. "'Doctor me!' he said to me," he said, "and so I doctored him," he said, "I gave him a small amount to drink, not much, not even half a teaspoon, I only gave him a little to drink," he said. "And so now, 'Leave it for me!' he said to me," he said; "'Oh my, no,'" he said, "'if the doctors find it, I will be in trouble,' he said to me -~ I said to him," he said; "'No, I will hide it in any case;'"—so then he gave him that medicine.

Right away, as he [Andrew] lef-~, as my brother-in-law got ready to sleep, he took one teaspoon, the next morning already again he took one teaspoon, he was very sick, for two days he was really sick, he had taken too much of it, eh? But then, after two days, then he got up and was cured; in that way he was cured (for many years, you know, for he died not long ago, of a heart attack), in that way he was cured of the cancer, by using that medicine. And so this brother-in-law of mine, he used to be well known everywhere, for he had also lived all over the States. It was really like wildfire, that is how word about this medicine spread, really from everywhere, from absolutely everywhere people were coming day and night, day and night they came; they were coming from everywhere to be doctored.

Did I once hear him say, ever, "Wait a while!"—not once; not once have I heard him say, "Wait a while!" to those who came to be doctored -~, right away, even while he was in the midst of a meal or just about to start the meal, he would get up and, without having finished the meal, doctor the people, hey, he doctored so very many. An enormous number of cars used to be parked here, and he used the tipi here (the poles still stand over there), he would make a fire inside, and there he would doctor the people; I would help him with things there as he doctored the people; they came here from absolutely everywhere, [and he doctored them] no matter what was wrong with them. Many times I was amazed, for I used to be the doubtful one, "It seems, it seems as though they cannot recover," I would think of them. Ohohohoh, you would be amazed, often I used to be so amazed, that he cured all of them.

At one particular time, towards the beginning, at one time two men came here and one of them came inside, "I have brought my brother," he said. "But he is not at home," I said to him, Andrew was not at home, "he has gone off somewhere," I said to him, "but he will be back any time now," I said to him. "We will drive around, then, for a little while, we will go about and look at the reserve," he said, and out of the door they were, they were gone. It was not long, about half an hour or a little more than that, when they already came driving back again, "Come in!" I said to them, "I will give you a drink of tea," I said to them. And so they came in, and to my surprise one was on crutches;

he was an older person, he must have been about forty years or more. And so they sat over there, then; and so Andrew arrived soon after. Oh my, we were surprised at that time how they had already heard about that medicine, the word must have spread so fast, everywhere had my brother-in-law told about the fact that he was cured.

"I have come to place my trust in you," that man said, "for you to doctor my younger brother here," he said (I believe it was his younger brother, or else his older brother), "he is over forty years old," he said; "the doctors are unable to do anything for him; he was simply sent home, and since he was twelve years old, he has had a bad leg," he said. From the time he was twelve years old, since that time had he been sick, and he was over forty; since they were unable to do anything for him. He had a cut about a foot in length, it was here, right along his thigh, as a matter of fact it was up to—

[*external break*]

[FA:] Now.

And blood and pus were oozing from there, it really looked horrible, "Well, hey, under these circumstances, how on earth will he succeed in doctoring him?" I thought of him [Andrew], he had suffered from this since he was twelve years old and could not even bend his leg, eh? and he was over forty.

And so he doctored him, then, he placed a very small amount of that medicine on him, like this [*gesture*], and also gave him some to drink. And so (oh yes, he did the following, he [Andrew] was very much surprised, too), he put a gun there on the coffee table, and then he put a hundred dollar bill there, oh my, now Andrew was really surprised, for he did not want to accept anything like this and, of course, he also would not be able to say "No," he just looked at it, oh my, he was surprised to be paid so much and have them come to place their trust in him. So then they went home, after we had fed them they drove home (they were from over there, west of Battleford, their name was paskimin, and he [Andrew] also was related to them, through her -~, through his mother, so he was related to them but he didn't know yet, eh? at that time).

So they went home. After about one week had gone by, all of a sudden they drove up again, you know that cut was only about an inch open? Already he was being cured, yes! one inch, a little -~ an inch and a half perhaps, that was all that the cut was still open, eh? That medicine had done him so much good, within two weeks or perhaps one week after they had gone off. And again he gave them of that medicine, some more. They even brought us potatoes and things like that, you know; they were so happy. Again they went home, and then, when they drove up after another week, another two weeks I believe, already there was nothing left of that sore, he was cured.

[FA:] He was cured.

That man is still in good health, I saw him at a Sundance over there at
Whitefish Lake last year, they held a Sundance there, that man is in good health,
you know; it is strange, I wonder what had been wrong with him, for him to
have had that sore for so long. And then I asked about him this year, a certain
woman had been at Whitefish, "And how is he now?"—"They are well," she
said, "there is nothing wrong with him," she said.

And I was also amazed at another case of his doctoring someone, we had
gone over to Little Pine's and we went to church, he [Andrew] went to conduct
the service in the church; then, after the service, a certain man came to fetch
us and invited us back to his home. Hey, I was glad, "We are probably going to
have a meal, we have been invited home," I thought, the first thing I thought
about, of course [laughter]. As we drove up at the house, following him along,
"Wow, it looks as though there were no woman living here," I thought; we went
in, and it was true indeed, it was a bachelor's place, his brother lived there and
he was sick. Oh oh my, I felt sorry for this man, he sat without a shirt, eh? all
over his body and his face he was covered with scabs, he had thick scabs literally all over, he could not even turn his head, his neck was so stiff -~, oh, he
looked terrible; oh my, I felt sorry for him. "I want you to doctor this younger
brother of mine," he said (I believe it was his younger brother, or else he said
"his older brother"), "I hear you have a medicine," he said to him [Andrew],
-~ he said. It so happened that Andrew had indeed taken that medicine with
him, he used to take it around with him all the time. Oh my, then he straight
away smudged it [the medicine] and burnt this, he used sweetgrass—and that
is one thing I failed to tell about at the beginning. My late grandfather who
with his wife had raised me, he was such a good person, he would make a fire
immediately after getting up, and then he would make a smudge of sweetgrass
and would pray and worship early in the morning, and finally he used to sing
his song, I have never heard anyone else sing that song; and it seems as though
I still hear him, and I am not able to sing that song either, it has such a lonely
sound; at last my late grandfather would go on to weep. That is what I failed
to tell about when I told about him, the sweetgrass—and when I came over
here [to Sandy Lake], I really had grown up seeing much of the Cree rites, of
Cree worship and all kinds of things like that; and that is one thing I think
of very highly. And when I came over here, the people over here were really
White, for they had thrown away their medicine-bundles long ago, they had
been told by the Anglican priests when they first reached them, "Burn all of
them!" they had repeatedly been told by them, and I was truly sorry for them
that they had made a mistake, but of course they very much tried to be White,
they acted terribly White, I found it very alien when I first came to live over
here; I of course had been raised very much in the Cree tradition, and I have

always thought very highly of Cree worship and the Cree rites. And so I used to discuss these with my late husband, the Cree rites and Cree worship, "Well, go on! No!" he used to say to me, but I still did not cease talking to him. "It is true," I used to tell him, "it is powerful, the Cree form of worship is what has been given to the Crees by the powers. This form of worship is powerful, and it is also clean, it is only because you do not understand it."—"We were not raised like that," he used to say to me.

But then, finally, we used to go over there to Morley to the Ecumenical Conference, we went there every year, and there he was taught a great deal, and finally he began to understand it. And, indeed, at last he began to think very highly of Cree worship, and finally he, too, used sweetgrass for smudging. And so he would make a smudge with it when someone came over here, both praying and worshipping when he doctored someone; finally I converted him to things like that, so that he began to be fully convinced of the Cree form of worship; and finally, towards the end of his life, he was entirely convinced of it.

And to this day I think extremely highly of this myself, these forms of worship—the Anglican liturgy, the Roman Catholic liturgy, and the Cree rites, these are the three for me. Although I do not in any way dislike those others [the fundamentalists], but, "Beware of false prophets," it is said in the Bible.

[AA:] [*aside:*] That is it for now.

[*external break*]

—*2000*

Bertha O'Watch
Nakoda · 1914–2012 · Carry-the-Kettle

Bertha O'Watch was from Carry-the-Kettle Nakoda First Nation. She was born northwest of Indian Head, delivered "by her father near the wagon in which her parents were travelling." Her Dakota and Nakoda name was *zit'dana to winya*, or "Blue Bird Woman." The selections below were recorded and translated by Linda A. Cumberland in her 2005 dissertation, *A Grammar of Assiniboine: A Siouan Language of the Northern Plains*. The second story presents Įktómi, a Sioux trickster, or more accurately known as Elder Brother, similar to the Cree *wīsahkēcāhk* or the Saulteaux *nēnapohš*.

Big Snake

This is another story about this reserve, the Skeleton Hill people, or Carry The Kettle people. Long ago there used to be a big lake down here [narrator indicates an area some distance behind her house]. I've seen that lake. There, us, my husband['s father] and his friend were swimming, they say.

They had gotten way out into the middle of the lake, they say. His friend said, "Friend, look in the water, there's something there," he said, they say. So then he looked down. Wait, I misspoke—it was my husband's *father* who was swimming with his friend; his name was Not A Young Man. It was his friend who looked in the water, and then… So then that thing, well! "Yes, Friend, it has horns, too." It was looking at them, in the water. Then, well! How he ran! He scrambled over the lake! He hurled himself through the water and they fled back to the lake's shore and they grabbed up their clothes and ran away. And, where the Mormon church is nowadays, there was a village there back then, they say. They went back there. And, they told everything, they say, to a man, uh, he was a holy man, called Mountain Man. They told him about it. Then he prayed. "Ah! You frightened my grandchildren!" he said. "Four days from now they will come to get you." Then everyone was waiting expectantly. Back then all this brush wasn't here, I think [indicating the trees behind the house]. All at once he told them. "They are coming now!" he said, they say. Then they all looked to where there was a small cloud hovering over the lake, constantly. So there where it was, there were lightning bolts. Then there were many bolts of lightning like that, all because of the Thunder being smacking the lake with a loud cracking sound, he shot it [the snake]. And they pulled it out, they say. It was a big snake. Its head wasn't visible. Its tail was a big round ball, they say. When it moved its tail again, there was another bolt of lightning and it was still; they lifted it up taking it back. That's the end of this story.

—*2005*

Įktómi and Fox

This is one of Įktómi's stories that I will tell again. Įktómi always fooled everyone. He shot a buffalo and butchered it, and took all the best parts.

So then a fox came along. "Older brother, I'm hungry. Give me some of that," he said. So he took tripe and finally he grudgingly cut some off. He said, "Take this over to the water and wash it and eat it! Bring it back here!" he said, they say. So the fox ran over there to the creek and ate it up there. As he came back, he craftily pretended to be lame. He came back and said, "Older Brother, the salmon snatched it away from me," he said. (Įktómi) gave him another piece. Again, he got up and went and ate it up. When he came back, he said the same thing as before. The fourth time, therefore, he took it and again, oh! so over there, (Įktómi) went and stood out of sight. (Fox) ate the omasum. Įktómi [came] back again over here and sat down. That fox was coming back. Now he said this [same thing], "Older Brother," he said, "the fish grabbed it away from me." (Ịktómi) knocked him down, they say. He even knocked him dead. (Fox) recovered from it.

(Ịktómi) was hungry, they say. He was not good (i.e., behaved in a manner contrary to proper behavior); he didn't even share; all by himself, he ate until he was full and he lay down. "My Buttocks, watch over this meat for me. No one is to eat it up on me," he said. He said it and then he lay down. Now he was sleeping, so the fox called for all the small animals. [He called for] the mouse, too. That one pulled fur from the buffalo hide with his mouth and stuffed it all into (Ịktómi's) rump. So he kept doing that. Oh! so then they all ate up the meat. They did that and they all headed out in different directions. Ịktómi got up and kept looking around for where he had put his meat. They had all eaten it up. Oh! he was angry! "My Buttocks, you are bad! I told you to watch over this meat for me; they all ate it up on me," he said. They had stuffed his rump with buffalo fur so that he couldn't fart. That is all. So then he really beat his own rump. He said, "I told you to watch over it for me. You didn't do it, and they all ate it up on me," he said, and he really beat his own rump, they say. He didn't know that they had stuffed it full of buffalo fur meanwhile [while he was sleeping]. That is all.

—2005

Arsene Fontaine
Dene · 1918–1993 · La Loche

Arsene Joseph Fontaine was born in 1918, likely at La Loche or West La Loche. He married Philomene Piche (also called Ts'ekui Chogh). Arsene and Philomene made their living by hunting, fishing, and trapping, and also growing vegetables. The following story is from an interview for the *Dene Elders Project*.

The Story of the Bear

One time I was up north and I had a .22 rifle, a single shot. So I went looking for beaver up the river. I was coming back and I saw a bear, lying there, you know. So I just put my shells in there—I had mostly only small shells you know, .22 short. I had only about two of them long ones so I don't want to shoot them right away so I started shooting with those short shells, you know.

I don't feel the bear's so fat, and he had a fight before me with another bear. You could see his right finger scratched all over.

So I made him mad I guess. He got up and he was just hollering, and he came at me. I had a sharp knife there and I was just going to pull it out. I didn't want to run away you know. If you run away he just jumps on you and then he would kill me. So I can't run away. My brother was about three miles away from me that time. But my brother could hear from that place, about three miles. That bear he was hollering. Boy he made a big noise. But I don't run away. When I run away he will kill me so I have to stand. I was just against a tree and I held my .22 and I grabbed my knife.

But the way I figure … the old people they used to tell me that the bear, they don't bite a person first. They said they grab him first. That's what they say. Then they start a fight and that's the time they bite. So the way I figure, when he grab me I'll cut him so his hand will go away from me.

I used to think about that when I was in the bush, if something happened like that. Maybe that's the only way you could save yourself.

So I had a sharp knife, you know. And the bear just got mad at me and came to me. Oh, he came real close. And I hollered to him, "Don't bite me. Don't bite me bear," I said.

He just stopped right away and just stood up and put his hands out, so I shot him. He came down, then went a little way again. Then he turned and every time he turned around he looked at me. Boy did he holler! He was so mad, you know. And the way I figure, when he comes to me like that, I'll cut his hand and I'll put my .22 in his mouth and that way maybe my bullets will stop him.

But he didn't come to me. He didn't want to grab me I guess. Every time I hollered to him he just stopped right there. He did that about three or four times. Then he came in slow so I started shooting. I shot him so many times and the bullet goes inside. At last he was going away, towards the hill. He fell down there. I hurt him too much because I shot him many times.

So I just sat down, and boy, he comes to me again. He still wants to get me. I just sat there. I know he won't get up so I just sat there, and I had those two long bullets, you know. So I put those in and I was just waiting. You know those big spruce trees on the high land? Well, he grabbed that big spruce and he just took it out. He was so strong. Then he came close to me and I started shooting him again.

Finally I killed him. His fat was much. No wonder the bullet didn't go through. That's the way it is if there's very much fat. That bear had had a fight before me. He had torn his fingernails … so that's what made him hurt. That's why he was slow I guess. He didn't run much. When he came to me he didn't run. I'm lucky that way.

—*19??*

Howard Adams

Métis · 1921–2001 · St. Louis

Howard Adams grew up in the Métis community of St. Louis on the South Saskatchewan River, south of Prince Albert. He completed his B.A. at the University of British Columbia and took graduate studies at University of California, Berkeley, becoming the first Métis Ph.D. He taught at the University of Saskatchewan and University of California, Davis, and became a strong voice of Métis rights in the 1960s and 1970s. The selection below is a brief excerpt from his 1975 book, *Prison of Grass: Canada from a Native Point of View*, which brought a new wave of political consciousness and articulation of the cultural, historical, and psychological aspects of colonialism for First Nations, Inuit, and Métis peoples.

Excerpt from *Prison of Grass*

In the struggle for liberation, the native people are asked to put their confidence in the good intentions of the colonizers. While it is true that certain decolonization is taking place, it is false to pretend that it is the result of the changing nature of man and of the state. The optimism that prevails today for liberation is not based on the fact that capitalism is becoming more humane or that colonialism is becoming more just. It is simply that the advanced liberal corporate state is able to co-opt native nationalism and revolutionary consciousness. Even our own revolutionary rhetoric has become an integral part of advanced capitalism.

We are told that the enemy, colonialism, is the historical oppressor. But we must make no mistake that our oppression is in the forms and institutions of colonialism, and in its manifestations, such as racial stereotypes, Indian bureaucracies, welfare, prisons, etc. Only by transforming the objective conditions can we put a final end to colonialism. For example, we must change the authoritarian schools and government departments, the economic elite who control the masses and the government, the chauvinist relationships that exist between men and women.

The Indians and Métis are now concerned with giving a native dimension to their lives and actions because identity helps in the struggle against colonialism. This struggle for liberation is a long and arduous one, yet it is for this reason that it must be fought without respite and without compromise. We have to do this by working at all levels in the liberation struggle. For instance, some members are able to work at the neighborhood level in simple organizational and education work, while others can work in a broader way, mobilizing for civil-rights actions and extra-parliamentary confrontations. Finally, there must be a group of natives who are willing and able to work at the sophisticated level of guerilla warfare, both urban and rural. The racism and colonialism of capitalism will always hold us captive in misery, violence, and exploitation. It is time that we recognized our own power and faced the fact that our solutions lie within ourselves. Revolution can be made only by those who are in a state of revolution.

—1975

Annie Benonie
Dene · 1925–2011 · Brochet, Wollaston Lake

Annie Benonie (nee Dzeylion) was born in 1925 in Brochet, Manitoba. She is of Dene ancestry, and her parents were Alphonse Dzeylion and Marie Joseyounen, of Dogrib heritage. She married at the age of fourteen, and later moved to Wollaston Lake in 1943. The selection below comes from *The Wollaston Interviews*, a collection of Saskatchewan Dene stories developed by Lois Dalby and Lynda Holland: "The Wollaston Interviews were gathered in 1980 by Mike and Carol Constantineau, teachers at the Wollaston Lake School, with help from students and community members." The stories were told in Dene and translated by Marianne Kkaillther. Other storytellers in the *Interviews* include Joe Joseyounen, Algina Sha'oulle, Flora Kkaikka, Joseph Aze, and Modeste Dzeylion. Annie Benonie's stories emphasize the importance of preserving an understanding of tradition for survival in modern life.

A Person That Always Stays Alone

Years ago, a long time ago, a Dene person, a person that always stays alone, was walking around on his way home. That Dene lived in a tent and every time he went home he heard strange noises at his place. Every time he went home he saw a ptarmigan coming out of his tent. He really wanted to know why it was so and he said, "I'll go home ahead of time to find out what this strange noise is and why the ptarmigan keeps flying out of the tent."

The next time he went home he didn't hardly make any noise. As he walked he could hear strange things coming from the tent. When he got near he opened the tent and he saw a lady there that was a ptarmigan. She changed herself into a lady again. The Dene man wasn't married and he didn't have any woman so he married the ptarmigan woman.

The man was making some snowshoes and he told his wife that she can do the netting on the snowshoes for him. His wife didn't know how to do the netting on the snowshoes so she transformed herself into a ptarmigan and she was making the snowshoes really fast.

From then on women knew how to do the netting on the snowshoes.

Years ago in the past the teenagers used to walk on the lake and all of a sudden they could hear a child crying on the ice. They looked but they couldn't find him. And those teenage girls would fix their hair and then they would go out looking for the child again. Many days passed and still they couldn't find him, and still the baby was crying.

Then there was a small old woman who asked the teenagers what they were looking for. She asked them if she could help them look for the baby. All of a sudden she said she could hear the child. Then she found some caribou droppings on the ground. It was just like sand. She was digging under the caribou droppings, under the ground, and she found a little child, a small baby.

The old woman took the child home and raised that little child from caribou droppings. The child grew up. When he was a young man he started hunting for the old woman. Even when he was an adult he was kind of small. (People in that village made fun of him, he was so small.)

One night the boy went hunting and he was gone almost all night. The old woman was scared and she started crying in her tent. She knew that he was a caribou child and she thought that the young child had left her.

Late that night the boy finally came home and found his grandmother crying. When he went in the house he told his grandmother to take his snowshoes off for him, and to untie the belt around his waist. He took off his clothes and inside, around his tummy, he had tied dry caribou tongues. When his grandmother untied his jacket all those tongues fell out. He told his grandmother to go with him tomorrow to where the caribou were.

The next day his grandmother went with him. When they got to where he had killed a lot of caribou his grandmother started cutting up the meat. She used the ribs of the caribou to make a knife. While she was doing the meat the boy asked his grandmother to show that she could cook a caribou head for him. So they went to make a fire to cook the caribou. When she cooked it for the boy, he didn't hardly eat. He gave some caribou head meat to the crows. Then he put on his snowshoes and started taking a walk in the bush.

And the boy transformed himself into a caribou. Then he started walking to where the people were staying. He walked around the lake, to make tracks.

The next day people thought there were a lot of caribou so they went hunting. They followed the tracks and came to a bare river hut. They went over the little hill…then the tracks turned to snowshoes again. The boy was lying down behind the hill. Then they saw that the boy could transform himself into any kind of animal. (This way he played a trick on the people who had teased him.)

That's the end of that legend.

The other legend is about a bear and a squirrel. The bear and the squirrel were always travelling with each other to see who did the best. They were by a little pond and the bear said, "Let's see who can climb up the tree the first." When they were ready for the race the squirrel was fast so he went up the tree first. The bear told the squirrel that he was just making a joke on him.

Then the bear said, "The one that throws a stone in the water that floats, he's the best. The bear went first. When he threw some stones in the water they fell to the bottom. Then the squirrel got dry wood, threw it on the lake, and it was floating.

Then the bear told the squirrel he wanted to start again. The squirrel said that a bear always wants to sleep at night. The squirrel said they should have a contest when the sun almost sets. Then the bear said when he closes his eyes he couldn't see anything but he could use his bum to move around. The squirrel told him, "What if I poked your bum with a stick," and the bear said, "If I used my paws then I could feel It." Then the squirrel said, "What if you were putting your paws on the ground and you poked your paws on the stick." Then the bear was chasing the squirrel again and said, "Let's see who can climb up the tree first." The bear caught up to the squirrel and again he said he was just lying. Then the squirrel made a fire. I don't know how in the past they could make a fire, but he made a fire. The squirrel was near the campfire and he turned his back against the heat. Some of the fur on his back was burned and it looked yellowish. And his eyes, from the smoke, were like when a person cries. (And that's why squirrels look like this today.)

Here's another story from the past. I remember it from my grandfather. Years in the past people were different from people nowdays. Maybe in the future we Dene people can't always live the white man's way.

Years in the past people used teepees. In the middle of the teepee they made a fire and inside the teepee, for the floor, they had spruce branches. To clean the floor all they had to do was to throw the old ones in the fire and some more spruce branches from the woods.

Nowdays people are using canvas for their tents and they use needles and thread to sew. In the past people used sinew and "alie" for sewing. They used to sew porcupine quills on moccasins and then beads.

When it was warm in the spring the men went hunting for beaver. The beaver used to live in their houses, under the water. They used a spear to hit their houses and when the beaver came out of the water they used snares like rabbit snares to catch them by their necks and drag them out. Then they used a club and hit them on the head.

That's how men used to hunt. Will your kids do that too? Nowdays people use traps for the beaver. They make a hole in the ice and then put the trap down. What if they didn't have any traps to catch a beaver with? How can you get a beaver now?

—1980

George Klyne

Métis · 1925–2015 · Katepwa

George Klyne was born in 1925 in the Indian Head hospital, the fifth child to Henry Klyne and Vera (nee Amyotte). He grew up in the Métis communities near Katepwa, leaving school at an early age to work the farms in the valley. Later, he married Rose Sparvier from Cowessess First Nation, and they settled in Indian Head, raising nine children.

A renowned storyteller and jigger, George was an avid supporter of Métis culture throughout his life.

The selection below is one of his many oral stories and reflects his beloved wit. It was transcribed by his grandson, Jesse Archibald-Barber.

The Trapper and the Snare

Back in the 1920s or '30s, during a really long winter, this one trapper and his family nearly run out of food. All they had left was a small chunk of bread, you know. But instead of eating it, the trapper decides to use it as bait to try and catch a rabbit.

So he goes into the woods and sets a snare on top of a large rock, and he puts the chunk of bread in the middle. When he comes back the next day, he sees rabbit tracks around the rock there, but the snare's not been set off, and the bread's gone.

Scratching his head, he goes back home. His neighbour says, "What are you going to do? You have no bait to catch rabbits now," he says. The trapper thinks for a while, then he says, "I know what to do."

The next day he goes back to the rock and sets the snare, and then he takes one of his bootlaces and cuts it into little bits and places them there in the middle. The next day, he comes back, but again the snare's not been set off, and all the bits of bootlace are gone. So he takes his other bootlace and cuts it up too and places it there in the snare, but again the next day the bait is gone and there's still no rabbit.

Not only that, but the snare was gone too, you know. See, the rabbit got so used to eating the shoelaces that he must've gone right ahead and eaten the snare too!

So he goes back home, and the neighbour says, "What are you going to do now? You have nothing left to trap with. Your family's gonna starve," he says.

"Don't know," the trapper says, "but I'll think of something." So he sits in his chair all night. The next morning he has an idea. He grabs a can of pepper from the cupboard, and he goes out to that rock, and he pours a small pile on top there.

Well, everyone back home thinks he's gone crazy, but the next morning he goes back, and there it was: a rabbit lying dead beside that rock!

When he goes back home, the neighbour is so surprised. "By George, how did you get that rabbit?" he says.

"Well, I took some pepper up to that rock, and I poured a small pile on top there. And when the rabbit came up and sniffed that pile of pepper, he sneezed so hard, he smashed his head right against that rock!"

—*2008*

Alexander Wolfe
Saulteaux · 1927–2002 · Sakimay

Alexander Wolfe was a Saulteaux storyteller from Sakimay First Nation. Notably, he collected his family's stories and published them in *Earth Elder Stories*. These stories tell the oral history of Pinayzitt, a Saulteaux leader, and his descendants, as they made the transition from a life moving on the Plains to settling on the reserve. Although these are oral stories originally told in the Saulteaux language, they were not recorded and then transcribed and translated like many of the other stories in this anthology; instead, Wolfe himself wrote these stories in English. The selection below exemplifies the trans-generational transmission of oral traditions, as Wolfe recounts a story as told by Earth Elder and retold by Standing Through the Earth.

The Sound of Dancing
told by Earth Elder, retold by Standing Through the Earth

Many years ago when Indians roamed this land, hunting and gathering for their survival, it was not uncommon for small groups to fall victim to raiding parties of hostile Indians of other tribes. The following account is of one little boy who survived to tell the tale of what happened to his people.

The camp was small. It was winter when the attack came. So ferocious that there was no hope of survival. The grandfather, covered only with a buffalo robe, fled with his grandson in hand. Their flight was short-lived as the grandfather was soon struck down by blows. In a last attempt to save his grandson, he grabbed him and threw himself on top of the boy, covering both of them with his buffalo robe.

As time went by everything became quiet.

The boy asked his grandfather, "How long will we be here?" The grandfather answered, "I will try to keep you as long as I can."

With this the boy fell asleep lying under the robe with his grandfather. In time the boy awoke. He could hear his grandfather talking with people, as if they were visiting. He wondered who they were, but did not dare ask his grandfather, because he knew that when older people were speaking it was impolite to interrupt. One was supposed to listen and learn from what they spoke about. Again, he fell back to sleep. At times when the boy awoke all would be quiet, as if it were night, and again he would keep silent lest he waken Grandfather, who was asleep. It was at these quiet times that he could hear in the distance the sounds of a drum with people singing, the sounds of people as they danced, and people speaking in remembrance of those gone before them. All this puzzled the boy, and at times when he awoke and Grandfather was awake he longed to ask him, but always Grandfather was talking to someone else.

After some time had gone by, the boy awoke again and all was quiet. He wondered, was it really nighttime? Why was it so quiet? Without disturbing Grandfather the boy slowly lifted the buffalo robe, just a tiny bit and peeked out. It was daylight. As the boy lay beside Grandfather he wondered what was happening to him and the place where they were. Again he heard Grandfather awaken and begin talking to the others as he always did. The boy waited for the right time to speak, to ask Grandfather why there were times of quiet, why he heard in the distance people singing and speaking of those who were no longer with them. Why all these things? Even now Grandfather was speaking to someone, as if he was visiting. Yet he never left. How long was he to lie here beside his grandfather. Grandfather had said, "I will try to keep you as long as I can."

When the right time came and Grandfather was silent for a moment the boy spoke, "Grandfather, why is it there are times when everything is quiet and in the distance I hear people. Then at other times you seem awake, you talk to others as if you were visiting. Why all these things, and how long are we to be here?"

Grandfather spoke, "My grandson, the time has come for you to go. I have kept my promise for I have kept you as long as I could. Now you must leave. But first I will speak of the things you ask. When my day ends, your day begins. With that you must leave. When it is quiet it is my night, and I must begin to prepare for my next day, just as you must be quiet in your night and rest for your next day. Those that you hear in the distance are your people; they are in their day. It is their time to sing and dance, to remember those of us who are no longer there, to remember what we had to say about life and how it should be lived. You must tell all that I tell you to your people—to those who will accept your word, and even to those who will doubt you. You must remember how to use those things that are yours and to share with others, even with us who are here. The times when I speak to others here are during my day. There are many who are here. We also have our song and dance, and in time to come you will be here. For this reason your tears shall not flow when you leave here at the end of my day to begin your day. When you leave here you will go due south. After you have made four camps you will reach your people. Go, my grandson, it is time to begin your day and tell all that I have told you.

With this the boy lifted the buffalo robe which covered him and his grandfather. It was daylight. Spring had come. The snow had melted on the hills. Only the bushes and the low spots had snow. Gently he covered Grandfather, whom he now knew had been gone for many days. Grandfather's spirit had kept him warm and alive. As he looked at the remains of those who had fallen in the attack, he felt a lump in his throat, but Grandfather had said that no tears should flow. He knew if he cried Grandfather would hear. Slowly the boy began to walk, his face to the south. When evening came he made camp. In the quiet of the evening the boy remembered all that Grandfather had said. To the north the northern lights danced. He remembered grandfather's words: we also have our song and dance. On the morning of the fourth camp, as the boy walked along, he smelled wood smoke and, going further over a ridge, he sighted a camp. He had found his people.

When the boy told what his grandfather had said and how he had survived, there were some who questioned his story and demanded to see the place where the attack had taken place during the past winter. In this the boy saw Grandfather's words coming true because he had said there would be those who did not accept his story of survival. In due time the boy led a group of men to the site. There they found the remains of those who had died in the attack. Grandfather still lay there covered with the buffalo robe as the grandson had left him.

—1987

Jim Kâ-Nîpitêhtêw

Plains Cree · ??–1996 · Onion Lake

Jim Kâ-Nîpitêhtêw was from Onion Lake and was a respected elder who spoke only Cree. This selection is a transcription and translation of a speech given in 1989, while Kâ-Nîpitêhtêw was a senior member of the Council of Elders at the Saskatchewan Indian Cultural College in Saskatoon. It was translated by Freda Ahenakew when she was the Director of the Saskatchewan Indian

Languages Institute, and was published by the University of Manitoba Press in 1998.

The speech is a type of *kakeskihkemowina*, or "counselling discourse," where Kâ-Nîpitêhtêw recounts the events, told to him by his father, at the Treaty Six signing, and calls for proper attention and respect when using the pipestem and performing the rituals. His primary concern is for the authenticity and authority of carrying on the tradition, and not to let the thread of transmission break. It is significant, as it provides a Cree view of the Treaty Six signing, as opposed to the Anglo-Canadian view as found in the Morris records published in 1880. Kâ-Nîpitêhtêw's account reveals several inconsistencies in the Morris account, and that there was more to the ceremony than Morris, or his interpreter Jackes, understood.

The Pipestem and the Making of Treaty Six

Introduction

Well, this which I am about to discuss, I wonder if I will be able to discuss it with proper faithfulness, just as my late father had told me the story about it, here [at the Saskatchewan Indian Languages Institute] where they wish that I should be able to discuss it, this pipestem as it is called; although I had most properly been told about it also by my father's brother, where he had kept this, where his grandfather had left this pipestem behind.

Well, I am very grateful of course that these our relatives who work for us in this place [at the Saskatchewan Indian Languages Institute] will have it [the pipestem] as their witness of what these promises are which have been made to us; that they want for a person [*i.e.* me] to tell about this story, just as he knows it, just as he heard it in his own hearing. Just as I myself used to be told the story by my late father, that is how I am going to tell it to them. I wonder if I will be able to tell it exactly, just as he used to tell it to me. It cannot be helped that my memory, too, lapses, but to the extent that I know this story, I will nevertheless try to tell it to them. This, for instance, I will discuss first, this which our grandfather *cascakiskwês* has left behind, the pipestem.

Part I

"At that time, when they gathered here at *nipiy kâ-pitihkwêk*, where they were going to sell the land, at that time it was used," my late father used to say. "Well, the situation had everyone speaking with great concern. The old men spoke about this with great concern, they were full of regret that where Our Father had put us down on this earth that we should populate it, that this was going to be sold in their name, that was what they spoke about with great concern." That he used to say at that time.

Well, a certain old man, one old man, had in fact foretold what was going to happen, the situation in which we find ourselves at present; well, it is sad indeed that the old men are not many, it would have been very good if one had worked on this earlier, while they were numerous, so that we would hear them discussing this with their authority on that kind [the audio-recorder]; but now the story is only something from our hearing, how the story had been told to us, now that is all we have to fall back upon. That is why I for one am grateful that they are working on this, that they are thinking of our grandchildren and great-grandchildren, because young people do not pay any attention to trying to learn about it, how the story is told about this, and this then must be the wish of those who are going to try to record this story, now this is what I am going to tell about at present.

He, my late father, used to say this, "Well, a certain old man had in fact foretold it, rising from his seat; then he had foretold it: 'The people must have something to rely upon as testimony, and we who are Crees do have something to rely upon as testimony; that which is called the pipestem, that is all upon which we can rely as testimony. When he, our brother the White-Man, made these promises to us, he did promise us that no human walking on two legs upon the surface of the earth would ever be able to break the promises made to us. Thus, it was then that he had asked him:

> «Do you speak the truth in this which you have promised me, that no one will ever be in a position to be able to break the promises which you have made to us? For you have come between us, you have come between the All-Father and us, where he has given us the sustenance upon which we live, you have come between him and us; in coming to promise us that you are going to look after us, do you speak the truth in this which you have promised us; here where you have come representing the Queen, will it never end, that which you have promised us?
>
> Behold it! Lo, here as far as you can see, as far as the corners of the earth reach, as many buffalo as your eyes can grasp, the All-Father has given us all these to live upon; will you be able to provide for us to the same extent so long as this world shall exist?»

Thus he spoke to him, to the one who had come representing the Queen;

> «Do you speak the truth in this which you have promised us, that no 'human walking on two legs,' as you put it, will ever be able to break that, look, which you have promised us.»
>
> «No, I have not bought the water from you, nor the animals upon which you live, I have not bought them from you; also not the fish, I have not bought that either; and the various kinds of berries upon which you live, I also have not bought those.»

Thus he spoke, the one who had come representing the Queen,'" my late father used to say when telling about this;

Part II

> «Indeed, do you speak the truth in that you will forever look after me to this extent?»

he had said to that one;

> «If you speak the truth, hold then this pipestem; do you speak the truth in this which you have promised us—Yes, or no?»—
>   «Yes!»

he said, and when they had made him hold the pipestem, then he had taken this pipestem,

> «Indeed! No human walking on two legs will ever be able to break what I am hereby promising you, I will never pay you in full for your land, I will forever make continuous payments to you for it. No, I do not buy from you what is deep beneath this land, only one foot deep whence the White-Man makes his living, that is what I buy from you, Indeed, from here on, any monies drawn from beneath the ground, let people understand that this is one benefit which the Crees will continue to be paid from their homeland;»

thus then he spoke, the one who had come to make the purchase for them;

> «Now that which I said, what you ask me about, that no one will ever be able to break it, it is true! it is true! no one will be able to break it. This is what I said, I do not buy the water, nor the lakes, from you, nor the fish; only enough land [i.e., one foot deep] for the White-Man to make his living. Where he homesteads, he will make a well, and that is the water he will use. Well, that is why I said to you that I am not buying the lakes from you, and I am also not buying the Rocky Mountains; I am only buying this whence the White-Man will make his living.»

Thus then they had these promises made to them, by that one.

Part III

That is why they had used that [the pipestem], "In the future, when these things are discussed, this is the bible of the Cree which he held, swearing upon it in response that no one would ever be able to break the promises he had made to us;" thus then spoke these old men.

> «*Indeed, thus now the promises which I have made to you, forever,*
> *so long as the sun shall cross the sky, so long as the rivers shall run,*
> *so long as the grass shall grow, that is how long these promises I have*
> *made to you will last;*»

thus then our grandfathers had been told. (And that is what the White-Man is now tampering with, trying to change our status.)

Part IV

"Indeed, there then again this old man had spoken," my late father used to say, "'I do regret it greatly, I regret it, since Our Father has given us this our land upon which to live, that this our land should have been sold. But, if that does not happen [*i.e.*, if we do not accept the treaty], if the Whites then increasingly crowd the land, it will be then that they will fight us over the land,' that old man had then said," my late father used to say, And that is what is before us at the present time.

Supplement

> "*Assuming there were here on the other side -~ on the other side of a*
> *hill, if there on a hillside on the other side there were gunshots heard,*
> *the Cree Indians will never be conscripted to be handed over into*
> *military service;*"

thus then he had also promised.

> "*These promises, as many as I have made to you, all this will hold*
> *forever;*"

thus then had the promises been made to that Cree who had sold our land.

Conclusion

Well, as I tell this story, just so I, too, had it told to me by my late father; I wonder if I tell this properly, just as he used to tell me this story, it is this that I have told to these my grandchildren.

But it will be very good when one is going to discuss Treaty Six, that there should be an old person, or an old woman, with her, too, bringing along something valuable, there to add her own story, so that we might think of our grandchildren. If the Whites overpower us when they are going to make laws for us, we will live in great misery; not only will the old people live in misery, but the children, too, who are coming after us in their various ages will live in misery, thus, as for me, I usually think.

Indeed, this is the story I am telling those who want me to tell them the story about it. It would have been very good to have photographed this pipestem here, the one upon which the old man had relied as testimony.

That was the last time it was used, the pipestem, where one first used it with the Whites, it was here at *pêhonânihk* as it is called, that is where the Sioux had brought along that pipestem; that was the last time it was used.

Indeed, this is all I know of the story as I have been told it.

—*May 2, 1989*

Augie Merasty
Woods Cree · 1930–2017 · Sturgeon Landing

Joseph Auguste (Augie) Merasty was born in 1930 at Sturgeon Landing. The selections below are brief excerpts from his memoir *The Education of Augie Merasty*, published in 2015. With the aid of writer David Carpenter, Merasty recounts his time at St. Therese Residential School from 1935 to 1944, where he and other students endured physical, psychological, and sexual abuse.

Excerpts from *The Education of Augie Merasty*

Hard Times

We used to enjoy going out miles away from the school, going on picnics, either to the beach or going fishing at the rapids north of the school. It felt so nice to get out of the enclosed playground. Most of the time, we were forced to stay within the yard, which was surrounded by a high barbed-wire fence. It felt like getting out of prison. But I recall many times I was detained and was not able to join the crowd going to these good times if I was penalized for whispering during silence, or poking someone in the ribs, or swearing in Cree, as I did several times. I once wrote down "I will not whisper during silence" five hundred times while everyone was gone out of the school area.

I really can't recall just how many times I was made to pay for such minor offences. I was once made to walk about twenty miles in –40°F weather with a fellow student, Abner Joseph, back to where we walked the day before, across the big lake with a strong wind blowing. I imagine the wind chill factor was about –60°F. Just because we lost one mitten each. We were very nervous and scared all the way, as we were only about eleven or twelve years old at the time. And we saw some fresh wolf tracks about six miles out on the lake and kept our eyes busy looking every which way, expecting to see some wolves following us. And we were only carrying sticks three feet long and two inches around. Not much defence against an animal like a wolf. We came back without the lost mittens as the wind and snow had covered everything that could be lost. That was January 1941, and it was that meanest of all nuns, Sister St. Mercy, who had forced us to walk in that godawful weather, only to come back empty-handed. We, of course, got the strap, twenty strokes on both hands.

Also my left eye still waters and aches where I was hit a number of times by two Sisters who worked for four or five years as boys' keepers. Sister St. Mercy again and Sister St. Joy, who was Sister Mercy's disciple. Sister St. Mercy trained her well, at different times. They really enjoyed causing pain and other kinds of suffering as punishment for the smallest infractions. I think they were paranoid in the position they had, being masters of a lower race of creatures, Indians, as we were called.

"Indians from the bush, what can you expect?" was Sister Mercy's favourite phrase.

They wanted to show who was superior, and no rule or order was to be broken or spoken against. They wanted to impress upon us that all this was for our own good and the will of God, and that the order of nuns, brothers, and fathers of the Oblate Mary Immaculate (OMI) were to some degree servants of God on Earth, and we must take any punishment without complaints. To be disobedient was a sin in the eyes of God.

In the springtime when the cattle were mating, and all the animals were in the open yards, if we laughed too much or too loud while the bulls were doing their thing, we used to get whipped on the butts with a hose three feet long. We were chased away to another part of the schoolyard so we could not watch what was going on with the mating bulls and cows.

We also spent much time watching chickens and roosters doing what they did best. We were allowed to watch the chickens all we wanted without inter-ference, and we used to make bets with whatever we had in hand—nickels, candy, or glass marbles, which the principal Father Aquinas Merton gave us occasionally. We used to make bets on how many times the rooster could mount the hens in thirty minutes. We all kept tabs. One white rooster did it nine times within thirty minutes. It was one of the lighter entertainments we enjoyed many times without interference or punishment.

During the nine years I was at school at St. Therese, even though all those chickens laid eggs, not one student ever once tasted one egg at mealtime. I was once caught with three eggs I picked up outside the chicken yard where some wandering hens laid, and was made to eat them raw, right in front of my fellow watchers. Brer Lepeigne must have thought we had gone right into the chicken coop to steal from the hens.

Every morning at breakfast, we ate rotten porridge and dry bread that was hard as cardboard. We always watched an impeccably white-clothed cart eight feet long being wheeled to the Fathers' and Brothers' dining room. Right through the centre of the refectory for all us boys and girls to turn and watch, licking our chops, all the beautiful food going past us ten feet away. It happened almost on a daily basis. Our keepers, one on the girls' side and one on the boys' side, banged on their clappers, and we were told to get back to our porridge and don't turn our heads again or it would be detention or another kind of penance.

Sometimes on feast days like Christmas, Easter, New Years, and other Saints' feast days, we saw even nicer food being wheeled by. It was absolutely gorgeous, especially when we were eating rotten fish or other distasteful crap. Especially during the Bishop's visit (Rev. Martin Lajeunesse). On these days we all saw roast turkey, or steaks, roast chicken, doughnuts, and cake. Fresh cake. We used to drool and sigh, and of course we were ordered to get back to our rotten food. "Eat or I'll make you eat it, one way or another."

I always wondered why our keepers and teachers talked about Jesus, Mary, and Joseph and all the love they had for mankind, and Jesus being born in poverty, extreme poverty, and we should try to emulate him and learn to take punishment for our wrongs to pay here on Earth and not later in Hell or Purgatory. Apparently they didn't know it was suffering enough to see all that beautiful food being wheeled by and only getting a smell of it. I know they never practiced what they preached, not one iota. Do to others what you want them to do unto you. Be kind to others. Jesus will love you for it, and so on, and on and on and on, all the talking and preaching in church and classrooms. And what they did to us and how they administered their little regime did not mean a thing to them. They never really practiced what they preached, period.

Whenever there were visits of Bishop M. Lajeunesse or visits from chiefs or members of council from any Indian reserve, they used to make us dress in our best clothing, provide concerts, and they even served us some edible food, beef stew or something. And they treated those northern visitors with good food and everything nice, and of course that chief or counsellor would get up at the end of the concert and speak from the stage facing all 110 children, telling us how lucky we were to be looked after in such a school as St. Therese Residential, and we should be thankful to God and to the administration for such blessings.

Oh, God, I used to think, *what hypocrisy*. Somebody sure pulled the wool over their eyes, because that is how it was meant to look, and it happened time after time.

Sometimes for punishment we were made to kneel on the cold cement floor from 8:30 p.m. until almost midnight, after everyone had gone to bed upstairs. We would fall asleep on the cold cement floor before Sister Mercy came or sent for her co-worker Sister Joy to tell us to go to bed upstairs. Then we were woken up early in the morning to go to church. We were usually awakened at 7:30 a.m., like it or not. All we used for toothpaste was salt, which the sister carried in a saucer. Salt, something we didn't even get to use at mealtime. Yet the cows and horses were getting all they wanted in blocks in the fields.

These incidents I have written about happened many times, and I have long lost count of the number of times they happened, but it was the same thing, punishment and abuse over and over again, even before these two nuns and others abused me.

Father Lazzardo among the Children

Every morning we were made to haul wood, large logs for the boilers and smaller stuff for the kitchen, which was located about two hundred feet away. We did this for Sister Virginia Rose, who was a nice person but a terrible cook. One morning Father Lazzardo was either in a hurry or in a very bad mood. I was at the top of the long stairway, approximately thirty or thirty-five steps to the boiler room, and there were three other boys with armloads of kitchen wood, and I had the large blocks of wood for the boiler. I heard the door open behind me and I didn't quite hear what Father Lazzardo was mumbling about. Now I can't recall if he did this on purpose or pushed me to get out of the way. He was bringing into the place a small table or chair or something.

All I can remember was waking up in the school's infirmary, a medical room we called it, with two hospital beds. I had a big gash in the back of my head on the left side. Soon I was taken to bed back at our dormitory. I should have been taken to St. Anthony's Hospital in The Pas, Manitoba, but they kept me in the dormitory for a whole month. I ended up with a headful of lice because I couldn't comb my hair or even scratch near the wound.

Right after my tumble down the stairs, I used to wonder, how long before I succumb forever or get operated on? All because of that injury caused by Father Lazzardo. I know now why I was not taken to the hospital. They were afraid I might talk too much and maybe expose the person who harmed me. And all the time I was in that dormitory alone and very lonely. I had my head bandaged, I was not supposed to scratch my head, and the lice were getting worse, and I just wanted to scratch my head so badly.

Another thing I can't forget. I have another scar on the front part of my forehead from being kicked hard by Brother Friedrich Gruenwald for whispering during silence in lineup time on our way to classes. I hit the sharp part of the door latch with my forehead from that kick.

These wounds on my head are still visible, and I will gladly shave my hair from those areas to prove it. Also the back of my right wrist. For the last sixty years or so I have felt awful pain, throbbing pain and headaches day and night on the left side and the back of my head. Also dizzy spells all these years and especially the last twenty or so.

Now, back to Father Lazzardo. I first learned this story from a cousin, who attended St. Therese's after I had left in 1944. By this time, Father Lazzardo had become the principal of our school. Father Lazzardo had trouble holding down his sex drive, which surfaced when he became the school principal. He had replaced Father Bernard Pommier. Sometime around the early 1950s, he asked the girls' keeper for two girls to come and clean his bedroom. As it happened, two of the huskier, heavy-set girls were sent to help the priest with this job. Both girls were fifteen years old. These were Angelina Robertson and Louise Deschambault (now dead). Angelina was sent across the hallway to clean Mr. Cameron's room, and Louise was given the order to clean Lazzardo's room about ten minutes later.

As some of us were told a few times by Angelina, while cleaning Scotty Cameron's room, she heard the sound of screaming and pounding on the walls, like someone getting attacked viciously. She dropped her things and ran to the room, whence this screaming for help had come. She said she kicked open the door and was shaken to see Father Lazzardo, half on top of Louise with one hand inside her dress and panties, and the girl screaming like a banshee. Angelina herself started to scream, at which time Lazzardo jumped off the girl, with one hand lowered to his fly, which presumably was open and ready for action.

He told Angelina to go and finish her work and wait for Louise. He closed the door with Louise still crying, and Angelina heard the Father telling Louise he was only playing, and he wanted to see what her reaction would be if things like this ever happened. He said for Louise not to tell anyone about this incident. Louise cried all that time in his room without doing any more work. Shortly after, he gave her a bunch of candy and some chocolates.

A long time before that, this same priest beat me with his fists until I bled from my nose and mouth, and kicked me in the ribs. He left us all with memories that we won't forget.

—2015

Helen Francis
Métis · b. 1931 · Cumberland House

Helen Francis (nee Cook) was born in 1931 in Cumberland House, the second child of Walter and Mabel Cook. Her father was of Cree and English ancestry, from the Cook and Fidler families, and her mother was of Norwegian and Swedish descent. She married Thomas Francis, and spent four decades of missionary work with him. After raising four children, she enrolled in the University of Regina and graduated with a B.A. in English in 1991. The selections here are from her book *Struggle to Survive: A Métis Woman's Story*, a family history that recounts life around Cumberland House, her marriage, and her conversion to Christianity.

Life on the Trapline

The season for trapping muskrats opened in March when the snow was still knee-deep and the lakes and rivers frozen solid. Because the northern region was still in the grip of winter, a dual-purpose transportation was needed to get to the trap-lines. By the time trapping season closed, the return journey would be made over open water so at the beginning of the season another mode of travel was necessary.

A canoe was secured to the sled with a cord and, for those who owned one, a team of dogs were hitched to the sled. The canoe was loaded with provisions and the wife and children bundled in feather robes that were warm and cosy. By then the dogs were straining in their harness, impatient to start.

Dad never liked dogs. He had good reason for disliking them. Grannie said he was almost bitten once when he was about 4. The time I recall him using a team of dogs to move to the trap-line, the entire journey was beset with the team's refusal to cooperate and Dad's exasperation. As far as I am able to determine Dad never owned dogs of his own.

In later years after we had grown up and left home, Dad went alone to his trapline on foot, pulling a sleigh on which he packed his provisions. In one of our visits to Cumberland after the grid road opened the way to make it more accessible, we gave Dad a ride to the point of entry from which he trekked the remaining distance to his cabin; about 7 miles, he told us. We sat in the car and watched him until he disappeared through the heavily wooded forest. I knew even as I watched him go into the bush that his days as a trapper were numbered. A painful arthritic condition in his knees would soon rob him of the only occupation he'd known. He loved the solitude of a trapper's life and I never heard him complain about the meagre returns of the furs he caught. Trapping was in his blood, as those of us, his offspring, discerned each spring when a restlessness would overtake him, a subdued kind of agitation we termed, *"the call of the wild."*

Bombardier

A new machine called a bombardier had recently come to the northern region to make winter travel less arduous. The vehicle's construction was ideally suited to drive over frozen lakes and rivers as well as deep snow, conditions which prevailed for two thirds of the year. To those of us unfamiliar with the French language we called it a *bom-ba-deer.*

When the DNR was informed that a bombadeer was designated for Cumberland House, Tom was assigned to pick it up in Flin Flon. My cousin Ruby, hearing that Tom and I were going to Flin Flon, asked if she could come with us. I saw no reason for refusing except for being in her fifth-month of pregnancy. But we'd be travelling in relative comfort both there and back. Besides, she had a brother, Rod, who lived in Flin Flon and with whom she could visit and spend the night.

We rode the bombadeer to The Pas, one that was already being used to transport passengers, and from there we caught the train to Flin Flon. After spending the night in the Manitoba town we were anxious to be on our way the following morning.

Before we left, the DNR men told Tom about a short-cut that would reduce the distance and lessen the time it would otherwise take to get home via The Pas. As the pencil-thin line on the map indicated, the cross-country route was not much more than a bush trail, but one for which the bombadeer was built to maneuver. So, for reasons relating to time and distance, Tom decided to take the shorter route to Cumberland and get home by early evening.

After Tom sent a radio-message to the DNR in Cumberland House to inform the senior officer we'd arrive home that evening, the three of us embarked on our journey across country. Despite the gas fumes and the noise of the engine, travelling in a bombadeer was a novelty that aroused a sense of adventure and a measure of excitement. We drove the length of Beaver Lake along the East shore until we reached land. Then, as we approached timber, Tom followed a separation through the trees which alone marked the path of an ancient trail. After about an hour or two into the bush, the motor began to cough and to sputter. Unfamiliar with the machine, Tom would stop, busily fuss over whatever he thought was causing the problem, and coax it back to life before we could advance another mile or two.

Due to the time Tom spent on the now barely limping bombadeer together with yet another reversal in the form of fallen trees, our repeated stops were stretching the miles to a much greater length. Our stops were now alternately caused by the ailing motor and the windfall which now blocked our trail with increased frequency. One of us would keep our foot on the gas pedal while the other two would remove the fallen tree. With the decreased power of the engine our lights dimmed and the interior grew unbearably cold. In one of our stops as Tom worked on the motor, Ruby and I kept warm beside the bonfire we had lit. Finally, coming to a clearing which indicated a lake, we had no choice but to camp for the night, if sitting up by the campfire all night can be called camping. The bombadeer had sputtered and died and our day's exertion had wearied us to the bone. Once more building a fire, we made tea, hungrily ate some lunch from the emergency rations that were kept in the bombadeer, and dreamed about home.

Sitting around the fire just to keep from freezing, we shifted our position regularly enough to keep more evenly warmed and wakeful. Falling asleep was out of the question. Out in the open in the middle of December sleep meant certain death. The stillness of the night was broken only by the crackling sound of sparks from the fire we kept feeding, and the distant sound of wolves which we fervently hoped would keep their distance.

Desperate for even a few minutes of sleep I filled a cast-iron skillet with some live coals and took it into the bombadeer to use as a heater while I dozed. My invention proved ineffective. The smoke was suffocating and my feet almost froze.

When, at the first light of dawn, we saw that the lake by which we camped was much smaller than Pine Island (the lake adjacent to Cumberland,) we took turns poring over the map to pinpoint our probable location. Our misconception of the distance we had come was now determined by the alarming discovery that a 12-mile trek through the bush still lay before us, with an additional 12-mile hike across the frozen Pine Island Lake. It was far more than we bargained for when we so happily began our journey from Flin Flon.

Carefully deliberating the next move—whether to wait for a rescuer or to start walking—we unanimously settled for the latter choice. Despite knowing a message was sent before we left Flin Flon, we had no way of knowing if the message arrived. Knowing only that we could not survive another night without sleep in subzero temperatures, we started out on what began as the longest walk any of us had ever attempted. Before we left, however, I changed my footwear from the winter boots I wore to some mukluks that were in the bombadeer.

Equipped with a teapail, tea, matches, a small axe, the remainder of the sandwiches, a map and some lumps of sugar, we crossed the small lake to the timberline. Tired from lack of sleep, the short distance we covered on the lake taxed our already depleted energy. Taking off the extra coat I had put on, I discarded it to dispense with the extra weight.

Tom offered to break trail for us while Ruby and I walked single file behind him. The snow was knee-deep with, as before, only the opening in the trees indicating where the trail, in a prior century, had been blazed and undoubtedly well trodden.

Stopping to make tea and eat our frozen sandwiches, we were as grateful for the rest as we were for the food. I was conscious of how inviting the soft snow looked. Even as we reluctantly got to our feet the struggle against the temptation to lay down in its fluffy depth and sleep took every ounce of determination we could muster.

Though already dark when we emerged from the woods, the outline of what we knew this time to be Pine Island Lake was clearly discernible. Although fatigued beyond words, we felt heartened at the sight. We stopped long enough to again make tea and eat the last of our lunch; one frozen apple for each of us.

Discarding the axe and teapail, we made our way down to the shoreline. Underneath the deep snow that covered the shoreline my feet sank into some slush, soaking my mukluks. It was not what I needed to begin our trudge across the 12-mile expanse of frozen lake. Once on the hard surface, walking became less demanding than it had been in the deep snow. But, with my mukluks freezing, I had another worry to be concerned about. To prevent my feet from freezing I kept my toes in motion, wiggling them back and forth while I walked.

And about halfway across the lake we saw the lights of the village in the distance. Most people were still using coal oil lamps, and though the lights were feeble it was a cheering thought to know the village was in sight.

The stars shone brightly in a clear sky but then, before we knew it we were in the midst of a snow squall. Our visibility completely obliterated by the swirling snow, we pressed on toward what we hoped was the right direction to the village. By now Ruby was urging us to leave her behind so as not to hinder us from the pace we tried to maintain. She was beginning to hallucinate from loss of sleep and the exerted effort to keep up with us. The sudden snow squall had no doubt disoriented her to some degree as well. But we refused to leave her to what we knew was certain death. I slapped her, gingerly at first, and then harder at her own pleading. It helped to waken her from the sleepwalking state she had slipped into. She told me she was dreaming and in her dream she was in a hotel room that had wallpaper with stars on the ceiling.

At one point while walking across the lake, we came to a heave in the ice. It was too dark to see what lay on the other side of the bank and we stood there for awhile wondering what to do next. Our fear of the possibility of open water on the other side kept us momentarily undecided about whether to risk climbing over or following the ice heave to wherever it might lead. Tom settled it by offering to climb over and if we heard a splash, he said, that we should then follow the ice-heave. We avoided talking about Tom's rescue should he fall in. Thankfully, Tom landed on solid ice and the two of us climbed over to continue our walk toward home.

When the snow squall lifted, we could no longer see the lights. Thinking we might have lost our direction in the whiteout, we plodded on anyway. Still following behind Tom with Ruby behind me, my own eyes began to play tricks on me. Tom looked like he was skating instead of walking. And sometimes the shoreline appeared close, only to recede in the next moment in the far distance. I knew then that if we did not soon find the village we would perish.

Even as that reality registered, I noticed that we had entered a point of land with a scattered growth of willows. Unsure at first whether the land we stood on was just another hallucination, I tried to differentiate between what was real or just another trick of the eyes. Reaching out to touch the willows and finding they were real, I tried to fix the location in my mind. Only faintly familiar at first, full recognition dawned on me; it was the island adjacent to Cumberland on which the government farm stood. Excited to know we were just across the river from Cumberland and so close to home, I burst out: "I know where we are!" as I pointed in the direction of the Bigstone River.

I tried to run in my haste to cross the river and get to the first house. Even then death was close on our heels, as evidenced in the light of the following day.

Completely oblivious to the danger, and hardly able to walk leave alone run, I fell a couple of times. Within a half hour, we knocked on the door of Dad's house. Grannie let us in. Absolutely incapable of taking one more step we spent the night there. Tom was the first one to conk out, sitting upright in Grannie's rocking chair with a half-eaten piece of bannock still clutched in his hand. Ruby and I explained our late arrival to Grannie. It was 2:30 in the morning. Grannie clucked and shook her head with wonderment that we had survived at all. With brief stops twice to make tea, and a stop now and again to give Ruby a few minutes to rest, we had taken 16 hours to walk the 24–25 miles home. Although it had not occurred to me at the time, munching on the sugar lumps that we had stuck in our pockets had no doubt given the extra energy we needed.

Driving back to retrieve our abandoned vehicle with a hired bombadeer and its driver the next day, Tom made the startling discovery. At the mouth of the river where we had crossed just a few hours earlier, the water was now flowing. We had crossed over on ice that was barely strong enough to hold us up. Our footprints, still visible in the snow on each side of the river, had since disappeared into the water that was now flowing down the centre.

Tom also found that, had we followed the ice-heave as we might easily have chosen to do, we would have ended up going away from the village instead of toward it.

Also, if Tom had known the source of the problem in the bombadeer, some methyl hydrate would have prevented our unforgettable ordeal. The driver who was hired to take Tom back to the location was more familiar with the machine and he told Tom the problem had been a frozen gasline. As it turns out, Ruby and I escaped with some frozen toes which blistered and later healed, while Tom's gallant trail-breaking left him so stiff he could barely walk home the following day to where we lived.

Four months later Ruby gave birth to a healthy baby boy!

—1997

Herbert Walker
Nakoda · 1931–2012 · Carry-the-Kettle

Herbert Walker was a member of Carry-the-Kettle Nakoda First Nation. The selection below was recorded by Emily Kay Schudel in her 1997 dissertation, *Elicitation and Analysis of Nakoda Texts from Southern Saskatchewan.*

Mink and Coyote

I am going to tell a story. A mink once lived around several sloughs. One day he met a coyote on a flat place. The mink said "My brother, you are carrying a jackrabbit in your mouth. Jackrabbits are very fast. How did you catch one?" The coyote said, "It was not hard to catch him because my legs are very long." The mink then said, "I will also catch one of them sometime." Then the coyote laughed so hard he fell over. The mink asked the coyote, "Why are you laughing so hard?" The coyote said, "Your belly drags so close to the ground, how could you catch one of them?" So then the mink said to the coyote, "It is true, you are a very fast runner. But I am a good swimmer," he said. "I just thought of something. We will race around this lake. Whoever gets back first will take the jackrabbit." Then the coyote said "I'll win it anyway," he said. And the mink said "No matter what, we will try it anyway" he said. "OK," said the coyote, "OK," he said. So then the coyote rand around the lake. The mink also started to swim in the water. The coyote lazily trotted. After a time, he looked up. The mink was already further ahead in front of him. So the coyote sped up to pass the mink. Several times he did this, but every time he looked up, he saw the mink still in front of him. Finally he looked once more and the mink was behind him. The coyote then slowed down again. He thought about the jackrabbit. After a time, he came to where they had left the jackrabbit, but there was nothing there. The coyote was thirsty so he went and stood in the water and then he saw something. He looked up and in a tree was the mink and a crow talking together and eating leisurely. The coyote said "Brothers, give me some." The mink was already full so he threw down what was left. Then the coyote happily ate. And so they all laughed a lot.

—*1997*

Freda Ahenakew
Plains Cree · 1932–2011 · Ahtahkakoop, Sandy Lake

Freda Ahenakew was born in 1932 on the Ahtahkakoop First Nation. She attended the St. Alban's Residential School in Prince Albert. Later she attended the Prince Albert Collegiate Institute. She earned a Bachelor of Education from the University of Saskatchewan in 1979, and taught at the Saskatchewan Indian Cultural College in Saskatoon. She then earned a Master of Arts in Cree linguistics at the University of Manitoba in 1984, and was an assistant professor in Native Studies at the University of Saskatchewan from 1983 to 1985, and the director of the Saskatchewan Indian Languagues Institute from 1985 to 1989. She was then a professor of Native Studies at the University of Manitoba until retiring in 1996. She was a member of the Order of Canada and received the Saskatchewan Order of Merit. Throughout her career, Freda published many children's stories and edited many collections of Cree oral stories and speeches. The selection below is from a transcript recorded and edited by Freda in January 1990 and can be found in Sarah Whitecalf's *kinêhiyâwiwininaw nêhiyawêwin / The Cree Language Is Our Identity: The La Ronge Lectures of Sarah Whitecalf*, edited and translated by H.C. Wolfart and Freda Ahenakew, as part of the *Publications of the Algonquian Text Society*.

Excerpt from *kinêhiyâwiwininaw nêhiyawêwin*

I [Speaking Cree and Speaking English]
FA: "tanisi itêyihtam aya ôma nêhiyawêwin, tânisi ê-isi-miywâsik kika-ayâhk, ka-nihtâ-nêhiyawêhk," ê-itwêt ana oskinîkîs.

SA: [1] êkosi mâka êtikwê anima kâ-itwêt awa oskinîkiw, miywâsin, kîspin ta-kakwê-nisitohtamêk êkwa mîna ta-kakwê-mitoni-wîcihisoyêk anima, ôma nêhiyawêwin kîspin kinôhtê-kiskêyihtênâwâw. ôma ôtê kâ-itapiyâhk sâskwatôn, êkosi isi ôma nikakwêcimikawinân kîkway, kîkway ê-nôhtê-kiskêyihtahkik êkosi isi ôma, pâh-pêyak ômisi isi nikî-kitotikonânak, "kîkwây anima êwako? tânisi anima êwako ê-itwêmakahk pîkiskwêwin?" êkosi itwêwak, êwako anima ê-kakwêcimikoyâhkok, êkosi wiya ê-kiskêyihtamâhk anima, kîkwây kâ-nôhtê-kiskêyihtahkik, êkosi nitati-wîhtamawânânak, êkosi ê-isîhcikêyâhk ôtê sâskwatôn; êkwa pêyakwayak anima êkosi isi ôma ê-apiyâhk, êkwa pêyakwayak

mîna ihtakon (kiskêyihtam awa anima ita mâna ê-apiyâhk), êkota pisisik kêhtê-
ayak. êkota êkwa êkonik kâ-nitawêyihtahkik, mêkwâc ôma êwako ôma êkwa
kâ-nôcihtâcik, êkota anima niwîcihiwân.

[2] nêhiyawêwin êkwa êwako, namôya piko ôma kiyânaw ôma kâ-isi-nêhiyawêyahk,
namôya piko êwako, nanâtohk ôki wêcîpwayâniwak nahkawiyiniwak
pwâtak, osk-âyak ôki mistahi ê-wanihtâcik pîkiskwêwin; êkwa ôki ê-itwêcik
nahkawiyiniwak wîstawâw, mihcêt aniki osk-âyak namôya ê-âpacihtâcik
anima nahkawêwin, wîstawâw otisi-pîkiskwêwiniwâw, êkosi êkwa aniki
kêhtê-ayak nitawêyihtamwak wîstawâw otôsk-âyimiwâwa ta-âpacihtâyit anima
onahkawêwiniwâw; namôya wî-âpacihtâwak êwako anima opîkiskwêwiniwâw
ôki osk-âyak, iyâyaw ôma âkayâsîmowin, êwako mistahi, namôya kakêtihk
ayiwâk âpacihtâwak. namôya mîna ê-wî-itwêyâhk, ê-pakwâtamawâyâhkok
osk-âyak ôma kâ-itatoskêcik, ôma kâ-âkayâsîmocik, tâpwê mistahi miywâsin
ôma, kâ-itatoskêyêk, âkayâsîmowin ôma ohci mistahi kimiyo-âpacihtânâwâw;
cikêmâ namôya miywâsin êkâ ta-âkayâsîmot ayisiyiniw – mâcika niya ôma,
îh ê-nôtokwêwiyân, seventy êkwa ê-ati-itahtopiponêyân, namôya ê-ohci-
iskôlowiyân, namôya iskôl ê-ohci-itohtêyân, êwako ohci mitoni niya nêhiyaw,
nêhiyaw-iskwêw mitoni niya; êwako ohci nikî-otinikawin anita sâskwatôn, êkota
anima, êkosi isi ôma kîkway ta-wîcihakik osk-âyak ta-wîhtamawakik, êwako
ôma, osâm ê-nêhiyawêyân mitoni, êkosi êkwa, êkota êkwa anima êkwa, êwako
ôma êkwa ta-kakwê-kiskinohamawakik ôma nêhiyawêwin ôki; êkwa, êwako
ôma êkwa kâ-kiskinohamâsoyêk ôma kâ-âkayâsîmoyêk, mitoni nahiyikohk
miywâsin ê-âkayâsîmoyêk ê-kiskinohamâsoyêk; mâka êkwa, ay-âpihtaw
iyikohk tâpiskôc ta-kî-âpacihtâyêk, kinêhiyawânâwâw, êkosi êkwa, kwayask
êkwa anita ta-kakwê-pimipayihtâyêk anima kâ-nêhiyawêyêk; êkâ ta-kakwê-
pônihtâyêk, êkâ ta-kakwê-wanikiskisiyêk anima kâ-nêhiyawêyêk. îh niya,
namôya ê-nihtâ-âkayâsîmoyân, kîtahtawê, mitoni ita kâ-wanwêhkâkawiyân,
piko ê-itwêstamâkawiyân; hâw, âsay niya êkota namôya nitâpacihtân anima,
êkâ âkayâsîmowin ê-ayâyân, mihcêt êkosi isi niwîtapimâwak nêtê sâskwatôn,
ê-itwêstamâkawiyân, ôki kâ-âkayâsîmocik ôki, mihcêt ahpô môniyâsak êkota
apiwak, êkonik êkwa aniki, piko êkwa ta-âkayâsîmowiht ayisk, ta-kitotihcik,
tânisi anima kâ-itwêyâhk anima niyanân kâ-nêhiyawêyâhk, êkwa êkwa aniki
ta-nisitohtahkik môniyâsak, môniyâskwêwak. êkosi anima ayi, êkosi êkotê
ê-isi-pimipayik, êkosi mitoni nitâh-takahkêyihtên êwako ôma, kiyâm kikâh-
nanâskomitinâwâw, kiyâm êkâ ta-kakwê-pakici-wêpinamêk kinêhiyâwiwininaw,
nêhiyawêwin, kiyâm ê-mamâyîyêk ê-pîkiskwêyêk, âhci piko ta-kâh-kocîyêk
ômisi isi, ta-kakwê-nêhiyawi-pîkiskwêyêk sôskwâc, mitoni miywâsin;
tâpiskôc niyanân awa niwîcêwâkan ê-nôtokwêwiyâhk, namôya kakêtihk âsay
nimiywêyihtênân, osk-âyak oski-iskwêw ta-pê-nêhiyawêmototâkoyâhk, mîna

oskinîkiw – kanakê nîso pîkiskwêwina ta-âpacihtât ta-nêhiyawêt, âsay mitoni
nimiyomahcihonân, tâpiskôc kwayask ê-nêhiyawêt nititihtawâw oskinîkiw
oskinîkiskwêw kâ-pîkiskwêt êkosi isi kâ-nêhiyawêt. êwako ani anima pêyak,
êkosi niyanân ôtê ôma kâ-isîhcikêyâhk sâskwatôn, tâh-têpi iyikohk ta-apiyâhk
ômatowihk, êkosi anima ê-isi-kitotâyâhkok osk-âyak.

I [Speaking Cree and Speaking English]

FA: "What does she think about the Cree language, what value is there in the
ability to speak fluent Cree," that young man said.

SA: [1] In response to what this young man said, there is value indeed in trying to
understand the Cree language and also in trying to study it in earnest if you want
to learn it. When we sit as elders over there in Saskatoon [at the Saskatchewan
Indian Cultural College], they have asked us things like these, they want to know
things like these, they have addressed us, each in turn, with, "What is this? What
does this word mean?" these are some of the questions they ask us, and as we
know the answers to what they want to know, we simply go on to tell them, this
is what we do there in Saskatoon; and for this we sit in a certain room, there is a
certain room (she [Freda Ahenakew] knows the room [the boardroom] where
we sit), and there the elders sit every time. And there, when they want to know
something, when they are working on a specific topic, there I am part of the group.
[2] It is true not only for the Cree language, the language we speak, not for
that language alone but for the various tribes, The Chipewyans [Dene] and
the Saulteaux and the Dakotas, that the young people have lost much of their
language; and the Saulteaux say the same, that many of the young people do
not use Saulteaux, their own language, and therefore these elders, too, want
their young people to use their Saulteaux language; but the young people will
not use their own language but, rather, English, they use a lot of that, they
use English a great deal more. We are not going to say that we dislike it when
they speak English in their work, for it is indeed very valuable for you, you put
English to very good use in your work; of course it is not good if a person cannot speak English—such as I myself, for instance, look, I am an old woman,
I am approaching seventy, I never went to school, I never set foot in a school,
and because of that I am truly a Cree, I am truly a Cree woman; because of
that I was chosen for the work in Saskatoon, to help the young people and tell
them about these things, this is the reason, because I truly speak Cree, and
therefore to try to teach them the Cree language there; when you are students
in an English-speaking school, it is entirely appropriate for you to speak English
in school; but then you should use both of them, about half and half, you do
speak Cree and therefore you should make a serious effort to keep speaking

your Cree; you should try [not] to give it up, you should try not to forget
your Cree. Look at me, I cannot speak English, at times when I am seriously
stumped [without English], I have to have someone interpret for me; now, in
that case I am helpless for I do not speak English, and there in Saskatoon I sit
[as an expert] with many who only speak English, and then I have someone
interpret for me, and there even are many Whites in the audience, and for all of
those, now, someone has to say in English what we are saying in Cree in order
for them to be lectured and for the Whites, the White women to understand
it. That is the way it is, and that is how it works there, and therefore I am very
pleased and I would thank you if you tried not to let go of our Creeness, the
Cree language, even if you make mistakes when you speak, you should still
keep trying like this, you should continue with your efforts to speak in Cree,
it is truly valuable; we, for example, my partner [Freda Ahenakew] and I, as
old women, we are so very pleased when young people, young women, come
to speak to us in Cree, and also young men—even if they use only one or two
words in Cree, we already feel very pleased, it sounds to me as if they spoke
real Cree when young men and women speak Cree like that. That is one of the
things we do there in Saskatoon, when we sit in a place like this from time to
time, this is what we say when we lecture the young people.

—1993

Hubert Gunn

Saulteaux · 1933–1995 · Cowessess First Nation

Hubert Gunn was Saulteaux from Cowessess
First Nation. He attended Marieval
Residential School, receiving a grade six
education. This, he said, qualified him for
"manure-forkin', hay-pitchin' and wood-
choppin'." He was a veteran of the Korean
War and also served as a band councillor
on the Cowessess Reserve, as well as a Land
Claims Specialist, researching illegal land
surrenders and other treaty-related issues.
His stories, including the one here, tell of
everyday life on the reserve when farms were
not yet mechanized and a few dollars could
be earned by selling wood or performing
casual labour for farmers.

A Lamp to Read By

It was a nice, warm, sunny fall day. A good day to haul a load of wood to town
and sell it in that district the Indians call "German Town." The residents in that
end of town were predominantly of German extraction and most of them liked
to get a deal on a load of wood. The sharp blade of the axe bit deep into the dry
poplar tree. Old Gus grunted as he pushed the tree down and started trimming

the limbs off. The ring of the axe echoed through the bush. He guessed that there were at least twenty or thirty loads of good dry wood left in this part of the reserve. He would be back again soon, but this log would complete today's load.

Old Gus stopped to take a grey, nearly empty package of tobacco out of the little bib of his faded overalls. The cigarette papers that accompanied his tobacco were Chantecler's. There was a rooster on the red cover, drawn in black ink. Gus referred to them as the "Rooster" brand.

Gus now fashioned a cigarette, rolling expertly. Then, lighting a match by whipping it across the seat of his overalls, he puffed contentedly on the cigarette. He was eyeing the team of blacks who were trying to reach a tuft of grass, causing the wagon to creep ahead a few feet.

"Whoa!" yelled Gus, at the same time grabbing the lines and jerking the animals' heads up.

"Allus tryin to eat when there's work to be done," he grumbled.

Gus was still peeved about events earlier that day. At times, the horses were hard to catch, like this morning when they somehow sensed there was work to do. At other times he could fool them by putting a handful of gravel in the pail he usually fed them from. They would come trotting up to him, expecting to get a treat of grain when he shook the pail. But this morning they must have remembered and were not fooled by the old trick. They came close, necks stretched way out, trying to sniff at the pail to see if there was really oats in it.

Just as he going to drop the pail and grab their halters, Old Dick, the wiser one, turned around as fast as a cutting horse and after kicking his heels up in the air a couple of times and bucking, he raced out of sight into the bush, switching his tail with Old Billie close behind.

It was at times like this that Gus felt like shooting his horses. He ran crashing and tripping through the bush, swearing. At last, his chest heaving, Gus stopped to lean against a tree to catch his breath and plan another strategy. Rolling a smoke, but looking out the corner of his eye under the brim of his tattered straw hat, he spied Dick's head, only partially concealed by the brush, calmly peering back at him. Gus began to whistle as he walked over in that direction, at the same time trying to make it look as though he had given up trying to catch them. Suddenly he made a dive and grabbed Dick's halter.

"Just for that—no oats for you," he said triumphantly. Billie followed meekly behind.

Gus cut four three-foot stakes and squared the ends. He put them in the stake holders of the wagon and loaded the poplar poles. He stepped back and surveyed the load. "Damn nice load," he said to himself. He threw his axe on top of the load and climbed up after it. He drove out of the bush, carefully skirting old stumps sticking up out of the ground.

Getting near town, he stopped and rearranged the logs to make it look like a really good load, which it was. He generally had to haggle the deal for the five dollars he got for his wood.

He pulled into town under the railroad overpass. The yard engines passing back and forth overhead made the horses nervous. They lifted their heads and pranced. "They'll think I have a fine team of lively horses," said Gus, proud of the way the team was acting. When he got to Herman Buckt's place, he pulled into the yard and noticed the curtains fluttering inside the kitchen window.

He got off the wagon and knocked on the door. Herman came out the door, pretending he had not seen Gus before. He shook Gus' hand and said,

"So, I see you vant to sell me a load of vood, yah."

Herman walked around inspecting the load of wood. He peered under it and over it and slipped in behind the team to see if the bottom of the logs were rotten. He went back to see how small the ends were, and was trying to climb up on the load when Gus stopped him.

"Four dollars," said Herman.

"Four fifty," Gus answered.

Herman was adamant, "Four dollars."

"But I worked hard and had to come a long way to bring such a nice load of wood to town for you."

"No matter, all the money me and the vife get is the old age pension."

"I need the money, and besides I didn't have my dinner yet. If you won't buy the wood, I'll go someplace else."

"Vell, four fifty. No more."

Gus knew he had won. "Four fifty and dinner to boot."

"All right, all right," said Herman, throwing up his hands as if he were being robbed. But he, too, had won.

While Gus unloaded, Herman went inside to tell his wife to prepare a meal. Gus tied a horse on each side of the wagon and split the bundle of hay he had on the wagon between them.

He thanked Mrs. Buckt for the baloney and potatoes and with the money in his pocket, hitched up the team and drove down town. He tied up near the pool hall, where the Indians from the reserve gathered whenever they came to town. As soon as he walked in he was greeted warmly by his friends who were standing by the first table playing poker pool.

"Grab a cue, Gus," said one. "We just started."

At that moment Gus thought about his old lady and her last words when he left the house that morning.

"And don't forget the lamp chimney this time. Come home early and no pool and no drinking!" At the awful impact of the thought, he backed out of the pool room and went to the general store.

"Well, Gus, long time no see," Mr. Lesser, the store keeper greeted. "What would you like?"

"Well, Mr. Lesser, my old wife's been nagging at me all week."

"What for?" asked Mr. Lesser.

"Well, the last time I came in, I forgot to buy a replacement for that damn lamp chimney our grandchild broke on us. Before I go and play pool and stay till midnight, like last time, and catch hell again, I thought I'd better get what I need first."

"Wise move," beamed Mr. Lesser, starting to get the items on the list Gus presented him with. "Come here, Gus, I'll show you a lamp chimney the kids won't be able to break so easy."

The store keeper took a package from the shelf and unwrapped a lamp chimney and threw it on the floor. It smashed into a hundred pieces as Gus jumped back in alarm. He then took another chimney from the shelf and throwing it on the floor, laughed as Gus jumped back again, expecting to see glass all over the place. Gus was amazed as he looked down at the fragile looking chimney, still in one piece.

"Well, I'll be dawgonned," said Gus. "Let's see that trick again."

"That was no trick, it's a new kind of lamp chimney," said Mr. Lesser. "You just have to be careful it don't hit any iron, like a nail or anything like that."

Walking out with his box of groceries and looking at the lamp chimney in its brown paper wrapping, Gus kept saying to himself over and over, "Well, I'll be damned, just wait till I show Sarah this one."

Twenty miles away, Sarah, Gus' sharp-tongued old wife, was cooking supper for herself, knowing that she would eat alone. She put another stick of wood in the stove. Gus did not get drunk every time he went to town, only once in a while, just when she least expected it. If he got drunk today, her mood would not let him hear the end of it for days on end.

Seeing that it was getting dark, Sarah cut a piece of cloth from one of Gus' old flannel shirts and placing it in a saucer, poured some melted grease over it. She lit the wick and watched as the room lit up dimly with the makeshift "bitch lamp."

It was nearly midnight when she heard the dogs barking, and going outside she heard the wagon creaking in the distance. She went inside and made another fire in the stove. Gus would be hungry. The dogs were setting up a racket, yelping and barking as they recognized their master.

The wagon stopped and Gus came in carrying the box of groceries and, looking at the sputtering bitch lamp, he started to unwrap a parcel. Sarah was trying to sniff at Gus' breath to see if she could detect the smell of liquor. She was looking at him closely in the fitful light.

His wife waiting, Gus finally got the wrapping paper off the lamp chimney and said,

"Look, Sarah. I bought a lamp chimney, a new kind, if you drop it, it won't break." Sarah, her suspicions now aroused, stepped closer, wondering what Gus meant. Gus said, "Watch this."

He threw the chimney on the floor. It hit a nail and smashed into a hundred pieces. Only then did Gus remember the store keeper's words "…as long as it doesn't hit anything iron, like a nail or anything like that…"

Sarah, frustrated after waiting all these days for a lamp chimney so she could read, grabbed the broom and chased Gus outside, yelling at the top of her voice,

"Get out, you drunken old fool! You can sleep outside with the dogs again."

Old Gus unharnessed the horses and giving them each a syrup pail of oats before letting them go, grumbled to himself, "Now what do you suppose got into the old lady to say that I was drunk like that?"

The dogs were staying away from Gus, just in case he was really drunk. They did not want to be within kicking distance. They watched him uneasily…but with some sympathy.

—1990

Vicki Wilson
Dakota-Cree · White Bear

Vicki Wilson is originally from White Bear First Nation. Throughout her life she has been active in the Indigenous women's movement. She has served as an Elder for the Saskatchewan Urban Native Teacher Education Program and the First Nations University of Canada. The selections below were originally published in *The Strength of Women: Âhkamêyimowak* (2011).

It was to me like we had lost our childhood

I'm an Assiniboine Cree, and I was born on White Bear reserve. I grew up when the Indian agents were still living on the reserve, and you weren't allowed to visit each other. I was raised traditionally by my grandparents most of the time, 'til I was about seven or eight, and then I was hauled away to a residential school. I cannot even remember the year that was, it was so long ago. I don't have a lot of good memories about being there. I think the only thing I learned from it was that you must speak English. I learned how to sew and I learned how to suppress my feelings, my anger. That's still with me after many, many years. I believe that I stayed in there for about roughly eight years—that's school years.

The only thing I can recall as being a good thing about residential schools is that we all learned how to speak English. When we were first taken away to school, I didn't speak a word of English. I spoke Cree at the time. By the time we came home at the end of June, we'd forgotten our language. We used to get our ears pulled if we were caught talking to each other.

We had friends, but it was a lonely feeling because we had never been away from home. You know, living with my grandparents we were treated with dignity, we weren't yelled at and we had chores and stuff to do. We learned some of our history from our grandmothers. Our grandmothers were the ones that looked after the children, both boys and girls. We weren't separated like we were at the school, where boys did this and girls were on the other side of the building.

I think it was about three hundred to four hundred children. I will always remember the day we got picked up to go, just in a big cattle truck, with benches where you could sit down and they put us all. We were the third pickup. It started in Manitoba and went into the Dakota reserves. No, I think we were the second pickup. I think they came to White Bear and picked us up, and then they stopped at Carry the Kettle and drove us to Lebret. At that time we didn't know where the heck we were going. One thing I always wondered was, who decided who was Catholic and who wasn't, because my family went to two different residential schools, one in Brandon, and some of us went over there. So I wondered, who decided that? I still wonder, but I haven't found out yet.

When we first arrived, we all had to line up and get our hair cut off, and then they deloused us. We all had to have a shower—it was an ice cold shower. They never gave us a towel. We were all standing in a row shivering, and we couldn't leave till the last person was done. I think we were all marched upstairs. We had never been in a concrete building in our lives, and it was so cold and inhumane and sort of dehumanized you. I don't think anyone slept that night, because kids were whimpering and crying, and we didn't know what was going to happen to us. We thought they were going to kill us eventually. I remember that because the boys were somewhere else in another part of the building. I remember I was left-handed, but I still could use both hands for cutting or writing. I was a left-handed person, and they used to put a mitt on you or some kind of tie to the desk, so you wouldn't use your left hand. You had to write with your right. I wasn't the only one; there were several of us.

So this went on 'til, like I said, by the end of September we couldn't speak our language, because we weren't allowed to speak it at all. And when we went home, the first thing I did was I went to my grandparents' place. My grandmother just cried when she saw me. I had no hair—they had cut it over my ears and I looked ugly. And that's what she said, she said, "You stink and you look ugly." I didn't know what she meant, because I couldn't talk to her, I couldn't talk Cree by this time. So I had my aunt with me and I said, "What is she saying?" The smell was because of the lye soap we used—we used it for shampoo and everything—and I guess you get used to smelling yourself all the time, you didn't know others smelled it on you, the lye soap. Then she started crying, and so did I for that matter. We were supposed to ignore our grandparents, because we were told they were a bunch of pagans and we had to pray for them. We ignored them because once they tell you long enough you start believing it yourself.

It was to me like we had lost our childhood. We lost so much. There was no comforting—you couldn't comfort other kids when they were crying, and I didn't have my brothers there yet. When they did finally enter the same school, the only times we saw them was when we went to mass in the morning. We couldn't look, we had to look straight ahead in the chapel, but we always managed to see them when they were there. Once, I didn't see my little brother for three days and I thought maybe he was dead, maybe they had killed him.

I have heard that the Lebret residential school is torn down now. I don't know what it looked like. It became nicer I guess over the years, because I had nieces that wanted to go there. They said it was better than home, because they came from big families.

You had to put a hold on your anger. I was very angry for many years. When I went home, my father was doing the same things. He wouldn't allow us to speak our language, and he didn't believe in ceremonies and stuff like that. He was the second generation that went to residential school. I think that just made me angrier. I think the last two years I was in that school, I became very... I was a troublemaker, I guess. I started questioning things. I wouldn't do things that the nuns told me. One of the things they did to us was they had a board in the dining room and you had little stars and they would put these little stars on it, if you were good. I think the last year I was there I had a bunch of black stars, and by this time I didn't care because I knew I wasn't going back to that school ever again. So I did things just to get those black stars. To me, it was my way of getting back at them, and still today I laugh about it. Like, I've learned to deal with a lot of the anger and stuff, but it stayed with me for many years. I guess my father was doing the same thing, not so much my mom, but my dad.

We learned how to hate. You couldn't trust anybody, especially the church, I learned that. I used to think to myself, one of these days, no one's going to tell me what to do, and then I was about fourteen, fifteen when that happened. My way of protest was that I never went to church when my family did because I was still angry about the churches. Look how they treated us. They're supposed to be kind and trying to save us, and they sure didn't practice that. And I carried that with me for a long time. I guess I acted out by doing a lot of crazy things. I said I would never do that to anybody, force them to go somewhere they didn't believe in. I remember trying to do that to my ex, I was trying to make him come with me. I said, why am I doing this when it was done to me? So we never got married in the church, and my mom was quite disappointed. I was one who thought, never baptize your children. I was really chastised by my brothers—they're saying that my kids are going to go to hell and things like that. I said, when they are old enough they can make their own choices, and today they've tried it. Before, when they were sixteen, they went to summer churches with their friends, and it wasn't what they wanted, and it was kind of scary. I kind of felt guilty about it, but I don't anymore, because none of them have joined a church, and none of their children are baptized. We do quite well without doing that.

Most of us in that generation didn't finish school because there were no high schools, it was all residential schools. So, we went back about two years later, we were supposed to be connecting high schools, and I think that about nine of us went back. I don't know why. Sometimes I wondered how I was able to go back after those bad, bad experiences. I left home because I couldn't stand it there anymore. That's when I decided to go back to Lebret. I was starting high school. Two years later, we were released from there. We really didn't graduate, not like today how students graduate from whatever. There were never any ceremonies, nothing. They just gave you a set of clothes, whether you fit them or not, and sent you home.

Like I said, there were nine of us that started, and I think I was the last one to leave because I didn't have any money to go home. I didn't want to go home anyway. We didn't have a teacher; they called them priests, they called them brothers. Ours had a little room and counted a bunch of books in front of us and then left us—he never taught us anything. So the students were gradually leaving. They did not live as far as I did, so I was the last one to leave. I just happened to run into my auntie, so I financed my way home.

I got as far as Regina. I remember I had another auntie there and I ended up staying because I didn't want to go back to the reserve. So I worked.

You'd be exposing yourself

I worked at a lot of places. I saw a lot of racism, discrimination in those days. I was about sixteen or eighteen, I guess. I lived in Regina, where Indians used to get escorted out of cafes—they didn't serve Indians. We used to just leave, we never questioned it. It was just the way it was.

I stayed with another aunt of mine in Regina, and she was very good, but she was also very stern. We had to work to contribute to the household expenses, and look after our own clothing. I remember working at Sears and I waitressed all night at a cafe that's no longer there in Regina. I decided to stay at the YWCA. I remember coming home because I worked the night shift from eleven to seven or so and I was going to come in and just sleep. These ladies at the YWCA asked me to leave because they thought I was out all night, and they went and checked my bed and it was made up and I wasn't there. I hadn't told anybody that I had just come off the night shift, so I left and went back to my auntie's.

They had industrial courses at Lebret, so a few of us went back several years later, after trying high school. We took a sewing course, and I was there for three years, three school years. That was pretty interesting because I had learned how to sew and how to design my own clothing. The last year we were supposed to go to Montreal to design school, but the principal disagreed, he said no, he didn't allow it, because Indians shouldn't go there. We asked why, and he said, "Because you'd be exposing yourself." And we didn't really know what he meant, you know, how can you be a designer and expose yourself? We didn't know what it meant. I left after that, but that's one thing I'm grateful for, I can sew and design my own clothes.

I think that is one of the reasons I left Saskatchewan in the late 1950s, was because of the racism that was happening in Saskatchewan. I think I've learned a lot, had a lot of experiences and did a lot of travelling. I got married and lived on the west coast. My children were brought up in Vancouver. I believe it was my children that brought me home, back to Saskatchewan. I was teaching them that they were plains Indians, and then they couldn't identify with the west coast. So we came back in 1971 and I've been here since. I'll always attribute that to my daughters because they wanted to come back. It took me four trips back to Vancouver to discover that I didn't belong there. My home was here, my ancestors were born in the plains. So we came back.

One of the things I learned is how to listen to people, especially my elders, my mothers, and especially my relations, you know. The importance of going back home. All the things I had learned before I went to residential school were coming back to me. A lot of times you put things on the back burner and just forget about it.

—*2011*

Bernelda Wheeler
Cree-Nakoda-Saulteaux · 1937–2005 · Gordon First Nation

Bernelda Wheeler was born on the Muskopetung First Nation. She was of Cree, Nakoda, and Saulteaux descent, and a member of the Gordon First Nation. In 1946, her family left Saskatchewan and settled in northern Manitoba. She attended the

Birtle and Brandon residential schools, and high school in Churchill, graduating in 1955. She worked extensively in radio, including working as host, producer, and journalist on CBC's *Our Native Land* from 1972 to 1982. She also worked as an actor, including roles in Tomson Highway's *The Rez Sisters*, in the 1998 mini-series *Big Bear*, and in *Christmas at* *Wapos Bay*. In the 1980s, she began writing, contributing extensively to Aboriginal children's literature. She also worked in print journalism for *Eagle Feather News* in Saskatoon. In 2005, just days before her passing, she was chosen as a recipient of the Lifetime Achievement Award by the Anskohk Aboriginal Literature Festival.

Our Beloved Land and You

Great Grandfather
In stories we learned of you and yours
Stories of times long gone
That travelled through them that came before
And came to us and ours
Of the great grandfather who journeyed the land
Our beloved land
And you

Small Boy
Clever and fast, who questioned life
Who ran and played and watched
You they chose to leave and learn
Then bring your teachings back to them
To live, to change the ways of the folk of the land
Our beloved land
And you

Young Man
Your wife and your small ones
All at home learning a strange new way
From a different world, a way
Those strangers brought. A way they said
Was the only way for you and yours, the prairie folk of
Our beloved land
And you

Church Man
You followed that way your whole life through

The half-remembered stories say
    And while you walked your eldest son
Hunted the bison while others played
He fished the rivers, the lakes of the land
    Our beloved land
    And you

His father
    You knew that food was scarce
        In those times that were then new
            Times when the others slaughtered all
When bison were less, new shelters cold
Small spaces to shield those ones within, on the land
    Our beloved land
    And you

Wise One
    You knew of the ways, of shelters shared
        The ways of the ones without
            The ones who knew a home no more
    The ones who shivered and shook
The ones who starved, the ones in the valleys of the land
    Our beloved land
    And you

You cried
    In a homeland losing its own
        Losing its life, its lives, its strength
            Grasping and gasping for love and soul
    Turning to others for strength and food
Knowing full well that all was there, there on the land
    Our beloved land
    And you

Giver of all
    You gave of yours, of shelter, of struggle and love
        To the ones who had lost, to the ones without
            You gave of your son and his will to work
    You gave to the hungry and cold
These were the ways, the ways of old on the land

Our beloved land
And you

Teacher of old
　　Trudging those prairie trails, in snow, in heat and sleet,
　　　Taking the teachings, the new but the old
　　　　Teachings you learned from them
　　　You made them yours within your soul
　　Then shared with those of the hills and plains on the land
　　　Our beloved land
　　　And you

Of their faith
　　You they scorned, thought you simple, inept, those strangers
　　　On our land. They paid you half a wage—they did
　　　　Then threatened to take the half away
　　　You stole their time—their time! They said
　　To share, to give, to love, those heathens on our land
　　　Our beloved land
　　　And you

With your head held high
　　Take it, you said. Take the whole half pay
　　　Abandon me if you dare
　　　　I'm here to do a job for God
　　　My God of the prairie, of valley, berries and birds
　　I'll do my job, it's here with these, these of the plains on
　　　Our beloved land
　　　And you

At treaty time
　　Spoke the words of a foreign tongue
　　　Spoke the words of your own
　　　　Signed the papers, the treaty was made
　　　The lands were gone for the others to use
　　A small reserve was all you had on this land
　　　Our beloved land
　　　And you

With strength and tenacity
    You did your job and journeyed the plains
        You taught your folk and prayed to God
            In your solitary way. You knew the trees
        And streams and lakes as your journeys took you far
Far over valleys, forest and hills. Far over prairie land
        Our beloved land
        And you

In your stubborn way
    Refused to yield when your old age came
        Refused to rest though weary and worn
            Still you trudged the trails to teach
        The ways of strength for body and soul
The ways of a God who loved the folk, folk of the land
        Our beloved land
        And you

Your soaring soul
    You left to those who still live on
        Legacies that will not die
            Of the stubborn strength
        Of the one who broke the trails to another way
The one whose tenacity held to the ways of the land
        Our beloved land
        And you

—2001

Maria Campbell
Métis · b. 1940

Maria Campbell was born in 1940 in northwest Saskatchewan. Her mother died when she was just twelve, and she had to leave school to help her father, a trapper, take care of her seven younger siblings. The person she was closest to was her great-grandmother, Cheechum.

The publication of Campbell's *Halfbreed* in 1973 is often considered the beginning of modern Indigenous literature in Canada. In it, Campbell recounts growing up, leaving home, falling into alcohol and drug addiction and prostitution, recovering, and later joining Native rights movements. The writing of the book itself represents her own healing journey, as Campbell says: "I had a whole lot of stuff inside me that I had to write to find out who I was, to heal myself."

The selection below is from another of her renowned works, *Stories of the Road Allowance People*, which includes Michif stories by Campbell and illustrations by Sherry Farrell Racette.

Jacob

Mistupuch he was my granmudder.
He come from Muskeg
dat was before he was a reservation.
My granmudder he was about twenty-eight when he
marry my granfawder.
Dat was real ole for a woman to marry in dem days
But he was an Indian doctor
I guess dats why he wait so long.

Ooh he was a good doctor too
All the peoples dey say dat about him.
He doctor everybody dat come to him
an he birt all dah babies too.
Jus about everybody my age
my granmudder he birt dem.

He marry my granfawder around 1890.
Dat old man he come to him for doctoring
and when he get better
he never leave him again.

Dey get married dah Indian way
an after dat my granfawder
he help him with all hees doctoring.
Dats dah way he use to be a long time ago.
If dah woman he work
den dah man he help him an if dah man he work
dah woman he help.
You never heerd peoples fighting over whose job he was
dey all know what dey got to do to stay alive.

My granfawder his name he was Kannap
but dah whitemans dey call him Jim Boy
so hees Indian name he gets los.

Dats why we don know who his peoples dey are.
We los lots of our relations like dat.
Dey get dah whitemans name
den no body
he knows who his peoples dey are anymore.

Sometimes me
I tink dats dah reason why we have such a hard time
us peoples.
Our roots dey gets broken so many times.
Hees hard to be strong you know
when you don got far to look back for help.

Dah whitemans
he can look back tousands of years
cause him
he write everything down.
But us peoples
we use dah membering
an we pass it on by telling stories an singing songs.
Sometimes we even dance dah membering.

But all dis trouble you know
he start after we got dah new names
cause wit dah new names
he come a new language an a new way of living.
Once a long time ago
I could 'ave told you dah story of my granfawder Kannap
an all his peoples but no more.
All I can tell you now
is about Jim Boy
an hees story hees not very ole.

Well my granmudder Mistupuch
he never gets a whitemans name an him
he knowed lots of stories.
Dat ole lady
he even knowed dah songs.
He always use to tell me
one about an ole man call Jacob.

Dat old man you know
he don live to far from here.
Well hees gone now
but dis story he was about him when he was alive.

Jacob him
he gets one of dem new names when dey put him in dah
residential school.
He was a jus small boy when he go
an he don come home for twelve years.

Twelve years!
Dats a long time to be gone from your peoples.
He can come home you know
cause dah school he was damn near two hundred miles
away.
His Mommy and Daddy dey can go and see him
cause deres no roads in dem days
an dah Indians dey don gots many horses
'specially to travel dat far.

Dats true you know
not many peoples in dem days dey have horses.
Its only in dah comic books an dah picture shows dey
gots lots of horses.
He was never like dat in dah real life.

Well Jacob him
he stay in dat school all dem years an when he come
home he was a man.
While he was gone
his Mommy and Daddy dey die so he gots nobody.
An on top of dat
nobody he knowed him cause he gots a new name.
My granmudder
he say dat ole man he have a hell of time.
No body he can understand dat
unless he happen to him.

Dem peoples dat go away to dem schools
an come back you know dey really suffer.
No matter how many stories we tell
we'll never be able to tell
what dem schools dey done to dah peoples
an all dere relations.

Well anyways
Jacob he was jus plain pitiful
He can talk his own language
He don know how to live in dah bush.
Its a good ting da peoples dey was kine
cause dey help him dah very bes dey can.
Well a couple of summers later
he meet dis girl
an dey gets married.

Dat girl he was kine an real smart too.
He teach Jacob how to make an Indian living.
Dey have a good life togedder an after a few years
dey have a boy.
Not long after dat
dey raise two little girls dat was orphans.
Jacob and his wife dey was good peoples
Boat of dem dey was hard working
an all dah peoples
dey respec dem an dey come to Jacob for advice.

But dah good times dey was too good to las
cause one day
dah Preeses
dey comes to dah village with dah policemans.
Dey come to take dah kids to dah school.

When dey get to Jacob hees house
he tell dem dey can take his kids.
Dah Prees he tell him
he have to lets dem go cause dats the law.
Well dah Prees
he have a big book

an dat book he gots dah names
of all dah kids
an who dey belongs to.

He open dat book an ask Jacob for his name
an den he look it up.
"Jacob" he say
"you know better you went to dah school an you know
dah edjication hees important."

My granmudder Mistupuch
he say Jacob he tell that Prees
"Yes I go to dah school
an dats why I don wan my kids to go.
All dere is in dat place is suffering."

Dah Prees he wasn happy about dat
an he say to Jacob
"But the peoples dey have to suffer Jacob
cause dah Jesus he suffer."
"But dah Jesus he never lose his language an
hees peoples" Jacob tell him.
"He stay home in hees own land and he do hees
suffering."

Well da Prees him
he gets mad
an he tell him it's a sin to tink like dat
an hees gonna end up in purgatory for dem kind of
words.

But Jacob he don care
cause far as hees concern
purgatory
he can be worse den the hell he live with trying to
learn hees language and hees Indian ways.

He tell dat Prees
he don even know who his people dey are.

"Dah Jesus he knowed his Mommy and Daddy"
Jacob he tell him
"and he always knowed who his people dey are."

Well
dah Prees he tell him
if he wans to know who hees peoples dey are
he can tell him dat
an he open in dah book again.

"Your Dad hees Indian name he was Awchak"
dah prees he say
"I tink dat means Star in your language.
He never gets a new name cause he never become a
Christian."

Jacob he tell my granmudder
dat when da Prees he say hees Dad hees name
his wife he start to cry real hard.

"Jacob someday you'll tank the God we done dis."
dah Prees he tell him
an dey start loading up dah kids on dah big wagons.
All dah kids dey was crying an screaming
An dah mudders
dey was chasing dah wagons.

Dah ole womans
dey was all singing dah det song
an none of the mans
dey can do anyting.
Dey can
cause the policemans dey gots guns.

When dah wagons dey was all gone
Jacob he look for hees wife but he can find him no
place.
An ole woman he see him an he call to him
"Pay api noosim"

"Come an sit down my granchild I mus talk to you.
Hees hard for me to tell you dis but dat Prees
hees book he bring us bad news today.
He tell you dat Awchak he was your Daddy.
My granchild
Awchak he was your wife's Daddy too."

Jacob he tell my granmudder
he can cry when he hear dat.
He can even hurt inside.
Dat night he go looking
an he fine hees wife in dah bush
Dat woman he kill hisself.

Jacob he say
dah ole womans
dey stay wit him for a long time
an dey sing healing songs an dey try to help him
But he say he can feel nutting.
Maybe if he did
he would have done dah same ting.
For many years Jacob he was like dat
just dead inside.
Dah peoples dey try to talk wit him
but it was no use.
Hees kids dey growed up
an dey come home an live wit him.
"I made dem suffer" he tell my granmudder.
"Dem kids dey try so hard to help me."

Den one day
his daughter he get married an he have a baby.
He bring it to Jacob to see.
Jacob he say
he look at dat lil baby
an he start to cry and he can stop.
He say he cry for himself an his wife
an den he cry for his Mommy and Daddy.
When he was done

he sing dah healing songs dah ole womans
dey sing to him a long time ago.

Well you know
Jacob he die when he was an ole ole man.
An all hees life
he write in a big book
dah Indian names of all dah Mommies and Daddies.
An beside dem
he write dah old names and
dah new names of all dere kids.

An for dah res of hees life
he fight dah government to build schools on the
reservation.
"The good God he wouldn of make babies come
from Mommies and Daddies"
he use to say
"if he didn want dem to stay home
an learn dere language
an dere Indian ways."
You know
dat ole man was right.
No body he can do dat.
Take all dah babies away. Hees jus not right.
Long time ago
dah old peoples dey use to do dah naming
an dey do dah teaching too.

If dah parents dey have troubles
den dah aunties and dah uncles
or somebody in dah family
he help out till dah parents dey gets dere life work
out.
But no one
no one
he ever take dah babies away from dere peoples.

You know my ole granmudder
Mistupuch
he have lots of stories about people like Jacob.
Good ole peoples
dat work hard so tings will be better for us.
We should never forget dem ole peoples.

—1995

Buffy Sainte-Marie
Plains Cree · b. 1941 · Piapot

Buffy Sainte-Marie was born on the Piapot First Nation. She was raised by foster parents in Maine and Massachusetts, but rediscovered her Cree heritage at a powwow when she was eighteen. Sainte-Marie has had significant successes as a singer and songwriter from her early twenties. One of her best-known songs, "Until It's Time For You To Go," has been recorded in seven languages by more than a hundred artists, from Elvis Presley to the Boston Pops, and her song "Up Where We Belong" won an Academy Award for best song. Her song "Universal Soldier" became one of the anthems of the peace movement, and it continues to be sung in that context. The selections below are only two of the hundreds of songs she has recorded.

Now That the Buffalo's Gone

Can you remember the times
That you have held your head high
and told all your friends of your Indian claim
Proud good lady and proud good man
Some great great grandfather from Indian blood came
and you feel in your heart for these ones

Oh it's written in books and in song
that we've been mistreated and wronged
Well over and over I hear those same words
from you good lady and you good man
Well listen to me if you care where we stand
and you feel you're a part of these ones

When a war between nations is lost
the loser we know pays the cost
but even when Germany fell to your hands

consider dear lady, consider dear man
you left them their pride and you left them their land
and what have you done to these ones

Has a change come about my dear man
or are you still taking our lands
A treaty forever your senators sign
They do dear lady, they do dear man
and the treaties are broken again and again
and what will you do for these ones

Oh it's all in the past you can say
but it's still going on here today
The governments now want the Navaho land
that of the Inuit and the Cheyenne
It's here and it's now you can help us dear man
Now that the buffalo's gone.

—1964

My Country 'Tis of Thy People You're Dying

Now that your big eyes are finally opened.
Now that you're wondering, "How must they feel?"
meaning them that you've chased across Canada's movie screens;
Now that you're wondering, "How can it be real?"
that the ones you've called colourful, noble and proud
in your school propaganda,
They starve in their splendour.
You asked for our comment, I simply will render:
My country 'tis of thy people you're dying.

Now that the long houses "breed superstition"
you force us to send our children away
to your schools where they're taught to despise their traditions
Forbid them their languages; then further say that
Canadian history really began
when explorers set sail out of Europe and stress
that the nations of leeches who conquered these lands
were the biggest, and bravest, and boldest, and best.
And yet where in your history books is the tale

of the genocide basic to this country's birth?
Of the preachers who lied? And the peoples who died?
How the nation of patriots returned to their earth?
And where does it tell of the starvation hell
where the children were herded,
and raped and converted
And when do we rescue the missing and murdered?
My country 'tis of thy people you're dying

A few of the conquered have somehow survived
Their blood runs the redder though genes have been paled.
From Arctic Inuvik to Niagra Falls
the wounded, the losers, the robbed sing their tale.
From Vancouver Island to the Labrador Sea
the white nation fattened while others grew lean.
Oh the tricked and evicted they know what I mean:
My country 'tis of thy people you're dying.

The past it just crumbled; the future just threatens
Our life blood is shut up in your papers and banks,
And now here you come, with a bill in your hand
and surprise in your eyes, that we're lacking in thanks
for the blessings of civilization you brought us
The lessons you've taught us. The ruin you've wrought us.
Oh see what our trust in O Canada got us.
My country 'tis of thy people you're dying.

Now that the rivers are dumps for your chemicals
Now that the forests are dead like the moon
Now that my life's to be known as your heritage.
Now that even the graves have been robbed.
Now that our own sacred way is your novelty.
Hands on our hearts We salute you your victory:
Choke on your true white and scarlet hypocrisy.
Pity your blindness—how you never see

that the eagles of war whose wings lent you glory,
are never no more than buzzards & crows:
Push some wrens from their nest;

steal their eggs; change their story.
The mockingbird sings it; It's all that she knows.

"Oh what can I do?" say a powerless few
with a lump in your throat and a tear in your eye:
Can't you see how their poverty's profiting you?
My country 'tis of thy people you're dying.

—*1966, revised 2016*

Gloria Mehlmann
Cree-Saulteaux · Cowessess

Gloria Mehlmann grew up on the Cowessess First Nation. Her memoir, *Gifted to Learn*, gives an account of her experiences as a public school teacher in Regina and her efforts to shape the curriculum to better reflect First Nations history. In her short stories, Mehlmann writes about life on the reserve during the decade when the men were overseas fighting in the Second World War.

The selection below, which first appeared in *Atlantis* magazine in 2005, provides a fascinating portrayal of life growing up on Cowessess and the chilling effects of residential schools.

Pin Cherry Morning

We three gathered in the doorway of the porch and stood in a pool of morning light. A perfect light—summery and clear. A light that sharpened the red glow of pin cherries beyond the fence wherein each berry marked its depth with a fine black line that ended in a tiny dot, like a pin. The bright light of mid-morning deepened the shadows in the bushes from which hung feathery branches of green and silvery-grey that turned and shifted as if by some unknown force. The thought of pin cherry flavour etching the roof of the mouth in a splinter-burst of tartness, made my jaws ache, made my mouth water.

With the ripe ones, the mouth watering comes twice, I knew. First, the thought of the first bite and its abrupt grab at your jaws in a bright, phantom taste. Second, the actual clamp down of teeth that releases a spring of juices that twist your mouth into new shapes, and even makes your eyes water, if a berry is sour.

Eating pin cherries meant sitting on the tree-pole fence and getting your nerve up. It meant reaching and then grabbing unto a branch where you pulled and raked off a handful and then removed leaves and bits of non-berry to swiftly fill your mouth with one, then two, and more.

The clear air sculpted the cheeks of Tony and Leta, my seven year old brother and little sister who was four. We stood together wondering what to do first: hunt for swimming holes in the bushes where the land dips and fills with rain water, catch tadpoles quivering in small see-through pools near croaking green frogs and toads that look like tired stones, blow feathered dandelion heads off their stalks away into the wind, or find tiger lily "pencils" to sketch with.

"Let's pick berries to see who can eat them without making a face," I say.

Leta doesn't want to, and she says no to a game of tag between the sweet-smelling rows of corn and snow peas on struts, and no to watching the horses in the shaded side of the barn swishing their tails at blue bottle flies. I didn't like to go near the flies. Their bites stung if you weren't watching. I couldn't look at them, sometimes, even with my eyes at the ready—when the rest of me just wasn't. Blue bottles dug through the skin of a horse, Tony said. He knew their babies were inside, in the raised bumps where eggs had been laid. Leta and I once went along to see.

Gladys, our horse, stood lazy in the heat of the sun and twitched her back into rolling rills where invisible gnats danced. Tony put a halter on her and tied her to the corral. She ate carrots pulled from the garden out of our freshly scented hands. Tony told us he'd squeeze the lump and we should watch the top of it. We sat ourselves near Gladys' rump and waited. Tony found a ripe one, he said. We looked. It was near the middle of the horse's back. I knew I wanted to see, and that I couldn't make myself cover my eyes. I knew I couldn't look away once I began. This feeling of my body wanting to run away and my mind wanting to know was strong. I stayed. Proof was coming that such horrible things are real. I marveled that Tony could do this. That he was willing to touch. His tanned hands reached and he placed his thumbs on the flat sides of the lump, and said watch.

"Hold on to Gladys' tail," he called, which I did so that she couldn't switch our faces with her long, black, stinging hairs.

Thumbs came together. Slowly and firmly at first—and then, pop! Out came a dollop of white pus and then up came a short, ridged, creamy maggot, fat as a finger. Part of my mind screamed. It's true! Things are true, even if they are hidden and you can't see. Even under you on a horse you might ride. My skin shriveled as goose bumps of horror rose.

Tony said, "See! I told you!" and then he said, "Roddy ate one for money, you know!"

My mind was saying no oh no oh no when Tony added, "Want me to prove it?" But I was already running, hiding what was possible from my mind.

The three of us sat in the heart of this new day. Leta didn't want to see the horses, and I didn't want the bluebottles. The porch steps grew hot under our feet.

"I know!" Tony said, "Let's see if the robin's eggs are hatched!" His eyes were bright.

Since it is the best idea, we carefully climb down, descending in bare feet down the slivered stairs, cautiously now across patches of prickly grass, past the thistles and a circle of broken glass so that there'll be no days of soaking feet in hot salt water to keep a vein of blood from blackening and running up the inside of one's leg—while siblings move free as wind and water.

The nest has held four beautiful eggs of a miraculous blue all this week. It is a hue of blue mixed from the lightest blue of the evening sky and the greeny white of the burbling stream that catches the morning light. Mom says it is a blue very different from natural things, just the same. It is a blue decided upon by a painter who makes men and children hunt everywhere else and never find it. Now Mom rests quietly inside, out of the heat.

Sometimes, I'd come face to face with what I hadn't hunted for, a thing so strange I hid myself away. One was the cat, a striped orange stray that wasn't our pet. It hung around the barn a lot. There was cruelty when that cat played with its prey, I saw. It gave the mouse hope and then took it away, again and again; it was, "You are free to go," and then, "Oh, no, you don't!" The end was the same, a helpless dob of mouse, sluggish with fear, finally killed. A tiny mouse had made a monster of the cat, and so I hid that day.

I didn't hide about the cow. The cow lost her red and white, wavy-furred calf and she bawled and crashed through the bushes for days, hunting. She ran across our yard and into the fields, her milk sack swinging. We found out much later that rustlers had come to the reserve. Mom said the cow bawled because her udder was full to bursting and needed to be sucked where she hurt. I thought it might be the love of a mother for its missing baby. I wanted it to be that. Otherwise, I couldn't explain to myself the sadness in the cow's call, unless it was a mother's tears. Animals suffered in silence, I knew, like when they gave birth. A bitch in a secret corner of a haystack nearest the barn wall looked for mercy whenever you stared down at her soft mounds of new-borns. Sometimes, in a short burst, an animal called out very suddenly, like when a rabbit was caught in a snare at night, or when a pup got itself stuck someplace. The rest was voiceless.

Our excited anticipation of peering into a sweet robin's nest pulled us forward on tender and watchful feet. Four year old Leta carried herself with the fierce confidence of a bear cub, a little ball of fur used to the watchful gaze of its mother that gives the gentlest smacks in moments of mild direction. The touchstone of getting what you want.

I was Coyote, however, scolded for seeking the boundaries where wildness feeds itself. There might be rules whispered in bear cubs' ears, earnest, sure, and secret. I didn't know these rules and wouldn't keep them. A cub, though, knew to pull itself out of a jam by executing a sweet jump with a half turn. I had neither grins nor sweetness to display, being different. Coyotes keep to the edges of peripheral fields that are neatly trimmed, avoided altogether if there is a Mama bear with a rolling cub crossing.

The world of the bear and the coyote are different, "miles apart" my elders have said. Something tossed over a fence, from the bear's domain, piques the nostrils with smells that are lively and keen in all their variability in the snout— odour-sharpness not the only point of location in the depths of coyote mind. Northern lights sharpen the coyote's wit, the stream cleans its teeth, and a flurry of a pheasant thrills the coyote's fur and lifts its life-sniffing paws. Coyote.

I was given the name Coyote. I could live that way, apart. I stayed out of the baby bear's way. A Coyote is older than a bear cub by a whole year, I knew and it watched and listened for help and trust and a mothers' love in all the growing things.

One peek and it was true. The robins were out! The blue ovals were shattered now, lying in cracked ruins on the floor of the nest. Four reddish-brown sacs of breathing heat-gobs rested there, their dark eyes covered and bulging under a coat of skin. The mother robin was out hunting for food to give to such ugly, fascinating bits of life. Leta pitched herself forward, a cub wanting to see.

"Don't touch!" I called out, behind her. "Mom says if you touch, the mother bird will know and she'll leave her babies to die."

Leta sulked.

Tony considered. "We could take a spoon or something and lay them in a saucer. We could really see against the white."

"That would still be touching!" I said, "I'll tell Mom if you do!"

"We could look at just one and put it right back," Tony said, "I can do it carefully."

"You might drop it!" I shuddered at the thought of such tiny nakedness getting caught in a branch, or worse, tumbling to the ground and into what kind of heap!

Tony said I was a scaredy cat and a tattle tale. Yes, I think, and a coyote that leaves baby birds alone. A coyote that is too curious, still...

Leta slipped into the house and came back with a white saucer. She handed it to Tony. I ran and hid in the porch. But the part of me that wanted to see the operation hung on to the rest of me. I went out, and I didn't call Mom.

The shock I felt was the same as the time Dogin and his twin bother, Big-shyman, called to us to come outside and see a trick that Dogin made up with frogs. Our mothers and we were visiting at Kokum's house, our evening meal done.

"Yes, come!" Dogin called, "You never seen this before!"

That erased my reluctance—seeing something new, the impossible. However, there was usually trouble whenever we joined Winnie's boys. Something either got broken, someone got upset, or there'd be a fight. Tony, Leta, and I never came out on top. Skunkie their big sister, older than all of us, stuck up for the little eight year old twin brothers, no questions asked. She did this by direct physical force, like twisting our arm till we cried and then laughing with cruel scorn at our tears. She'd beat us all and leave us crying together in shame.

I was glad that Skunkie would soon return to the residential school in Marieval because I wanted to reverse the shame I felt, once and for all. I told Tony and Leta my plan. We'd wait in the bushes between our house and their aunt's, where Dogin and Big-shy-man visited most days. We'd ambush them now that Skunkie was gone. It thrilled me and gave me a feeling of cold, too, this certainty of a battle won. When the day arrived, Dogin and Big-shy-man, I knew, would come up the footpath that led from their place, across the stream, past Kokum's, then past our place, and finally through the bushes near our house to their Aunt Flora's, a big, white house standing where the bushes cut away.

I was tense as I crouched in a stand of furry-leafed willows, spear grass, and foxglove where sweet revenge and triumph were contemplated. I told Tony that he and Leta could take on Big-shy-man, the smaller of the two, who cried easily and was considered by us a coward. His mean little mouth pouted innocently whenever his mother wanted answers and he needed only to point at his chosen culprit for the slaps to ring. Though this distressed me and I would take great delight in beating it down, I wanted Dogin. I wanted him to myself, and I insisted on it.

He was as tall as me and every bit as skinny. I knew my knuckles would blast with pain when they connected with his sharp bones. I didn't care. Just last week, he slapped me across the face while Skunkie stood there daring me to hit back. I wasn't about to give into the prodding of a solid 13 year old. She had finished off my seven year old brother, Tony, when he sassed her, didn't she? Worse, she'd pushed little Leta, that day, and forced her to walk backward till she fell in a bear cub heap beside Tony who nose bled and who blubbered like he shouldn't.

Now, "Take that!" Dogin had said to me, smiling brightly.

My face stung and my cheek lit with a painful burn. As if that wasn't enough, Skunkie laughed in my face. She called me a dumb Ojibway, too, and put her arms protectively around her brothers. I wanted to call her a dumb Cree but that was half my family and she had already insulted the whole of my Mom's side. Had I called her a dumb half-breed my Mom would have whipped me. Add to this, Skunkie had the colouring of her father, light brown hair and blue-green eyes that I admired, and wanted.

Walking away, she turned to call to Tony, "Damn good for you!"

Coyotes don't take this lying down, I told myself. But then there I was, down.

At last Dogin and Big-shy-man approached, singing a foolish made up tune. When I stepped out of the bushes I asked Tony to separate the boys. The twins realized their situation in the full.

"It's you against me, Dogin, no one else. So you better fight for your life because you're gonna to get it, this time!"

He knitted his brows in a solid ridge of black, and stood considering his opponent. He put up his fists, and without calling ready I cracked him a punch, square on the nose. Dogin saw his nose spurt blood and screamed for his brother, who was stubbornly trying to tangle with Tony, to run for it.

I didn't want the fight to be over that soon. I had pictured a couple of swift kicks, a head-shaking hair-pull, and a loud, satisfying, open-handed slap on that face. But they ran like lightning and we couldn't leave Leta who had managed to stay out of the battle and who would surely tell Mom, now.

So now here they were, after supper at Kokum's, calling us from the table to join them outside. The thing I had never seen before called just as hard.

I matched my steps to Tony's as he burst into a sprint behind the twins whose speed had picked up down the path. We slammed into our favourite spots in a patch in the road and waited; this, our rallying point, was only a widened hollow in the path connecting our homes. We all played there, our activities over time widening the space that always felt like major territory. The dry mud, ground to a fine powder, felt good to our bare feet.

On this early evening hour, when the sun stretched our shadows to the trees, Dogin went over to a clump of tall grass and came back with a jar. The sealing jar had a live frog in it. Mom and Kokum and all our aunts forever warned us never to touch a frog or we'd get warts all over our hands. So I said I wasn't going to touch it, and Dogin said to just shut up and watch.

He removed the frog from its jar and laid it on its back in the dust. He stroked its white stomach and pressed his thumb on its chin so that it lay stretched out and still, its hind feet like hands reaching. Its heart throbbed under pallid skin. Then Dogin did a horrible, hair-raising thing. He carefully grabbed the two hind legs, one in each hand and waited. "See, he's breathing," he said, and with a jerk, he pulled the legs apart so fast and hard that the frog's body split and its black guts spilled out unto the ground. I screamed. Tony cried out "Aghhhh!" over my screams. I hid my face in my arms hearing the sound of Tony puking and the pealing laughter of Dogin—and Big-shy-man's scornful squeal of a final triumph.

Mom cried when we told her. She said that bad things would happen to us all now, and that we had better be as good as can be so that Dad could come home from the war. For a coyote that might mean not looking at some things, I told myself.

There was another time I very much wanted to hide and not look; but I didn't on account of my little cousin, Marcy. Uncle Earl's big black dog, Frank, licked little Marcy's crotch, that day. How it started, no one knew. She was six. I was six. I had stepped into the room off the kitchen, where Uncle Earl sat with tea and bannock biscuits, and when I looked out the window I caught sight of this. It was strange behaviour for a dog and stranger still to see Marcy holding her panty down and presenting herself to the dog's long, red tongue. I looked at Uncle Earl who lowered his eyes; but he secretly watched the shocking scene, too, despite the need to cherish privacy. It was such an ordinary summer day, otherwise, with the sky very blue and the grass very green and Marcy very, very young. She was so unknowing, in fact, that she had not idea she could be seen; she thought being behind the house was all that was needed, never mind people on the inside, and never mind the window where she saw only reflected sky and trees where the sunlight played tricks.

Mom stepped into the room and stood stalk still. She turned beet-red and said to me, as if something was about to break, "Go and tell Marcy to come in, now!"

The rest was trying to put shame in its place, for Mom. Winnie, mom's best friend, walked into the house later that day to ask what the trouble was. Mom cried that she was so ashamed to have such a thing happen in front of a male relative.

"A girl that young—and so—dirty!" she said. And that was when I wanted to hide but didn't, for Marcy.

Winnie said, yes, she was young. Too young to feel shame. "Besides," she said, "Think—what does any of it mean with everyone so mixed up about things?"

Mixed up or not, the scene to me was the beginning of beguilement. Like a coyote, I eavesdropped and opened my eyes for answers to strangeness everywhere. Because everyone was mixed up—I could tell that would be interesting.

Cousin Roddy was mixed up. Take the day, on the way to town, when he was badly upset. Kokum and my aunts and Mom had to pull him off the wagon and tell him to walk behind till he stopped being a wild man. He yelled and screamed and cried so much, Mom said, because a bad man did terrible things to him in Round Lake School.

The sun was bright and purply lilacs scented the air that day. We got ready to go to town, some 12 miles away. For the trip, Kokum had borrowed a team of horses from Martin Delacroix, a bachelor, who lived in his house across the small stream separating their houses. We needed salt, flour, sugar, and lard, Kokum told him, and green liniment for her legs that were swollen with arthritis and that made her varicose veins pain, too.

The women had to decide what to do with Roddy who was acting up. They couldn't just leave him at home; neither could Martin nor Winnie stay at the house to look after him. He was fourteen and big for his age. His behaviour today would get worse. Mom, Kokum and the aunts stood outside beside the wagon that had slowly filled with blankets to sit on, a box of bannock and a big, dented milk can filled with water. Flies buzzed and sorted themselves out around us.

Twittering canaries and bluebirds flew in and around the garden and lit briefly on the barb-wire fence then flicked off toward the stream. The aunts and Mom stood thinking in their floral summer dresses, ironed earlier that morning, their open-weave second-hand sweaters hanging like sacks over their shoulders. Mom's dark curls were soft and full and she looked nice in her tweed jacket, a man's cut down. Roddy would soon become violent, they said. What would they do with him then, and on the road? The little girls were too young to be left at home. Leta and I could sit on laps, I offered. Aunt Mary's legs were stiff and unbendable with arthritis now and it was impossible for her to climb up and step down—and who could lift her? She, not Roddy, would have to stay home alone, Kokum decided.

Roddy had had fits before. When these began he made choking sounds deep inside him, so deep that he couldn't be found and pulled out, the women said. There were no men to help, either. They were at war across the sea, fighting for the King. They'd just have to risk taking Roddy along, Mom said. Right now he lay on the bed, curled up on his side, saying he couldn't and wouldn't go. His tears showed sadness, not anger yet. And this was a sure sign, the aunts told one another.

Roddy was my second cousin who came to stay with Kokum, on Cowesses, because Aunt Georgina, his mother, brought him back to the reserve from Regina where she was trying to make a living on her own. The residential school, in Lebret, returned Roddy to her the year she left for the city, when he turned 13. It was obvious, Aunt Georgina said, that when he got home he wasn't the person he was meant to be; he was a stranger, broken down. Those bright inquisitive eyes of his were gone.

For a while in their little apartment in Regina, near the General Hospital, he was fine. He swept the courts and did odd jobs for the janitor, for a quarter, every so often. He kept himself clean and tidy.

Aunt Georgina worked as a cleaning lady at "the General." At noon hour, she'd slip home to see Roddy, her work thankfully close by. But soon, he showed no real interest in the places she took him. He acted nervous when out, and sad too, often wanting just to go home. At first Aunt Georgina didn't notice anything. Then one day, after work, she found her newspaper torn up into little bits and strewn in the middle of the living room floor. Roddy refused to answer her questions about it. Another time, he'd grabbed a butcher knife from the kitchen counter and plunged its point into the fabric of the chesterfield in several places. This time, he denied knowledge of it; he seemed as earnestly shocked and worried as she. He cried a lot nights and more frequently during the day, so Georgina brought him home to Kokum's, begging for help.

That was the reason Kokum had him and now asked him to walk into town behind the team and wagon. Half way to town, his eyes grew wild and he hit Tony quite suddenly in the back of the head. No one saw it coming and now Tony lay across Aunt Ena's lap sobbing. This made Roddy flail his arms and legs and scream, in an agony no one understood. Mom told Miriam to grab the reins. She then helped Ena and Kokum wrestle and hold Roddy down in the wagon. They tied a twine plaited rope around his waist. Ena grabbed the reins and the rest of the women pulled Roddy off the wagon. Now he stood there puzzled, trying to smile. His crooked smile was wiped away by sadness and then by anger that took turns in his face as he stood waiting.

Then everyone but he climbed back up and Kokum said giddy-up. The wagon began to move. The rope tightened and Roddy lurched forward. For the next long while, Roddy cried and pleaded and howled and ran up as though afraid. He yelled and screamed and fell back but the wagon kept going. I stared at the strange, terrible sight. Cars passed us and the dust whirled. Roddy grew dustier and more tear-streaked; still, Kokum kept the team plodding, on and on. The aunts cried silently, like her, I saw.

"He needs to go to the hospital," Aunt Ena said.

"We can't leave him there. They'll take him away," Miriam said, and now she too cried.

I tried to keep my eyes open and not turn my face away. But my eyes stung and so I cried, too, because everyone else was, and there was sadness mixed in with other things. Even a coyote's eye couldn't pierce it all.

The sun was burning our backs as we hunched over the robin's nest. Tony had run in for a table spoon and now held it behind him. The new robin sacks throbbed inertly as the gnats and flies buzzed and sizzled next to the nest. Sunlight dappled the ruins and feathery leaves swayed and skip-danced overhead. Swallows and sparrows chirped and trilled in the trees. The air was light on our cheeks.

"Don't you dare!" I whispered sharply to Tony as he brought the spoon nearer the nest.

"Yes!" countered the cub.

"You'll see." Tony was calm. He was intent. I ran away and hid.

My fingers were my earplugs and my knees held them tight to my ears as I sat on the porch step, my eyes shut so tight they hurt. To my left, and down a ways, something was taking place and I couldn't move. Suddenly Tony was speaking to me; he stood above me and asked me to look.

"I got them unto the saucer. Come and look before I put them back!"

"No!"

"Why not?"

"I can't. I don't want to!"

"They're all right. You're scared for nothing. Come and look at how clear you can see. Then I'll put them back. 'Promise.'"

He pulled me up by the hand and I opened my coyote eyes. He pulled me carefully toward the site where Leta sat, her back to us, holding the saucer of birds on her lap. Then Tony screamed, "No, Leta, quit it!"

He was so genuinely horrified that I had to look.

Leta sat there, calmly cutting across the neck of one of the baby birds with a kitchen knife. One already lay separated. There was a sudden and horrible silence without movement.—Except for the sharp rasp of that knife and that small, terrible centre of calm. The territories of the bear and the coyote had been crossed, utterly. Tony's mouth was twisted as he stood there, tears falling, unable to speak.

It wasn't because of the pin cherries.

—*2005*

Doug Cuthand

Cree · b. 1946 · Little Pine

Doug Cuthand is from Little Pine First Nation. A journalist and an independent film producer and director, his numerous features and columns in daily newspapers and other print media have made his a respected voice in Saskatchewan. For decades, his columns have provided important perspectives on the history of the treaties and education, and many of them have been collected in *Tapwe: Selected Columns of Doug Cuthand* and *Askiwina: A Cree World*.

On Canada Day, Remember That Canada Was Built on the Treaties

Canada Day is our national holiday, and while we may not go nuts with the same passion as the Americans do three days later on Independence Day, we nevertheless have much to celebrate.

There are many yardsticks for determining a nation's greatness, but I look to European pickpockets who prize a Canadian passport above all others. A Canadian passport commands the highest price on the black market. Forget the separatists, forget the grumpy old men in the Conservative Party, and forget all the prophets of gloom. The thieves know who is number one.

So how did we become number one? Whom do we thank?

Our history is unique in that with the exception of the conquest of Quebec, Canada was expanded and developed by peaceful means. And the treaties with the First Nations set us apart as a special place.

The role that the First Nations played in the history of Canada is seldom seen in a positive light, but, in reality, the First Nations in the west played a pivotal role in the establishment of Canada as a nation.

The year 2001 is the 125th anniversary of the signing of Treaty Number Six, which ceded large tracts of Alberta and Saskatchewan to Canada. In 1876, two significant events occurred in Indian country. First, the Battle of the Little Big Horn took place, and second, Treaty Number Six was negotiated and signed in Canada.

The Canadian government was worried about the peaceful settlement of the west. *In The Treaties of Canada with the Indians*, Lieutenant Governor Alexander Morris writes that "the gravest of the questions presented for solution ... was the securing of the alliance of the Indian tribes and maintaining friendly relations with them."

Americans were waging a genocidal war against the Indian Nations within their boundaries, and it was spilling over into Canada. American traders were entering the country illegally, and in 1873, there had been a massacre of Assiniboine people in the Cypress Hills.

Also, Sitting Bull would seek asylum in Canada, and later the Nez Percé, under the leadership of Chief Joseph, would try to make it to safety in Canada.

The American philosophy of Manifest Destiny was in force and the Canadian West was filling up with settlers. Earlier, the Americans had fought a war with Mexico and gained the territories of Texas, Arizona, New Mexico, and California. They were now casting greedy eyes on the land to the north.

President James Monroe had earlier stated that the boundary between the United States and Canada should be set at the 55th parallel of latitude. The pressure was clearly on Canada to secure the West before it was lost to the United States.

The numbered treaties began in the so-called Northwest Angle, which was the territory between the western shore of Lake Superior, Fort Francis, and present-day Winnipeg. Treaty One and Treaty Two were located in southern Manitoba and contained different terms than Treaty Three or the Northwest Angle Treaty.

Treaty Three set the pattern that the other numbered treaties would follow.

It was established that the leaders of the First Nations would speak for their people in negotiations, and the leaders would be regarded as heads of state. The warriors and the Northwest Mounted Police held equal status. The treaties were therefore international in character and were made in the name of the Crown, and so should stand up to the vagaries of future politicians.

It was also made clear on both sides that what was negotiated in the future would apply to all. Therefore, Treaty Six may have the medicine chest clause that assures health care, but it was added to future treaties and applies to all because of the spirit of the negotiations. The numbered treaties are incremental and apply equally to all.

However, as an emerging nation that wasn't yet a decade old, Canada received an enormous land base that was assured to remain Canadian. At the time, the westward expansion of the United States posed a real problem for Canada. The Americans were eyeing the western Prairies with greed and a belief in their Manifest Destiny. It was crucial that Canada secure this vast land mass.

After the negotiations were concluded, the Chiefs received red treaty coats to wear on official occasions and to reflect their rank as leaders and representatives of the Crown. They also received a large silver treaty medal and a flag. At that time, Canada still used the flag of Great Britain, the Union Jack. With these symbolic gifts, the treaty negotiators extended Canadian sovereignty over the ceded land. The Chiefs would represent the Crown, and they would fly the flag. This meant that the Americans would have a difficult time taking the Prairies since they legally belonged to Canada.

At the time, the West was sparsely settled and American whiskey traders were moving in. The Cypress Hills Massacre was a result of American fur traders importing genocidal tactics. The First Nations feared the Americans and chose to remain in Canada. Sitting Bull knew of the protection the Crown afforded, and he sought sanctuary in Canada following the Battle of the Little Big Horn.

The First Nations to the south of us fared much worse. Treaties were negotiated at gunpoint, and genocide was the alternative.

Once, I met a group of Aboriginal health educators who'd been to the States to see what programs were being developed and implemented there. Their reaction was, "Thank God we live in Canada." Apparently, there were no innovative programs, and health and education were poorly funded. Schools and clinics were housed in old buildings and budgets were low. It made them thankful that we live in a country that provided meaningful programs in spite of complaints from our leaders.

In the United States, services are provided to Native Americans with an attitude of largesse. There are no treaties of substance, and the country's constitution provides no protection as Canada's constitution does to its First Nations people.

For a brief time, Canada sought an alliance with the First Nations to secure a land that would some day be the envy of the world. The early Chiefs saw themselves as allies with the Crown and Canada, and the government treated them as such. As the West opened to settlement, though, it became apparent that this alliance would change.

The First Nations were partners in the development and establishment of Canada as a country. The First Nations could have made a treaty with the United States, but the choice was Canada, a decision that many more people would also make in the future.

Is 125 Years Such a Long Time?

In the summer of 2001, the 125th anniversary of the signing of Treaty Number Six was commemorated at Fort Carlton, one of the locations where the original treaty signing ceremonies took place.

Treaty Six was negotiated and signed at Forts Carlton and Pitt in Saskatchewan. Later, in 1889, an adhesion was signed for the Lac La Ronge and Montreal Lake First Nations at the north end of Montreal Lake.

My First Nation, Little Pine, signed an adhesion to Treaty Six at Fort Walsh in 1879 along with Chief Lucky Man. They were an independent and difficult group, traits that exist to the present day. Later, Chief Big Bear and his people also signed Treaty Six, but the events of the North West Rebellion overtook them, Big Bear was sent to jail, and the band members were dispersed among the Cree reserves in the Battlefords area and Alberta.

And it isn't as though the treaties are that old. In the 1950s, the Saulteaux and Witchekan Lake First Nations signed adhesion to Treaty Six and received reserve land. The Treaty Land Entitlement Agreement of 1992 recognized the land still owing to First Nations under the terms of Treaty Six.

But I have always wondered about the two solitudes that exist around the treaties: while the First Nations revere them and use them as the basis of their political and historical relationship with Canada, the other side virtually ignores them.

It wasn't always this way. The 50th Anniversary or Jubilee of Treaty Number Six in 1936 was a major event. It was held on the Mistawasis First Nation and attracted a large group of dignitaries and speakers. Apparently, there was even a guy there with a bi-plane selling rides.

My father attended the Jubilee. He told me that Grey Owl, the famous writer and naturalist, was in attendance among the dignitaries. When Grey Owl spoke, he used Cree, but every Cree speaker there knew that he spoke with the accent of someone who had learned the language. Nobody pointed this out, and they let him go on playing Indian.

In 1976, we commemorated the Centennial of the signing of Treaty Number Six. This time, the Beardy's First Nation was the host. Once again, the dignitaries and their spear-carriers showed up, and copies of the original treaty medals were handed out to the present-day Chiefs.

These gatherings have never been viewed as celebrations because the treaties were never fully implemented and we gave up so much. Instead, the milestones have been regarded as commemorating the past and honouring the future.

But the treaties are not old, molding documents. They are part of Canada's national fabric. They are woven into the Constitution. Section 35 affirms existing Aboriginal and treaty rights. The Supreme Court has recognized this, and has pointed out in its decisions that the treaties must be given a "broad and liberal interpretation." In other words, where ambiguity exists, the decision must favour the First Nations.

The treaties read like the colonial documents that they were. The British were famous for promising one thing and doing another; it's how they built their empire.

The text of the treaties promises peace and friendship, a schoolhouse on the reserve, land for families, and other economic and social rights. However, because the treaties were written over a century ago, they're silent on important issues like resource revenue sharing and First Nations governance. Naturally, they also lack consideration of advances in technology over the past century.

Over the years, our leaders have maintained that the treaties cannot be translated literally. Instead, they must be interpreted in their broader spirit and intent. In this way, the text of the treaties makes sense in a modern-day context.

In addition, our leaders have maintained that the treaties between the First Nations and the Crown are international treaties between sovereigns. This, of course, is disputed by the Canadian government, but recourse to international courts, tribunals, and organizations like the United Nations still exists. These are not routes that many First Nations leaders want to take because of the time and expense involved. Instead, the Canadian government must get onside and educate the public about their legal and historical obligations. Inaction is leading to ignorance and misunderstanding.

As a result of the government's resistance, we have ongoing battles with fishermen on both coasts as First Nations fishermen try to exercise their fishing rights and make a living for themselves and their families.

In Saskatchewan, we have a situation where only Indians living on reserves have treaty rights. The federal government has successfully dumped the off-reserve First Nations people on the Province, in spite of the federal government's constitutional responsibility for First Nations people regardless of where they live.

So now we have over 125 years of history behind our treaties. I wonder what the future will hold, and whether the treaties will continue to grow and define our relationship with Canada. The First Nations know which way to go; now it's up to Canada.

An Indian University: Why Not?

In 1996, the Saskatchewan Indian Federated College (SIFC) in Regina celebrated its twentieth anniversary. The SIFC is now considered the flagship of post-secondary education in Canada, but getting there wasn't easy.

In 1972, the Federation of Saskatchewan Indians released a report as a result of a two-year task force on Indian education in the province. The report was an exhaustive examination coordinated by Rodney Soonias from the Red Pheasant First Nation, who now practises law in Alberta.

The report examined all aspects of Indian education and concluded that the best way for Indian people to benefit from education was to take control of it themselves. This message was taken to a Chiefs' meeting, where a strong endorsement was received to adopt a policy of Indian control of Indian education. This was to be a major battle cry of the 1970s.

Previously, Indian education had been the function of the Department of Indian Affairs, and they had created a sorry legacy. The Department's policy was to abdicate their responsibility to the church-run boarding schools, and, later, to dump Indian students on local municipalities by providing money for integrated schools. Both policies failed because they were one-way streets with no parental or community involvement.

The early 1970s was a period of unrest and school strikes. Parents refused to send their children to school off the reserve and insisted on control of their educational programs.

The institution that became the focal point for the implementation of this policy was the Saskatchewan Indian Cultural Centre. The Cultural Centre, an institution of the FSI, was able to receive relatively stable funding, and it became the developmental institution for the policy of Indian control.

The education task force called for the development of a post-secondary academic institution, and the late Ida Wasacase was hired to develop the idea.

The first discussions were with the University of Saskatchewan, which couldn't accept the idea of an independent institution, and so discussions fell through. Meanwhile, the President of the University of Regina, Dr. Lloyd Barber, was sympathetic and worked with FSI officials to develop a college with federated status with the U of R.

Lloyd had an interesting position in the scheme of things. His position was unique because he had an inside view of Indian country. He had been appointed Indian Claims Commissioner as a part of the terms of the 1969 White Paper on Indian Policy. The First Nations leadership had roundly rejected this policy, and Lloyd was caught in the crossfire. He was rejected and ignored as part of the political climate of the day. He sat in his office in Regina and watched the tumbleweeds roll by.

The FSI Chief, Dave Ahenakew, and Sol Sanderson, his Executive Director, met regularly with Barber and briefed him on the issues. He was onside for the establishment of the Federated College.

In 1976, the Federated College became a reality.

In the early days, the college was a crazy place, with lots of freewheeling and political brinkmanship. There was no established funding, and Indian Affairs resisted at every turn. It finally took the political muscle of the FSI to force a funding formula.

The college became a magnet for pioneers and innovators. At one time, the staff of the College was the most international of all the University of Regina's faculties and departments. We had people from Jamaica, Barbados, and Hong Kong. The staff members that passed through the college were of a calibre that they went on to succeed in their future professions. For example, Glenda Simms went on to head the Status of Women, and Gerald MacMaster went on to head up the First Nations Art Department of the Museum of Civilization in Ottawa. Gerald is now an art curator with the National Museum of the American Indian in Washington, DC.

Over the past twenty years, starting with the first graduate, Piapot's Sharon Carriere, the college has graduated over 1,450 students.

The march of progress is a strange procession. It is headed up by the dreamers and pioneers, followed by the builders who make the dream a reality, and finally come the administrators and bureaucrats who make an institution permanent.

The SIFC began as an idea and existed in rented space that was begged, borrowed, and stolen from the University. The Federated College has now undergone major change. The name has been changed to The First Nations University of Canada, and they occupy an exciting new building on the Regina Campus.

But a university cannot be seen as merely an edifice; it is a living centre of free thought that must first exist in the hearts and minds of the staff and students. The college leaders must keep this in mind as they head into the future.

—2005

Margaret Reynolds
Dene · b. 1947 · English River

Margaret Reynolds is Dene from the English River First Nation. Throughout her life, she has worked extensively as a storyteller and knowledge keeper throughout Saskatchewan. The selections below are from *Dene Stories*, originally published by the Saskatchewan Indian Cultural Centre in 1979. Notably, the third selection is about Crowhead, a Dene trickster figure.

The Snow Man

A long time ago, the people of northern Saskatchewan were starving and beginning to die because winter would not go away. For two years the moose, deer and caribou did not grow new horns as they always did in the spring and the ducks and geese did not return from the south. Ice on the lakes and rivers grew thicker and thicker. In their attempts to make holes from which to fish, the people would heat rocks and throw them on the ice but it would still not melt. Something had to be done quickly or all of the people would die.

Finally, in desperation, one man decided to go to Fond-du-Lac to try to snare partridges which he heard were very numerous in that area. After dividing the meagre food supplies with his family, he set out across the ice and snow. Several days later, he met a very strange-looking man who was all frosty and white. Behind this person trailed a storm of snow. Immediately the hunter realized that this creature was Yatth Dene, the Snowman. No wonder winter wouldn't go away! Yatth Dene was staying in Saskatchewan all year around.

Thinking very quickly, the hunter decided that he must fool Yatth Dene into going back up north for the summer.

"What are you doing here?" he shouted to the Snowman. "Don't you realize that the people up north are killing your children while you spend your time here?"

Yatth Dene, remembering his children whom he had left in the north, immediately fled in that direction to see them again.

Since that time Yatth Dene comes to Saskatchewan only in October and leaves again in March to visit his children who stay in the north.

Every summer the moose, deer and caribou grow new horns, the birds return from the south, and the people are happy because they have plenty of food.

The One Who Crossed

Many years before people lived in tribes as we know them today, a woman named Na Ne Ya, was fleeing for her life with her two small children. They had become separated from their people and were now being pursued by enemies. After running for many miles, they came to the shores of a great lake. Na Ne Ya had no canoe with which to cross and to go back would mean sure death in the hands of her enemies.

There was nowhere to go! Na Ne Ya sat down and began to cry, but her misery was soon interrupted by a wolf which came towards her wagging his tail in a friendly way. As she and the children watched, the wolf walked a short distance out into the water then returned to her. He did this several times as if trying to indicate that she should follow him. But how could she escape this way? Neither she nor the children could swim and to walk in the lake would surely mean death by drowning.

The wolf came to Na Ne Ya, licked away her tears and beckoned her to follow him into the lake. Death was all that she would find if she did not escape, so she and the children followed the wolf into the lake. Expecting the water to get deeper, she was surprised that it was no deeper than her ankles. For two days they walked and the water stayed the same depth. After the second day they were safely across the lake. But as she sat on the shore beside her exhausted children, Na Ne Ya wondered where they should go now. Her native land was far across the lake and she knew no one here.

As Na Ne Ya sat deep in thought, staring across the water, she saw something moving. Her first thought was that her enemies had followed her. She watched, paralyzed with fear. As they came closer, she saw that it was not her enemies—but a great herd of caribou. Here was food for her and the children. Quickly she ran from the shore and hid behind a ledge of rocks until the caribou came ashore. She sprang out of her hiding place and with her hunting knife, killed one. Now they could eat!

The Caribou were quickly moving away and Na Ne Ya knew that if they were to obtain a steady source of food, they should stay with the caribou. After their meal, she called the children to follow her. The oldest refused to go, so finally she left him there. As she left, he was still sitting by the fire, happily eating the caribou that had been killed.

This boy was to become the father of the Eskimo people, while the child who went with Na Ne Ya became the father of the DENE people.

Crowhead

Crowhead, a legendary hero of the Dene, always wore a crow-skin which was his medicine. This cape warned him of the approach of enemies.

One day two girls angered Crowhead by making fun of his cape.

"We'll make a birchbark canoe and leave this place," he said to the orphan he had raised as his grandson.

In a small valley, they found some birchbark and began to cut it. As they were doing this, some people on the other side of the valley began to throw snowballs at them. Crowhead told his grandson not to mind them. They took the birchbark and returned back to the camp.

At the camp, they found that the Cree had killed all the Dene. Crowhead put the bodies in a heap and went to build his canoe. Worms appeared on the bodies. Crowhead put his cape over the bodies and lay down on it. He told his grandson to wake him up at noon the next day. While Crowhead was sleeping worms crawled into his nose, ears and mouth.

At noon, the boy woke his grandfather and they left in the canoe and paddled north to the Barren Grounds. When they arrived there, they stopped and Crowhead made many small lodges. He then lay down and used his medicine.

"Let all the dead be in the lodges," prayed Crowhead. At this time all the worms emerged from his nose and mouth, and by his magic became people once more.

After the Cree had killed the Dene, they started to go home. Crowhead used his medicine to change the direction they were going. The Cree were surprised to find themselves back near the place Crowhead and his grandson were. When they saw the man and the boy, they decided to kill them immediately.

"Grandfather! Wake up! The Crees are here!" shouted the boy.

Crowhead awoke and saw the Cree coming to the shore in their canoes. He took the boy down to the river and hid him under the bark of a rotten birch tree and quickly made holes in the bark through which the boy could peek.

"Stay in here and watch," he told his grandson.

Crowhead was a small man. He went down to the river with a blanket over him and pretended to be mourning the death of his relatives. The Cree saw him and thought he was a child.

"There is no use in killing a child with a pointed arrow," they said.

They used blunt arrows that just bounced off Crowhead. The Cree landed at the shore and Crowhead ran off into the bush. They chased him, throwing off his blanket; he quickly turned to face them. He wore his crow-skin cape and protected himself with a deer horn.

The Cree were surprised! They had expected a child, not a man! He ran at them and broke each man's right arm and left leg. The Cree were afraid—this was Crowhead! They tried to run, but he ran ahead and smashed their canoes.

Crowhead called the boy out and told him to take a spear.

"Take it and kill the enemies, grandson," he said.

Because of his grandfather's powerful medicine, the young boy was able to do this.

One of the Crees, who lay dying, said, "If it were only you, without Crowhead, you couldn't do this!" The Cree had recognized Crowhead's powerful medicine.

Later when the boy went to find his grandfather he could not find him. He ran all over, searching frantically, and finally, several days later, he saw Crowhead approaching.

"Why are you crying, my boy?" he asked.

"I thought you were lost!" he replied.

"Well, there is no time to cry. Our people are all alive. Let's go back to the lodges," said Crowhead.

The two set out, and as they approached they could hear laughter and singing. They also heard some crying and went to a lodge to find out what was wrong.

"Two of our people are missing. We think the Crees killed them!" wailed one woman.

She looked up and recognized the two missing people. Everyone was together and happy. All were alive except the two girls who had laughed at Crowhead's cape. He did not give them life again.

—1979

Tom Jackson
Cree · b. 1948 · One Arrow

Tom Jackson was born on the One Arrow Cree Nation. He is an actor, singer, producer, and activist, well-known as the creator of the Huron Carole, a touring musical production that raises donations for local food banks, and for his role of Chief Peter Kenidi on CBC Television's *North of 60*. Dubbed "minstrel with a message," Jackson has also had a prolific career as a singer and songwriter, and his songwriting has become his vehicle for social change. He has been the recipient of numerous awards, including the Humanitarian Award by the Canadian Academy of Recording Arts and Sciences. The songs below were released on Jackson's 2015 album *Ballads Not Bullets*.

Blue Water

In her eyes we will always be equals
One blue drop in her forest rain
Hear her voice in the cry of the eagles
Singin' love is gonna lead the way

We all need blue water
We all need to lead the way
We all need blue water
We all need to lead the way

We'll sail the seven seas and find a new direction
Thirsty tears we will wash away
There are thorns in the crown of perfection
But love is gonna lead the way

We all need blue water
We all need to lead the way

We all need blue water
We all need to lead the way

There will always be rainbows
There will always be a better day
I believe there is a kingdom in tomorrow
And a child of love will lead the way

The world's future is in our hands
It is our home and our native land
We all need to understand

We all need blue water
We all need to lead the way
We all need blue water
We all need to lead the way

—2015

Vacation
(by Tom Jackson and David Cramer)

Teach the way to the children
The harmony that grows within
Can light the spark and rise again
The flame that's died in holy men

Take me on a vacation
Where liberty is free
Take me on a vacation

Take me on a vacation
Where liberty is free
Take me on a vacation

Dictator feed the old regime
Young people seek democracy
Man hunt black gold in my country
They make big hole the land she bleed

Chorus

The bird of prey sit in the tree
The woman seek equality
Let me go swim in her sea
And keep big shark away from me

Chorus

Teach the way to the children
The harmony that grows within
Can light the spark and rise again
The flame that's died in holy men

Chorus (repeat)

—2015

Elder

The Creator has given us a song
We all have a song
We must sing it loud
It makes us strong
It makes us proud

It is a birthright
We own it
It's forged by
Love, peace and wellness

A musical compass
Guided by compassion
Inspiring hope
To imagine defiance
Against oppression
And the sounds of silence

A song that is sung and celebrated
It will not be denied

We all have a path
You must find yours

And when you do
He will walk it with you

The earth is our mother
Be humble and believe
That the land was in the cradle
Before man was conceived

When you feel the cool of the summer fountain
Feel the strength of the Father
In the mountain

Like the sun and the moon give light
Mother Earth gives life

We must protect her

—*2015*

Priscilla Settee
Cree · b. 1948 · Cumberland House

Priscilla Settee is from Cumberland House. She has worked extensively as an activist for Indigenous women's rights throughout her life, helping to open a shelter in Prince Albert for women facing domestic violence. She has also been on the board of the Indigenous Women's Network, and in 2013 she was awarded the Queen Elizabeth II Diamond Jubilee Medal for her work. She is the director of the Indigenous Peoples program at the University of Saskatchewan.

The selection below is from the Introduction to *The Strength of Women: Âhkamêyimowak*.

Introduction to *The Strength of Women: Âhkamêyimowak*

There is a force among women which I call âhkamêyimowak, or persistence, that provides the strength for women to carry on in the face of extreme adversity. Âhkamêyimowak is a Cree word and embodies the strength that drives women to survive, flourish and work for change within their communities. Women are the unsung heroes of their communities, often using minimal resources to challenge oppressive structures and to create powerful alternatives in the arts, in education and the workplace.

In the Indigenous world, stories are a means of transmitting vital information from within our community as well as outside of our communities. The stories of women are central to my life and my work as a university professor and community activist. What sets [*The Strength of Women*] apart from other books about women is the central role of culture, the tenacity of women's spirit and the importance of political activism. These stories will, I hope, inspire future generations with pride, commitment and hope.

Since the early 1970s, I have worked with Indigenous women at the local, regional, national and, later, international levels, setting up homes for battered women and addressing other human rights abuses such as structural unemployment, inadequate housing, and the failure of mainstream education to assist our youth. Since the late 1970s, the global community has been my home and my working space. Over the years, I have developed relationships with colleagues and friends as I learned about Indigenous struggles in many regions of the world. I have been inspired to learn the stories and saddened to realize the inequities that exist not only in faraway places in the world but also right here at home.

I believe that it is important to analyze the situation of our Indigenous communities within a larger context—a set of relations, as it were. Relations are something fundamental to Indigenous communities the world over. Besides our human relationships, there is a bigger set of relationships that keep some people marginalized and others in positions of power. *The Strength of Women* tells the stories of both sets of relationships. Some women tell powerful stories and others describe institutional relationships that keep Indigenous women in Canada—along with women generally, people of colour and Indigenous peoples and youth around the world—in the margins. In both cases, the clarity of vision that comes from existing in the margins is astounding and compelling.

In the Cree world view, a core value is *miyo-wichihtowin*, which means "having good relations." Individually and collectively, people are instructed by cultural teachings to strive to conduct themselves in ways that create positive relationships with our extended community. The concept of extended community and family is fundamental in Indigenous communities. Aunts, uncles and grandparents are surrogate parents. The community is an extension of the family.

The idea of relationship is extended to the animals and the natural environment as well. These are ones who cannot speak for themselves, but whose existence is essential to human survival. The extended community takes in all relationships, human and nonhuman, and is reflected in our interdependence. The women of Sheshashiu, Labrador, and Grassy Narrows, Ontario, have stood up to environmental polluters and risked being thrown in jail to protect their homelands. Reference is made to the concept of "all my relations," which means that all living things are related and must be cared for by one another. Service to humanity is primary.

Cree values are embedded in natural laws called *wakohtowin*. The circle symbol reflects the equality of all people and their capacity to care for, nurture, protect and heal one another and the land. It is important to emphasize the holism of non-industrialized Indigenous peoples. As a university professor, I try to help my non-Indigenous students see their relationships with Indigenous peoples. We share environments, communities, lands and resources. Our human survival is interconnected.

Community norms have been disrupted by colonialism, including the intentional breakup of families, communities and nations, by imposed borders, residential schools and the accommodation of new settler populations, who now have third, fourth and fifth generations. We say that all people except Indigenous peoples are immigrants and some have seniority, usually the ones that make all the rules.

The Western capitalist system promotes educational individualism and moving ahead of fellow human beings; this undermines what is at the heart of the concept of *wakohtowin*, the betterment of all our relations. Historically and today, our domestic and political issues originate in our relationships with the church and the state and their establishment of empires. The establishment of empires has meant the deconstruction of traditional cultures and their economic systems. As part of the legacy of colonialism through the residential school experience, children were routinely sexually and physically abused, humiliated and beaten for speaking their language. So many children died from abuse, disease and loneliness as a result of this horrific time in history that some refer to the residential school period as the Indigenous holocaust.

Colonization has been particularly devastating for Native women. Economic analyses fail to describe the multiple ways women have disproportionately suffered under colonization from sexual violence and forced sterilization to the undermining of women's central role as community organizers, planners and leaders. One of the tragic aspects of Canadian history is the disappearances and deaths of over five hundred young Native women. Many had been fostered or adopted at a young age. Some had been incarcerated and had unresolved personal issues and addictions. While some were involved in prostitution and risky lifestyles, many were simply in the wrong place at the wrong time. Many were homeless, most lived in poverty, and all were targeted as Aboriginal women. To this day, public and societal indifference continues to leave Aboriginal women at risk.

Indigenous women are the unrecognized backbone of our communities, who build social support networks and keep our culture intact through their struggles to establish relevant educational institutions and keep our languages alive. Women preserve the social, cultural and natural foundations of their communities and establish norms that retain traditions and challenge undemocratic practices. Women's economic contributions are seldom counted. Women challenge the status quo by being on the front lines when the world's wealthiest transnational corporations carve up our lands and pillage them through free trade agreements and multinational investment agreements, with the license of undemocratic bodies such as the World Trade Organization and their financial partners.

Women from Canoe Lake in northern Saskatchewan worked on the front lines when our communities were being clear-cut by forest company giants. Women, including elders, were jailed in Sheshashiu, Labrador, while attempting to stop NATO war games on their lands. Today, women fight racist elements in the state and sexist elements in their communities. Many university classes I have taught are attended predominantly by women who sustain families single-handedly, and become educated in order to provide for their families. There is a saying that a nation is not conquered until the hearts of its women are on the ground. We are living proof that hearts can rise, hope can flourish, peace can exist and a new world can be built.

Colonization's continuing legacy is now transforming our communities into globalized market places at the fringe of "development." Many urban marginalized people immigrate from northern communities that suffer from economically deprived conditions and lack economic infrastructure and services expected in southern communities.

UNIFEF's report on child poverty in developed countries ranks Canada near the bottom for children's well-being, at 17 out of 23 countries. Single mothers and their children under the age of seven live in poverty. A UN human rights committee noted that the number of food banks in Canada grew from 75 in 1984 to 625 by 1998. Another UN committee on human rights criticized Canada for adopting policies that have increased poverty and homelessness among many vulnerable groups (such as children and woman) during a time of strong economic growth and increasing affluence.

In Canada, human rights violations have meant a "boil-water" condition in large numbers of communities, epidemic suicide rates among our youth, structural unemployment rates of 60 per cent and more for the majority of our communities, early death from preventable diseases, outstanding land claims and outstanding residential school settlements. This, while both provincial and federal governments make record profits on our resources, which have never been signed away or ceded.

Clear cuts, mercury poisoning, oil exploration, sour gas plants, bombing ranges, dams and mines have taken tremendous tolls on communities, causing never-before-seen cancers, mercury poisonings and loss of traditional economies, which are replaced with capital-intensive projects that export profits outside the communities and leave communities poisoned and unfit for human survival, forcing people to urban centres where they face housing crises and gang threats.

Currently in Canada there are a number of front-line attacks on Indigenous sacred lands: The Lubicon Cree, who are fighting further oil exploration in an area where treaties or First Nations land entitlement have not been settled. Dudley George, an Anishnabe man, was murdered by Ontario Provincial Police for defending his land at Ipperwash Park, Ontario, in 1995. Today, the people of the Mohawk nation are engaged in violent opposition and attacks within their own territories. In northern Saskatchewan, the Buffalo River Dene Nation have taken their case to the World Court to challenge the loss of traditional hunting territories. These four cases are the tip of longstanding claims against the governments of Saskatchewan and Canada. In March 2008, several leaders from Ontario were jailed for opposing uranium and platinum mining.

Provincial prisons are filled to capacity. So desperate is the situation in the Saskatoon provincial jail that prisoners are stockpiled in small cells and forced to use pails for toilets.

The questions I ask are, is this what the original treaties were signed for? Is this what free and informed consent is about? Is this what human rights amount to while daily the wealth of the top income earners in Canada amounts to millions and billions of dollars? These are conditions that make a sham of the Canadian constitution, under which Indigenous peoples are promised protection. Indigenous peoples have the constitutional right to have prior, informed consent to what happens on their lands.

Indigenous peoples feel the impact of globalization, which is no more than a continuation of the brutal economic and political processes of colonialism and imperialism of the past centuries. These conditions have motivated millions of Indigenous peoples to build linkages and develop the United Nations Declaration on the Rights of Indigenous Peoples. The most comprehensive non-binding agreement ever written, it has the endorsement of the world's some 370 million Indigenous peoples, or 7 per cent of the world's population. Indigenous peoples are no insignificant force. They are from diverse geographical and cultural backgrounds, with a tremendous range of knowledges that have contributed greatly to global food security but have never been acknowledged or compensated. Since colonization, they share commonalities such as: lack of basic health care; limited access to education; loss of control over land; abject poverty; displacement; human rights violations; and economic and social marginalization. In 2007, the Declaration of the Rights of Indigenous Peoples was ratified without the support of Canada, Australia and New Zealand, the countries with the most significant Indigenous populations. In its opposition to the declaration, our federal government claimed, incredibly, that the declaration contravenes Canadian laws, including the Canadian constitution and the Charter of Rights and Freedoms. Despite Canada's intransigence and arrogance, the declaration represents a commitment by the signatories to meaningfully consult and engage in partnerships in legislation and policy that will affect Aboriginal people in Canada. The failure of the Canadian government to ratify the declaration is a cause of great concern, but the declaration is a victory for people who strive for democracy.

What is to be done?

There is a need to right the historical wrongs. Treaty land entitlement and Métis claims must be settled to ensure royalties from lands and resources are paid to fund economic development. Emphasis must be placed on social economies and putting women and families at the centre of development and economic analysis. As Indigenous peoples, we are not asking for handouts, we are demanding that the terms of treaties be honoured, those treaties that granted new immigrants rights and conditions to share our lands. For First Peoples, these rights are spelled out in section 23 of Canada's constitution. Even before the Canadian constitution, it is important for people to understand, Indigenous peoples always had people-centred economies, but also ones that lived within natural laws and had respect for nature. It is good that other people are starting to share the value and importance in such simple and sustainable concepts. As people recently removed from the land, we welcome partnerships that promote sustainable development, as we believe the current development process is irrelevant, costly and hugely unsustainable.

As Indigenous peoples struggle with the shackles of colonialism, it is important to draw on the strength and wisdom of ancient values, wisdom and knowledge to create strong and vibrant communities. We ask you to share with us in that collective process. As though he had sat around a campfire and listened to the wisdom of my ancestors, my colleague Dr. David Korten, author of several books on social economics, has stated:

> Humanity's collective demand on the regenerative capacity of Earth's ecosystem grew to exceed the limit of what can be sustained. To create a world that works for all, public policy must give priority not to aggregate growth, but to using the resources of planet and society equitably and sustainably to provide healthy, fulfilling lives for all people and other living beings. It means reorganizing economic life to produce more of the things that people need—like food, shelter, clothing, education and health care—and less of the costly things we do not—like military hardware, pollution, traffic jams and white collar

crime. Hope for the human future rests, therefore, not with institu-
tions of power, but with the millions of individuals like you who have
gathered here, to see solutions to the reality of our collective crisis.

As the great Dakota visionary Chief Sitting Bull urged, "Let us put our minds together and see what future we can make for our children." His thoughts are echoed in the preamble to the 2000 Earth Charter:

We stand at a critical moment in Earth's history, a time when humanity
must choose its future. As the world becomes increasingly interdependent
and fragile, the future at once holds great peril and great promise. To
move forward we must recognize that in the midst of a magnificent
diversity of cultures and life forms we are one human family and one
Earth community with a common destiny. We must join together to
bring forth a sustainable global society founded on respect for nature,
universal human rights, economic justice and a culture of peace.

—2011

Beth Cuthand
Cree · b. 1949 · Little Pine

Beth Cuthand is from the Little Pine Cree Nation and grew up in Saskatchewan and Alberta. Cuthand attributes her love of stories and writing to the times travelling with her father, Stan Cuthand, an Anglican minister who visited communities throughout the prairies. She worked as a journalist from 1975 to 1983 before teaching at the Saskatchewan Indian Federated College (now First Nations University) from 1986 to 1992. She holds a master's degree in creative writing from the University of Arizona, and has published two books of poetry, *Horse Dance to Emerald Mountain* (1987) and *Voices in the Waterfall* (1989). Her poetry is characterized by a sharp humour and a sense of the oral voice from the past within the present.

Were You There
for Joy Harjo

Were you there
on the White Sands?
Did you feel that primal wind
caressing the pores of you skin?
Did you smell the salt
of the old sea or

hear the silence roar
louder than the bombs
that blew on
Hiroshima or Nagasaki?

Were you there in Ottawa
when we rose as one
spontaneously
like a prayer for
all that we had been
and ever hoped to become?

Did you feel it then?
The whispered words of beings
older than their
laws or constitutions?

Were you there in the pine forest
in communion with those old trees
who keen for the people
laden with their burden
of grief and disrespect?

Were you there when the army
attacked the Kanesatake?
Did you feel the wind
shift
and blow the tear gas
back
on the Destroyers?

Were you there on the hill
when we called the Thunder?

It rained

and the land was green.

—1990, 1992

For All the Settlers Who Secretly Sing
for Sharon Butala

You have seen my ancestors
riding in buckskins
down the coulee into the trees.
You have watched them
frightened that it is you who intrudes
awed, that it is you who sees.

You have met the hawk
soaring above you as you sit
still
waiting for the land to speak
to you who have not heard her
since you fled your lands across the seas.

At night you dream of drums
and hear voices singing
high in the night sky
and you wonder if the northern lights
are more than they appear to be.

And you hold these questions
in your heart not daring to ask
the indigenous people who hold
themselves aloof from settler voices
chattering.
You know they think no one listens
and you understand
the stillness it requires
               and the faith
               and the faith
to hear the heart beat of the land
as one solitude not two.

And you dare not tell the others
her song rises in you
yet it rises and you sing

secretly   to the land
              to the land

And then she knows sister/brother,
that you belong here too.

—*1992*

Blair Stonechild

Cree-Saulteaux · b. 1950 · Muscowpetung

Blair Stonechild is Cree and Saulteaux, and is from Muscowpetung. He is a professor of Indigenous Studies at First Nations University of Canada. His works include *Loyal Till Death: Indians and the North-West Rebellion*; *The New Buffalo: The Struggle for Aboriginal Post-Secondary Education in Canada*; *Buffy Sainte-Marie: It's My Way*; and *The Knowledge Seeker: Embracing Indigenous Spirituality*. The selection below is a brief excerpt from Stonechild's seminal work, *The New Buffalo*, an important study that helped conceptualize a new vision for Indigenous education, while still connecting it to tradition.

Excerpt from *The New Buffalo*

In the process of claiming sovereignty over Canada, the British Crown assumed control over all the land and its resources in exchange for benefits that would be given to First Nations. The spirit of the treaties is such that First Nations were to receive something of significant value, and, in the case of the Numbered Treaties, this was largely represented by the demand for education that would enable future generations to share in the bounty of Canada. This access to opportunity extends to post-secondary education and implies that First Nations individuals should have unlimited access to any training for which they qualify. In addition, Aboriginal people should have the right to establish and control post-secondary institutions as a means of ensuring culturally appropriate and effective programs. Such a measure of compensation is modest indeed when compared to the value of resources from which Aboriginal peoples have been alienated. Given the removal of Aboriginal peoples from their original ownership of the vast resource wealth of the land, and lacking any major redirection of natural or financial resources, there exists, at the least, a moral justification for Canada to provide adequate funding for Aboriginal higher education.

The issue of jurisdiction over First Nations post-secondary education is complex and controversial. The federal government's current policy is to limit First Nations aspirations by delivering such education as a social program only in order to bring First Nations participation rates to a level comparable to the rest of society. The difficulty with such a strategy is that it does not deal directly with the notion of rights, and until this is done, perception will exist that government can arbitrarily cut funding at any time. The federal government must be explicit about its intentions by enacting legislation that will empower Aboriginal higher education institutions with the benefit of permanent funding. Canadians and their governments need to accept the notion that First Nations are a part of the national landscape, as are provinces and municipalities, and that Aboriginal citizens, treaty or otherwise, have legitimate entitlements to funded post-secondary education, both as individuals and in terms of controlling their own institutions.

Such unique collective rights are politically difficult to justify because they run counter to the liberal ideology of equal rights for all individuals, and, therefore, are highly unpopular for Parliament to entrench in legislation. However, the product of such a policy could be well-functioning Aboriginal communities with highly educated and motivated individuals who will be committed to, and play an important role in, contributing to the vision of the country. Being allowed to pursue this "new buffalo" will mean that future generations of Aboriginal peoples will not only have a special and unique ability to participate in post-secondary education, but will be able to acquire the tools that can one day enable them to contribute at the highest levels to the country they know as their homeland.

The challenges of finding more equitable means of delivering Aboriginal post-secondary education and of building Aboriginal self-government capacity will be a major test of governments' resolve to bring about major improvements in the lives of Aboriginal peoples.

—*2006*

Rita Bouvier

Métis · b. 1951 · Ile-a-la-Crosse

Rita Bouvier was born in Ile-a-la-Crosse. She holds a master's degree in Education from the University of Saskatchewan and has taught in the areas of Indigenous education and social justice. She has worked for the Saskatchewan Northern Governance Task Force, the Gabriel Dumont Institute of Native Studies and Applied Research, and the Independent Oversight Committee on Métis Elections Saskatchewan. She has also served as a Coordinator with the Canadian Council on Learning–Aboriginal Learning Knowledge Centre partnership at the University of Saskatchewan. She has published three books of poetry: *Blueberry Clouds* (1999), *papîyâhtak* (2004), and *nakamowin'sa* (2015). The selections below explore memory, language, family relations, politics, and history within the context of the Aboriginal experience in Canada.

Running Dream

I am deer leaping
over thick brush
air scented
cranberries over-ripened
earth's perfume
I have travelled here once
yet, I have never been
an arched stone way
leading from the forest
to the open sea
all around me now
the forest has fallen
a man on the road
cautions me
return, return, return
I gaze back
the forest now
a sketch of ancient ruins
a sea so green
a sky so blue

—1999

bannock and oranges

the alarm clock sounds
far, far away, uncertain
of place, perhaps too many
hotel rooms. I can't count.

they are all the same
a dull bedspread here
a bedside table there.
lamps, always too many
a chair for company
that never arrives.
an empty, dank smell
everywhere I turn; me
wishing I was home
except this morning.

something on the table
catches the morning light
memory brings clarity.
bannock and oranges
still, against a backdrop
of freshly washed linen
as I had left them late
last night when I returned
to my nowhere hotel room
after a visit with my mom.

a schooled eye can see
that what was once ordinary
is not so in morning light
the preparation like communion
between your wrinkled hands.

I remember watching you
slice the bannock—aroma fresh
toasting it medium, and then
buttering it, sparingly
my unique preference
among nine siblings
juice spurting on your hands
as you sectioned oranges
placed them in a scrubbed
plastic recycled yogurt tub
so I would not go without

no still life can be more beautiful than
bannock wrapped in freshly washed
pressed white linen graced with
sectioned oranges in a recycled yogurt tub

—2004

Riel is dead, and I am alive

I listen passively while strangers
claim monopoly of the truth.
one claims *Riel is a hero,*
while the other insists, *Riel was mad*

I can feel a tension rising, a sterile talk
presenting the life of a living people,
sometime in eighteen eighty five.
now, some time in nineteen ninety five

a celebration of some odd sort.
I want to scream. listen you idiots,
Riel is dead! and I am alive!
instead, I sit there mute and voiceless.

the truth unravelling, as academics
parade their lines, and cultural imperialists
wave their flags. this time the gatling gun
is academic discourse, followed

by a weak response of political rhetoric.
all mumbo-jumbo for a past, that is
irreconcilable. this much I know
when I remember—I remember

my mother—her hands tender, to touch
my grandmother—her eyes, blue, the sky
my great grandmother—a story, a star gazer
who could read plants, animals and the sky.

—2004

songs to sing

it was here in the Northwest,
the free traders and coureur de bois
of the XY, Northwest and Hudson's Bay companies
arrived from the east singing their songs,
searching for riches the land held.
it was here they stayed, were swallowed
into the place of no good-byes;
just *kitahtawî kawâpimtonaw*—
a humbling gesture to the energy of
this place that gives and takes on its own terms.

it was here they learned the importance of
wahkohtowin from our mothers—fire keepers,

who knew *askiya*'s contours and medicines
feeding the body, the mind and the spirit.
reverence, not too strong a word for its generosity.

here in the Northwest,
the free traders and coureur de bois
voyaged the York boat brigades each spring;
no river or portage ever too long
or arduous, as long as they had fifty songs to sing.

it is said that as they launched their boats
white pelicans soared above them in kinship
for their journeys up and down the *misinipî*, north
to the McKenzie, northeast to Hudson's Bay, sometimes
southeast to *kihcikamî* and west to the Rocky Mountains.

wingtip to wingtip they flew directly above paddlers
like veteran pilots on a mission, bidding farewell—a safe journey
down the waterways, the rapids like wild white horses and snakes.
and then, it is said, the pelicans soared back again
on reconnaissance   returning to their flock.

it is said that by day they were accompanied
by the mnemonic sonic songs of
kiŷasak—gulls, *les cilowî*—sandpipers
terns and shorebirds of all kinds;
the men paddling in perfect time   fifty songs to sing.

it is said that by night, they were guided
by a new silver moon as it paled—
hallowed be thy name. all the while
the waves cresting over sparkling rough waters;
the paddlers mesmerized   fifty songs to sing.

it was also here in the Northwest,
the free traders and coureur de bois fought family
in competition for rich furs
until trade   and then food declined;
the land exhausted   no song to sing.

a new way of being arrived, a slight shift in the wind—
an ominous hush telling of what was yet to come.
when it came, they say
it blew in from the south—*sāwanohk ohci*
hungry, feeding like a wild man-animal—

piyakwan wihtikō wīnō.
it gorged itself, eating
oils and minerals, diamonds   and spirits
with which it is blessed *holy Mary,*
mother of God, wīcihinān—help us.

still though, when the wind rests for the night
and the moon comes out to show her shine
slip-sliding, shuffling across the night sky
to an old paddling song from days gone by,
you too, will hear the chorus line they sing,

alouette, gentille alouette,
the paddlers on their way home their flock awaiting.

—*2015*

little lemon yellow sailboat

eyes half open, I awaken
bright morning light streaming
through the window overlooking the Gorge.

on the far bank sits
a little lemon yellow sailboat
marooned   no owner in sight.
my heart skips   remembering
that little rowboat with oars
my papa built   sized to fit.

to à la Grosielle I would row,
embarking on many as trips as necessary
to carry all my cousins to the tiny island.

the island a perfect size for children
to wander—to play on the sandbars
with pelicans and gulls all day.

across the way, under a canopy of pines
the figure of a man rises.
in slow, measured time

he walks over to the lemon
yellow sailboat on the shoreline
its paler yellow sail in the wind.

there is a glint of something shiny—
a ceremonial movement
of hand to mouth as he drinks.

he stands still for the longest time
looking down the inlet and then
walks the perimeter of his sailboat.

he climbs in, places the bottle on the ledge,
and begins wringing a rag over the edge.
done, he returns to the shaded canopy.

there, he sits waiting …
while I drift into the blue beyond   floating
in my little rowboat   borne up into clouds.

—*2015*

SkyBlue Mary Morin

Métis-Cree · b. 1951 · Ile-a-la-Crosse

SkyBlue Mary Morin was born in Ile-a-la-Crosse, of Cree and Métis ancestry. Her work has appeared in several anthologies, including: *Seventh Generation: Contemporary Native Writing* (1989); *Writing the Circle: Native Women of Western Canada* (1990); and *Let the Drums Be Your Heart: New Native Voices* (1996). Her poetry expresses the spiritual path in life, the blessings of the Creator, and the power and strength of women.

As You Lie Sleeping

As You lie sleeping
in the winter season
I marvel at your Beauty.
Such a short time to rest

preparing for the work ahead,
My Mother, the Earth Mother
from whence Life comes
in the circle of Life.

Our Mother, the Earth Mother
I see and feel your pain
constantly having to Heal
the wounds of profit makers.
I want to expel my insides
as I watch the chemicals
spew forth from Your Body.
The Scourge and Rape continues.

As Thunder comes to awaken
you from much needed slumber
I see your Rebirth, New Growth.
As you become Forceful
carrying Floods to distant places,
providing paths for Hurricanes,
Quaking from your Insides
I am certain you are strong.
But can you last, Earth Mother?
I pray the offerings of Tobacco
I give to you will help.
I pray our Respect grows
for your Sacredness,
and keeps you Strong;
for should you Cease,
so will the People.

—*1995*

Legacy of Residential Schools

Kayas oma, ka machi payak pi mat so win.... Long ago since the beginning of Life
E kis ki na ma ko yahk ta sa ki hi yahk Kihchi Manito.... taught to respect the
　　Great Spirit
E kis ki na ma ko na me yo pi ma ti so win.... the Teachings of the harmony
　　Way of Life
that whatever we do in life.... would affect the next Seven Generations.

"Kihchi Manito ka ka na wemik, awasis.... Creator will always be with you
    my child
Father Sky gives sacred breath of Life.... Mother Earth nourishes with food
    and water
Always honor Father Sky and Mother Earth.... they will honor you with Life
Your Indigenous nature name, your kinship with Creation: Mother Earth and
    Father Sky, Grandmother Moon and Grandfather Sun."

Respect for the Mi'kmaq, the Montagnais, the Algonquin, the Huron
Respect for the Iroquois Confederacy, the Six Nations Hau de no sau nee:
    the Mohawk,
the Oneida, the Onandaga, the Cayuga, the Seneca, the Tuscarora
Respect for the Abenaki, the Odanak, the Wabu-Aki, the Anishnawbe Ojibwa
Respect for the Nehiyo Cree, the Assiniboine, the Stoney
Respect for the Blackfoot Confederacy Niitsitapi: the Blackfeet Nation, the
    Peigan Nation, the Kanai Nation, the Siksika Nation
Respect for the Coast Salish: the Nootka, the Kwakiutl, the Bella Bella, the
    Bella Coola, the Haisla, the Nisgaa, the Haida, the Tlingit
Respect for the Dene Nation: the Denesuline (Chipewyan), the Tli Cho, the
    Yellowknives, the Gwich'in, the Slavey, the K'asho Got'ine and the Tsuut'ina
Respect for the Inuit, the Inuvialuit, the Innu and the Halfbreed Métis

Government made laws for First Nations, Inuit, Inuvialuit, Innu and Halfbreed
    Métis Nations
the 1857 Gradual Civilization Act passed to assimilate Indians
started with Prime Minister McDonald's directive.... "to take the Indian out
    of the child."
1870 to 1910 Period of Assimilation.... was colonization, a period of devasta-
    tion, demoralization
mutual objectives of government and churches, assimilate native children
    into Canadian society
Slavery was abolished in 1838 in the British Colonies, abolished 1865 in the U.S.A.
But, Canada enslaved First Nations, Inuit, Inuvialuit, Innu and Halfbreed
    Métis children.

1876 Indian Act enacted under The British North America Act, Britain's
    Constitution
Treaties with the Crown across the land making Indians British subjects of
    the British Crown
Kept them on lands reserved for Indians....

Left the halfbreeds fallen through the cracks of their society, the Halfbreeds
who set up camps on Road Allowance ditches, open land between highway
and settlers' lands.

Indian Chiefs forced to starvation finally took Treaty in 1882.... learned of
broken Treaty promises in 1885
Indian Act prohibited cultural ceremonies and ceremonial dances.... kill the
culture and you will kill the Indian Nations
Chiefs protested they were not subjects of the Queen, that the land did not
belong to the Queen
imprisoned Chiefs who hid their people for survival.... wrongfully accused,
tried for treason
sentenced to years in stone prison institutions, died shortly after surviving
government prisons
Warrior Chief portraits hang on prison institution walls to commemorate
spoils of war.

1885 Battle of Batoche led by Louis Riel.... the Halfbreed Métis Nation fought
for land and a "way of life", their culture and language
The Halfbreed Métis got small settlements of land.... some got scrip worth a
dollar an acre
the dollar for the acre of land that they sold.... when they needed food to feed
their children
many Halfbreed Métis continued to live in tents on Road Allowance ditches
or "the other side of the tracks" the uninhabited side of town, in shacks and
tents
or the poor side of town, the ghetto where the poorest people lived in the
poorest housing
To deal with the halfbreed problem after Battle of Batoche, government created experimental work farms for the Halfbreed Métis.... to teach new
skills of survival....
taking away their hunting and trapping skills.... leasing land that would never
be theirs.

1895 Indian Act prohibited gatherings and ceremonies that shared goods and
money
Sharing, the very basis of our cultural teachings, basis of a nation's community
survival
helping each other through the hard times, supporting each other through
the winter seasons

government stopped the economy of humanity.... all part of controlling economic status
enfranchised Indians, took their status away.... all part of controlling their
status in life.
still, First Nations, Métis, Inuit, Inuvialuit and Innu
enlisted in the Army & Navy, to help Canada fight in the War.

Then the mass exodus of children from Indian Reserves, Métis and Inuit
communities
By horse, by wagon, by car, by truck or by plane
Exodus to Industrial Schools for learning, mostly as child labor to service the
Industrial schools
Exodus later to Residential Schools on lands reserved for Indians
compulsory attendance for children seven to fifteen years
children forcibly taken from their families by Indian agents....
by red coated Northwest Mounted Police then the Royal Canadian Mounted
Police
arresting mothers and fathers if they stood in the way....
the dark era of our parents, grandparents and great grandparents.

To take the Indian out of the child.... stop the language, call it the devil's
language, machi manito pe kes kwe win, or evil, machias.... and.... it is not
good, mwe me yo sik....
learn the language, use it against them in a broken attempt at speaking our
Mother's tongue.... insensitive to dialect, inflection and gender.
Break their hearts through emotional abuse.... with names like savage, pagan
and heathen
Put those racist names in school books, use them in schools as ownership and
spoils of war.
Tell them lies like your parents don't want you.... don't love you
Take their kinship away.... cut the ties to cousins, aunties and uncles, grand-
parents and great grandparents
So they will forever lose their connection to family and community.

E pe oh ti nah chik awa si sahk.... they took the children away
O papa wa ekwa o mama wa e ma to chik.... while mothers and fathers cried
Carrying the hurt and pain, anger and rage for more than a hundred years.

"Believe in the Great Spirit my child, Kihchi Manito, as you are taken away
by the Indian agent

Believe in your heart, your parents, your family, your community loves you.

Your heart, the way of love, sah ki hi to win, will keep you strong.... to keep the nation alive

Your heart pumps the life blood of our nation.... your blood, the life blood of proud ancestors.

Believe in the Great Creator my child.... Kihchi Manito, Great Spirit will keep your Spirit strong

Your kinship with nature Mother Earth and Father Sky

Grandmother Moon and Grandfather Sun will keep you strong.

Life is a Circle, my child as our ancestors have taught us through oral history

since time immemorial since the beginning of all life.... What goes around will come around."

E man sah ki we sta ka ya.... they cut their hair.... their spiritual connection to Mother Earth

while indigenous children with long sacred hair stood in fear of long robed priests and nuns

As they force children to memorize, recite foreign prayers.... learn the hierarchy of a new god

force through spiritual abuse.... where traditional native songs and chants turn into hymns

taking away their nature name.... giving children names of saints to take the child's soul

taking away children's name giving them a number.... that would forever replay in their mind

force through mental abuse.... calling children dumb and stupid.... to believe the craziness

as if the nuns and priests weren't crazy trying to change their god's creation....

force through physical abuse, beating the language out of children.... hits to the head with wooden rulers and sticks, sometimes wooden planks.... straps with a machinery belt....

making children wash their bodies in lye soap, brush their teeth 'till they bled

physical pain forever implanted in the body and brain.

force through sexual abuse the final assault.... raping children, teaching children to rape,

their attempt to break the Spirit, Heart, Mind, Body.... our medicine wheel of Life.

From a Circle of Life taught children to jump into square boxes and form straight lines

counting 1 little, 2 little, 3 little Indians, made a song about counting our little Indians....
took away their sacred feathers, medicine pouches and animal kinship ties
dressed them in foreign clothes and foreign uniforms where everyone dressed the same
teaching little boys to march all with military precision preparing them for the Army
dressed in business ties for photo ops with the Indian agent.... and government inspectors who came to government inspect their schools.

By 1931, eighty Residential schools colonized First Nations, Inuit, Inuvialuit, Innu and Métis Children, compulsory attendance for all children now six to sixteen years
Breaking children's bones if they didn't listen.... no one would know or question an accident
hiding children's dead bodies behind residential school buildings to hide their crimes
Using children as sexual objects.... no one will know or believe that a man of god did this
Breaking children's spirit by teaching them the fear of God and burning in hell
Fear of their own Pipe Ceremonies, Sweat lodges, Yuwipi and Sundance ceremonies
Fear of their own sacred objects: prayer pipes, ceremonial rattles and drums
so they will ever be fearful to return to their culture.

Children's spirits lurk from hiding places.... behind those residential school walls
where children left their spirits to protect themselves.... from residential school horrors
crying alone children, beaten children, raped children, broken spirit children.

In 1996, the last government run Indian Residential School closed
Over 150,000 Indian Residential School survivors survived the horrors of abuse
thousands and thousands of former Indian Residential School students
launched lawsuit after lawsuit of wrongs done, lost language and lost culture.
that would have bankrupt the Canadian government.
A court ordered Indian Residential School Class Action Settlement Agreement
offered compensation for the Common Experience of loss of language and culture
common experience of braided hair cut and bodies washed in lye soap
common experience of strappings with machinery belts and wooden yard sticks.

In the independent assessment process compensation on physical harm and
    sexual abuse
Residential School Survivors need to prove their allegations against church
    and government
Residential School Survivors' experiences are questioned for truth
Survivors have to prove they were at a Residential School, prove their abuse
    and name their abusers
Survivors say, they are being abused again through the process of compensation
as old wounds open.... reignite the trauma that needs to begin the healing
    process....

And then, Reconciliation to tell their Residential School experience to docu-
    ment the wrongs
to teach Canadian Society through the Truth and Reconciliation Commission.
Residential school stories accepted as truth, to be heard as a person, experi-
    ence validated
This is all part of the healing process of Residential School Survivors.
Apartheid through the Residential School system lost six generations of children
this is what the Canadian government has done.... the vision of Sir John A
    McDonald.

Now, we pick up the pieces of our legacy of our life experience through colo-
    nization
the legacy of First Nations, Inuit, Inuvialuit, Innu and Métis nations
Today, some Residential School Survivors live with their private pain
not wanting to relive painful trauma and horrors of residential school experience
Today, many Residential School survivors are living forgotten and homeless
Rough sleeping on the streets, parks, back alleys and dumpsters
This is our sixth generation of grieving survivors from Residential Schools
homeless, society's system of exclusion.... homeless discriminated because
    they are homeless
society excludes instead of includes.... the numbers keep increasing
homeless in the grieving state of addiction.... drinking and drugging to kill
    heartfelt pain
homeless chased away from street agencies by other homeless
acts of territory and desperation perpetuate society's exclusion.

Today's Seventh Generation.... some homeless youth at risk, couch surfing
    with friends
not knowing they are homeless....

some lost youth lost in hopelessness and addictions, drowning in abandon-
    ment to suicide
We need to give youth spiritual hope there is a better tomorrow,
Rekindling love of self and cultural pride to increase self-esteem
Showing our youth cultural pride through showing our own cultural pride
Healing their hearts with love and understanding
Honouring their bodies with sacred touch only, with sacred and loving words
    only....
Reclaiming the sacredness of kinship and relationships, reclaiming kinship
    of aunties and uncles and cousins, reconnecting with Elders, reclaiming
    their place in community
Guiding their wandering spirits through spiritual connection to life
teaching youth spiritual strength through ceremonies
So, they may find hope and strength of heart and spirit when all else fails.
We have always been there for them.... they need to know.

Today's Seventh Generation, our leaders of tomorrow
taught through the Haudonasaunee Great Tree of Life, the Way of the Mide wewin
The Way of the Seven Rites of the Lakota, they Way of the Medicine Societies
the Way of the Sacred Pipe, the Way of the Sweatlodge Purification Ceremony
The Way of the Yuwipi, the Way of the Sundance
The Way of the Potlatch, the Way of the Tea Dance
And the Way of the Purification Ceremony smudge
Today's Seventh Generation, taught through the Seven Sacred Laws of Life
We need to teach and reach through cultural experience each generation to come
Need to show our youth love, love of Creator, Mother Earth, community and
    family
And to reconnect with them through the natural laws of the land.

The Seven Sacred Teachings....
need to teach our youth Respect.... through respecting sacredness of life
need to teach our youth Courage.... it takes courage to do what is right
they were born to be brave like their ancestors before them braver than brave....
need to teach our youth Honesty.... to walk the Red Road in an honest way
to be honest with others and true to their word
Need to teach our youth Wisdom.... from the blood of our ancestors
Show them that they have sacred wisdom within.... ke mam to ni chi kahn
Need to teach our youth Humility of humbleness and service to others
to give thanks to the Creator at sunrise for life and at sunset for the day
Need to teach our youth Truth to live with truth, integrity and honor.

Today's Seventh Generation, carrying on a healing legacy
using the Teachings of the Four Directions, the Circle of Life: spirit, mind,
    heart and body
Reclaiming ceremonies, sacred songs and prayers to Creator
Reclaiming teachings of Fasting and Vision Quest
Teaching youth about their culture, respect and connection to the land
Kinship with Mother Earth, Father Sky, Grandmother Moon and Grandfather Sun
Because they will be the teachers when the earth changes come
And every nation will seek their help and understanding

For all my relations.... Kah ke yo ni wah ko ma ka nahk....
Residential School Survivors have truly survived a holocaust....
Honour their stories as they purge their pain....
teach their history to the generations to come.... the legacy imposed by colonizers.

Iko si anma.... Kah ke yo ni wah koh ma ka nahk....
That is all.... All My Relations

—2015

Jo-Ann Episkenew

Métis · 1952–2016 · Regina

Jo-Ann Episkenew (nee Thom) was born in 1952. She was Métis, originally from Manitoba but a long-time resident of Saskatchewan. In 2006, Episkenew was awarded a Ph.D. from Ernst-Moritz-Arndt University in Greifswald, Germany, making her the first Indigenous Canadian to receive a Ph.D. from a German university.

She was a professor at the First Nations University of Canada and the Director of the Indigenous Peoples' Health Research Centre. The selections here are from her 2009 award-winning book on residential school literature, *Taking Back Our Spirits: Indigenous Literature, Public Policy, and Healing.*

Excerpt from *Taking Back Our Spirits*

Policies that Controlled Indian Education

[...] Because they fall under the jurisdiction of the federal government, Status Indians often fall into a jurisdictional quagmire when dealing with areas designated as provincial responsibility under the Canadian Constitution. Even though education in Canada falls under provincial jurisdiction, the education of Status Indians became the responsibility of the federal government. Thus, it was the federal government that was responsible for the policy that created residential schools for Indian children.

Of all the policies that the colonial regime initiated, the policy that established and regulated the residential school system had, and continues to have, the most far-reaching destructive effects on both Indians and not-Indians in this country. Over the last twenty years, many former students have publicly revealed that school officials abused them in every way possible: culturally, physically, emotionally, sexually, and spiritually. Government and church records not only confirm these reports, they also provide evidence that school officials neglected the students by failing often to adequately provide the necessities of life: food, clothing, health care, and, ironically, education. Currently former students have filed more than 10,000 civil suits against the Government of Canada and the churches that operated the schools for their abuse of Indigenous children. The Anglican Church of Canada teeters on the brink of bankruptcy because of these suits. John S. Milloy writes that "in thought and deed the establishment of this school system was an act of profound cruelty rooted in non-Aboriginal pride and intolerance and in the certitude and insularity of purported cultural superiority." Former students agree.

Colonial officials reasoned that, by controlling the education of Indian children, they could bring about the complete assimilation of the remnants of the Indian tribes into civilized society. To that end, they looked for an appropriate model after which to design an educational system for Indian children. Indian leaders agreed that their children needed to learn "the cunning of the Whiteman" and favoured the day schools that had been operating on a number of reserves for many years. The colonial officials disagreed. Because the children spent the greater part of their days at home, their families exerted a stronger influence than did schools. The children who attended day school were not being assimilated into colonial society. They still thought and behaved as Indians. Even worse, the colonial officials discovered that these children could become formidable political adversaries when they merged the European-style schooling with their traditional Indigenous education. This had already happened with some of the highly educated Métis of Red River and was beginning to happen with some of the graduates of Indian day schools. Day-school education had armed these children with the skills they needed to negotiate and argue with colonial officials and had made their graduates skilled advocates on behalf of their people. This was not the end that the colonial regime desired. Another alternative, then, one that the regime could control, was necessary. Turning their gaze to the few church-run residential schools that were already in operation and to the American industrial schools for Indians, colonial officials found the model that would become the cornerstone of their assimilationist policies.

The colonial officials and the churches considered adult Indians lost causes but believed that there could be hope for the children if all things Indian were eradicated from their thinking. They reasoned that, by removing Indian children from their families and communities and placing them in an environment where they would be taught to think, act, and believe as civilized Christians, Indian children could be completely resocialized. In his 1887 memorandum to Prime Minister John A. MacDonald, then Deputy Superintendent of Indian Affairs Lawrence Vankoughnet quotes a clergyman whose words formed the principles for the residential school policy; he writes:

> *Give me the children and you may have the parents, or words to that effect, were uttered by a zealous divine in his anxiety to add to the number of whom his Church called her children. And the principle laid down by that astute reasoner is an excellent one on which to act in working out that most difficult problem—the intellectual emancipation of the Indian, and its natural sequel, his elevation to a status equal to that of his white brother. This can only be done through education....Only by a persistent continuance in a thoroughly systematic course of educating (using the word in its fullest and most practical sense) the children, will the final hoped and long striven for result be attained.*

Since Christianization was a component of the "long striven for result[s]," Indians could not be assimilated into civilized society if they were not Christianized. Consequently, the colonial bureaucrats assigned the churches a central role in the implementation of the policy. The residential schools would become a concrete representation of the colonial regime's "ideological commitment to suppress the native culture as rapidly as possible and fashion a new generation of Indian children raised in isolation from their parents, in the image of the white man." Thus, the Indians who did not disappear as a result of disease would disappear by way of education.

The churches already had experience delivering European Christian education to Indian communities because re-education had always comprised an important component of their missionary agenda. The churches had established both day schools and the first residential schools many years before the colonial regime considered positioning schooling at the centre of its Indian policy. Day schools had achieved a moderate degree of success, but church officials had difficulties persuading Indian parents to send their children away from their communities to attend the boarding schools. Indian parents wanted their children to attend school to learn the "cunning of the Whiteman"; however, they also wanted their children to be educated in their own communities where the extended family was the cornerstone of not only their societies but also their educational system. Furthermore, Indigenous people doted on their children and wanted to keep them at home where they would be safe, which was another thing that the colonial officials found problematic. Because of their strong familial ties, few students stayed for long at boarding schools where they experienced great loneliness. Some clergy, such as Father Lacombe in Alberta, recognized this as a problem and "did their 'best to prevent these departures,' but to no avail. The constant 'excuse to go,' rooted in the pain of separation, 'was and is always the same—We are lonesome.' Nothing would make them stay."

In addition to being situated far away from the children's loved ones, residential schools had earned a poor reputation in many Indian communities. Former students returned with stories of inadequate food and abuse at the hands of the staff, and as a result many students refused to stay at school. Rather than improving conditions as a means to improve student retention, the churches complained relentlessly to the colonial regime. As a result, in 1920, the colonial regime amended the *Indian Act* to make school attendance mandatory for every Indian child between the ages of seven and fifteen. If the children did not attend, truant officers or police would investigate. The courts would fine or even incarcerate parents who did not comply. From 1920 onward, the policy that created and regulated resident schools and their students would eventually affect every Indian in Canada.

Beneath their rhetoric of noblesse oblige and moral superiority, the colonial regime had other, more self-serving, motives for removing children from their homes and placing them in the residential schools. By the time of Confederation, Indian communities were in a severely weakened state. Disease had reduced their populations while the number of European immigrants continued to grow. Indians had suffered severe economic losses because the colonizers no longer needed them as important trading partners. At the same time, their traditional economy was laid to waste as European immigrants and their descendants claimed more and more land. Buffalo herds on the Great Plains were shrinking in number. Indian nations were concerned for their very survival. Yet, despite their weakened state, the colonial regime and their settlers still feared the Indians. A goal of the Canadian government policy that mandated attendance at residential school was to coerce Indian people to obey the dictates of the empire. Their means of achieving this goal was to hold Indian children hostage during their stay in residential school. Both churches and colonial officials agreed that Indians would be less likely to engage in hostile and disruptive acts if their children remained in the custody of the schools.

Residential education became the keystone of the colonizers' Indian policy, whose aim was to eradicate all things Indian in Indian children. The classroom activities comprised but a small component of the overall assimilation strategies that the regime ordered the schools to employ. Each school was to become "a circle—an all-encompassing environment of resocialization. The curriculum was not simply an academic schedule or practical trades training but comprised the whole life of the child in the school." Understanding culture as the complete life way of a people, the regime mandated school officials to change every aspect of the children's culture: their dress, food, language, religion, manner of working, and interpersonal relations. When they first arrived at school, school officials issued new clothes to the children and destroyed their old ones. The next act was to cut their hair. Agnes Grant, in her study of the effects of residential schools on former students, describes how soul-destroying this seemingly trivial alteration in appearance was to many Indian children. But changing the students' appearance was only the beginning. Understanding that language is a critical vehicle of cultural transmission, colonial officials identified eradication of the students' Native languages, followed by their acquisition of English, as paramount to their resocialization efforts. Accordingly, colonial officials developed a policy that ordered schools to prohibit students from speaking in their Native language with a goal of ensuring that students spoke and thought in English. To achieve that goal, school officials punished students who they caught speaking in their Native languages. Often that punishment was swift and severe. Many former residential school students talk about "losing" their ability to speak in their Native languages. What is more likely is that their language development was curtailed because they could only speak covertly and only to other children. By the time they left school, many students had forgotten some words and had never learned others. Speaking only to other children, except during brief holiday periods, these children had had no chance to expand and enrich their knowledge of their Native languages and to acquire the sophistication in language expected of adults. They continued to speak as if they were children. Most of these children became only minimally proficient in English, often learning their new language from francophone priests and nuns who were barely conversant in English themselves. Although the students now dressed like White children and spoke a nominal amount of English, they still thought, worked, and related like Indians, albeit confused and frightened ones.

Colonial officials planned that the Canadian schools, like their US industrial counterparts, would teach basic literacy and numeracy for part of the school day with the remainder of the day devoted to instruction in the trades for boys and domestic education for girls, thereby applying the same gendered division of labour as was the norm of the colonizer culture. This segregation of the curriculum by gender as defined by European patriarchal conventions and its subsequent privileging of the masculine was very damaging to Indian students and to future generations of Indian people. Although the division of labour in Indian societies was typically gendered, the gender roles were not the same as those of European societies, and the masculine was not automatically privileged. In those nations that engaged in agriculture, for example, farming was typically women's work. Women from those nations would sneer at any men who attempted to usurp their role by attempting to farm. Indeed, some Indian societies considered the women to be the owners of the land. How shocked young Indian boys were when school officials ordered them to work on the school farms. By attempting to make them over into farmers, the school officials effectively emasculated these young men.

Gender complementarity was more often the norm in Indigenous cultures than was the gender hierarchy that prevailed in colonial society. Often women were strong political leaders or healers, and nowhere in this country were women mere appendages to their men. Together, men and women formed the circle—a central symbol in many Indigenous nations—with each gender comprising and supporting one-half of the circle that was their community. Women and men were deemed to be of equal worth because, without the support of both genders, the circle would collapse. In the same way, women and men in Indigenous societies fulfilled roles and functions that were complementary in order to support their communities and, thus, ensure the survival of their people. By imposing a European patriarchal and hierarchical model of gender roles and values onto the curriculum of residential schools, the colonial regime committed another direct assault on Indian cultures. Through the curriculum, they taught Indian children to devalue their own societal norms and, worse yet, to devalue the women in their communities—their grandmothers, mothers, aunts, sisters, future wives, and daughters.

Because the colonial regime did not provide the schools with adequate funding, school officials had to find ways to make up the chronic funding shortfalls. Under the industrial school model, each student worked in a trade that supported the operation of the schools, which were designed to be self-sustaining. Boys worked in the barns and chicken coops, and girls worked in the tailor shops and kitchens. School officials sold agricultural produce to make ends meet rather than using it to provide students with healthy diets. Although their work supported the production of food, the students' diets were often poor, and the quantity of food they received was minimal. Furthermore, because the colonial regime funded them on a per-student basis, the schools admitted as many Indian children as possible resulting in over-crowded conditions where diseases, such as tuberculosis, flourished. Because the students' diets were poor, their health care inadequate, and their living conditions cramped, the death rates of Indian students were inordinately high. Ironically, without the children's labour, the schools could not function as businesses, yet running the business of the schools became more important than providing a good, or even adequate, education for the students. At many schools, the students knew that food was available and were aware that the staff ate a much more substantial and appealing diet than they did. This has become a theme in literature about residential school, such as Maddie Harper's *Mush Hole*, Lee Maracle's "Charlie," and Oskiniko Larry Loyie's "Ora Pro Nobis," to name but a few. The children's awareness of this injustice—of how little value both colonial regime and churches place on them—caused them to feel enormous bitterness.

Perhaps it was the emotional starvation, rather than the physical, that has had the most damaging effects not only on the children who attended the residential schools but on their children and grandchildren as well. Students felt bitter about the absence of emotional support and the cruelty of the punishments that school officials meted out at school. Because many staff believed that Indians indulged and spoiled their children, school officials were very deliberate in their efforts to ensure that no form of emotional comfort was available for the children. To that end, they instituted the truly mean-spirited policy of discouraging student contact with siblings of the same sex and prohibiting contact with siblings of the opposite sex.

Government policies of fiscal restraint resulted in the residential schools being rarely able to attract top-quality staff. Few teachers considered residential schools desirable places to work, and as a result most top-quality teachers, and indeed even mediocre ones, sought employment elsewhere. The challenges of resocializing a people whom most Whites thought of as savages while being housed in chronically underfunded, isolated institutions made residential school employment unattractive to teachers who had other options. Thus, residential schools became convenient "dumping ground[s] for less-competent church staff." Not surprisingly, the teachers and staff who were hired often lacked the stock of educational resources and strategies that might have enhanced the prospects of success for the colonial regime's grand experiment in resocialization. Without such resources to draw upon, teachers and staff often turned to violence—both physical and emotional—to coerce children to learn and obey. The schools' primary focus quickly shifted from resocializing Indian children into civilized people to enforcing order and discipline. School officials punished students cruelly in a variety of circumstances.

However, there was an even darker side to residential school staffing. Because they afforded staff unlimited access to children, absolute power over those children, and little scrutiny, residential schools attracted disproportionate numbers of pedophiles, who were free to wreak havoc on generations of Indian children. It should come as no surprise to learn that, as time progressed and students suffered physical, sexual, and emotional abuse at the hands of the school staff, some learned to abuse each other. This is part of the psychopathology of abuse. Children learned from example and experience. Often student abuse of other students was institutionalized and incorporated into the structure of the schools. School officials appointed children to monitor, and often discipline, other children—a practice that missionaries also employed with adult Indians to monitor the behaviour of their converts on the reserves. In "Returning," Louise Halfe remembers "the girl with the big lips" who hit the other children with rulers, abusing them on behalf of the nuns. By demonstrating favouritism to some children and not others, school officials effectively divided the students as a community and instilled fear, suspicion, and distrust. Many former students clearly remember learning to abuse each other, both verbally and physically. As a result, the children learned to mistrust their classmates and isolate themselves from others. And, above all, the children felt anger but, having no outlet to express their anger, they repressed their feelings and suffered intense shame.

Shame had been part of the hidden curriculum of residential schools since their inception. In the minds of the school officials, both teachers and staff, the Indian children in their care were savages from an inferior race in need of civilizing. They did not hesitate to communicate this to the children, and, not surprisingly, the children learned to feel ashamed of their very identities as Indigenous people. Shame and fear were also part of the missionary agenda of the schools. As part of the process of converting Indians to Christianity, school officials taught students that they were pagan savages and, therefore, would burn in hell if they persisted in practising their traditional ways. Beatrice Lavallee, an elder from the Piapot First Nation, told how, as a young child, she would on countless occasions come home from residential school terrified that her *Kohkom* (Nêhiyawêwin for "your grandmother") would go to hell because she was not a Christian. Like Lavallee, the students were isolated from any alternative discourse and, as a result, believed their teachers.

Predictably, Indigenous children at residential school began to exhibit behaviour that today would be labelled post-traumatic shock response. PTSR coupled with cultural differences resulted in students being reluctant to make eye contact or speak up in class. Having experience teaching White children only, many staff members interpreted this behaviour as a sign of their students' inherent racial inferiority. Rarely did these supposed educational experts bear in mind that the students were terrified. Students were not afraid to tell their families and communities about the physical and emotional abuse that they experienced at residential school, however. Stories of beatings at the hands of school officials were commonplace in Indigenous communities, and students learned quickly that their families had neither the power nor the influence necessary to protect them. In his memoir *Indian School Days*, Basil Johnston explains how students often felt shame for and anger towards their parents because they were unable to protect them from the agents of the colonial regime. Neither the family nor the children had the power to stop the physical and emotional abuse that the children endured at school. Indeed, their powerlessness seemed to be proof of what the schools taught them. If the power to defend one's self and one's family is a measurement of worth, then Indigenous people had less worth than White people did.

The students who had been sexually abused were much more reticent to tell family members about their experiences—feelings of terror caused them to keep silent. The foundation of the contract implicit between sexual abusers and their victims is silence, and abusers use every method at their disposal to ensure that their victims keep the secret. Although stories of the sexual abuse of Indian children did not become public until well after the last residential school closed, the consequences of this abuse revealed itself in Indigenous communities where some children who had been abused grew up to abuse others. In "Nitotem," Louise Halfe describes how a young man rages against women on the reserve, raping them while remembering the nun who abused him.

Given the children's soul-destroying experiences at the residential schools, it should come as no surprise to learn that the students continued to suffer emotionally and socially long after they left school. The negative consequences of the education that students received at the residential schools became apparent as early on as 1913, when Indian agents began to notify the colonial officials that when the children returned to their reserve they did not display any of the positive effects of education that the officials had projected. Instead, they were "stranded between cultures, deviants from the norms of both." The schools' wanton disregard for the identity formation of their students and the way that those students fit into their societies tore at the social fabric of Indigenous society and affected relationships within Indigenous communities and with settler society. In its 1992 memorandum to the deputy minister of Indian Affairs, the Assembly of First Nations explains: "The residential school led to a disruption in the transference of parenting skills from one generation to the next. Without these skills, many survivors had had difficulties in raising their own children. In residential schools they learned that adults often exert power and control through abuse. The lessons learned in childhood are often repeated in adulthood with the result that many survivors of the residential school system often inflict abuse on their own children. These children in turn use the same tools on their own children." Therefore, the pattern continues so that, often, Indigenous people who did not attend residential school still exhibit the same behaviours as those who did. Both Vera Manuel in her play "Strength of Indian Women" and Robert Arthur Alexie in his novel *Porcupines and China Dolls* describe the intergenerational effects of residential schools.

By the second or third generation of Indigenous children attending residential school, "the Department [of Indian Affairs] had to struggle with the consequences for Aboriginal people of Canadian economic development and its own assimilative policies: broken communities, dysfunctional families, and their 'neglected' children." Churchill points out that

> in the end, of course, the racial biases of the settlers were such that there were precious few jobs for graduates, even of those demeaning varieties. Thus "disemployed," they were mostly forced into a posture of seemingly immutable material dependency upon those who most despised them. What the residential schools in effect produced were generations of increasingly desperate and dysfunctional human beings, incapable of valuing themselves as Indians and neither assimilated nor assimilable into the dominant society which had rendered them thus. Given the sheer impossibility of their situation, the self-negating pathologies evidenced by residential school graduates were, or should have been, perfectly predictable.

As part of the colonial regime's policy of assimilation, residential schools failed. Few students succeeded academically, and those who lived to return to their communities came home emotionally wounded and uneducated in the ways of both White and Indigenous societies. Residential schools, then, have contributed to the positioning of Indigenous people as an underclass in Canadian society.

The regime was well aware of the failure of its policy of assimilation as early as 1946, following receipt of a report on that policy written by a joint committee of the House of Commons and Senate. Nevertheless, the colonial regime persisted with the policies with only minor revisions until the last school closed in 1986. Buckley writes that "the tragedy is the educational system that they got, which no way fitted them for Canadian society. It was a cheap and cheerless package judged good enough for an unimportant minority." The damage that these schools inflicted on Indigenous communities is unparalleled.

—*2009*

Erroll Kinistino
Cree · b. 1952 · Ochapowace

Erroll Kinistino is from the Ochapowace First Nation. He works as an actor, drama instructor, director, writer, and singer. He is best known for his role as Leon in the CBC television series *North of 60*, and for playing the role of Creature Nataways in the first run of Tomson Highway's *Dry Lips Oughta Move to Kapuskasing*. Kinistino continues to work in film, television, theatre, and music, and has become a respected and familiar presence in performance projects throughout the province.

The selection below is one of Kinistino's many songs. He says: "the song was written about my mother Rosalie Kinistino (nee Belanger) in her house on the edge of the Ochapowace Lonesome Prairie. This song was inspired by a painting, by her cousin Maurice Louson, Chewat, from the Kahkewistahaw First Nation. It was also written after she purchased a white 2003 Pontiac, Grand Prix, GT, with her Common Experience Payment from attending the Brandon Indian Residential School, 1939–1949."

Kokom's Kaddillac

Do you wanna ride, Kokom's Kaddillac?
Do you wanna drive, Kokom's Kaddillac?

She came a long way, from the Red River cart,
The Horse and the buggy, with her Indian heart.

Kokom's Kaddillac, (Hey yah Hey!)
Kokom's Kaddillac, (Hey yah Hey!)

Do you wanna ride, Kokom's Kaddillac?
Do you wanna drive, Kokom's Kaddillac?

Geronimo asks her, "Where you get your wheels?"
Big Bear's in the back, trying to grab the wheel, of

Kokom's Kaddillac, (Hey yah Hey!)
Kokom's Kaddillac, (Hey yah Hey!)

(Bridge)
(Hey Hey Hey!) (Hey Hey Hey!)
Kokom's Kadillac!

Do you wanna ride, Rosebud's Kaddillac?
Do you wanna drive, Rosebud's Kaddillac?

She came a long ways, from Ochap Lonesome prairie,
With Mushom's oxen, and his Model A!

Kokom's Kaddillac, (Hey yah Hey!)
Kokom's Kaddillac, (Hey yah Hey!)
(fade out)
(Hey Hey Hey!)
(Hey Hey Hey!)
Kokom's Kaddillac!

(stop)
"Poor old Noko, thinks it's a Cadillac!"

P. O. N. T. I. A. C.

—*2008*

Sky Dancer Louise Bernice Halfe
Cree · b. 1953 · Saskatoon

Louise Bernice Halfe, or Sky Dancer, was born in 1953 on the Saddle Lake Reserve in Alberta. At the age of seven, she was sent away to Blue Quills Residential School, but left for the public school at the age of sixteen. She received her B.A. in Social Work at the University of Regina in 1991 and worked in Saskatchewan in drug and addiction counselling. She was first published in 1990, in *Writing the Circle: Native Women of Western Canada*, soon becoming one of Canada's foremost Indigenous poets. She has since published *Bear Bones and Feathers* (1994), *Blue Marrow* (2004), *The Crooked Good* (2007), and *Burning in this Midnight Dream* (2016).

Crying for Voice

I must pull frog
pry its webbed feet
from snails in
my throat.

Kneel, fold my hands
invite weasel to untangle
my braids.

Boil duck, rabbit, fish
scoop out brain,
eyes and tongue
roll them
inside my gut.

Pull out tapeworm
chop onions, grind peppercorns
fill the intestine
with fresh blood.

Boil bible and tripe
clean off grass,
boil and boil
pebbles bubbling
soup.

Suck marrow from tiny bones
fill the place
where frog left slime
and salted snails
fell.

I'm fluttering wind
tobacco floating
against my face
mosquitoes up my nostrils
swatting memories
inside marrow.

—1994

Nōhkom, Medicine Bear

A shuffling brown bear
snorting and puffing
ambles up the stairs.

In her den
covered wall to wall
herbs hang ... carrot roots, yarrow,
camomile, rat-root,
and *cācāmosikan*.

To the centre of the room she waddles
sits with one leg out, the other hugged close.
She bends over her roots and leaves
sniffs, snorts and tastes them
as she sorts them into piles.

She grinds the chosen few
on a small tire grater,
dust-devils settling into mole hills.
Her large brown paws take a patch
of soft deer skin
and wraps her poultice
until hundreds of tiny bundle-chains
swing from the rafters.

The brown laboring bear
Nōhkom, the medicine woman
alone in her attic den
smoking slim cigarettes
wears the perfume of sage, sweetgrass
and earth medicine ties.

Nōhkom, the medicine bear
healer of troubled spirits.
A red kerchief on her head,
blonde-white braids hang below her breasts.
She hums her medicine songs
shuffling alone in her den where
no light penetrates, no secrets escape.

She bends and her skirt drapes
over her aged beaded moccasins.
She brushes the potions off her apron.
A long day's work complete

Nōhkom ambles down the stairs
sweeps her long skirt behind her
drapes her paws on the stair rails
leaves her dark den and its medicine powers
to work in silence.

—*1994*

Der Poop

der poop
forgive me for writing on dis newspaper
i found it in da outhouse, saw lines
dat said you is sorry
some of my indian friends say is good but
some of dem say you sorry don't walk
so i was sitting here dinking dat we
maybe dalk
say, i always want to dell you stay
out of my pissness
if me wants to dalk to trees
and build nests in house
dats hup to me
if me wants to pitch my dent
and feed da ghost bannock hen berries
and maybe drow some indian popcorn
for you geezuz dats hup to me
i don't hask forgiveness not want
hand mary's, or a step ladder to heaven
me is happy with da sky, da bird *Iyiniwak*,
four-legged *Iyiniwak*, i is happy
sorry mean dat i don't need yous church
and yous priest telling me what to do
sorry mean dat i free to dalk to *Manitou*
the spirits and plant *Iyiniwak*.
dats all for now, poop
maybe we dalk again next time i see you
in da newspaper.

—*1994*

Excerpt from *Blue Marrow*

Keeper of the Stories—*âcimowinis*

They hobbled, limped, shuffled,
pink, purple, blues, reds, yellows,
white, black, printed blazed
calico dresses, shawls,
kerchiefs, blankets.
Dried flowers, old sweat
and sweet perfume, they teased,
laughed, joked and gossiped.
Ran their fingers through each
swinging hand. Pipe smoke
swirled. Men drumming our songs.

I watch them. Hundreds of my husband's family.
They've travelled across Canada, the United States,
rejoice at recognizing one another, some for the first time.
Each has brought a book they've lovingly compiled.
It contains the history of their migration
from England, Norway, and into the Dakotas.
They are scattered throughout Turtle Island.
They marvel at the trek of their ancestors.
The click of wine glasses echoes through the arbour
of this large family gathering. And five Indians.
I the eldest, my children and two other Indian youth.
They are not yet aware how this affects their lives.
Who are we? Adopted. I gather inward.
How many of my relatives were cattled
onto the reservation during their settlement?
How much of my people's blood was spilled
for this migration? Laughter and wonder
as fingers move across the atlas. This is where
great-granddad Arne crossed on the barge.
This is where great-great-granddad travelled
and preached the law of the land where his
wife Isobel taught the little savages to read.
My lips are tight from stretching when my
small family is introduced alongside the

large extended family. Later,
driving home, I weave a story for my children—
how their great-grandma rode sidesaddle,
waving her .22 in the air trying to scare
those relatives away. I tell them
how my relatives lived around the fort,
starving and freezing,
waiting for diluted spirits
and handouts from my husband's family.
I tell them
how their little children died wrapped in
smallpox blankets.
My breath
won't come anymore.
I stare
at the wheatfields.

—2004

tipiyawēwisīw—ownership of one's self

I come from a breed of leaders
though I wonder if they had taken scrip
like our cousins the Métis
we would have been feathers in the wind.

In 1892, my great-grandfather, my *cāpān*
Papaschase gave this message,

My children, surrender the land.
This is a better decision for our people.
The palefaces are coming against us again,
for they are full of greed, lust and murder.
If we resist they will utterly exterminate us, yes,
even to the little ones in their mother's arms.
They are not evil.
They are like little children who are lost
because they do not understand the teachings
of the Great Spirit.
We made peace and we promised
the Great White Mother
that we would make war no more.

This is beautiful land.
It is wrong that we should stain the soil
of the land of the Red Sun with the blood
of our white brothers.
We accept this and seek a new road
for our people. We must find the pathway
that leads to the stars.
I have spoken.

Mother's father was *kehīwin*, Chief of Long Lake
my grandfather, my *cāpān*, was *pāhpāscēs*
my father's father, William
was a Saddle Lake councillor.
They were gentle men,
though I am told their will was steel.

The wind that blew from the east
saw our people herded into land rejected
by the white settlers.
These grandfathers witnessed the nation's quake,
watched their children enter the brick walls.
We, the children followed.

I was called One Who Speaks With One Mouth
papθyakītōn, always searching
behind the questions.
But I never inquired enough how to find my way.
I stumbled within this silenced history.

—*2015*

āniskōstēw—connecting

I cannot say for sure what happened
to my mother and father.

The story said,
she went to St. Anthony's Residential School
and he went to Blue Quills.
They slept on straw mattresses and
attended classes for half a day.

Mother worked as a seamstress,
a kitchen helper, a dining room servant,
or laboured in the laundry room.
Father carried feed for the pigs,
cut hay for the cattle and
toiled in the massive garden.

That little story is bigger than I can tell.
 Before them were *nōhkom* and *nimosōm*.
She was a medicine woman
whose sweat lodge was hidden away,
wore prayer beads
and always had a pipe dangling
from her mouth.
nimsōm had his own car
back in the fifties
and he plowed his own land.
He was a wealthy man because
they lived in a house while we had a cabin.
He lifted the sweat rocks
for *nōhkom*.
That is as far back
as I can take you.

All the Old Man said is that
I have nothing to weep about
compared to them.

I know now where the confusion began.
She was a tough mistress, that confusion.
We were all caught in her web.
Her history is covered in blisters, welts
and open sores. You already know that part.
We came later.
We were the children
that mother and father tried
yes, tried to raise.

How scared *nimosōm* and *nōhkom* were.
They knew what the priests, and nuns,

supervisors did at those schools.
We all left, all of us.
Confusion was in our wind.
We no longer knew
where to turn.

That is where my footsteps began
where my footprints
appear in snow, in grass.
 I don't like walking backwards.

Old ones haunt my thoughts
tiny spirits that brush
the colour off my wings.
I need them now
to help others understand what happened.
It wasn't their fault.
It wasn't our fault.

Confusion was the ultimate glutton.
He came from far away
wore black robes and carried a crucifix.
He was armed with laws, blankets
and guns.
He fixed us with a treaty
that he soon forgot.

Sometimes the end is told before the beginning.
One must walk backwards on footprints
that walked forward
for the story to be told.

I will try this backward walk.

—2015

John Cuthand
Plains Cree · b. 1953 · Little Pine

John Cuthand was born in Prince Albert. He began a career in journalism in 1974 after he "wrote an angry rebuttal to a Canadian politician's remarks about Indians." Over the next decade he worked as a writer and editor for several Indian newspapers.

Cuthand's stories reflect over three centuries of his family's stories. "Naska" captures a vivid picture of the spiritual significance of the Saskatchewan River. While "The Search for Chief Lucky Man" was originally published in 1985, a significant change was made in 2016 to indicate that the author is the last living person of the many who worked together in the search for Lucky Man.

Naska

Her home was the deep water pools of the South Saskatchewan River. Here among the water plants, rocks and sandbars she passed the day and avoided the only enemy she ever knew—the bright burning sun. She hunted alone and without remorse, for such is the way of the big northern pike.

Her name was Naska. She was in her prime, weighing over thirty-five pounds and stretching almost a yard. Her shining, well-muscled body was white on the bottom, a mottled green and white along the sides and dark green on top. Her mouth was a maze of needle-sharp teeth. Smaller fish avoided her. And only the hard-shelled painted turtle could afford to ignore her approach.

When the hot summer sun drove her into the deepest reaches of the river, she would hover, her fins circling, facing the current a foot or so above the bottom. It was here, in these long hours, that the waters told her stories. The river sang as it flowed over and around the deep water rocks. It spoke in the soft rustle of the water weeds and in the gurgle and murmur of water pouring around the few scattered boulders breaking the glassy surface.

The voice said, "I am the ancient daughter of ice mountain, born when the freezing sky allowed him dominion over the south. I am the blood of ice mountain, born from his death before the warming sky. I am ancient and I am mystery. I am swift-flowing water. I am Saskatchewan."

In the black of the late night she rose with the morning star. She fed until the star was high and fading. When the first rays of the shimmering sun cast long shadows, she herself was like a shadow sinking into her deep water pools. She surfaced with the setting of the sun, fed, then slid deeper when the night became black.

On cloudy days she ranged beyond her familiar haunts. In the fall, with the gradual cooling of the water, her range extended further still. In winter, when the ice sealed off the surface and the sun no longer warmed the water, she roamed as she pleased. She much preferred the colder water. In mid-summer she was sluggish, but that was also the time when the river sang to her.

One time it told her ice mountain had never been entirely defeated by warming sky. "He rules still in one quarter of the sun's cycle. He covers me with his cloak and speaks to me in the booming thunder of my cracking ice mantle. He is father. In his death I was born. In his rebirth, I die. I am ancient but he is ageless."

In the time of the full moon Naska would rise and seek different prey. The moon's glow concealed her, but she could see them. They were the night creatures that live between water and land. For them the beckoning, seemingly peaceful waters held terror. Quick, violent death came with a splash and a swirl of black water. Where a gosling or a baby muskrat once swam, all that remained was an expanding ripple.

The big fish did not think in terms of right and wrong. Hunger, insatiable hunger, drove her and she killed only to live.

Among her moonlit prey the story spread of a water demon in the form of an enormous fish. The story was told in the haunting lonely laughter of the loons, the croaking chorus of the frightened frogs, and the chatterings of the milling ducks. The moonlight sighting of a long, shining back lolling over the water drove them further down the sandy bank away from that terrible place. The hunted lived in fear and they feared her most of all. If Naska knew of their fear, she didn't care. Generations of her kind before her and from her had ruled and would rule the river's waters. For the river in its mysterious way had willed it so.

She had been the mother of many. Perhaps some were among her kill, for the female pike takes no part in the raising of her young. Perhaps one or two would grow to her size if they survived the slaughter of the first years. One and one alone, however, was destined to become mistress of the river. The river in its way had willed it so. Naska was the survivor and heir of a mother who once ruled these waters as she did. This she did not know. She knew only that the river was her home and the river's spirit her sole benefactor.

One night, when the autumn moon was full and the great fish was on the hunt, a wandering band of antelope came to the river's edge. They waded out into the shallows and were drinking their fill, when their sharp-eyed leader spied a great shining back coming toward them. He watched intently, expecting an enormous snake, for snakes were creatures they knew well. A great finned tail curved upward, then sliced down, scarcely breaking the surface. "This is no snake," thought the antelope, "it is a creature solely bound to the water spirit."

The great fish felt a curious pulse from the shallows and veered toward it. This was not the fluttering sound of webbed feet, her usual prey. It was the feel of something large, many large creatures.

The antelope, alert as always, sensed that something very alien was close. They stiffened, raising their heads to sniff the wind. Only the leader gazed at the smooth, flowing water directly in front of them.

Naska followed the river bottom and rose as it rose. She came as close as boldness could take her before caution and the rising river bottom forced her off.

The leader was the first to notice the ruffled water above the shallow-running fish. The V-shaped wake came directly toward them, then moved away in a sharp curve. The antelope were nervous but their curiosity got the better of them. They watched in fascination as the dark shadow beneath the now churning water glided by, first one way then another, more slowly and closer with every pass.

Naska could not see straight ahead, because her eyes were on either side of her head. Cruising first one way then another allowed each eye to scrutinize in turn. The antelope froze in place, only their eyes tracked the meandering fish.

The shadow slowed, then hung motionless, her body curved in an arc, head and tail lowered—the defiant attack stance of her kind. Her cold, unblinking eye peered from beneath the water. The antelope peered back. Both sensed danger, but both were too fascinated to turn back. Neither one moved. All was quiet and still except for the murmuring water and the distant night sounds. The stand-off was finally broken by a single, curious antelope advancing a few hesitant steps. It paused in mid-step, ears forward, eyes shining. The dark shadow turned to meet him. The pronghorn's nostrils flared. Genuine fear was rising in him now, in spite of his curiosity.

In this position Naska could not see, but other more acute senses compensated. Her body felt the change in water pressure. Sensitive pores surrounding her mouth tasted the water. The tingling of these senses was her warning, but she wasn't quick enough. Her world exploded. The pronghorn struck with slashing hooves. He felt his first strike hit, then searing pain gripped his left front leg. He turned and leapt to the river bank. The others, as if one, instantly followed.

The herd left the river valley, trotting toward the rising morning star, now above the high prairie hills to the east. One limped, streaming blood from a deep gash to its front leg.

The pronghorn's slashing attack had cut deep, narrowly missing Naska's spine. Her reaction had been fast: a violent counter attack followed by a darting retreat. She left tasting blood.

The fight was brief but the effects devastating. Naska's needle-like sharp teeth had torn flesh as she shook her massive head from side to side. The pronghorn's small hooves, honed to a fine edge by climbing the rocky high ground, cut and crushed. Naska was lucky to be alive.

She retreated to the safety of deep water where, unmoving for many days, she nursed her wounds.

As she hovered, death close at hand, the river spoke to her again. "My riddles are written in your colours and patterns, in the coiled shell of the water snail and in the advance and retreat of my morning mist. All is there for those who seek. The willows know and bow before the river winds. I am as the veins of their stems and that of the animals. My sisters both young and old bring life to the land in the endless cycle of wind and water. We are ancient and honour only ice mountain and his creator. My father feels the deep stirrings of growth again.

His advance will come soon, with the passing of ten thousand cycles of the sun. Death is always close at hand, but you, my defiant one, will live to hunt again."

The cold water of winter revived her. For the remainder of her days, though, she wore a distinct crescent-shaped scar high upon her back.

The spring brought high, murky water. The great, restless river cut new channels and deep holes. Fish, both hunter and prey, sought the sanctuary of the river's deepest pools. A strange truce resulted. Clustered together in desperate, common survival they faced into the current, awaiting the river's ebb. They ignored one another; choosing not to eat until the peril passed. Overhead, the river carried a deadly cargo of uprooted trees and smaller debris. In another time the fish would welcome the shade and shelter of a beached river log, but for now the debris was an adversary to be avoided. The gentle river was showing its wrathful side.

Naska's strong body was rocked by the swirling water and her sensitive gills ached from the heavily silted water

In time the river subsided. The fish returned to their former roles. Hunter stalked prey and sought the safety of weed beds and shallow water. Naska hunted with renewed vigor over a territory she now knew only by instinct. For the river bed had been forever changed by the river's rampage.

Just as the butterfly changes and renews itself in the cocoon so too did Saskatchewan in the cleansing flood of the early spring. Life more bounteous than before returned with the subsiding waters.

The spring also brought subtle but significant change. The fishes of the north moved south, and Naska challenged their invasion. Goldeye, pickerel and the odd wandering pike all bore the tell-tale wounds of Naska's wrath.

One day a new threat appeared. It was a creature she had never met before. It was big and moved slowly like a log carried by the current. Her other senses told her it was a living being.

At any other time her actions would have been predictable. But this intruder made her pause. It was bigger than she, much bigger. She approached slowly, her back arched and her broad tail making slow, deliberate sweeps. The stranger kept to its slow, steady course along the river bottom, unconcerned by her approach. Naska's fury rose. Her body tensed, then she shot out of the gloom in dauntless attack. Her jaws did not grip. The intruder was far too large. She came at it again and again. Her teeth broke on a craggy back. The fight was entirely her own. The giant fish did not fight back. Almost with contempt it seemed, the giant continued its fluid movement slowly and methodically down river.

Naska launched a final attack. By luck or misfortune she struck the giant's tail fin. She felt flesh tearing, then saw the huge fin sweeping toward her. A powerful blow stunned her. She recovered in time to witness the long tapering tail of Namew the sturgeon vanishing down river. Their chance encounter was over.

The ice mountain's rule had come and gone many times before Naska grew too tired for the hunt. The smaller fish grew bold and she found it hard to catch them. Almost in disdain they drifted by her jaws, only to dart away when she moved to attack. What once took but an instant was now painfully slow. Her lightning-quick reflexes were gone. Her meals became slow-moving crayfish and frogs. On her last hunts, in complete contempt, the little fish followed her, seeking the remains of what little food she could find but not swallow. Naska's body ached and she spent much more time in solitude on the river bottom. Here she awaited the return of the comforting voice of the river spirit, but no voice was heard.

The time came when the moon was full and no shining back was seen breaking the river's surface. The moon waned and the night creatures along the edge of the land and water felt safe.

The morning star was at its highest point and the eastern sky was bright with early dawn. The sun rose red and fairweather clouds of violet and gold floated across the sky.

Naska's movements were slowing. Her gills once flushed with red blood grew pale and sickly. She didn't know why, only instinct drew her from her hovering place to the weed bed. With painful effort she dosed her tired mouth over a single water plant. Then with a turn of her massive head she pulled it free. Straining against the current, she carried this hard-won prize back to her chosen place. No prey had taken so much effort as this simple task.

She faced into the current for the final time. The rising sun now bathed the river bottom in a soft half-light. Only the dying remained. Her gills stopped moving. Her mouth opened and closed a final time, freeing the water plant. Her tired body shook with her death rattle. She briefly drifted with the current, then rose slowly toward the sun. One eye saw blackness, the other a brilliant broken circle of light. The light grew in intensity. A bright light she would only see once filled her being. Then all was blackness.

Wind and current brought the limp corpse to the water's edge. It drifted to a sandbar where it rocked back and forth with the lapping waves. The birds of the air feasted. Before the coming of the next sunrise, mighty Naska's body was reduced to bones and a toothy, grinning skull.

The night creatures, once timid of her mere approach, now rejoiced in her death. And so began a night of steady tatoo, celebrating the end of their once formidable foe. The frogs croaked together of a great victory, but theirs was not a valid boast. Only death had won.

In the spring the rushing water swept the bones along the river bottom where they collected in a shallow river hollow. Swirling silt covered them. A stand of water plants began to grow thick and lush from the calcium-rich sediment.

Along the wandering river, in the back water of a shallow place, small fish—the survivors of uncountable hatchlings—flittered among weeds, pursuing water bugs and minute creatures. Others, much larger but no older, stalked tadpoles. They all feared the deep water where the larger fish lurked ever hungry for a meal of their kind. In time, the pull of instinct or perhaps destiny called the bold one to the deep, alluring water. She paused at a lush stand of water plants and hovered beside it. The water-filtered sun, moving in zebra-like patterns over her back, shone on a curious crescent-shaped birth mark. The singing river called her in the soft rustle of the water weeds and in the gurgle and murmur of water pouring around the few scattered boulders breaking the glassy surface.

The bold one swam deeper, down a sandy decline, past the last of the weed bed, and into the unknown reaches of the deep calling river.

—1985

The Search for Chief Lucky Man

In the early 1980s I travelled to Rocky Boy Reservation in central Montana in search of my grandfather's American history. It is known he came as a twelve year old refugee to escape the persecution the Cree and Assiniboine faced following the Uprising of 1885. He returned to Canada in 1896 when Queen Victoria granted amnesty. During this time the unwanted Cree and Assiniboine refugees suffered.

I read archive accounts of how one band fed off poisoned coyote carcasses in order to survive during a cold winter. Then there was an editorial out of Havre stating that Cree children could live off barbed wire and thrive on the diet. Their story is kept alive in bits and pieces by storytellers and in the archives of the Glenbow Museum and the Montana Historical Society. It's these missing pieces that I wanted to know. In the end my journey was both an unexpected and mystical experience. It was as though it was meant to happen and my history became very much alive.

I was raised with my family history and like my father shared a life long interest in oral history and archival research. I have found those who know their kinship also know their history. It was on the Rocky Boy Reservation I met some Montana relatives who welcomed me. Stories were shared and I eventually came to understand much more. I was greatly assisted by Geneva and Bill Stump, Art Rainingbird and Four Souls, who I met only months before his death. Four Souls was the grandson of Little Bear and spiritual leader of the Rocky Boy Cree. His successor was Raining Bird.

There is a spirit that goes with gifting. Gifting should be non-exploitative and beneficial to both the giver and receiver. Everyone should be happy in the end. I believe this happened during those memorable days.

The Rocky Boy Reservation is located south east of Havre near Box Elder. It is sheltered by high hills and the Bear Paw Mountains. The land remains largely untouched prairie. At sunset, as shadows move across the face of the westernmost mountain what appear to be the claw marks of an enormous bear are seen in sharp relief and then mysteriously disappear. The experience can be quite eerie. This is how the Bear Paw Mountains got their name.

I found to my great sadness that I may have literally driven over some long ago relatives. In the early 1960's the main street of Havre was paved using gravel taken from an area near old Fort Assiniboine. Among the gravel were many Indian graves. These were simply mixed in with asphalt and made into a pavement. The practice was finally stopped but not before considerable damage was done. These bones remain to this day a part of main street Havre.

My search brought new insight and in the sharing I came across the history of a little known Chief named Papewes, the Lucky Man. What began as a search for my grandfather also became a search for this remarkable man.

His story and the story of the Montana refugees began in Saskatchewan during the Uprising of 1885. The Lucky Man was a father-in-law to Chief Little Bear and both brother-in-law and counselor to Chief Big Bear. The renowned Chief Big Bear was the last principal Chief to enter into Treaty Six. He stubbornly demanded better Treaty terms and held out despite incredible hardship. Lucky Man at the insistence of Chief Big Bear entered into Treaty Six. Big Bear wanted the old, the women and children to enter into Treaty to receive rations. The rest held out as best as they could. Lucky Man's band stayed among relatives on Little Pine's Reserve awaiting a reserve. Fighting broke out before they chose their reserve and it would be at the end of the next century before they finally gained their new reserve.

Riel's Métis and Indian allies surrendered at Batoche. Poundmaker and allied bands, undefeated in battle, surrendered at Fort Battleford. Only Chief Big Bear's people remained. The Cree fought a running battle as three Canadian army columns converged on them. The camp splintered with those who surrendered and those who refused. A large group under Little Bear escaped down the spine of the Thick Wood Hills. They crossed the North Saskatchewan River, then moved west, hiding by day and traveling by night until they reached the north shore of Tramping Lake. They then moved south through sparsely inhabited prairie and plain. They masterfully eluded their pursuers and crossed into the United States where they found safety.

It is said Chief Lucky Man held a grandchild's hand and sang as they crossed the Cypress hills within sight of the Bear Paw mountains and safety. I was told the site of Lucky Man and a daughter's graves was known to the Windy Boy family whose ancestor was buried nearby.

Lucky Man and his daughter died of small pox in 1901 while attending a sun dance near the Milk River. Her name is unknown. It is believed she was about nineteen years old at the time of her death. They are buried side by side in an old tradition still followed by their descendants, with head to the north and feet to the south. A black stone marked his grave and a small circle of stones marked her grave. They were in a cluster of seven graves. Mrs. Windy Boy, a descendant of those buried here, would tell us ninety years later where to find the subtle signs of those we sought. I returned to Saskatoon from this initial trip carrying information for those whose ancestor's graves were known to the Rocky Boy Cree. I approached the late Chief Andrew King of the Lucky Man First Nation. He was a direct descendant of Lucky Man and the Chief who eventually gained the land promised his ancestor over one hundred years before. He was very interested and requested the help of the late Eli Bear from Little Pine First Nation and an *oskâpêwis* (assistant) to the late Jim Kahneepahtehtehow, a head Elder from Onion Lake First Nation.

The help of "Old Jim" proved invaluable. His father had been a ceremonialist in Big Bear's Band and Elder Kahneepahtehtehow knew his history and culture very well. He told us the time we lived in had been predicted a long time ago. In the prophecies a time would come for old things to return from the earth. The rediscovery of long ago ancestors was a part of this. We were instructed on the proper protocol for approaching the Elders of the Rocky Boy Cree and how to address the ancestors when we found their resting places. It was to be a gathering of families once scattered so long ago but now coming together with common purpose. It was a time to shed healing tears.

Chief King, Eli and I left Saskatoon in late May. We stayed in Swift Current overnight. During the night Chief King had an astonishing experience. He was visited by a ghost. He awoke in the middle of the night and saw a long ago Indian, tall with braided hair smiling at him. The apparition disappeared and Chief King slept peacefully through the rest of the night.

We gathered at Geneva and Bill Stump's place on Rocky Boy Reservation. I was saddened to learn Four Souls, grandson of Little Bear and the head Elder of the Rocky Boy Cree, had passed away. They said he met a beautiful death. He had gone with some people to the high mountain meadows to round up horses. Four Souls said he was tired and stayed behind. When the people returned he was missing. The eventually found him lying peacefully in a meadow filled with wildflowers. The people said this was a good way for a Cree man to die and there was no tragedy in a life well lived.

We presented our pipes and spiritual offerings to their Elders. Art Rainingbird was their spiritual leader and Chief King spoke on our behalf. Chief King's address was brief and emotional. He repeated the information I had provided him and requested their help in locating the grave of his ancestor. They accepted our pipes and offerings. We prayed and smoked together. They then agreed to help us, with concern the grave sites should remain undisturbed.

I noticed the women Elders spoke through Geneva Stump. She had been provided with a photograph they identified as Lucky Man. I had been told in order to find Lucky Man, I must first find his famous son-in-law Little Bear. The photograph they presented contained both. There was no photograph known to us of Chief Lucky Man until this moment. The tall man standing to the left of the photograph was the same long ago Indian who appeared in a vision to Chief King the night before. Perhaps one of the women is his daughter. We had found Lucky Man. Chief King cried.

We were taken to a place outside Havre Montana. I was shown the site of the 1901 sun dance. It was a good place. Nearby we were taken to a field of low rolling short grass prairie. The crocus were in bloom, the meadowlarks were singing and the sky was a brilliant blue. Everything felt right.

Mrs. Windy Boy came here since she was a child. Her family tended ancestors graves in the spring of every year. They had shown her the site of Chief Lucky Man and his daughter's graves. She had always remembered and it was she who helped us. It was strange we never met her but her presence was definitely felt and appreciated through the intercession of Geneva Stump. She had told Geneva to look for a dip between two hills and then follow the dip down until we found a circle of stones. This was the grave of Lucky Man's daughter and next to it we would find a black stone, the grave of Lucky Man.

Chief King and Eli went off in separate directions looking for the two hills and the dip in between. I was about to search myself when Geneva told me to stay put. She had never been here herself but she clearly sensed something I didn't. She told me we should have a cigarette and talk about nothing in particular. Looking back now, I can see she was teaching me something. We smoked and engaged in idle conversation then she said, "Do you see it?" I looked around but could not see the two hills and I told her so. "Look there" she said and pointed with her head. I looked again and then I saw it. The two hills were barely a ripple on the crest of a gradual grassy slope leading to the banks of the Milk River. Between them was a slight dip. I could have spent all day looking for it and never found it. It was a subtle mystery, barely discernable, yet there.

We followed the dip about ten feet and then found the circle of stones, pebbles of white shale in a rough circle barely eight inches across. This was Lucky Man's daughter's grave and next to it, barely four feet toward the river, a small black rock of shale barely the size of a man's palm, the grave of Lucky Man. My heart was beating fast and my skin felt prickly. We were on hallowed ground.

There wasn't much said and there wasn't any need to say very much at all. We made a sweet grass smudge and prayers were given as old Jim had instructed. We were to speak to the ancestors gently and lovingly. Again everything felt right. I shared a sweat with the Stumps that evening and left the next morning refreshed and at peace.

There are times I reflect on those moments, for something important and mysterious happened for us all. I often think of the daughter and how sad it is, the women are largely forgotten in the histories, yet it was the women who enabled us to find the hallowed ground. I wonder was it she, who as a child held the hand of her father as he sang crossing the Cypress Hills to safety? I also see them crossing safely hand in hand from this world to the bountiful Green Grass World, where there is no winter, no want and no suffering. I believe Chief King has joined them and all the others who were with us but have since passed on. I am now the only one alive of all those people who worked together at that time.

There are many stories which are subtle and mysterious like the changing face of the Bear Paw mountains and I believe they are important because they tell us something of who we really are.

—1995, revised 2016

Solomon Ratt
Woods Cree · b. 1954 · Stanley Mission

Solomon Ratt was born on the banks of the Churchill River while his family was on its way to the winter camp. After his mother went into labour, the men built a cabin at the edge of water, in which he was born. Ratt attended the Prince Albert Indian Residential school and later the INAC boarding-out program. He went on to earn his master's degree at the Univeristy of Regina. He is a professor of Cree language and literature at the First Nations University of Canada, and he has published numerous books on Cree language learning. The selections below are from his book *nīhithaw ācimowina*, or *Woods Cree Stories*, written in Cree syllabics and Roman orthography, and translated by Ratt into English.

Grandmother's Bay

A long time ago people would travel about in search of game that would keep them alive. One autumn these people from Stanley Mission travelled from there.

They camped along the way at Otter Lake, in one of the big bays in the area. They were there for one night. In the morning they decided that they would have to leave behind an old lady who was slowing them down because she was on the verge of keeling over from old age.

In that bay they left her with a small canoe and all her tools. The old lady thought nothing of this because that was the way things were done in those days.

One evening the old lady saw a moose swimming across the lake. Hey, quickly she jumped into the canoe. Taking with her a rope and a small axe, she chased the moose. Hey, she was able to snare the moose and then she hit the moose on the head. She had herself some game!

In the spring her relatives travelled back and there they found her still eating dry meat. Apparently she had eaten that moose she had killed all winter.

From that time on that bay where the old woman had spent the winter alone was known as Grandmother's Bay.

Buffalo Wings

A long time ago our Grandfathers were skillful hunters. Listen, I will tell a story about them. Have you ever eaten that food known as 'Buffalo Wings'? Those are buffalo wings—they are tasty!

Okay, I will tell you … long ago when the Cree people went hunting buffalo they would not kill them. They were satisfied with knocking off their wings, that's how skillful they were! True! All they would do would be to cut off the wings from the buffalo … they, too, liked the taste of buffalo wings.

They were true to their mark. They rarely killed the buffalo. Eventually the buffalo became numerous, and eventually the buffalo started to be born without wings. It's because of "evolution"—yes, that thing known as "evolution" is the reason that today the buffalo are born without wings. It's true! Our Grandfathers were very skilled hunters!

Eventually the buffalo became very numerous over there in the Prairies, no longer having any wings. That is why when the people from across the ocean arrived, these Caucasians, they never did see buffalo with wings.

But it is a wonder, they are so inventive.

They can still cook, and sell, buffalo wings.

They are truly tasty!

—2014

Janice Acoose
Saulteaux · b. 1954 · Sakimay

Janice Acoose is a member of the Sakimay First Nation and the *Ninankawe* Marival Métis. She attended the Cowessess Indian Residential School in the 1960s. Acoose was the first Native Affairs columnist for the *Saskatoon Star-Phoenix* and contributed to papers across the province. She completed her Ph.D. at the University of Saskatchewan, and she has published a number of critical works, including *Iskwewak-Kah'Ki Yaw Ni Wahkomakanak: Neither Indian Princess or Easy Squaw* (1996), a groundbreaking book in Indigenous literary criticism in Canada.

The selection below is a radio play, co-written by Janice Acoose and Brenda Zeman, and edited by Wayne Schmalz. Originally a co-production between CBC Radio and Ka-Top-Aim Media Productions, Saskatoon, it first aired on "Ambience," 8 February 1986. The work relates the story of Acoose's grandfather, Paul Acoose, a noted runner, who was the son of Samuel Acoose, an esteemed Buffalo Runner, who in turn descended from Quewich, who travelled with Chief *waywayseecappo*.

Paul Acoose: Man Standing Above Ground

Janice: Running has always been a tradition in my family. It was thoughts of my mooshum that inspired me as I first played with the idea of becoming a runner myself. Finally one day I thought, Janice Acoose, you are the granddaughter of Paul Acoose, one of the great long-distance runners, so what are you doing? Get out there and run. It's in your blood! (*Street sounds, birds. She begins to run*).

I remember that first morning I went out to run. It was a warm day in March. The last of winter's cold was disappearing. It reminded me of another such morning a long time ago, the first time I met my mooshum. (*Street cross-fades to sound of pow wow drums, singing*). My dad told us we were going to the reserve to a pow wow. You know, coming from the city, the only knowledge I had of my people were images I had seen in movies, rough and wild-looking creatures. When we drove through the gate I saw a number of tents set up. There were children and dogs running about. Almost immediately my dad's face broke out in a wide grin. And then I saw this man coming towards us. The sound of bells tinkled from his moccasins as they softly struck the ground. His face was painted up and he wore a bonnet of feathers. "Grandfather?" I said. And I remember him replying, "Noosisim, I'm your mooshum. You call me mooshum." (*Street traffic, running come up again*).

My memories were interrupted by city traffic that squeezed me to the outer limits of the road, like I was an intruder. So I turned around and started running towards open country.

My mooshum always hated cars. He would never ride in them. He walked everywhere.

I remember the first time I discovered he was a runner. A moonyaw, or whiteman, had come out to the reserve to paint his picture. I asked him why that man was there. He motioned for me to sit down beside him and then he began to tell me his story. He talked about his father, Old Samuel Acoose, and his grandfather, Quewich, both famous runners. He told me of places he had raced in, places that seemed like they were on the other side of the world, like Madison Square Garden in New York City, Vancouver and Winnipeg. As he talked, the age disappeared and he looked strong and proud.

I reminded myself that I have a long way to go to achieve the kind of inner strength he had, and I turned and headed for home. As I ran I thought of how he must have felt when he returned home from racing. He was a hero, a world-class runner. But on the reserve, every aspect of his life was controlled by an Indian Agent.

My mooshum was a proud man, rich in the knowledge of his culture, yet prohibited by law from carrying on the traditions of his grandfathers. I can still hear him proudly speaking of the rain dance and the joy he felt as a grass dancer. But I also remember the Sunday ritual, when he would worship the Christian god. Rather than hold his head high in pride as he did when he spoke of the rain dance, he hung his head as he entered the house of worship.

Anger came over me as I remembered the way he was treated. But almost as soon as it came, it was gone.

I thought of the year when I watched my grandparents grow old. My kokum bedridden with illness, my mooshum always by her side. When she slept, he would sit with us kids, him in the middle and us all around. He told us then about the strengths and the beliefs of our people, the Saulteaux. He tried to teach us our language and instill values within us by telling us stories. I remember one thing, "Never throw your hair away when you comb it." He said your hair is your strength. He reached into his pocket and showed me a little white bear. He told me he kept his and my kookum's hair and always wrapped it around the white bear. This always kept them safe. Then he put it back in the pocket closest to his heart.

My kokum and mooshum were two unique spirits. Their home on the reserve was a special meeting place for all my cousins, aunts and uncles. That special feeling isn't there anymore.

As I got to the last part of my run I slowed down to a walk, so I could cool down. Because of all the running, my legs were numb and my feet felt as though they weren't touching the ground! It was then I finally really understood my grandfather's name—Acoose, "Man Standing Above Ground."

An old man once told me my mooshum was like One Who Runs with the Clouds. Often I would try to imagine how it might have been for him when he learned that like his father and his grandfathers, he too had a special gift for running.

My mooshum, Paul Acoose, was born near the time of the Riel Resistance in 1885. Tuberculosis, typhoid and scurvy were destroying our people. On the

Kahkewistahaw Reserve in the Qu'Appelle Valley, within three years, ninety-one people died. One of these was mooshum's mother.

Young Paul: My mother she had me that time the saskatoons bloom when the half-breeds they fight the government. That time my mother she died. There was no milk, *(laughs)* they gave me rabbit soup instead.

When I was growing up on the Kahkewistahaw, my grandmother she raised me. I was brought up to the Lebret School when I was about eight years to be educated. *(laughs)* Ooh... I was no good at all. They teach me to speak English. *(chuckles)* But it was no use for me.

One day my dad he come for me at Lebret. He takes me to Sakimay in the Qu'Appelle Valley. I was grown about sixteen years I think.

Outdoor sounds

Old Acoose: N'Egosis, you are away too long. You forget our ways. Ma Noo, come we run together.

Young Paul: Ah Papa, you are too old. *(laughs)*

Old Acoose: Ah-hah! We see about Old Acoose. Ampay. Come on, we run down valley over the hill.

Young Paul: Cowine, Papa, that's too far for you!

The sound of running, breathing.

Janice: My mooshum took off like a jack rabbit. His father, old Acoose, let him get ahead. Then he began to run with long loping strides, arms low and easy at his sides. They ran through the valley, young Paul still in the lead. But Old Acoose was a good runner. Soon they were even.

Old Acoose: *(teasing)* Come on, N'Egosis, are you not a good runner?

Janice: Paul, he struggled to keep up with his father, but it was no use. Old Acoose pulled ahead, running easily around and over the gopher holes.

Paul slumps down on the ground.

Old Acoose: *(from a distance)* Whooo boy! You a good runner, come on, catch up!

Young Paul: *(to himself)* Ta ya, sure enough he runs good. I bet he can still catch and beat that old man.

Old Acoose: Ah-hah boy, maybe it's enough. We stop now *(comes towards Paul)*. Come sit down. *(teasing)* You're a good runner, my boy.

Young Paul: Hummmm!

Old Acoose: Long time ago, Quewich, your old mooshum, he beat me too.

Young Paul: Grandfather, he beat you?

Old Acoose: That old man, he still wants to race with me sometimes *(chuckles)*. He thinks of the days when he chased the buffalo. One time when I was a baby, our people they were hungry. Sure there were many buffalo those days but they run fast. It was hard to catch them. One day your mooshum Quewich he asks the Creator for help.

Young Paul: Is that when he put on the buffalo robe??

Old Acoose: Ah-hah, he put on the buffalo robe, then he go out and find the buffalo. He call them like this: *(high pitch cry)* "Ah Hah!" The buffalo they get mad. They try to run mooshum into the ground but your mooshum too smart, he too fast. He get them buffalo running after him till the buffalo they get tired and stop. Then the hunters they come and shoot their arrows. Hoo hoo, the people they get lots of meat!

Young Paul: Mooshum, he stay in front of all the buffalo? How he runs like that?

Old Acoose: N'Quewich, he say to me, the Creator gives us many things. He gives us the strong medicine to run and to catch the buffalo!

Young Paul: I know our Creator! Is He the same as the one they call God at the Lebret School?

Old Acoose: N'Egosis, there is the same Creator for all. Many times I look to the Creator after our people make treaty. We don't get what they promise, our people were starving.

Young Paul: Is that the time you run down seven elk?

Old Acoose: *(remembering)* Ah-hah!

Young Paul: The buffalo and the elk they are all gone now. At Lebret School they teach me to farm and make shoes. So for what do I look to the Creator. Why the Creator give me the strong medicine to run?

Old Acoose: Ah hey, N'Egosis, maybe your time not come yet.

Music Bridge

Janice: In the early 1900s, long-distance running became very popular. No self-respecting small town sports day was complete without a race.

In Grenfell, Saskatchewan, Ernie Welsh was the town favourite. But twelve miles away at Sakimay Reserve, my mooshum Paul, who was nineteen then, was ready to challenge him. Arrangements were made for the Grenfell champ to race the Sakimay Indian—that's what they called him. But before he could get to the starting line, my mooshum had to run the twelve into town. For him, that was just a warm up.

Annie Yule, author or Grenfell's history book, Grit and Growth saw Paul Acoose run when she was a girl.

Yule: Ernie Welsh was quite a long-distance runner at that time and there was a certain amount of rivalry there. But, of course, Paul could run so much better. He ran for miles and miles. It was swift and it was graceful.

Janice: John McLeod was a prominent man in Grenfell. At various times he was principal, businessman, postmaster and Presbyterian Sunday School teacher. Billy Patterson was a former student of McLeod's and worked at the Dominion Bank. His friends called him "Billy Pat." Later Billy Pat would become Premier and Lieutenant-Governor of Saskatchewan.

Annie Yule explains why they got interested in Paul Acoose.

Yule: Well, certainly the gambling aspect was part of it. I suppose love of the sport might have had something to do with it, but I'm pretty sure that the gambling aspect was a big part of it.

Janice: McLeod and Patterson were intrigued with what they saw at the Grenfell sports days. But mooshum had only faced local competition. They were real anxious to see how he'd do against the big boys in Regina.

Sound of crowd cheering.

On Dominion Day, July 1st, 1907, my mooshum came home as Saskatchewan amateur road racing champion. The whole town of Grenfell welcomed him and John McLeod was there to shake his hand.

McLeod: Ladies and gentlemen. Ladies and gentlemen. This noble Saulteaux here in front of you is a credit to his race, a credit to this town and a credit to Saskatchewan. As you know, I'm not a man to mince words. At times this has gotten me in hot water. *(knowing chuckle from the crowd)* Wait a minute, wait a minute, you'll like what I have to say. In my opinion, as a sportsman, Paul Acoose is a good runner. He won the ten-and-a-half-mile race in Regina in sixty-four minutes and four seconds, the nearest fella a full eight minutes back! A runner with ability like this should have every chance to become a great runner. So, Billy Pat and I and a few of the boys have been figuring ways and means to send Acoose here to the hotbed of road racing—Hamilton, Ontario! *(Cheers, applause.)* I think Acoose can give those eastern boys a run for their money...and our's too!

Janice: Mooshum didn't make it to Hamilton that fall. But his fame was growing in western Canada. By Labour Day, 1908, he had become the amateur five-mile track champion of Saskatchewan and the three- and five-mile road champ of Western Canada.

Somehow that August, in all the running madness, there was time for marriage. Following the old way, my mooshum, Paul Acoose, and kokum—her name was Madeleine O'Shoupe—had been promised to each other when very young. My kokum Madeleine was an Irish orphan with bright carrot red hair. She was the adopted daughter of Chief O'Shoupe, a distinguished and honourable Saulteaux. Their marriage united two respected families and would last for seventy years.

Music Bridge

For our people, running was a spiritual ritual. It was a gift from the Creator. I remember my mooshum said he wore eagle plumes attached to his back when he ran in races.

Up until a few years before World War I, there was money to be made in professional long-distance running. And there was a big demand for Indian runners. From the point of view of white promoters and spectators, they had romantic appeal. They were often seen as the last vestige of a noble breed.

That's why a Winnipeg promoter named F. Nelson Smith had a meeting with mooshum Paul at the Grenfell Hotel in April of 1909. His purpose: to convince my mooshum to turn professional.

Bar-room sounds

Smith: Sorry, I can't offer you a drink Acoose. That'd be illegal. It was hard enough persuading them to let you in here.
    Now, the way I see it, Acoose, you've got a problem. All the talent in the world but you still need a shot at the big time. Know what I mean?
Acoose: Ah-hah.

Smith: And Acoose, you need promotional saavy to get you to those big races I'm talkin' 'bout. That's why you need me.

Acoose: Ah-hah

Smith: I'm glad we're talkin' the same language, Acoose. We're gonna get along just fine. Now, here's what I'd like to do for you. I promise you a fifteen-mile race with the English champion, Fred Appleby, for a purse of five hundred dollars... minus expenses of course. And then, I'll get you a race with that other Indian fella...Tom Longboat. How's that, Acoose?

Acoose: Longboat, I like that. I'll beat him.

Smith: I can see it now. We'll call it "The Redskin Running Championship of the World!" What do you think of that, Acoose?...Never mind, just put your name here on this line. Your X will be all right.

Janice: The Appleby-Acoose race was arranged for May seventeenth at the Happyland Athletic Ground in Winnipeg, Manitoba. On the day of the race, a Winnipeg Free Press reporter caught up with Paul and F. Nelson Smith.

Racetrack sounds in background

Reporter: Acoose! *Winnipeg Free Press* here. What kind of condition you in? Reckon you're fit?

Acoose: Ah-hah.

Reporter: Can you be a bit more specific?

Acoose: I feel pretty goo...

Smith: *(interrupting)* Acoose has come on wonderfully in the past two months. His trainer tells me he's running twenty-six miles and finishing strong. He's going two workouts a day, morning and afternoon, getting ready for his professional debut. Look at him! At 5'8" and 127 pounds, this Indian here is in the shape of his life!

Reporter: *(writing)* Okay, got all that...Appleby was quoted as saying he was lured to Winnipeg under false pretences. He says he expected a relay race against some western runners. He had no idea he'd be racing one man for fifteen miles. What do you say to that, Acoose?

Acoose: Appleby...

Smith: *(interjecting)* We deny any wrongdoing in this race. Personally, I think Appleby's running scared. And for good reason. Let me put it this way: If I was a gambling man *(chuckles)* I'd be sweet on Acoose.

Announcer: Gentlemen...to your marks. *(Gunshot.)* They're off! *(Cheering crowd.)*

Reporter: Hummmm, this Acoose is interesting. *(writing)* Like all of his race, he is flat–footed, creating at times the impression of a shuffle. His gait is ungainly but deceptive, and he travels easily despite an apparent awkwardness.

Announcer: Hold on to your hats, ladies and gentlemen! We're on world record pace!

Reporter: A world record! At the five-mile point, he's scarcely winded!

Announcer: And it's Acoose, the Grenfell Indian in the lead!

Reporter: Amazing! *(writing)* Acoose is rather unkempt and somewhat inclined to indifference. But, I dare say, with a little more polish the Indian may develop into a really high-class man.

Announcer: And it's the bell lap in this fifteen miler! Acoose is still on world record pace! And...with half a lap to go, he's picking it up! *(Wildly cheering crowd.)*

Ladies and gentlemen...in 1 hour 22 minutes and 22 seconds...Paul Acoose has himself a new world record!

Reporter: *(After race.) Winnipeg Free Press* again. Tell me, Mr. Acoose, how do you feel?

Acoose: *(breathing heavily)* All right.

Reporter: You broke the world record! What's your next challenge?

Acoose: *(firmly)* Tom Longboat.

Janice: Appleby sure didn't like losing to my mooshum and he demanded a rematch. The following week's stakes were higher. After mooshum's world record performance many people bet big money on him.

Typically, he wore moccasins. Appleby wore shoes with thick soles. Only a short distance into the race a gambling enthusiast threw tacks on the track to stop my mooshum. He kept running by Appleby and was able to romp to victory. Immediately, mooshum's trainer offered a ten-thousand-dollar stake to anyone who thought he could beat my mooshum fairly. There were no takers.

Mooshum Paul ran many professional races in 1909, sometimes under a handicap of two. That September, for example, he was seasick crossing from Vancouver to Victoria but he got better, and beat a two-man relay team over a twelve-mile course at the Victoria Athletic Grounds.

Mooshum was winning, but his races were mostly against western runners and a few touring English professionals. The real competition was in eastern Canada and the northeastern United States. To really test himself, mooshum had to go there.

So in January of 1910 he headed east. To him, there was only one man to beat: his equal and kindred spirit, the Onondaga Indian from the Six Nations Reserve in Ontario, the celebrated Tom Longboat! By the time mooshum arrived in Toronto, Longboat had been through the professional running mill. In fact, compared to the experienced Longboat, my mooshum was like a babe in the woods.

My mooshum and Tom Longboat finally met on March 30th, 1910 at the Riverdale Arena in Toronto for an indoor twelve-mile race.

Racetrack sounds, cheering crowd, gunshot.

Announcer: And they're off! Two fine specimens of Indians running here tonight, head to head, for the Redskin Championship of the World!...In the lead, the conqueror at Boston, the fella they had to dope to beat in London, England. The professional world champion against Alfie Shrubb in New York. The Indian they call "Wildfire." The Onondaga Wonder...Tom Longboat! And on his shoulder, the challenger, fresh from a second place run in a twenty-mile event in Madison Square Garden in New York City. In moccasins, the Grenfell Wonder...Paul Acoose!

Acoose claims he'll take the Longboat scalp back to Saskatchewan. He's fresh from his big international race in New York, but there are many in the know there tonight who say Acoose's showing was a fluke. They doubt he'll repeat. But, so far Acoose is staying on Longboat's shoulder.

And, at the eight-mile mark, it's still Longboat. Some say he's past his peak, on the way down, but you couldn't sell me on that tonight. Looks like he's still got a kick.

Don't count Acoose out yet. He's hanging in there. Longboat can't seem to shake him. It's a marvelous race...the famous Tom Longboat and the unheralded Paul Acoose...a blistering pace!

How much longer can they keep it up?

And now, at the ten-mile mark...Acoose is making a move! Acoose is pulling away from Longboat!...Longboat!...there's something the matter with Longboat! (*shocked*) Longboat's walking off the track! He's giving up the race to Acoose!

Ladies and gents, Paul Acoose just beat the world champion. Paul Acoose is the new Redskin Champion of the World!

Janice: Why Longboat quit part way through the race remains unknown. Perhaps he was sick. Perhaps the pace was too fast for him that night. But whatever the reason, for my mooshum it was a great victory. He won a good purse and a gold medal from the Six Nations Reserve.

He could have stayed in the east and gone to New York for the prestigious Marathon Derby at the Polo Grounds in early April. He could have raced for ten-thousand-dollar pots. But mooshum was anxious to go home. Instead of heading south, mooshum and promoter F. Nelson Smith boarded a west-bound train.

Train Sounds

Smith: Well, Acoose, it was just last spring you turned professional, you broke the world record and that was the start. And now, after this trip you've really caught the eye of the racing establishment. I didn't want to tell you, but you know Tom Flanagan? The man who manages Longboat?

Acoose: Ya. Flanagan. Longboat told me all about that fella.

Smith: Yes, well…Flanagan says he's sweet on you. He'd like to take over your contract. *(pause)* He's got big ideas for you, Acoose. There's money out there, Acoose! You've got a great future. I cou…I mean, you couldn't lose if you sign with Flanagan. Now, what I want you to do… *(pulls out a piece of paper)* is sign here … *(pause)* What's the matter, Acoose? Don't you want to sign?

Accose: I want to go home.

Smith: Yes, you're on your way home! Now sign.
Acoose: *(firmly)* I want to go home. I'm tired of running in circles.

Janice: My mooshum retired from professional running when he was twenty-five years old. But running would always be part of his life.

Paul Acoose, Man Standing Above Ground, died in 1978. He was ninety-eight years old. He was inducted into the Saskatchewan Sports Hall of Fame in 1983. Portraits of his father, Old Samuel Acoose, and his grandfather, Quewich, hang in the Legislative Building at Regina.

Voice: Think of the death of Acoose, fleet of foot, Who in his prime,
A herd of antelope, from sunrise, without rest, a hundred miles
Drove through rank prairie, loping like a wolf, tired them and slew them,
'ere the sun went down.
…There Acoose lay, silent amid the bracken, Gathered at last with the Algonquin Chieftains.
Then the tenebrous sunset was blown out, And all the smoky gold turned into cloud wrack.
Acoose slept forever amid the poplars. Swathed by the wind from the far-off Red Deer Where dinosaurs sleep, clamped in their rocky tombs.

Music.

—1986

Joseph Naytowhow
Plains-Woodland Cree · Sturgeon Lake First Nation

Joseph Naytowhow is a singer, songwriter, storyteller, and voice, stage and film actor from Sturgeon Lake First Nation in Saskatchewan. As a child, Joseph was influenced by his grandfather's traditional and ceremonial chants as well as the sounds of the fiddle and guitar. Today he is renowned for his unique style of Cree/

English storytelling, combined with original contemporary music and traditional First Nations drum and rattle songs.

An accomplished performer, Joseph is the recipient of the 2006 Canadian Aboriginal Music Award's Keeper of the Tradition Award and the 2005 Commemorative Medal for the Saskatchewan Centennial. In 2009, Joseph also received a Gemini Award for Best Individual or Ensemble Performance in an Animated Program or Series for his role in the Wapos Bay series. That same year, he was also awarded Best Emerging Male Actor at the Winnipeg Aboriginal Film Festival for his role in *Run: Broken Yet Brave*, and won Best Traditional Male Dancer at John Arcand's Fiddlefest in Saskatchewan. The selection below reflects both his traditional and contemporary storytelling styles.

Subtle Energy As Seen through the Eyes of a Nêhiyo (Cree Person)

It would be easy to assume that one can undertake discussion of subtle energy from the *nêhiyâwiwin* (Cree way of knowing and seeing), cultural perspective in the same manner one would discuss the Yogic çakra system as typically viewed in North America. Suffice it to say, in many cultures, subtle energy, and its maintenance, production and expenditure, is guarded for protective purposes and this is the case for the duration of one's life journey. Protocols exist as a means to ensure that protection. For example, the giving of a tobacco offering along with gifts is customary as one enters into the elder/teacher-student relationship of *nêhiyâwiwin*.

In our traditional language we have a word for someone who is entering into the spiritual gifting process. This concept is one requiring initiation and is known as *mamahtawisiwin* which generally means 'one who is spiritually gifted and/or is seen as having a special energy about them'. This energy is understood to be in association with the spirit world and guided from a source named *kise manito*, (holy/sacred being), through dream or waking state. *Mamahtawisiwin* recognizes that anyone earnest may enter into this domain. It's understood, however, that one always has a choice to undertake this journey.

As such, when my sudden government-enforced kidnapping occurred in Canada in 1959 as a child at six years of age, I'm quite positive that *mamahtawisiwin* was at play. How else would I have been protected from the potentially life threatening situation I'd been put through? Someone or something was watching over me. Maybe it's speculation, yet when I discovered later on in my life that I had come from a family which lived by this spiritual practice, *nêhiyâwiwin*, (Cree way of knowing and seeing), it explained a lot.

In *nêhiyâwiwin* there are many ceremonies that one can participate in from birth till death and my grandparents exposed me to many of them. For example, I remember the feasts we'd go to at the cemetery on the reserve in

June. They would refer to it as flower day. It was a ceremony that included those who had left this earth plane. Four male elders and a female elder would be selected to perform the annual ceremony of inviting, feasting with, and acknowledging our ancestors. We'd eat together and tidy the grave sites of the ones gone ahead. The stump of the tree that those elders sat under is still there. It now appears, however, further inside the cemetery, as other relatives who have died over the years have taken up the space around it. As I saw and observed, so has it come to be that I sit in this place where my elders once sat. That is the way of the *nêhyowak*, (Cree people), within the *nêhiyâwiwin* way of knowing and seeing.

Suffice it to say, to provide an in-depth explanation of subtle energy from the perspective of the spiritual tradition I was raised in would place me in a compromised position. It would require me to divulge details privy only to myself regarding the traditional knowledge/teachings, songs, stories and prayers shared in a private setting with me by my elder/teacher. Paramount to this sharing of traditional/spiritual knowledge is the establishment of a trust relationship between teacher and student.

For many years I served as an *oskâpêwis*, (new learner to the teaching), for many Indigenous elders. I began one such journey as an *oskâpêwis* for an elder from Mosquito First Nation while in my early thirties. I had many responsibilities which included driving him to ceremonies, medicine picking, grocery shopping, cooking, ceremony preparation, feast serving and being a noble friend. I had no expectations. Over time I learned Nakoda and *nêhiyo nîkamowina* (Cree songs), sacred stories and eventually earned the right to own my teacher's sacred pipe. I'd also learned that there is always someone, (generally elders), watching. A teacher is always on the lookout for a promising student because in *nêhiyâwiwin* s/he is by natural law expected to pass on their knowledge and skills on how to perform ceremonies. How you behave or conduct yourself around children, women, and elders can be considered the initial stage whereby one becomes introduced to the subtle energies embedded within *nêhiyâwiwin*. In the initial stages of gathering my medicine towards understanding the workings of subtle energy it was without a clear awareness of my own actions and their impact on the efficacy of medicine. Thankfully I later realized that my conduct in and out of the community was profoundly significant to the way of *nêhiyâwiwin* and *mamâhtiwisiwin*.

Prior to becoming an *oskâpêwis*, I was an academic student bereft of any traditional knowledge and *nêhiyâwiwin*. At that point in time I didn't even know I was of *nêhiyo* ancestry. This is typical of many Indigenous people who endured the residential school experience in this land now called Canada. This complete cultural annihilation would happen in the space of thirteen years and it was indeed a spiritual event that guided me to return to the sources of my original cultural knowledge. This awareness certainly wasn't taught at the university I'd attended. On the flip side, it was not just serendipity that I met an elder who happened to provide me with my first glimpse of *nêhiyâwiwin* and *mamahtawisiwin*. Then, and now, this spiritual world view makes sense to me as a means to experience soul transformation via the sudden and subtle cues I am thrust into from time to time. These teachings have led me to understand that these cues can occur within the *nêhiyâwiwin* (Cree way of seeing and knowing), and within my European cousins' way of seeing and knowing. My academic journey through university, though a continuation of colonization, is also an example of this energetic universality. There is a reason for where one happens to be and to experience life.

Fundamentally, I had to learn how to work with people, gather medicine, manage life's situations and wait for years before starting to experience *mamahtawisiwin* or, as I like to refer to it, 'unusual spiritual events on the path of spiritual awakening'. Coming from a people who dream I finally began receiving guidance both from elders and spirit.

Back in the 1990s, Ken Cohen, my spiritually learned adopted brother from Eldora, Colorado came to visit me in Saskatoon, Saskatchewan. He had been studying with many teachers from many Indigenous cultures. He wanted to meet Cree elders. I told him about Buffalo Child from Ermineskin First Nation, Alberta. I called Buffalo Child and he listened and said *'ahaw, pitohtik'*, (okay come on down). When Ken and I arrived, Buffalo Child seated us in the living room. Ken sang an honour song and we waited... and waited. Finally Buffalo Child sat down. He pulled out one of those small match books and began to read what was written on it. It said, 'two *spirit people* coming from the east'. Then Buffalo Child told us he'd decided to cancel all other plans that day when he received this message as a breath voice in his ear. Needless to say Ken and I sat staring at each other for some time.

As a young man in my late teens I encountered my first experience with what science might refer to as subtle energy. I was up north in Lac La Ronge, Saskatchewan in the early 1970's and had gone to visit Sam, a friend I'd made at the Prince Albert Student Residence, (formerly All Saints Indian School). We had returned from a lengthy canoe trip and I planned to be off the next day. I was asleep when a pressure came around my head area. It was as if someone had pushed the air around my head and gently touched my auric field. The feeling it gave me was not one of malevolence. I also knew it wasn't a dream as the air next to me was several degrees cooler. I tried to call out to Sam, but for some reason I wasn't able to. Eventually this 'visit', as I call it now, subsided. I believe that occurrence was what my elders talk about as *mamahtawisiwin*.

To this day I've never forgotten this experience and I have grown accustomed to expect other similar visits.

I have read upon occasion about the way in which medicine or spirit works in other cultures. For the most part I have lived to feel or sense the world around me. Over the years I was introduced to the healing arts by various respected elders/teachers within Indigenous and Buddhist traditions. I have also met people gifted with paranormal abilities. For many years my desperation and hunger for self understanding following forced removal from my people literally flung me into any spiritual and cultural opportunity I could find. Interestingly, I would at times discover my search experiences to be perilous. My practice these days is to remain aware and continue onward as usual. As my people often say, 'walk carefully, speak respectfully and watch how you think'.

—2016

Kim Soo Goodtrack
Lakota · b. 1955 · Wood Mountain

Kim Soo Goodtrack is a member of the Wood Mountain Lakota First Nation in southern Saskatchewan. Her great-grandmother walked to Wood Mountain with Sitting Bull when the Lakota people came to their traditional hunting lands In Canada, seeking refuge after the Battle of Little Bighorn.

Goodtrack is a visual artist and has had several art exhibits across Canada. She has also written the children's book *The ABC's of Our Spiritual Connection*, and she co-created and co-wrote the television shows *Art Zone* and *"Wakanhja" First Nations Children's Puppet Show*, both originally broadcast on APTN. Goodtrack also taught art classes in Vancouver public schools for over twenty years before returning to Wood Mountain. The selection below gives an insightfully comic view regarding the protocols of recording oral traditions.

Joe Flyingby's Tape Recorded History

Our dear Auntie Bea was a woman who was loved, feared and hated. She was outspoken that's for sure. My Sister and I loved her. We knew when to listen and we knew when to take cover! Or for that matter to stand up to her!

South Dakota summers were the perfect time to visit Auntie, sort of a religious Indianage…as compared to a pilgrimage! Many Lakota people were getting ready for the Sundance. It was a time to pray, visit, learn and prepare. The Sundance had been held for 25 years, since the early 70's on the Little Eagle Reservation.

My Sister was going to Sundance. She was excited and contemplative. We had sewn her dresses and packed her camping essentials. We would be going to the Sundance site the next day.

Auntie wanted us to go and visit with an elder and Medicine Man on the neighbouring reservation. She was giving orders, we were listening. "Take a tape recorder and record everything he says!" A directive that we were both hesitating to follow. "Take my car and watch out for the gumbo."

We had met Joe on our last trip to Standing Rock. My sister really adored him. She had such a respect for Joe, as did I. He was pure magic! He was clairvoyant, a healer and Spiritual leader in the Lakota community. Aunt Bea said he was one of the last REAL Medicine Men.

She told us that as a child Joe was his grandfather's eyes. Joe's grandfather was blind and also a Medicine Man. Joe was taught the old ways from a very young age. The whole Lakota community respected Joe. He was the first Medicine Man to hold a Sundance after the law banning Sundances was lifted in the early '70s.

We jumped into Auntie's old '79 Volvo station wagon, a standard no less, and proceeded to Little Eagle. It had rained earlier so the roads were a bit gummy but no troubles. I was driving; it seems I always do the driving!

One time I drove from Standing Buffalo, Saskatchewan to Standing Rock, South Dakota through a wicked lightening storm. The lightening was striking all around us as we drove; now that was scary! The brilliant bolts lit up the land. I was afraid we would get hit. But that trip is another story about another Sundance. How I digress!

Okay, so there we were coming up to the reserve. We didn't really know where old Joe's house was so we parked the car. Aunt Bea had given us the tape recorder. "Aren't you going to take the tape recorder?" I asked with big sister authority.

Sister replied, "No, I'm not going to take it, why don't you take it!" She said in a defiant little sister way. "I'm not going to take it, why don't you take it?" I retaliated, geeze it just seemed too presumptuous. Where's Mikey in a situation like this? So we left it in the car.

We took our tobacco bundle and headed down the street. It was a gift for Joe, a Lakota tradition. Auntie had wrapped the tobacco in some red cloth. As we walked it was funny how part of me had wanted to take the recorder, I guess to be a good niece and for posterity too.

We asked a kid where Joe lived and proceeded in the right direction. As we walked one could not escape the dire look of the yards, houses and cars. Something was amiss…a familiar sight on most reservations in Canada and the U.S.A. A look of despair, a feeling of numbness came over me.

We arrived at Joe's house and walked up to the door. His son was home, as was a young woman. They invited us into the humble home. It was clean and sparse with the smell of sweet grass in the air...the smell of comfort. Joe's son started on a barrage about the life and rights of a Lakota man.

I thought he was a braggart and somewhat of a sexist

I didn't voice my opinion, out of respect for Joe; we just sat on the couch and waited for Joe. We listened to the son's cultural rhetoric. He boasted about trading 15 horses for one of his wives, and how it was his right to get some more wives, blah, blah, blah! I don't know, it was the first and only time I met him, maybe I was judging him too harshly.

Joe was in the back bedroom. He came out and said hello and that he would be a minute or two. In front of us, on the coffee table there was a partially beaded prayer stick. On the walls were Lakota beaded bags, staffs and family pictures.

Eventually Joe invited Sister and me to enter his little back bedroom. His son did not follow. I was glad that he didn't follow us. I had had enough of his energy!

Joe's bedroom was clean and old-fashioned looking. His quilt was made out of various coloured pieces of fabric. There was no design element at all. Function was its main purpose. The quilt's edging was made out of old white sugar and flour sacks. You could still see some of the writing describing the contents of the sacks.

He had positioned two chairs near a small table. He gestured us to sit down. On the table there was a cassette tape player. Never in a million years did I think that is what Joe would do! Here he was ready to press play!

The tape was that of an Elder speaking Lakota. Joe explained that she was a woman in her nineties that had been recorded in the 1970s. He told us she had been a young child that had gone to the northern camp with Sitting Bull back in the old days of war and came back too.

I think Joe wanted us to hear the tape as our mother was from the northern camp. Wood Mountain Saskatchewan is where our mother was born. And this is where the Lakota had settled after the war. Mom's Grandmother had walked all the way up from the Wounded Knee area.

My sister and I have heard about the conditions of that walk from our living relatives...to this day! They still talk about it! Our People were starving to death on that walk north. Pursued by the U.S. army, there was no relenting. The People had to escape the murderous rampage.

Joe started the tape. The voice we heard was that of an older woman speaking Lakota. Joe started to interpret. Every now and then he paused the tape to explain something further. Here is my recollection of Joe's translation.

When the U.S.A. gave the Lakota permission to come back to their homeland, Standing Rock area, they decided to leave Canada. Some of The People stayed in Canada. However, the majority came back.

Upon arrival Sitting Bull and The People were greeted by the U.S. army. The army leader told them that they would be given rations, food and housing. Until then they were to surrender all of their weapons and take refuge in the army horse barns. The People surrendered all of their guns and knives.

The horse barns were dark and damp. The People did not want to cause any trouble so they went into the barns. The caged area was locked. The People had no freedom. True to their word the U.S. army did start to feed The People.

The dark and damp barn was not conducive to a healthy living. The People started getting sick. As they got sick they got weaker and weaker. They begged their capturers to release them but to no avail.

The People told the U.S. army to keep their weapons and rations. The People told the U.S. army that they did not have to build any houses if only to be let go. The army refused.

The People started to get sicker and sicker. Eventually one of the soldiers told someone not to eat the food as it was being poisoned. The People rejected the food from then on. The leader of the U.S. army was mad The People had stopped eating. He demanded that they eat!

All of a sudden the U.S army leader dropped into a coma. The army doctors were baffled by this. The leader lay on a bed with his eyes open, not moving, not eating and not talking. Days went by. The army doctors could not do anything for their leader. They knew he would die soon.

The doctors asked the Medicine Man if he could help. The Medicine Man was allowed to leave the locked area and look at the comatose leader. All The People were watching to see what would happen.

The Medicine Man touched behind the leader's ear. He pulled out a sewing needle. The leader sat up immediately. The doctors and soldiers were taken aback and in shock. They told the leader what had happened. The leader gave the order to release The People.

The doors were opened and The People walked away.

Joe turned off the tape. Sister and I didn't say much as we were in a bit of shock ourselves. We left Joes and went back to Auntie's house and told her what Joe had shared with us...recorded oral history. Joe and Auntie Bea are both in the Spirit world now. With respect I tell of this experience. With part of my heart they rest.

If I were to embellish on this story I would have said this. One of the soldiers must have fallen in love with a beautiful Lakota woman and was guilt ridden. How could one poison such a lovely woman?

The needle would have been secretly kept by a woman. How could one give up such a useful tool? She hid the needle in the hem of her dress and only gave it up when the Medicine Man asked The People if anyone had a weapon! Something had to be done to free everyone.

When the Medicine Man was given the pitiful needle as the only thing that resembled a weapon, he used it as a deterrent. The Medicine Man knew of the equilibrium nerve behind the ear and with his powers, embedded the needle into the U.S. army's leader's nerve behind the ear! Now of course this is sheer projection with a romantic twist!

I left my embellishment out to give you the words of Joe and the Elderly woman the best I could. You will never read this in the history books…one of the main reasons that I have written it down! I don't know what happened to that tape after Joe died. I hope someone in Joe's family kept it. And I really wish that we had taken Aunt Bea's advice and recorded Joe!

—2010

Harold Johnson
Cree · b. 1957 · La Ronge

Harold Johnson is from La Ronge. He has a Master of Law degree from Harvard University, and he practises law in La Ronge. He has served in the Canadian Navy and has worked in mining and logging. Johnson has published several novels, including *Billy Tinker* (2001), *Back Track* (2005), and *Charlie Muskrat* (2008). His work *Two Families:* *Treaties and Government* (2007) won a Saskatchewan Book Award, and he recently published the critically acclaimed book *Firewater: How Alcohol is Killing My People (and Yours)*. The selections below are from *Charlie Muskrat*, where Johnson uses the Cree trickster to parody Greek mythology and Christian theology.

Excerpts from *Charlie Muskrat*

Wesakicak's moccasins flopped on the marble steps all the way up Mount Olympus. The cool smooth stone felt kinda nice where the soles of his feet touched it through the holes in his moccasins. He was tired when he reached the top. Wesakicak felt his age. It was a long time since the beginning of the world. He refused to fly since 9/11, and it had been a tough paddle across the big pond to this far away place. The canoe trip reminded him of when Muskrat swam down in the water for land and the making of Turtle Island. That was a long time ago. Now there was this Charlie Muskrat thing to take care of.

He sat on the top step and leaned against a white smooth pillar. It wasn't as comfortable as leaning against a tree, but it supported his aching back. A man with a single long black braid down his back stopped on his way out and looked down at Wesakicak. He just stood there and looked, so Wesakicak asked "Who are you?"

"I'm Adonis." He pulled in his sagging stomach, rolled his shoulders back and pushed out his chest. "I'm one of the Greek gods."

"But, you're Chinese."

"I am not Chinese. I am Asiatic, according to the poets."

"I thought I was in the Greek Heaven."

"This is Mount Olympus, home of the great Zeus and all of his descendants."

"Who are you?" Wesakicak realized he had already asked that question, so he decided to ask it a different way. "Who are you related to?"

"I am Adonis. My father is my grandfather. My mother was Myrrha, but now she is a tree."

"Weird," Wesakicak thought.

"Barbarians are not allowed here." Adonis seemed unsure what else to say to Wesakicak.

"I had nothing to do with Barbara Ann. That must have been my cousin Nanabush. Us Cree don't fool around with white women."

"Oh, here is Hermes. Hermes, would you escort this barbarian off the mountain?"

"How come you got sea gulls in your shoes and in your hat?" Wesakicak asked Hermes.

"Those are not sea gulls. I am the messenger of Zeus and I have winged shoes and a winged hat. What are you doing here?"

"Who are you related to?" asked Wesakicak.

"Who wants to know?" The wings on his hat fluttered like a seagull defending a scrap of garbage on the beach.

"Me."

"Who's Me?"

"I thought you were Hermes, the guy who walks on seagulls"

"I am Hermes, and those are not seagulls. I am the god of travellers and thieves."

"Thieves?" asked Wesakicak.

"Yes, thieves. I was born at dawn and by noon I had stolen fifty head of cattle."

"You're a rustler."

"I am a messenger for Zeus." The wings folded back, stiffly.

"I thought you people hung rustlers. Almighty Voice was cannoned to death for killing his own cow."

"I know nothing about that. What is it you want here?"

"Oh yeah, you guys have the right to remain silent, I'd forgot that."

"I know nothing about that either."

"What do you know?"

"I know that when mortals die, I escort them to the house of Hades."

"Is that your, how do they say in the movies, your happy hunting grounds?" Now Wesakicak was getting somewhere.

"I know nothing about the hunting. It is told that there is a Plain of Asphodel but it is not written whether they hunt there. All I know for certain is that I take a Shade to the ferryman, Charon, and he takes them across the river Styx if they can pay the fare."

"Pay the fare? You mean with good deeds and valour and things like that?"

"No, they must pay the ferryman with money. They need a coin, an Obolos to cross."

"Hmm, that might not work. Charlie usually doesn't have any money."

"Who is Charlie?"

"I thought he might be one of yours. His father was Greek and his mother was Cree. She thought he said he was Creek. You know like the Indians in the States. But anyway, now we have Charlie and we don't know what to do with him."

"If he is a barbarian he cannot go to the house of Hades in any event. Perchance he is a Christian and can go to the Gates of Pearl and there state his case to Peter. There are many who follow the Christian road these days. In fact very few mortals seek the house of Hades anymore."

"Christian, you say. I never would've thought of that." Wesakicak looked out across the world from Mount Olympus. It was a good world, blue and green, white puffy clouds drifted lazily, easily across the sky. He thought about it. "Maybe Charlie was a Christian." He thought about it some more, closed his eyes and tried to imagine it.

Hermes and Adonis looked at each other, then again at Wesakicak. "Is he asleep?" Adonis asked.

"I know nothing." Hermes answered.

"Hey, barbarian." Adonis nudged Wesakicak with his toe.

"You have to move along now. You cannot sleep here."

Wesakicak opened his eyes, looked up at the two men in white dresses staring down at him. "I wasn't asleep." He lied. "I could just about imagine Charlie as a Christian."

"You will have to imagine it somewhere else." Adonis pulled in his stomach again.

"It's okay, my friends." Wesakicak leaned forward from the pillar. "I can see that Charlie would not like it here." He pushed himself to his feet. "I'll go check with him, see if he might wanna go somewhere else." He started down the long steps.

[...]

Wesakicak's moccasins beat a steady rhythm against the marble steps as he walked slowly down the stairs. He was looking for a place to finish the little nap he started and had cut short by Adonis' toe. This was a quiet place, a forgotten place. The only sound was the *wolp, wolp* of his moccasins. Well, going down was easier than going up. He would find some place at the bottom, a tree, maybe some shade, grass would be nice, lean back, close his eyes and dream.

"Behold, a barbarian." The purple-robed man sitting on the stairs put his doll aside. "Come, barbarian, sit here a while and converse with me." He turned to the man sitting a few steps below. "This will be interesting." The lower man picked up his laptop computer and set it on his knees."

"Sit, sit, Barbarian. You and I will have a debate. No not there. Move down a couple of steps. A free man should not have to look up at a barbarian." Wesakicak complied by sliding his butt down the steps. "There, that's better. Now for the record, I am Socrates and the scribe there is Plato, and your name is...?"

"Wesakicak"

"Wesakicak. What kind of name is that? Well no matter, we can expect barbarians to have strange names or else they would not be barbarians. Now, Barbarian," Socrates spread his hands. "I correct myself, Wesakicak. I should call you by your name for the sake of courtesy—for the sake of debate we will elevate you to the rank of a human. You have just come down from the towers of intrigue and petty gossip. Tell us, Wesakicak, what have you learned?"

Wesakicak leaned into the edge of the step behind him, leaned harder into it until it stretched out the ache in his muscles. Plato looked up from the screen in anticipation, his fingers on the keys. Socrates picked up his doll and set it on his lap.

"What kind of berries are those?" Wesakicak pointed his chin toward a bowl beside Socrates.

"These? These are olives. Would you like some?" He held the bowl out to Wesakicak. "Truly a barbarian, not to know the food of civilization," he remarked aside to Plato.

"These are like wild plums. They have a stone." Wesakicak tried one of the green ones. At first he wanted to spit, but that would not be polite. The fruit became more palatable as he nibbled the flesh from the pit. Not bad. He tried another.

"You see, Plato, the barbarian is always starving, never learned the art of cultivation and hence civilization. He follows the illusions and shadows of the forest and believes he understands the world. Tell me, Barbarian, what reason have you?"

Wesakicak spat a pit, fired the stone from between his teeth a good distance, wiggled his cheeks and fired another, and another, and another, and another, and finally spoke around the remaining stones in his mouth.

"My reason is to help Charlie," he gurgled.

"No, no, I did not mean your purpose, I meant your thoughts, your reason. You do reason, do you not?"

"My thoughts? You ask me my thoughts? My thoughts about what?"

"Now we are getting somewhere. Tell me your thoughts about the purpose of man. Why are we here? What is our greatest achievement?"

Wesakicak spat the few remaining stones, reached again for the bowl, but Socrates pulled it back. "Well, I guess the purpose of man is to live." Wesakicak snatched at the bowl, grabbed a handful, and sat back.

"To live. Very good, very good, perhaps we can converse, you and I. Now tell me, how shall we live?"

"We shall live," Wesakicak stalled, wriggled a few olive pits forward, spat, spat again, then continued. "We shall live like a family."

"Like a family? Do you mean we shall have a father figure in the lead, an eldest son, younger sons and then the rest following?"

"No, not like that. We should treat everyone as relatives with none above the other."

"None above the other. But how would you be organized? Who would be responsible?"

"Everyone should be responsible."

"Yes, yes, everyone responsible, granted, but who would make the decisions? Surely you would not allow women and the feeble-minded to decide for themselves."

"Who would decide for them?"

"In a civilized state, only the intelligent, the worthy, the very best minds would make the important decisions. Women and the feeble-minded must learn to obey."

Plato paused in his typing, struck a final key, waited while the compact printer buzzed a sheet of paper through, waited for the buzz to finish, pulled the sheet the rest of the way out, held it up and let it float away on the wind. He answered Wesakicak's quizzical look. "It is how we converse with the world."

Wesakicak tilted his head, still puzzled.

"The people read our words. They keep us alive here. For twenty centuries and more they have read our words. The word is the thing."

"So, if the people stop reading your words…"

"We fade into nothingness."

"You don't go up the steps to the top of the mountain?"

"Who would wish to? There is no intelligence up there, a clique of incestuous gossips, caught up in their own pettiness. You will find no insights on Mount Olympus." Plato readjusted the computer on his lap.

"You don't honour your forefathers?"

"They are not forefathers of ours." Socrates re-entered the conversation. "They only exist because the poets immortalized them. They have nothing to offer. In a perfect state there would be no need for the gods and especially not for the women among them."

"It appears to me, that you do not like women?" Wesakicak tried out formal speech. It did not fit his tongue, which at this time wriggled around olive flesh and pit. He spat. "What of your Mother? Your Grandmother?"

"Old women." Socrates bounced the doll on his knee. "They have a place in society. They are, after all, needed for procreation, but little more than that. They should be kept comfortable. But imagine if we allowed them into politics. Where would we be? It would lower the level of debate to the point where it would not be worth participating in any longer."

"You don't talk to your Mother?"

"Nor my father. It is the youth that we must communicate with. The youth with minds like clean slates upon which we inscribe ideas." Socrates patted the head of the doll. The doll smiled, turned adoring eyes up at the bearded face and buried his head in Socrates' shoulder. "You see, Wesakicak, if it were not for the youth, through these last long centuries, reading our words, we would not be here to debate with you. We would have faded into the dark of nothingness."

"What about your other place, that Hades place?"

"As my dear Plato here has said, we were saved from that forgotten place by our words. We are written here, Gutenberged here. We are always up to date. Hades has faded from memory, it barely exists now. We have exceeded that fate, surpassed it. We are forever."

"But surely," Wesakicak's tongue was getting into the rhythm of the conversation. "Your ideas must get old."

"Not at all. That is the beauty of it. So long as the conversation continues exclusively with the youth, our ideas will remain perpetually young. We are always modern."

"Don't you worry that you might lead them wrong."

"I deny that accusation." Socrates hugged the little boy. "I am not a corrupter of youth. I am their saviour. I have had enough of this foolish talk. Away with you now, Barbarian." Socrates clamped his mouth firmly shut. Plato closed the laptop. Wesakicak spread his hands questioning. "What did I say?"

Silence.

"Come now, we have just begun to visit." Wesakicak looked longingly at the bowl of olives.

The boy climbed down from Socrates' knee, gave Wesakicak a foul look, and walked away. Socrates followed, head high. Plato tucked the laptop under one arm and the bowl of olives under the other, shook his head at Wesakicak, as if to say "you are a pitiful person" and followed Socrates and the boy. They all walked stiffly with straight backs like people who have been insulted and want to show that they still have dignity.

Wesakicak sat a while on the marble steps and thought to himself, "Oh well, those funny little fruit didn't taste that good." And went to see if maybe Charlie Muskrat was a Christian.

[...]

Wesakicak opened his eyes in the mist. Yawned, stretched and scratched his ass. The Muses were still debating.

"If Strauss was a painter, would his art move the world?"

"If Churchill spoke poetry, would the world have followed him to war?"

Wesakicak checked the toe sticking through a hole in his moccasin. He scraped the crescent of black under the nail with a fingernail. The black was now under there. He scraped it with a thumbnail, now it was under there. Wesakicak looked around. No one was paying any attention to him. He scraped the thumbnail with the toenail, and pulled his moccasin over the dirt-encrusted digit.

"What you go and do that for?"

Wesakicak looked around to see who was talking to him. The man with one arm was talking to the man wearing shredded clothes that smelled of exploded dynamite, a cordite stink around him. He stuck a finger in his ear and wriggled it around. "What?" he asked as he cleaned out the other ear. "What a blast."

"Asshole!" The other man picked up his arm and stuck it back on.

"What you go and do that for?" asked a young woman looking around for her parcels. She pushed a dress back into its torn paper wrapping. "I was looking forward to wearing that." The dress fell out the other side of the package. "Oh well, I suppose I should be happy. I always thought you couldn't bring it with you."

Cordite Man looked around at the crowd that was gathering, forming in the mist. "Six, seven, eight." He counted with a pointing finger.

"What you go and do that for?"

"What you go and do that for?" they asked as they emerged.

"To go to heaven," answered Cordite Man, as he removed the wide leather belt with the bits of wire and the leftovers of exploded dynamite. He dropped the belt and never looked at it again.

"Well, here we are," said the man as he flexed his arm, good as new.

"What are you guys doing here?" asked Cordite Man.

"Same as you, idiot, come to heaven," said the old lady with the glass shard in her face and a hole in her chest. She looked around, got her bearings and started off toward the high, white wall with the shiny gate. Cordite Man followed her as did the young lady, and the man with two arms, and the rest. Wesakicak fell into line behind them.

"Rosella Stienne," said the old lady to the man in the white robe with the big book. He ran his finger down the page.

"Not today," he said.

"Do I look like I'm supposed to be here today?" snapped the old lady. "Try a little further ahead."

Peter flipped pages, found her name and stroked it off with a quill. "Next."

"Gloria Phyplia, You'll have to look a long ways ahead to find me."

"George Nexar."

"Erin Moore."

"Cassandra Laura Robinson."

Peter flipped pages, stroked names and waved each through the gate.

"Mustafa Goldstein," Cordite man stated proudly.

Peter flipped pages, stopped, started over, flipped more pages, looked up. "Sorry, Mustafa, your name isn't in the book."

Mustafa's once proud face fell. "How can that be?" Tears formed in the corners of his eyes.

"I am teasing you, my friend." Peter let out a little chuckle, some days are pure fun. "You're in here." He stroked out an entry and waved Mustafa in.

"How about Charlie Muskrat?" Wesakicak asked.

Peter checked the book, forward, forward some more. "Not here, Wesakicak."

"You know me?"

"Yes, Wesakicak, everyone knows about you. When we took the stories about you away from the Indians, we brought them up here. You're one of the favourites in the big library."

"Is that a fact? You're not trying to tease me now, are you?"

"I would never tease anyone who was older than myself. Especially not you, Wesakicak." Peter closed the book and rested his elbows on it. "So, my friend, why are we concerned with this Charlie Muskrat?"

"Oh nothing, I was just curious."

"Is he on his way?"

"I hope not. I was just wondering where he would go."

"Probably down in the valley. Just follow the river until you come to a forest. Ask the people there."

Wesakicak felt like he was getting somewhere now, as he headed away from the gate.

—2008

Bevann Fox
Cree · b. 1958 · Piapot

Bevann Fox is from Piapot First Nation and is a professional motivational speaker. As an artist of abstract acrylic paintings and sculptures, she often uses natural materials

in her work. The selections below are from
Fox's novel *Abstract Love*. They represent
a critical account of the residential school

experience, and the narrator's attempt to
heal from her past trauma.

Excerpts from *Abstract Love*

Chapter 6

[...]

Myrtle lived on the reserve just south of the biggest city she had ever seen. The
reserve was covered with lots of trees and hills. Her Grandparents she called
Kokom and Moshom. They took care of ten children. Her mother was there
too, but sometimes she left for awhile, probably for her sense of sanity. Myrtle's
mother had to get away from the house and reservation for awhile because she
worked so hard taking care of all of them. The days were hard work washing
clothes by hand, and scrubbing the walls and floors.

Once a week Myrtle was bathed in a big round silver tub in the same water
everyone else used. Myrtle hated bathing in the dirty water, particularly because
the younger kids often peed in it. In winter, her grandparents chopped ice from
the dam nearby and gathered snow to melt on the stove. The water was used
for drinking, cooking and washing. "It has to be clean," Moshom said. "Be
careful not to gather dirty snow."

One day, Moshom pulled them in a sleigh and Myrtle started to cry as she
stared at his back. His eyesight was weak and he was getting old. Myrtle thought
he was going to die. She wanted her Moshom to live forever. Who else would
take care of them? Later that night Myrtle asked him not to die. Moshom talked
with her about death but Myrtle still could not bear the thought of him dying.
She could not bear the thought of losing Moshom.

Kokom made fresh bannock every day and they ate deer, rabbit, duck and
prairie chickens. When there was no food to eat Moshom cut pickets and sold
them to nearby farmers. The kids helped Moshom carry the trees from the
bush. It was fun. Mostly they loved getting praise for the work they did. At
times they wanted to show Moshom and Kokom how strong they were and
competed with each other. There was complaining and arguing over who
pushed who into the bush of pinches. Pinches were like thistles that hurt and
sometimes stayed stuck in the skin.

They attended lodge ceremonies although Myrtle never participated. "A
long time ago we weren't allowed to practice the ceremonies. The Rain Dance
was a ceremony that was done every year. The government stopped the Indian
people from practicing the traditions passed on from my grandfathers. They

have control over everything we do," said Moshom. He talked about the Ghost Dance, the Shaky Tent, the piercing at the Rain Dance. She could not believe what happened in the ceremonies as she listened to him describe the different ceremonies. He said, "If you believe... you could move a mountain," and "you do not talk about what happens in the ceremonies, because it is very sacred." He went on to say, "The white men come around here being nosy with their cameras. The white ones, they want to look at everything under a microscope and they have to explain everything, make it like a test in science and sell it to make money."

Myrtle was startled, "Oh no! Moshom, I am too scared to go to ceremony and I won't tell anyone about them!"

Moshom smiled, "Why you afraid, don't be afraid. You must pray everyday, sometimes do a fast and give up something, a sacrifice like food and water. Go without food and water for one day." Moshom's words rang in her ear. "You put the Creator first, then you. You must believe in yourself!" When Moshom started his four-day fast he sometimes let Myrtle fast for a day or half a day. At the end of the day he prayed and gave Myrtle the blessed rainwater to drink. The soup and bannock he prayed over. He said, "Sometimes we take the simple things in life for granted." As Myrtle swallowed the fresh cool rainwater, she could feel it going down her throat. How she loved and appreciated that drink! And she thanked the Creator. The taste of soup and bannock was the most delicious meal ever! Myrtle thanked the Creator... she thanked the Creator for LIFE!

Myrtle attended powwows. Her dance outfits were later passed on to the younger children. The powwows were so much fun! Moshom set up camp and people from far away came to visit. At powwows there was so much laughter and excitement in the air. Everyday there was something to do and people to see. Moshom said, "A long time ago before the powwow became competitive and commercialized, the sweetgrass smudge scent carried for miles and miles." As he spoke, Myrtle could smell the sweetgrass scent far from the powwow grounds. She closed her eyes... but didn't know what commercialized meant.

Often, people who came to the powwows stayed on at Myrtle's family's home. Myrtle's grandparents gave the visitors gifts of fabrics, blankets, or beaded items. Visitors were treated like kings and queens in their home. The children were to wait on them, serve them meals and treat them with respect. They were to never stare at people because it was impolite and rude. Myrtle liked to stare at people and often Kokom scolded her and told her to stop staring in Cree, "Mitonay Poyou, kawiya wapamit."

Moshom and Kokom's home was warm and comfortable. It smelled nice, like apples and sage. Myrtle's Moshom helped people. People came to see him from near and far. He was a medicine man. Myrtle could hear the prayers, the songs, the special whistle blowing and the rattle shaking.

Moshom once told Myrtle about a woman with a sickness called cancer. Cancer ate the insides and it was very painful and those who had the sickness would die. Myrtle went with her Moshom to pick roots from the ground in the bush. He crushed the roots and made medicines to drink and smudge. She watched him make colours from the ground. The colours he used for special things like paint for the teepee.

Chapter 12

The ride to the boarding school was very long. Myrtle was scared, yet excited and wondered who would be there. "What will I learn, Moshom?"

"Learn all the good, leave the bad," Moshom said. Mrytle wondered what he meant by bad so she asked him the question again.

"You will learn how to read and write," he replied.

"Will you come for me?"

"Yes I come visit and you will come home for holidays, Christmas and summer," Moshom said. Myrtle felt lonesome already.

"Will the Queen be there?" Myrtle asked. No one answered. "Am I a red child?" She was so curious about the school.

"You listen in school and learn. Go to her school, her people will take care of you," said Moshom on the drive to the school.

Myrtle was proud of her light blue matching coat and hat with her little tiny light blue suitcase. She felt pretty and important, like a Queen she thought, "This is how the Queen of all the lands must feel. I hope she likes me."

The school was a red and brown brick building, it was big and scary and smelled like dough inside. The floor was all stone. When Myrtle and her family arrived, a black and white thing appeared and walked toward them. Accentuated by the long black and white dress that covered her head, her face was almost too white and she wore round wire glasses. She had a black necklace with a cross that hung around her neck. "Hello," she said, "my name is Sister." Myrtle thought she might be the Queen's sister.

"She is a nun," whispered Myrtle's cousin.

The nun smiled at them, she looked very kind as she explained "I will be in the little girls' dorm and I will look after Myrtle." The nun took Myrtle's blue suitcase and her hand. When Myrtle looked back, her family was gone. She began to cry.

The nun took Myrtle down a long hall to a big room with a cement floor and lots of small cupboards that sat one on top of the other. Suddenly, the nun stopped and said to Myrtle, "Get out of these dirty clothes!" She locked Myrtle's suitcase up high in the cupboard and threw a dress and apron at Myrtle hissing, "Put these on!"

Myrtle was shaking and she cried out. "Kokom, Moshom!"

Myrtle felt a hard slap land on her head and whip across the face. The nun kneeled down and shook Myrtle. "Don't you ever speak that pagan tongue again? Do you hear me, do you hear me?" The nun yelled as her face grew red. Myrtle felt the fear go through her little body. Her arms felt prickly and her legs couldn't move. She felt frozen as terror shot through her—she was numb with fear. Myrtle cried louder, screaming as the nun pulled her hair and slapped her again while jerking Myrtle back and forth by the hair.

"You little ugly dirty Indian. Change your clothes, you stink like a savage!" Myrtle felt the nun's spit thrown in her face and the nun's breath smelled of decay as she yelled at her. Myrtle wanted to vomit; she gagged and could not breathe. The nun continued to slap Myrtle. "You listen… don't talk that evil tongue again, now change out of those ugly dirty clothes and be quiet!"

Myrtle could not stop crying and shaking. "Stop that crying, you little dirty pagan Indian, I will give you something to cry about!" The nun screamed and again hit Myrtle across the face and yanked on her hair. She slammed Myrtle against the many tiny locker doors until Myrtle fell to the concrete floor. The nun looked as big as a giant lurking over Myrtle. The nun pulled Myrtle upright by the hair. Myrtle succumbed and changed her clothes, trying not to cry. She was frozen with fear, her heart pounded and her head throbbed with pain. The sobs stuck in Myrtle's chest making it burn like fire. The tears rolled hot down her cheeks and burned. She tried to blink them back, but they kept coming, gushing like a spring from underneath her closed eyelids. Her cheeks stung, burning from the slaps as more tears rolled down. Myrtle tasted the tears on her lips; it was like drinking tears from a cup. She could not stop her little body from trembling. Her whole body shook with fear.

The nun had forgotten to put Myrtle's blue coat away when she took the blue suitcase. "Let's put this ugly stink coat away and out of sight," and she locked her blue coat up high in the cupboard along with her other clothes and pretty blue suitcase. Myrtle's little body continued to shake with fear.

When Myrtle was fully dressed in the dress and apron the nun had thrown at her, the nun took Myrtle to another big room with many little girls like Myrtle. They were staring at Myrtle, watching as the nun sat her on a chair. The nun put a towel over Myrtle's shoulder like cape and began to cut Myrtle's long hair.

Myrtle thought of Moshom and what he had said about her hair. The tears rolled down her face more than ever. The nun buzzed the back of Myrtle's head and poured some liquid that smelled like gas onto Myrtle's scalp. Myrtle's forehead, ears and neck burned from the liquid. It felt like the nun had set her on fire. All the while, the nun slapped her head and yanked her hair. "You are shameful; your hair is full of bugs."

Myrtle's hair lay on the floor. The nun called a girl to come and sweep up "this dirty hair." The girl came and did as she was told but did not look at Myrtle. She took Myrtle's hair and put it in a garbage can.

Myrtle thought of her sacred hair and her heart broke for Moshom, for her, for her hair. No one ever touched her hair and threw it away like that. Her heart broke as the terror pulsed through her body. Myrtle was very scared. Her crying stopped but she continued to shake uncontrollably and gasped for air each time the nun hit her. Myrtle's nose was bleeding and the nun laughed at her and called her blood "pagan blood."

Myrtle saw her older cousin Kaya who arrived at the school before her. Kaya moved her lips saying "don't cry." Myrtle wanted to scream for Kaya, cry for her to help. Suddenly, Myrtle sat quietly, she was very still as she looked at Kaya. It was a comfort to look in Kaya's eyes. Myrtle kept focused on Kaya as she smiled at Myrtle. Myrtle still had blood leaking from her nose but she remained calm as she watched Kaya's eyes, Kaya smiling at her so peacefully. Myrtle sat still with her quiet jerking sobs held in her chest as her head was buzzed and shaved at the back.

Myrtle's heart beat fast as the fear continued to spread and settle deep within her little body. *I want to go home. Come and get me please. Please take me home now.*

—*2011*

Paul Seesequasis
Cree-Dakota-Ukrainian-German · b. 1958 · Melfort

Paul Seesequasis was born in Melfort, and he is of Plains Cree, Dakota, Ukrainian, and German ancestry. He is a writer, journalist, editor, storyteller, broadcaster, and arts policy advisor, serving thirteen years as a literary arts officer at the Canada Council for the Arts. His writing has been published in numerous books and journals, and he was the founding editor of *Aboriginal Voices*, an award-winning magazine. The selection below is an autobiographical parable that satirizes both the Indian Act and First Nations governance.

The Republic of Tricksterism

We were urban mixed-bloods. Shopping malls and beer parlors were our sacred grounds; as we reached adolescence in the 70s, the Sex Pistols and the Clash provided the tribal drums. Fallen between the seams and exiled from the reserves, we were the prisoners of bureaucratic apartheid, of red tape and parliamentary decrees.

Our tribal links were obscure, our colonial banishment confirmed by the Indian Act. White bureaucrats and tribal politicians alike were our oppressors.

"We are heading toward self-government," proclaimed Tobe, the Grand Chief of the Fermentation of Saskatchewan Indian Nations (FSIN) as he shook the hand of then Saskatchewan Premier Allan Blakeney.

In his hands Tobe, the Grand Chief, held a paper promising tens of millions of dollars; but that money and power were destined for only a select few. The Grand Chief's vision was obscured by power and long-legged blondes. He denounced Indian women who married white men, while blond secretaries and assistants crossed their legs in his plush office at the FSIN.

Mary Seesequasis, a.k.a. Ogresko, was born on Beardy's Reserve in central Saskatchewan on January 20, 1934, the first child of Sam Seesequasis, of Beardy's Reserve, and Mary Rose Nahtowenhow, of the Sturgeon Lake band. Sam, my *nimosom*, danced through life with gentleness and humour and became a leader in the community. Mary Rose, my *nohkom*, was large and became a bear when she laughed. She hunted rabbits, decapitated chickens, and farted in the direction of bureaucrats and posers.

They made love, had nine children, and seven lived to adulthood.

The Grand-Chief-to-be and his family lived downwind from my grandmother's farts. He was born the same day as my mother and they played together as children; they fell asleep infused with dreams of *Wesakaychuk* and *Pakakos*; they hid under the covers from the *wetigoes* and hairy hearts.

But their lives were destined to take far different paths. Tobe was born mixed-blood, his father Cree, his mother white. But the irony and humour of being mixed-race was lost on Tobe. He would grow up as a mixed-race "pure-blood"; purer than thou and given to exaggerating the quantity of his half-cup of tribal blood, Tobe lived in denial of his white parentage.

The Indian Act enabled Tobe to imagine himself a pure-blood. With Indian father and white mother, he was allowed to stay on the reserve. In 1950, my mother met and fell in love with a white man, Dennis Ogresko, and because she was *hisqueau*, she had to leave the reserve.

The hairy hearts ran amuck in 1950s Saskatchewan; cannibal spirits plagued the small towns and hid in grain elevators. It was open season on squaws, wagon-burners, and mixed-breeds. By courageously proclaiming brown-white love, my parents challenged the humourless segregational values of the time. Unable to hide on the reserve they learned to bear the taunts and jeers with laughter. That love could exist between races offended all the pure-breeds; and by making love, Dennis and Mary parented two cross-breed mutts—my brother and me.

We experienced childhood between the seams, spending summers on the reserve, winters in the city. We played without leashes; without pedigree, we learned to live with our genetic-mixture coats and our lack of papers. We pissed on the city trees, marked our traditional urban territories, and barked ferociously at the white poodles. It was the 1960s and my mother, now a registered nurse, worked at the Community Clinic in Prince Albert in northern Saskatchewan, where she healed the urban orphans and mixed-bloods who were now entering the cities in increasing numbers.

Tobe, the mixed-blood pure-blood, had grown up too. He became a tribal politician, a chief of the reserve, and a wearer of suits and ties. His hair was short and his speeches were long. He spoke of self-government and economic development, but his mind was focused on attending conferences and getting laid in hotels. With enthusiasm he joined Wild Jean's Indian Affairs Bandwagon and Wild West Show; and with conferences here and there and blondes to his left and right, he lived the modern-day chief's delight. Tobe sold his Pontiac— the Poor Old Nechee had thought it was a Cadillac—and actually bought a real Cadillac. He hired a blond chauffeur. But while Tobe played the colonial game, a revolution was brewing in Prince Albert.

Malcolm Norris was a Métis trickster, a *rigorueau*, and a shit-disturber and activist par excellence: a cofounder of the Métis Association of Alberta in the 1930s and an urban activist who cut through the lies of white bureaucrats and tribal politicians alike. Fate had landed him in Prince Albert and, in 1965, he and my mother became friends.

As a *rigorueau*, Malcom Norris was hated by the hairy hearts and the cannibal spirits. They envied his power, his ability to turn into a dog, a bear, or almost any kind of rodent he chose. From Malcolm, I learned to see the evil spirits around me. I felt the disapproving glares of the police, farmers, tribal politicians, and store owners. They were everywhere in the city and their numbers were increasing.

The cannibal spirits and the hairy hearts ruled the cities and reserves. They fed on both Indians and whites. "There just aren't enough of us *rigorueaus* left to stop them," Malcolm once told me. "These evil spirits," he explained, "feed on souls that are empty, rub against their bodies, and penetrate the skin. Sometimes a person can repel them if he is strong enough, or he can call on a *rigorueau* to drive the spirit away. But most people succumb and the cannibal spirits continue in their goal to create a world of hate. A world in which they can proliferate."

Then one day, Malcolm was missing. Search parties were organized and the mixed-bloods and urban orphans looked everywhere, but it was the squirrels, the rodent friends of the *rigorueau*, who led us to him. He had been dumped into a grain chute and his body was badly beaten. While the crows cawed mournfully and the stray dogs howled their lament, our procession carried Malcolm back to our house. He was laid on a bed and a group of women healers worked with him; after a few days, his heart began to beat again. Time passed and Malcolm cracked a smile. "My spirit has tasted life again, though parts of my body never will," he said. True, he was now paralyzed from the waist down.

But being confined to a wheelchair didn't slow Malcolm down. He wanted to take over the Prince Albert Friendship Centre and remove the metal detectors from the door. Those detectors beeped a warning any time someone without an Indian-blood status card tried to walk past them. He called a gathering of mixed-bloods and orphans, at which he spoke passionately about uniting all urban skins, mixed or full. "Burn your status cards!" he proclaimed. "And throw away your colonial pedigree papers. Don't let the white man define us. Let's define ourselves." The mixed-bloods and urban orphans from the streets cheered and, with Malcolm leading them, they grabbed trees as battering rams and forced their way into the Friendship Centre as the suits and ties, panic-stricken, climbed out the back windows. Leaving in such a rush, the suits didn't have time to shred their Indian Affairs hit list or their sacred status-card membership rolls. The Republic of Tricksterism, where humour rules and bureaucrats are banished, was proclaimed. "All skins are equal" was the first constitutional decree and a pair of red drawers became the new flag. Skins from the street came in to help the social workers heal themselves, and tribal lawyers were deprogrammed.

The Prince Albert Regional Tribal Council was in a panic. They passed resolutions and sent ultimatums to the Republic of Tricksterism, demanding that it abdicate power. "We are the chiefs," they reassured themselves, "the big white men in Ottawa say so." "Ah—go on," replied the Republic of Tricksterism. When even memos from the Department of Indian Affairs failed to dislodge the trickster upstarts, the Tribal Council called in its heavy: Tobe.

Tobe, now the second-in-command at the FSIN in Regina, arrived in Prince Albert with a hundred tribal goons. They were armed with baseball bats, dog repellent, and mace. "When we talk about self-government we mean it for us, not for them," Tobe proclaimed as the chiefs cheered, patted their beer bellies, and licked their fat lips in anticipation.

The assault came at dawn. Calling in the mounties, who donned full regalia and did a musical ride alongside them in honor of the chiefs, Tobe and the goons marched in a column toward the Friendship Centre. But the urban animals, the squirrels, raccoons, and foxes, ran out ahead of the approaching army and barked out a warning to the citizens of the Republic of Tricksterism.

"We must avert bloodshed," Malcolm observed to the citizens. "Violence is the tool of fools. It is with humor and irreverence that we urban animals must survive. Let them have their building back; let them issue their proclamations with dead trees; let them have their dubious titles like national chief; let them become the media stars: we'll find our humour back on the streets."

And so it came to be that Tobe and his goons recaptured the Prince Albert Friendship Centre without bloodshed. "These mixed-bloods are cowards," Tobe proclaimed. The joke was lost on him.

Malcolm Norris was captured by the tribal goons and brought before the Prince Albert Regional Tribal Council. "He must be punished as an example," proclaimed Tobe. "He has committed blasphemy and challenged our noble and sacred institutions."

"Spare him!" yelled the urban orphans and mixed-bloods but, as always the chiefs were deaf to the sounds of the streets. On a Sunday, surrounded by a procession of goons, Malcolm was forced to wheel his chair to the highest hill in Prince Albert. There he was nailed to a metal medicine wheel, his arms and legs spread in the four directions. Malcolm died soon after, and his body was taken by the goons and buried in an unmarked grave. The mixed-bloods and urban orphans mourned. Crows flew high and cawed his name to the clouds. A wake was held, and for four days the memory fires burned from street-corner garbage cans. On the fifth day the crows told the people that Malcolm had been resurrected but that he had come back as a termite.

The urban people rejoiced and Malcolm, in his new life form, moved into the regional Indian Affairs building and gnawed at the bureaucrats' desks until they dissolved into sawdust. Having completed his job in Prince Albert he found his way into a chief's pocket and made it to Ottawa.

Rumour has it that even today Malcolm, the termite, has led an army of termites into a certain national chief's organization where he is currently munching away at the legs of a certain national chief's chair. Meanwhile with the retaking of the Friendship Centre as another dishonourable feather in his war bonnet, Tobe ran for national leader of the FSIN and won the big chief position at that fermenting organization.

"Who better to speak the politicians' garble? Who better to hide the truth between platitudes of self-government and economic development than Tobe?" proclaimed the FSIN in their press release announcing his victory.

Then in May 1987, despite the opposition of the FSIN, C-31 became law. With the stroke of a bureaucratic pen, status was restored to those long denied, as if the government could, with a decree, instantly undo a hundred years of damage. "Hallelujah, we're Indians," was the ironic response of the mixed-bloods. Our hearts soared like drunken eagles. We donned our chicken-feather headdresses, our squirrel-tail bustles, and fancy-danced around the Midtown Plaza.

For my mother, a full-blood Cree woman, the seemingly gracious convening of status was a double irony that could be dealt with only with humour. In the FSIN offices, Tobe, the mixed-blood pure-blood, and his Indiancrats, were having a bad day. They grumbled, drank double shots of rye, and hit their blond secretaries.

But C-31 was only a temporary irritation for Tobe. He remained focused on his career. He wore blinders whenever he entered the city so as not to see the urban orphans. He talked about First Nations as if the cities did not exist. He became bloated with his power and gained weight by the hour. As the Honourable Heap Big Chief, he increased his salary and his belly respectively. Meanwhile Mary Seesequasis moved to Saskatoon and worked at the 20th Street Community Clinic where she administered to the mixed-bloods, the whores, dykes, queers, street people: everyone.

"We are not victims. We are survivors," was the motto she lived by. Tobe was a survivor too, but in a more dangerous game. My mother saw the Indian Act as a bad joke. Tobe embraced it as a career. His sense of humour was lost in the shuffle of colonial cards and his heart was hardened by the cannibal spirits.

Meanwhile Uncle Morris, having completed his job in Prince Albert, found his way into a chief's pocket and made it to Ottawa. Rumour has it that even today he has led an army of termites into a certain national chief's organization where he is currently munching away at the legs of that chief's chair.

—1991

Winona Wheeler
Cree-Nakoda-Saulteaux-English-Irish · b. 1958 · Saskatoon

Winona Wheeler is a member of the Ockekwi Sipi (Fisher River) Cree Nation in northern Manitoba, though her family comes from the George Gordon First Nation in Saskatchewan. She received her Ph.D. in 2000 from the University of California, Berkeley. She has lectured internationally, and has held appointments at Athabasca University and the First Nations University of Canada; she is currently an associate professor of Indigenous Studies at the University of Saskatchewan. She has served as the President of the Native American and Indigenous Studies Association and as a Keeper with the Walking With Our Sisters (Saskatoon) Exhibit.

In the selection below, Wheeler challenges the "Great Canadian myth" that missionaries invented the Cree writing system, privileging instead the oral accounts of the origins of Cree syllabics.

Calling Badger and the Symbols of the Spirit Language: The Cree Origins of the Syllabic System

Nêhiyawak, *Cree people*, were the first, and for a long time the only Indigenous peoples in present-day Western Canada with a written language. Composed of syllabic characters, the written form of nêhiyawêwin, the *Cree language*, can be found throughout Cree territory from Northern Quebec to Northeast British

Columbia, and south to Montana. Cree syllabics arrived among the people in the early 1800s and were used extensively until quite recently. Over time, as the English language replaced the daily usage of Cree, the Cree syllabary fell into disuse. Today only a handful of Cree speakers still know and use it, though in the last decade or so, interest in reviving and utilizing Cree syllabics has grown tremendously.

The origins of the Cree syllabary has long been credited to the ingenuity of the Rev. James Evans of the Wesleyan Methodist church. According to missionary records and other non-Indian documented accounts, Evans arrived among the muskego-wininiwak, *Swampy Cree People*, of Norway House in August of 1840 and by mid-November printed three hundred copies of the hymn "Jesus my all to Heaven has Gone" in Cree syllabics.[1] A remarkable feat for anyone who had only been among Cree people a few short months and who continued relying on interpreters for the duration of his time in Cree country. According to his biographer and other historical records, Evans' accomplishment, "upon which his enduring fame rests" was made possible by his fluency in the Ojibway language which allowed him to "master Cree easy" and also by the assistance of Chief Factor Donald Ross of the Hudson's Bay Company and his Native wife.[2]

This great Canadian myth has endured for over 160 years virtually unchallenged. Few question colonialist/conqueror renditions of the past and even fewer bothered asking Cree people directly about the origins of their writing system. A handful of anthropologists are aware that an Indigenous version exists in Cree oral histories but most, like David Mandelbaum, choose to disregard it in favor of the James Evans story.[3]

Mandelbaum recorded the origin story of the Cree syllabary from old Chief Fine Day of the Sweetgrass First Nation in the 1930s. According to Fine Day, a Wood Cree named Badger Call[4] died and returned to life with the gift of writing from the Spirit World.[5] Old Fine Day's grandson Wes Fineday told the story in more detail some time ago on the CBC radio program Morningside. Fineday the younger explained that Calling Badger came from the Stanley Mission area and lived ten to fifteen years before his grandfather's birth in 1846. On his way to a sacred society meeting one evening Calling Badger and two singers came upon a bright light and all three fell to the ground. Out of the light came a voice speaking Calling Badger's name. Soon after, Calling Badger fell ill and the people heard he had passed away. During his wake three days later, while preparing to roll him in buffalo robes for the funeral, the people discovered that his body was not stiff like a dead person's body should be. Against all customs and tradition the people agreed to the widow's request to let the body sit one more night. The next day Calling Badger's body was still not stiff so the old people began rubbing his back and chest. Soon his eyes opened and he told the people he had gone to the Fourth World, the spirit world, and there the spirits taught him many things. Calling Badger told the people of the things he was shown that prophesized events in the future, then he pulled out some pieces of birch bark with symbols on them. These symbols, he told the people, were to be used to write down the spirit languages, and for the Cree people to use to communicate among themselves.[6]

A few decades after David Mandelbaum's visit among the Plains Cree of Saskatchewan, anthropologist Verne Dusenbury was doing fieldwork among the Plains Cree on the Rocky Boy reservation in Montana. He was told a similar story by Raining Bird in December of 1959. According to Raining Bird "the spirits came to one good man and gave him some songs. When he mastered them, they taught him how to make a type of ink and then showed him how to write on white birch bark."[7] He also received many teachings about the spirits which he recorded in a birch bark book. When the one good man returned to his people he taught them how to read and write. "The Cree were very pleased with their new accomplishment, for by now the white men were in this country. The Cree knew that the white traders could read and write, so now they felt that they too were able to communicate among themselves just as well as did their white neighbors."[8]

In all the oral accounts of the origins of the Cree syllabary it was told that the missionaries learned Cree syllabics from the Cree. In the Fineday account Badger Call was told by the spirits that the missionaries would change the script and claim that the writing belonged to them. In the Raining Bird account the birch bark book with the teachings and Cree syllabary was stolen and taught to the missionaries who disregarded the spirit teachings, took the syllabary and claimed they invented it.

What we have here are two conflicting accounts of the origins of the Cree syllabic system, one found in Cree oral traditions that has long been disregarded, the other documented in primary sources and touted as the official version. The primary reasons why the Evans version prevails are first, because it supports colonialist discourse—Europeans were/are superior to Nehiyawak. Church historian Bruce Peel feeds into this discourse by ostentatiously proclaiming that "Evans used symbols to represent syllables and produced a script so simple that any unlettered Indian could master it within days."[9] The second reason why the Evans version prevails is because very little serious attention has been paid to the version stored in Cree oral traditions.

Anthropologist Verne Dunsenbery is one of the few scholars who challenged the Evans version in favor of the Cree. Before completely disregarding the Cree account, he implores, two factors should be considered:

*In the first place, the writing does not look like anything a white man,
and especially an Englishman, would invent. In the second place, an
interesting speculation arises concerning the possibility that the Cree
might have developed their own written form—much as Sequoia
did for the Cherokee—by what Kroeber calls 'stimulus diffusion.'*[10]

All other missionaries before Evans used the Roman alphabet to reduce
Indigenous languages to written form. The Cree syllabary is unique in that it
consists of a series of triangles, angles, and hooks of various configurations each
of which are mirrored in four directions. Each symbol depicts syllables rather
than individual sounds, and to these are added a number of accent characters
that represent terminal consonants and vowels.

Plains Cree Syllabary

▽	e	◁	i	▷	o	◁	a	◁̇	â
▽·	we	◁·	wi	▷·	wo	◁·	wa	◁̇·	wâ
∨	pe	∧	pi	>	po	<	pa	<̇	pâ
∪	te	∩	ti	⊃	to	⊂	ta	⊂̇	tâ
٩	ke	ᖘ	ki	◗	ko	b	ka	ḃ	kâ
⌐	ce	ᒋ	ci	⌐	co	ᒐ	ca	ᒐ̇	câ
⌐	me	ᒥ	mi	⌐	mo	ᒪ	ma	ᒪ̇	mâ
ᓄ	nw	ᓂ	ni	ᓄ	no	ᓇ	na	ᓇ̇	nâ
ᐢ	se	ᐧ	si	ᐧ	so	ᐢ	sa	ᐢ̇	sâ
ᔦ	ye	ᐧ	yi	ᐧ	yo	ᖬ	ya	ᖬ̇	yâ
·	w	ᑊ	m	°	w		
ᐟ	p	ᑉ	n	⅔	l		
ᐠ	t	ᐢ	s	ᔕ	r		
ᐠ	k	ᐟ	y	"	h		
–	c			×	hk		

Sequoyah's Cherokee alphabet has received far more serious attention as an
Indigenous invention, but unlike the Cree syllabary, no competing claims to
its invention threaten its Indigenous origins because it was so well recorded in
its making.[11] The Cherokee had already experienced considerable interaction
with European colonists and by the 1820s, when Sequoyah developed the syllabary, the Cherokee not only had direct knowledge of writing and its utility,
but many were literate in English.

According to Raymond Fogelson, Sequoyah's idea to create a writing system was definitely influenced by his contacts with Euroamericans, but it may

have also been influenced by old petroglyphs found throughout Cherokee territory.[12] After years of experimentation and study, Sequoyah eventually translated the Cherokee language into eighty-five "minimal sound units, to each of which he attached a particular symbol." While many of the symbols derive from the English alphabet none has the same corresponding sound value as in English and all denote syllables rather than letter sounds.[13] By the early 1820s the significance of the Cherokee syllabary was recognized, in 1828 the first issue of a bilingual newspaper the *Cherokee Phoenix* rolled off the Cherokee Nation press, and by 1830 most Cherokee people could read and write in their own language.[14] Missionaries were quick to recognize "the advantages of the syllabary over the awkward orthography they had tried to impose on the Cherokee language" and so among the earliest publications were the Bible and other religious tracts which were translated, typeset, and printed by the American Board of Foreign Missions.[15]

Like the Cherokee, the Cree also had upwards of two centuries of contact with Europeans, vis-à-vis the fur trade, and were well aware of the power of the written word. Unlike the Cherokee experience, however, Cree people had little or no chance to learn how to read and write because prior to Evans arriving in Norway House the only schools in Rupert's Land were located in the Red River settlement.[16] Also like the Cherokee, age-old petroglyphs abound in Cree territory, especially in the Canadian Shield area around Stanley Mission.

Given the circumstances in Cree country in the 1840s—long familiarity with the written word, age-old petroglyph archetypes, and the fact that James Evans was only among Cree speakers a few short months which is far too brief a period to learn the language—Dusenbury's claim that "it does not seem too incredulous to believe that the Cree may have developed a written form of their own language" is convincing.[17] Luckily, the Cherokee already knew how to read and write English and so were able to document the emergence of their own syllabary.

The 'official story' of the Cree syllabary has taken on a mythic quality in Canadian history. Like the 'Bering Strait' theory, the James Evans version of the origins of Cree syllabics has been propagated for so long, it has become 'fact' in Canadian minds. But it is only one version. The colonialist tendency to ignore or disbelieve the ability of Indigenous peoples to create remarkable engineering, scientific, and other intellectual accomplishments will continue until more challenges from Indigenous oral histories refute them.

—*2000*

Notes

1   Bruce Peel, "How the Bible Came to the Cree," *Alberta Historical Review* 6, 2 (1958), 15,16.

2   John McLean, *James Evans: Inventor of the Syllabic System of the Cree Language* (Toronto: William Briggs, 1890), 163.
3   David Mandelbaum, *The Plains Cree: An Ethnographic, Historical, and Comparative Study* (Regina: Canadian Plains Research Centre, 1987 reprint), 180.
4   Badger Call is also referred to as 'Calling Badger' and 'Badger Voice' or Mistanakowew.
5   Fine Day explained that he learned the syllabary from Strikes-him-on-the-back who learned it directly from Badger Call. Mandelbaum, *The Plains Cree*, 180.
6   Wes Fineday, "The Story of Calling Badger," CBC radio, Morningside (n.d.)
7   Verne Dusenbury, *The Montana Cree: A Study in Religious Persistence* (Norman: U of Oklahoma P, 1998 reprint), 267.
8   Ibid., 268.
9   Peel, "How the Bible," 15.
10 Dusenbury, *The Montana Cree*, 271.
11 Sequoyah's English name was George Guess. See Raymond D. Fogelson, "Sequoyah c.1770–1843 Inventor of the Cherokee syllabary," pp. 580–582 in Frederick E. Hoxie, ed., *Encyclopedia of North American Indians* (Boston: Houghton Mifflin Company, 1996); Rayna Green, "Sequoyah," pp. 146–147 in *The British Museum Encyclopedia of Native North America*, (Bloomington: Indiana UP, 1999).
12 Fogelson, "Sequoyah," 580.
13 Ibid.; Dusenbury, *The Montana Cree*, 271.
14 Ibid., 581; Green, "Sequoyah," 146.
15 Fogelson, "Sequoyah," 581.
16 See Winona Stevenson, "The Red River Indian Mission School and John West's 'Little Charges', 1829–1833," *Native Studies Review* 4, 1 & 2 (1988): 129–66.
17 Dusenbury, *The Montana Cree*, 271.

Connie Fife

Cree · 1961–2017 · Prince Albert

Connie Fife was born in Prince Albert. At the age of ten, she left Saskatchewan, travelling with her adoptive father on his Anglican missionary work. In the mid-1980s she helped found the Native Women's Resource Centre in Toronto. She attended the University of Toronto and later the En'owkin International School of Writing in Penticton. Her writing has appeared in numerous anthologies and journals, and she has published three collections of poetry, *Beneath the Naked Sun* (1992), *Speaking Through Jagged Rock* (1999), and *Poems for a New World* (2001).

i have become so many mountains

standing on the shoreline of history
pondering the forthcoming sunrise
or the very impossibility of it
i have become so many rivers

not a single current but many
leading to a whirlpool of countless places
i have become so many women
waking each morning with jaws clenched
determined to bite down on the impending day
i have become so many men
wondering which mask to remove
afraid of flailing skinless in the wind
i have become so many forests
whose tears slide down hillsides
then come to rest in shimmering pools of ice
i have become so many ancestors
who dance through empty houses
windows blown out by our laughter
i have become so many photographs
framed and frozen behind glass made of lies
whose eyes hold the truth despite the distortion
i have become so many songs
slipping off the tongues of entire nations
who sing me into the existence of memory
i have become so many landscapes,
scarred by the hands of the uncivilized
whose open wounds now swallow them whole
i have become so many poems
whose fingers caress me with their desire
while fighting for our lives breath by breath
i have become so many mountains and rivers
so many women and men singing
so many ancestors
so many photographs carried in my lungs
so many landscapes acting in revolutionary fashion
i have become so many movements
without having made the slightest motion.
standing in solitude on the shoreline of history

—1999

the knowing

the re-invention of oneself
through the tongues of whispering mountains
the re-arrangement of the universe

because a spider wrapped her legs around a star
the knowing
the remembering of stone's story
while walking down a dried riverbed
being serenaded by crickets singing the blues
because everyone except them has forgotten
the knowing
which trail to follow through dear-cut forests
which scent will lead you home
because a thousand-year-old bear still lives
amongst the dead bodies feeding off their memory
the knowing
the recollection of the loudness in silence
the clarity of unspoken words while sound crashes earthbound
because it is in what is not said that the truth sits
the knowing
the peeling back of ones own skin
to discover that the lizard sleeping against your spine
was born the same moment as you
because she knew that one day you
would need her sharp tongue to survive
the knowing
the rediscovery of crow perched on your shoulder
her claws leaving scratch marks against your heart
because you need to be reminded that you are alive
on days where you are numbed into speechlessness
the knowing
the glimpse of your reflection in the eyes of a stranger
who is leaning against the chest of a cedar tree
while cars spit at her then mock her existence
because she refuses to roll over on the sidewalk
and you need to be reminded of why you were born
the knowing
the recreating of ceremony at the hands of change
while wandering through unknown places
because history has turned us into our own lodges
when it tried to bound our mouths and tie our words
the knowing
the acknowledgment of ones ancestors
must become an ordinary event taking place with each breath

keeping them alive so their voices touch our skin
with urgency and desire in our ribcages
because it is their shadows that protect us
the knowing
the importance of embracing our places of remembering
because inside their bodies live our beloved
through their existence we are fed love on a plate of resistance
while we swallow stars dropped down our throats by spider

—1999

Berries and Ripened Poems

In the likelihood we should meet again
I have prepared a bowl of ripened poems
with which to ease our hunger,
laid out a tablecloth made from memories
each one tasting of wild berries wrapped in early morning dew.
I have sewn stars into a tapestry above each door frame,
drawn back the clouds and pulled the sheets
made from a laughing moon across the bed
beside which stands an empty gourd
waiting to be filled by our stories carried
across the heartlands of distance we will have travelled.

—1999

Yvette Nolan
Algonquin-Irish · b. 1961 · Prince Albert

Yvette Nolan was born in Prince Albert. She is a playwright, director, dramaturge, and educator. She was the first ever writer-in-residence at Brandon University in 1996, and she served as the artistic director of Native Earth Performing Arts in Toronto from 2003 to 2011. Her plays include *Annie Mae's Movement*, *Blade*, *Job's Wife*, *Flesh Offerings*, and *The Unplugging*. She coedited *Performing Indigeneity: New Essays on Canadian Theatre*. The selections below come from her critical work, *Medicine Shows: Indigenous Performance Culture* and from one of her plays, *The Birds*, an adaptation of the classical Greek play by Aristophanes.

Excerpts from *Medicine Shows*

Medicine, in my community, is not about curing, not even really about healing. Medicine is about connection, about health. Many of the First Nations attach teachings to the Medicine Wheel: a circle that embraces the directions, the seasons, the ages of a human being, the grandfather teachings. The Medicine of the Wheel is that it endeavours to teach us to apprehend the interconnectedness of all things. When someone talks about bad medicine, I understand the phrase to mean that someone is breaking something, a relationship or a rule or a social contract. Good medicine, on the other hand, makes community.

Medicine, in Indian country, also refers to the four traditional medicines of many First Nations: tobacco, sweetgrass, sage, and cedar. Like everything in Indigenous worldview, they are connected—to teachings, to directions. Tobacco connects us to the spiritual world, carrying our prayers to the Creator; sweetgrass reminds us of kindness, as it bends when it is stepped on; sage is for purification, cleansing our minds and hearts of bad feelings; and cedar is similarly for cleansing, and I have been taught that it is associated with strength and protection.

The drum, the same drum that Hollywood immortalized and bastardized with its *BUH-buh-buh-buh* rhythm, is also medicine. Our people talk about bringing back the drum, its circular shape the reminder of all the circles that we hold sacred: cycles of seasons and of life, directions, and equality (for no point on a circle is closer to the centre than any other). The drumbeat is the heartbeat of Mother Earth, and her heart beats like ours, not as Hollywood would have it. Bringing back the drum, then, is an acknowledgement that we have become disconnected from our ways, from our histories and our values, and we must work to become reconnected.

[...]

Indigenous theatre artists make medicine by reconnecting through ceremony, through the act of remembering, through building community, and by negotiating solidarities across communities. The act of staging these things reconnects who we are as Indigenous people with where we have come from, with our stories, with our ancestors. The things we know and the values we hold that manifest in the contemporary work that we put upon the stage make the Indigenous artist a conduit between the past and the future. Ceremony. Remembrance. Making Community. Survivance.

—*2015*

Ernie Louttit
Cree · b. 1961 · Saskatoon

Ernie Louttit was born in a remote northern Ontario community and is a member of the Missanabie Cree Band. He left high school to work for the Canadian National Railway, and at seventeen he joined the Canadian Forces, serving with the Princess Patricia's Canadian Light Infantry and military police. He joined the Saskatoon Police Service in 1987. At the time, he was only the city's third Indigenous police officer, and he became known on the streets as "Indian Ernie." The selection below is from his memoir, *Indian Ernie: Perspectives on Policing and Leadership*. It is significant for its account of the events surrounding the death of Neil Stonechild and other Indigenous men, including the claims about the notorious "Starlight Tours."

Excerpts from "Young Man Frozen"

In late November 1990, I never missed an issue of the local paper. In my early years with the Saskatoon Police Service, I had a hunger for the news and cared how the media portrayed us. It was my last day off, and I picked up the paper from a confectionery in the lobby of our apartment building. I read through the headlines, none of which I can remember now, and came across a small article describing what sounded like a death by misadventure. A young man had been found frozen to death by two workers in a field in the north end of Saskatoon's industrial area. I perked up and was immediately intrigued by the lack of detail. I decided I would find out what the real story was when I returned to work.

When I got to work, no one seemed to know a lot about the young man's death. Eventually, I found somebody in the station who knew that the dead person had been identified as Neil Stonechild. I recognized the name, but not having had a lot of dealings with him, I was not seized by the tragedy. I knew his younger brother Jake or Jason much better, and I felt bad for him. Jake fought his own demons, and his brother's death would surely make the battle more difficult.

I threw myself back into my work and listened for any developments or information about Neil Stonechild's death. I considered his death to be very unusual given his age and the location where his body was found. I trusted the investigation was in good hands.

I dealt with my calls and arrests, and the shift progressed normally. It was my practice to park my patrol car and walk the beat on 20th Street when I was between dispatches. I went to an arcade located at 20th Street West and Avenue G South, where I suspected drug trafficking was taking place. Some local toughs and young offenders hung out there, and I liked to make contacts or arrests there to keep things in line as much as possible. I walked in, let my eyes adjust to the dimness, and began to look over the patrons through the clouds of cigarette smoke. It was a small place, barely up to any building safety codes, with buzzing machines and bustling with young people. I saw Jake in a corner.

Jake came up to me and told me he was out on a temporary absence from a local youth detention facility. He was serving time for one offence or another—I did not ask him because I liked him and it didn't really matter either way. He asked if I'd heard about his brother Neil. I told him I had heard where and how he was found but did not know much more than that. Jake asked me to step off to the side, away from the other patrons. He then told me he had heard on the streets that two brothers had killed his brother, and some girl whose name started with the letter P was there. His brother Neil had been at a party in the north end and had gotten very loaded. He had been beaten, thrown into the trunk of a car, and dumped. Jake then asked if I could call his mom, Stella, because she really wanted some answers. I told him I would. Given our location, I felt I could not safely question him any further because the stigma of being seen talking to a police officer could pose a very real threat to Jake. After making it look like I was conducting a street check on him, Jake and I parted company.

I walked back to my patrol car and immediately made notes of what he had told me. It was close to the end of my shift, but I was pumped. Nothing offends me more than murder. If what Jake had said was true, this information could break the investigation of Neil Stonechild's death wide open and possibly give some closure to his family. All the persons involved were either young adults or young offenders, and all of them were known to the police. Sadly, they were all First Nations and Métis.

I told a couple of officers in the locker room, but no one knew what I was talking about as Neil Stonechild's death had happened on our days off and the one short newspaper article had attracted little attention. It's one of the perils of the police world—you can easily get information overload. There's always so much going on, an individual officer has trouble keeping track of things they are not directly involved in.

The relationship I had with some detectives was already strained, so I did not want to take this information to them until I knew more about the investigation. Some of the detectives made it a habit to demean uniformed officers and their efforts to assist investigators with their cases. I don't know if it was arrogance or a sense of entitlement or a combination of both. If you paid the proper deference to them and if they saw you as somebody who understood how important they were, then they would deal with you. Making sure you knew your place was more important to them than working co-operatively. These types of attitudes have hurt police forces since the beginning of organized policing. Arrogance can serve a steep bill at the end of the day.

Shortly after meeting Jake, I went to Central Records. Central Records is the depository for all reports left by the Saskatoon police service. It is manned by civilians who process every piece of documentation left by the police. The Central Records staff prepares court documents, enters warrants, and so much more. Without the staff of Central Records Department, our police service would grind to a halt.

I found the file number for the investigation of the death of Neil Stonechild on our local computer system. I asked the file clerk to retrieve the hardcopy for me. I felt like a thief because I had nothing to do with the investigation officially, but I did not want to go to the detectives unprepared and give them information they already had.

The file clerk brought me the file. I read the first few pages, then photocopied it so I could read it all later. I was glad nobody saw me except the clerk because by this time in my service I wasn't exactly sure who the "Friendlies" were anymore. I put the file into my metal clipboard and went back out onto the streets. Once I was back in my patrol car, I let the dispatcher know I was available for calls so I would not be questioned about why I was booked down at the station for long periods of time. In the early 1990s and still today, uniformed members had to account for their time and were subject to much more scrutiny than plainclothes investigators.

One of the reasons for the bad blood between some of the detectives and me was that I had reopened files they had concluded, investigated them, and laid charges. I had been sworn at, undermined, and turned in to my supervisors when these things happened. It did not deter me, it just made me wary.

There were a lot of things causing me concern in 1990 and 1991. The chasm between the new way of policing and the old way was widening. The days where longevity was the only required criteria for someone to become an investigator were becoming numbered, and whether they liked it or not, the days where they would only work with other white men were gone. It was the pain of each step and how long it took to make that concerned me, and I wondered if I would be there at the end of it all.

Once I was in my district, I pulled over and began to read the file in detail. I was shocked to see that the file had been concluded. The investigator's conclusion that Neil Stonechild had wandered up to the North Industrial Area to turn himself in at the Adult Correctional Centre was ludicrous. I had seen things written off during investigations before that raised my eyebrows, but nothing as serious as the death of a seventeen year old in suspicious circumstances.

I called Stella, Neil Stonechild's mother, and arranged to meet her. When I went to her home in the Confederation area of Saskatoon, I was greeted by a cordial and dignified woman. Her pain and frustration were obvious. A mother's grief is one of the strongest emotions. Some of Neil's siblings were there, and while they listened, they did not interrupt. It was clear that Stella was the leader of family. Stella told me basically what Jake had told me, but she gave me more background information on Neil. It was all third-party information. The legal term is hearsay, but I felt it gave investigative direction.

When Stella began to speak about how she and her family were being treated by the police, I didn't know what to say to her. This woman and her family wanted to be treated with respect and kept informed on the progress of the investigation. They'd received at best the barest minimum of consideration a police officer could give without getting himself fired. I could not understand why this had happened to them. I wondered what they thought of me, a uniformed officer who was not part of the investigation, coming to their home. I wanted to help and hopefully get some answers for the family. I also did not want to give them false hope. I have never forgotten the poise and dignity of Neil's mother. Her love for her family was unconditional. I told her I would do whatever I could.

I went to my staff sergeant and told him that I had information regarding the death of Neil Stonechild. He changed my duty hours so that I could have a meeting with the staff sergeant in charge of the Major Crimes and Morality sections. I was on night shift, and my normal hours were 7 p.m. to 7 a.m. The staff sergeant arranged for me to come to work at four o'clock in the afternoon before the plainclothes officers were done shift.

I came to work and steeled myself for the coming meeting. This was one time when the discipline I acquired in the army was working against me. I knew I had to defer to their rank and experience when I spoke to them. I wrote down my concerns in my notebook in point form. Most of my concerns had been raised by reading the file, and meeting with Stella added several more.

A junior uniformed officer was never warmly welcomed in the offices of the plainclothes investigators. There were none of the cordial greetings you would normally receive from coworkers. No "How are you doing? How's the job going?" or anything other than cold stares and that glad-you're-not-talking-to-me look.

I went upstairs and, as I expected, was greeted coldly. I spoke with the staff sergeant and tried to outline my concerns about the investigation for approximately five minutes. The staff sergeant did not crack a notebook and listened only long enough to give me the distinct feeling that he wanted no part of this. He told me I would have to speak to the assigned investigator, Sergeant Jarvis.

It went badly from the first words I spoke. I could tell his temper was up the moment he saw me darken his door. I was told the file was closed. The information I had was hearsay, and I was meddling in things I did not understand.

There is nothing I can recall from that meeting that was even remotely positive. My place in the food chain was made very clear to me. I do not like to use the word racist. I tried to avoid it or bully my way through those types of attitudes with work ethic and reason. I came out of his office forty-five minutes later shaking. I was so full of anger and frustration. He had implied that my meddling could be dealt with in many different ways. My future wife was seven months pregnant at the time and I had a lot to lose. I could only console myself with the thought that what is said is said and there was no way they could not at least revisit the investigation, do at least a little bit of digging, and give Neil Stonechild's death a second look.

I stayed angry for many years, though I didn't realize how angry I was until years later when I testified at the Stonechild Inquiry.

I went back on the street to work my night shift. As always happens, events conspired to force me to get my head back into the job of policing. There was a car chase with a stolen car that started in the Riversdale neighbourhood of Saskatoon and ended with the car crashing by the Victoria Bridge. The passenger bailed out and ran. I arrested the driver at gunpoint. I was still a police officer.

I called Stella when I returned to the day shift. I felt more in peril now and worried that meeting her would land me in serious trouble. When we met, I told her that the information she had given to me had been passed on to the investigator. I did not tell her what a complete disaster the meeting had been. I hoped against hope that the conversation in the office of the plainclothes investigators had prompted somebody to do something. The following shift, I contacted Stella again, and when I went to her house, she told me that she had not been contacted by anyone.

We both took to criticizing what had or had not happened as far as the Saskatoon police were concerned. I made heated comments along the lines that if Neil Stonechild had been a white youth, more would have been done. I felt the sting and anger of the indifference being shown to Stella and her family. It made me question the motives behind the disregarding of this family's grief. I told Stella there was not a lot more I could do.

I didn't realize at the time the stress this frustration was causing. My wife was almost ready to give birth when I noticed a bald spot on my head the size of a large coin. I thought I had brain cancer. I went to the doctor and was told it was a skin condition called alopecia, caused by stress.

Stella, God bless her, went to the local paper, and an extremely well-written article appeared on the front page detailing the death of Neil Stonechild and the treatment the family had received from the Saskatoon Police Service. Unfortunately, the article included some of the things I had said to her. I was quoted as a senior officer with the Saskatoon police. I was mortified. That evening on the news and in the follow-up articles in the paper, the information officer, holding a hefty file, told members of the media that a tremendous amount of work had gone into investigating Neil Stonechild's death. The chief of police and administration took the same stance. If I felt in peril before, now I felt in jeopardy.

My first son was born a couple of days later. I tried to tell my wife about everything that had happened so far, but a new baby trumps the goings-on at work. I felt isolated and very much on my own. I had given the Stonechild family false hope. I called Stella for the last time and told her she would have to deal with the investigators from here on in.

Still, the day-to-day, night-to-night dispatches and crimes in the life of the patrol officer did not stop because of what had transpired. I waited to be called in and questioned. I became swept up and seized with trying to right other wrongs. I had a harder attitude now and contempt for anyone who did not do their job. I waited and waited to be called in and dealt with for violating policy and interfering with another officer's investigation.

Nothing happened. It was like none of this had ever happened at all.

In 1991, the CBC produced a docudrama about the killing of Helen Betty Osborne in The Pas, Manitoba. I was asked to take a CBC reporter on a ride-along so she could get a perspective on the relationship between natives and police in Saskatoon. Every night after that, a segment of the docudrama "Conspiracy of Silence" was shown. They would show a clip of the ride-along on the national news. CNN and headline news also showed the clips. I took the reporter and her cameraman to calls and we dealt with drunken people, alarms, and all the normal goings-on of the night shift. What made it so ironic was that at the time, Neil Stonechild's tragic story had already started. The spotlight on The Pas and its citizens would be turned on the Saskatoon Police Service nine years later.

I very rarely submitted files for investigation after that. I did them myself. I put the Neil Stonechild file in my barracks box and forgot about it, though I never forgot the Stonechilds.

Over the next nine years, I solidified my attitudes and work ethic. I was a very aggressive patrol officer and aspired to nothing else. I did not seek promotion. It was always in the back [of] my mind that someday someone would talk about the death of Neil Stonechild and how he came to be found frozen to death in a field.

On 29 January 2000, the body of Rodney Naistus was found frozen to death in the Southwest Industrial Area of Saskatoon.

On 3 February 2000, the body of Lawrence Wegner was found frozen to death in the area of the Queen Elizabeth Power Plant southwest of the city of Saskatoon.

In February 2000, I came to work and walked into the station to find it enveloped in an atmosphere of tension and anger. Officers were muttering and speaking in low and angry voices. I was told a man named Darrell Night had come forward with an accusation that he had been driven out of town by two officers, dropped off in subzero temperatures, and made to walk back to the

city on his own. Mr. Night stated that he'd been dropped off in the same area
that Lawrence Wegner's body had been found.

Senior administration was aggressively interviewing the patrol officers who
were on duty that night. Mr. Night's accusations were serious, and interviews
were, by necessity, harsh and abrupt. Officers whose integrity had never been
questioned became defensive. One of the hardest things is to defend yourself from
an accusation if you had nothing to do with what you are being accused of. The
atmosphere was frantic. There was blood in the water. The media now had the
story, and the most tumultuous period of the Saskatoon Police Service had begun.

Accusations of murder and racism began. I watched as my coworkers began
to reel from blow after blow. Morale plummeted. We were called murderers
every day and every night. We were spit at, assaulted, and held in contempt. Of
course people still called for the police when they needed help, but everything
we did had an edge to it.

At this point, allegations were made that police across Western Canada,
and in Saskatoon in particular, were regularly driving First Nations people out
of their neighbourhoods and dropping them on the outskirts as a punitive and
expedient way of solving problems. The term "Starlight Tours" was taken from
a newspaper story written by a member of the Saskatoon Police Service in the
early nineties in what was supposed to be a humorous piece. He wrote a story
about dropping off a troublesome man outside of Saskatoon and making him
walk back to town to cool off. It was not funny then and is even less now. The
Night incident, in my opinion, happened because those officers were not being
supervised. They believed they could do what they did because there would
be no consequence. How very wrong they were.

[...]

The RCMP announced that they would not be reopening the Stonechild
investigation until the initial investigations into Darrell Night's allegations and
the deaths of Rodney Naistus, Lawrence Wegner, and Lloyd Dustyhorn were
completed. After the officers who dropped off Darrell Night were convicted,
the RCMP announced that Neil Stonechild's body would be exhumed.

The investigation of Neil Stonechild's death was emerging as the most serious
allegation against the Saskatoon Police Service. I hoped a new autopsy would
yield enough evidence to move the renewed investigation forward. There were
so many forces in play by this time, I was struggling to keep up. There were calls
for sweeping and all-encompassing inquests into the relationship between the
Saskatoon Police Service and the Aboriginal communities.

In the early part of 2002, I testified at the coroner's inquest into the death
of Lawrence Wegner. Another officer and I had gone to his apartment to
investigate a domestic dispute between Lawrence Wegner's roommate and

the roommate's girlfriend the day before he was found dead. The lawyer for the Wegner family was very aggressive, and his disdain for the police was very much in the forefront of his cross-examination.

I remembered the call. I didn't know Lawrence Wegner, and he was not the subject of the call. All I could recall of him was that he was a nervous man, reluctant to speak to the police about what was going on in the apartment. I remember getting off the stand and realizing that the tone set in the courtroom room would be the template for inquests to come. Yet no one from our administration or police association ever asked me about it. As a leader or a union rep, I would have been curious. It reminded me of the marked man scenario from basic training. You felt you were on our own. I am sure other officers felt the same.

In February 2003, the Saskatchewan Minister of Justice announced an inquiry into the death of Neil Stonechild. I knew an already ugly and difficult situation was about to get even uglier and more difficult. I knew I would be in the thick of it, and people would be hurt and reputations ruined.

I don't know where I heard it from, but I heard that the Stonechild report had been purged from the Saskatoon police records as part of a routine purging to free up space in our building. Throughout all the events and the stressful atmosphere, my copy of the report lay forgotten at the bottom of my barracks box in the basement of my home. It was the only copy of the report in existence.

My partner at the time had been designated a sniper with the Emergency Response team. I was happy for and proud of him. I told him I had some sniper material from my time in the service, and I would dig around my barracks box and bring it. A barracks box is basically an army-issued trunk for you to keep your kit in when deployed. I went downstairs and was rummaging through newspaper clippings and different paraphernalia from the army. Old leave passes, evaluations, and copies of old search warrants were scattered inside.

I found the report. I knew instinctively my life would change. My family would be affected. The police service would suffer. Individual reputations would be ruined. So many different people and organizations would read it and spin it whatever way it suited them.

I had been stressed trying to articulate what my concerns were [in] 1991. Now that I had the report in my hands, my concerns were there for everyone to see.

I brought the report upstairs. My wife, who knew a lot more than I thought about the stress I was feeling trying to give as much information as I could to the RCMP about my concerns from 1991, knew right away what I had in my hands. I contacted the RCMP investigator and our deputy chief and told them that I had found the report. I brought it down to the station. I remember thinking that I would be in trouble again because I had clearly violated policy by removing a report from the station. But I did know for certain now that the investigation would be in the spotlight, and the light would not be kind.

The next couple of months were a blur. I stayed on the streets and kept doing the job of policing. Taking calls, and taking abuse related to the unfolding events in Saskatoon policing, was not easy during this period. People didn't care who you were; all they saw was the uniform. What they heard or were told was that we were dangerous and racist. It is a tribute to the young officers—and invariably they are young officers who populate the front line of Patrol—who maintained their professionalism and worked throughout this period. Most of them did not even know who Staff Sergeant Jarvis, Chief Penkala, and Neil Stonechild were.

There were calls for the RCMP to take over policing in Saskatoon, lock, stock and barrel. There were calls for the dissolution of the Saskatoon Police Service as an entity. Not to put too fine a point on it, but four-hundred-plus people could have lost their jobs. I had four children and no other skills other than the army and policing, so the fear was real. On top of this, I had violated policy by keeping a report at my home.

Being charged with a *Police Act* discipline offence is an easy prospect in a profession where everything you do is scrutinized. The tension I felt was compounded by undiagnosed post-traumatic stress from the chase in 1999 and all the other things I had seen. I cannot believe my family and friends put up with me. So many battles are personal in people's lives, and the main reason they are personal is because the embattled do not share with people when the battle is occurring.

I do not know if I ever shared the angst I felt about Neil Stonechild's death with anyone. He was seventeen when he died. I was seventeen when I joined the army. I could relate to the promise seventeen held, and how easily at that age Neil's fate could have been mine, and my mother's anguish if it had. I was working on the railway, drinking and partying all over Northern Ontario, with my fate in the hands of strangers. There would I have gone but for the grace of God.

The indifference shown to his family angered me. Still, I loved being a police officer. I respected and admired most of the people I worked with. These mixed feelings and the nagging suspicion the senior administration had been willfully blind to the distress and grief of the Stonechild family made the following months like walking through the smoke of a forest fire.

[...]

—2013

James Tyman

Métis · 1963–2001 · Fort Qu'Appelle, Ile-a-la-Crosse

James Tyman was born in 1963 in Ile-a-la-Crosse. He was adopted and raised with a white family in Fort Qu'Appelle, during an era that has come to be called the "sixties scoop." He spent time in and out of the correctional system throughout his youth and adulthood. In 1987, after receiving a two-year sentence in the Saskatoon Correctional Centre, he began writing his memoir, *Inside Out*. In Tyman's words: "*Inside Out* was not written to seek pity nor was it done to ask forgiveness. I wrote this book to simply ask for understanding and acceptance for myself and all Native people." The selections below are taken from this memoir. Tyman reportedly died on the streets in 2001.

Excerpts from *Inside Out*

1972

[...]

I began to hate myself that year. I was getting teased by the white kids, and nothing I said seemed to matter. If I talked back it only made them taunt me more, until I just laughed along with them and then they would stop. But it hurt. I'd go home and look in the bathroom mirror and curse the colour of my skin. Why couldn't I be like the other kids? My parents treated me with love, but at school I learned of the Indians and their savage ways, how they scalped people, how they'd tie you across an anthill till the insects ate you alive. It chilled me to the bone to think of such a horrible death. I wondered if that was what the Indians did out on the reservations that surrounded Fort Qu'Appelle. We'd sit in class telling horror stories about how the Indians were going to come in and burn the village and scalp everybody. "But they'll leave you alone, Jimmy," a snooty kid would announce. "You're one of them." I hated her for saying those things.

"My family is white."

"Doesn't matter. They bought you. You're an Indian."

I'd go home and scrub my hands, hoping to wash the darkness off.

If I agreed with them, they'd leave me alone. But I was hurting inside. And I was learning to hate them and myself for being Indian.

I can look back now and see what I was doing and why, but I never told anyone. I never asked my parents about these stories about Indians. They were white, of course they'd confirm the stories. And on TV the Indians were blood-thirsty savages killing the white settlers, and the cavalry would have to be sent in to stop them. "Red devils." Yes, Indians were going to hell. The TV would not lie.

I should have asked my parents.

After school I wandered around town looking at the Indians and trying to figure out if what they said in school was true. They looked harmless enough, I thought. I knew I was an Indian, but according to my friends I didn't act like other Indians. What was an Indian supposed to act like? My mom and dad bought me? Could that be possible? I never asked them. I just kept it all inside.

1973
[...]

I was alone in the house one Saturday afternoon when I got the impulse to enter my parents' bedroom. I knew they kept our old report cards there, and I wanted to see the kinds of things the teachers used to write about my two older brothers. I didn't think they'd had as much trouble in school as I was having, but I thought comparing my behaviour with theirs might help me understand why I acted the way I did.

I was fumbling through some papers when I came across a large brown envelope marked "Saskatchewan Social Services Department." My head went light. There was a letter with "Adopt Indian Métis" in dark blue letters across the top. I must be a Métis Indian, I thought. I wondered what tribe that was. I knew we had Sioux Indians all around us on the reserves. But where was the Métis reserve? I read on: "Born in Ile-a-la-Crosse, Saskatchewan." Where the hell was that? My mom said I was born in Saskatoon. The letter gave those two bits of vital information; the rest was details of meetings for parents to attend in Regina. I read it three times. There was no hint of who I was, no name. But its impact on me was staggering.

Up until then I'd felt very close to my mother and father. Now I felt alienated; it was a mixture of love and hate, and my resentment was building. I wanted to know who my biological mom was, but who could I ask? My adopted mother? I couldn't figure out why they'd never told me anything.

It took a few days for me to realize I should look in the encyclopedia for a map of Saskatchewan and find out where Ile-a-la-Crosse was. I flashed through the index. There it was! "Ile-a-la-Crosse, G-5." I put one finger on G and the other on 5. Ile-a-la-Crosse was 200 miles northwest of Saskatoon. One road went there, and according to the map that's where it ended. Ile-a-la-Crosse was the end of the road, the end of civilization. I shut the encyclopedia. I was more confused than ever. I was alone in the house, so I went back to the drawer which contained my past.

I looked through the letters from the Social Services Department. Again there were meetings for my parents to attend, and one letter listing all the diseases I'd contracted. It was a long list. I tried to remember being so sick. There were no names on these letters, just "the subject."

"I'm a subject," I smiled to myself. Then I finally found some news: "Kenny Howard Martin was placed with William and Cecile Tyman on September 17th, 1967. His new name will be James Kenneth Tyman." I felt a heat rush. That was it! Now I know who I am. I have another family. But where are they?

[...]

—*1987. Saskatoon Correctional Centre*

Carol Daniels

Cree-Chipewyan · b. 1963 · Regina Beach

Carol Daniels was born in Regina. She is of Cree and Chipewyan descent from Sandy Bay, but was adopted at birth as part of the "sixties scoop." She has since reconnected with her family. A professional singer, drummer, artist, actor, and storyteller, she has also worked as a journalist for CBC Newsworld, becoming the first Aboriginal woman to anchor a national news broadcast in Canada, and she later became the host of *In-Vision News* on APTN. She works frequently as a touring artist for SaskCulture and the Saskatchewan Cultural Exchange Society. She published her semi-autobiographical novel *Bear Skin Diary* in 2015. The selection below addresses the impact of the "sixties scoop," and is published for the first time in this anthology.

Lori

Once more puff and Lori would have burned the tip of her finger. Her cigarette was right down to the filter. She didn't even notice. Preoccupied. Caught up in her own world. Today it is a world that includes angst and pronounced feelings of guilt.

Death will do that.

Lori didn't get a telephone call. No one told her, specifically. She found out by chance.

She's been looking for a used snow blower. Ever since her boys graduated and moved away to go to university, buying a snow blower has been on her list. Enough with the shoveling. She checks out the classifieds. Unlike some people, Lori does not make it a habit to read obituaries. But today, something about that section of the newspaper cannot be ignored. A familiar photo. As she reads, the melody of a wicked song flashes through her memory. Ding dong the witch is dead.

There is a funeral tomorrow for the woman who raised Lori.

Stroke? Something related to old age? Lori wonders.

But, those details are not important. Foster mommy has been dead to Lori for years, even though the old lady's body kept walking around. Even as a girl, Lori referred to her as a dead, cold zombie, who says mean things. Foster mommy's purpose in life? Seemingly, it was to pull wild flowers out by their roots, their colours too vibrant. Foster mommy tried the same with Lori, who was just a toddler when she came to that home.

"That's what killed that woman—not old age—just old and poisonous ideas." Lori scowls, finishing up another cigarette.

"So now what? Go to the funeral or pretend I didn't see this notice?" She snuffs out what's left of her smoke in the lid of an old Cheez Whiz jar. The action prompts childhood memories. Rushing back, unwelcomed, like a bloody leak in an overly-saturated feminine pad. Grossly uncomfortable, as Lori revisits a day when she was six.

The early autumn sunshine is magical streaming in through the window. Lori loves its warmth and the warmth of hot toast covered with melted Cheez Whiz. Her breakfast before heading off to school is always the same, as is the bullying on the playground. But she's used to the name-calling. Sadly, she hears it all the time—at home.

"Hurry up, schvartze, it's almost time to go," foster mommy pats Lori's head, "but take off that black sweater." A sharp command. Lori knows, she'll see the back of a hand if not immediately obedient.

The black sweater is a hand-me-down, even though foster mommy is given money to buy the little girl new clothes.

"You know I don't like you wearing black. Makes you look too dark. You're dark enough. Come along, schvartze doofkhu. You're always dawdling." The woman selects a pink poncho for Lori instead. The little girl stuffs the last bit of toast in her mouth before climbing in to the pink, knitted cape and heading out the door.

Unorthodox and abusive. Spare the rod, spoil the child. Lori goes through the same routine each day. The name-calling that starts at home, first thing in the morning, continues all day long. Darkie. Schvartze. Told she is ugly because of the colour of her skin.

Dark thoughts. Dark times.

Lori glances at the lipstick stain around another cigarette as emotions compete for attention. Should I be angry or sad? Pretend I didn't see this article? Miss the funeral? Is this something a decent person would do? Am I decent? The obit has unearthed bones, some with rot and sinew still hanging, even though Lori had gone out of her way to bury those dark memories.

It's been decades since Lori and old foster mommy even pretended to be close. Lori realizes the drift apart began the moment she turned 18. No more need for charade. That was the day the Department of Social Services stopped sending child benefits. The people she regarded as family never legally adopted her. Why? Lori banished that from her memory as well. Too painful. But this obit renders Lori helpless to stop the resurrection of hateful and stinging words.

Audible apparitions assault.

"You can't be serious. Adopt her? We'll lose all that money. And for what? She's going to be nothing but trouble. Destined to be. They all are, you know. She'll become a hooker and a drunk and a thief, that's the way they are. Rotten greasy Indians, those schvartze."

Lori lights another cigarette without realizing she's chain smoking. Her coping mechanism for when old voices haunt.

Schvartze.

When she was little, Lori once asked, "What does schvartze mean?" She remembers foster mommy fidgeting ever so slightly then making up a lie, "It means little one." But even back then, the explanation didn't fit. Every time an uncle or neighbour said the word, it was accompanied with maniacal laughter, taunting and finger pointing.

It wasn't until years later, when Lori was in university, that she finally discovered the meaning.

She stumbled upon an article while in the library, doing some research towards her degree in education.

The *Schwarze Pädagogik* is a German concept of child-raising, specifically designed to damage a child's emotional development. "Poisonous pedagogy." It happens when a parent believes that a child's behaviour indicates that child is infected with the "seeds of evil."

Another description she finds calls it—a psychological and sociological term for describing a subset of traditional child-raising methods, which modern sociologists and psychologists describe as repressive and harmful. It includes behaviours and communication that theorists consider to be manipulative or violent.

Further, Lori discovers the similar spelling—schvartze—which looks more like the word she's heard.

Shhh-vHUT-zhee, the word rolls off foster mommy's tongue, as much a part of her mouth as dental decay. She even told young Lori that all Indians are evil, savage, need to be taught a lesson, "You don't want to be like one of them."

Schvartze.

It is slang and racist and is often used in combination with the words lazy and stupid.

Schvartze.

As harmless a name as morning star—and just as potent. Being hit with a spiked weapon is exactly how Lori feels—realizing she's been vilified, scorned, assaulted—by people who promised to care for her. And she was just a child.

"Schvartze. You are inferior. You should be ashamed." For a long time, the child Lori believed this daily recitation.

Meantime, accomplished university student Lori no longer follows that creed but is mortified to discover a pejorative translation from German to English.

Schvartze. Nigger.

Lori's translation? Squaw, sick bitch, stupid loser.

This is how she sees me?

Its mortality wounds a piece of her soul. Do all parents act like this?

The forced remembrance brings a single tear. But Lori wills it not to fall. She's become a master at that.

She prays, "Wash away my guilt," crushing out yet another cigarette and reaching for the telephone book. She looks up a number wondering if she is still guided by childhood voices, which say, "Be decent. Make the phone call. What's wrong with you? Extend sympathy. That is what good people do."

Those childhood voices have grown faint over the years and Lori can barely hear them anymore. But still, they sound. Occasionally. Today, she responds to their whispers.

Not every memory is laced with vinegar. Foster mommy insisted that all children need to learn proper manners. So Lori was taught. But what is proper in this dilemma?

Maybe phoning is required?

For a moment, her emotional burden is lessened.

If I call, maybe I will find out that the old lady's final days were repentant? She hopes. Maybe old foster mommy has been wishing, for years, that I'd get in touch. So she can offer an apology?

A schvartze no more.

Lori grabs the telephone receiver. The tear drop that's been hanging there, naked, finally makes its way out.

"But what if I do go to the funeral and see that family again, what if they say that word again? Schvartze." Despite her best efforts, the tears begin to stream. Lori yells skyward, needing God to hear. Surely God will understand and offer forgiveness—on both sides?

Forgiveness.

It reminds Lori of a story and that helps her through this moment.

An Elder once told her, "There are two dogs that live inside you. One is mean and is always fighting and the other is good."

Lori asks, "So which one am I?"

The Elder responds, "That is up to you. The stronger one—is the one you feed the most."

Lori will feed the good one. Be good to herself even though others were not. She picks up the telephone receiver and dials.

"Good afternoon, Paradise Travel. How may I help you?"

Lori has called a travel agent. She wants to book a trip, to a place where she won't feel the cold anymore.

She's okay with that.

—*2015*

Floyd Favel Starr

Cree · b. 1964 · Poundmaker

Floyd Favel is from Poundmaker, and has written numerous plays and essays. The selection below, formerly titled *Governor of the Dew*, was workshopped by the Takwakin Performance Laboratory and the Montreal Playwrights Workshop in October 1997. It was premiered by the Globe Theatre in October 1999, performed by Andrea Menard, and was presented by the Globe Theatre and the National Arts Centre in Ottawa in September 2002, performed by Monique Mojica.

Author's Note: *Master of the Dew* is meant to be performed, not as a naturalistic drama, but by one performer accompanied by music. Cree orthography in the plays is by Jean Okimasis and Arok Wolvengrey. French words by Jean Frederic Messier.

Master of the Dew

Act 1

Narrator: This story goes something like this.
    It's been so long since I heard it.
    It's from another time, from another place,
    before I became a man
    in this whorehouse of the world.

    Back then we lived on the reserve,
    beside the creek bordered by shadowed paths
    of decaying birch and poplar leaves.
    The soft footfalls at twilight of long dead ancestors
    whispering through the branches and thorns.

    There, my mother would walk
    in the light between dreaming and waking
    checking her rabbit snares.

The winter morning broken by the sharp crack
of trees and ice, breaking with the cold.

Nimama, nikawiy,
Your smile brightened the world!

Now I have only faded photographs
and your words, your stories,
to evoke your memory
and to pay tribute to you.

May you weep for us
as we go forward
to our day of reckoning.
May the Great Spirit have pity
on us his orphaned children!

This is a story that my mother told me.

Mother: Once upon a time, an old woman,
Rose Billy, was at home
One still summer afternoon
When all we hear
Is the wind rushing through the grass.

Rose: *(chant)*

niya ôma nôcikwesiw	*I am an old woman*
Rose Billy kâ-isiyihkâsot	*I am called Rose Billy*
ôta niwîkin	*here I live*
e-peyakoyân	*I am alone*
e-kaskeyihtamân	*in solitude and loneliness*
ekwa mîna e-kitimâkisiyân	*and I am so poor*
ekwa mîna e-kitimâkisiyân	*and I am so poor*

(musical interlude)

niya ôma nôcikwesiw	*I am an old woman*
Rose Billy kâ-isiyihkâsot	*I am called Rose Billy*
ôta niwîkin	*here I live*
e-peyakoyân	*I am alone*

e-kaskeyihtamân	*in solitude and loneliness*
ekwa mîna e-kitimâkisiyân	*and I am so poor*
ekwa mîna e-kitimâkisiyân	*and I am so poor*

[*chant*]

Rose: I was at home.
I hear these steps on the porch. Mah!
There was a scratching sound on the door.
Who could it be? could it be my grandson
who has gone away to the city?
or could it be an old sweetheart
coming to warm these old bones?

So I open the door,
and standing there
is this old beaver.

wahwâ, mitoni nimâmaskâten	*Oh my, I was incredibly surprised!*
e-mamâhtâwahk!	*Such sacredness!*
ahm mosôm, tawâw	*Grandfather, welcome, there is room.*

Mother: The beaver entered
and sat beside the table.
The room was silent.
The beaver hung his head
and tears poured down his face.
His body heaved with his broken heart.

Beaver: I have lived my life in shame
and please nôsisim, don't judge me.

Rose: Mosôm, you know as well as I
that it is not us who can judge.

Beaver: tâpwe nôsisim, kitâpwân.   *So true grandchild, you speak truthfully.*
Kimiyopîkiskwân
You speak truthfully and with kindness
which I do not deserve.

Rose: I gave him some tea, lifting it to his mouth
   and he drank.
   I wiped the tears from his eyes
   and caressed his head.

   ahm âcimo!   *Come on, tell your story!*

Beaver: iyaw, kâya nânitaw iteyimin ôma kâ-wî-âcimoyân.
   Please do not think bad of me of what I will tell.
   This story happened over there at the shallows
   where the wagons used to cross.
   This story is about the time I fell in love.
   Yes, I was in love once.
   To look at me, you would find that hard to believe, cî?

Rose: No mosôm! you are still very handsome.
   One can tell that you have had many lovers!
   Your visit blesses me.

Beaver: Yes, I was in love once.
   It is difficult to speak about it.

   ahm nosisim, give me some more tea.

Mother: The old woman gave the beaver another drink of tea and wiped his mouth.

Beaver: It happened like this.

Young Beaver: One morning, I was up earlier than usual
   and I sat on the bank of the creek,
      looking at the red willows and poplars that lined the banks,
      listening to the birds singing us to wakefulness and vigilance.

   I breathed in the morning air.
   This is my home, this is my land, nitaskiy ôma!
   Someday I will be the Master of my tribe,
   and this is our land.
   I lifted my hand like this, and turned a half circle this way.

Then I lifted the other hand and turned in the opposite direction,
and said a little prayer,
wishing for long life and the health of our tribe
and for the unborn who come crying over the next horizon.

Beaver: How naive our prayers can be.
We never know what life will bring in the next sunrise.
We are so pitiful in our understanding of the Great Mystery called Life!

But I believed in my prayers.
Was that not enough I ask you?
Yes, if I have been blessed in this life,
at least i knew the taste of faith,
however brief in that long ago morning.
Praise the Creator!

Young Beaver: I went on my stomach and slid down the black mud slide
and splashed into the cool clear water,
frightening a school of jackfish ahead of me.

Mother: He made his way downwards to the narrows
where the shade is cool
and where members of his tribe gather
in the heat of the brief summer
to ceremony and to settle tribal disputes.

Here the horses came to drink at dawn,
silently, warily, like outlaws.
They were led by the dappled stallion
who stood off to the side, keeping watch,
nose testing the air for signs of danger.
New to this land,
they have been accepted by the different animal Nations
and given their space and freedom.

A distant solitude is in their nature.
Perhaps it is memories of their past suffering
to the far south and across the Big Water
that have made it difficult for them to trust.

Here they have found Peace.
Is it not true that
Peace is what we all seek?

Young Beaver: I emerged and saw some humans on the shore.
Their party consisted of a dozen horses
dark with sweat and carrying trade goods.
Slowly and silently I surveyed this party.
The bearded men laughed and called to each other
in a language that I had never heard before.
mitoni, e-miyohtakosicik. They sounded so nice.
One man sat in the shade
playing an instrument he held under his chin.
It made a high beautiful sound
that I felt all along my spine.

I drifted closer, seduced and curious.

And then, I saw her.
Her!
This young woman,
sitting on a rock by the creek,
her feet in the water.
How strange, her skin so smooth and bronzed,
her hair, so long, black and wavy.

Woman: *(singing)*

Mistahi nimoyekatane	*I cry a lot*
tapkoc onikamowin	*for the songs*
L'oiseau	*Of the birds*
ekwa kapataman	*and when I hear*
ton nom	*your name*

(chorus)

kespin kakocitaman	*if you could taste my heart*
mon Coeur	*my heart*
kakiskaytane	*you would know*
pekiskatsowin	*broken heartedness*
mway katch ketom	*never again*

na mosetan   *will I feel*
your breath, your lips
nomoyakatch ketwom kawapimitan   *never again will I see you*
ni wesakitahan   *my heart pains me*

nimoskotoyhan   *my heart weeps*
kamamtonatamn   *when I think*
opesimoyapiy l'soleil   *of the rainbow, the sun*
misatimak minikwecik   *the horses drinking*
d'leau   *the water*
ekwa kakesimocik   *and the prayers*
les guerriers   *of the warriors*
nitaskiy nisakihane   *I love my land*
nitaskiy nisakihane   *I love my land*

Young Beaver: Her eyes found mine
and I was never so aware of myself.
I knew shame.

I returned her gaze,
in spite of my shame.

Beaver: What could I do when faced with such a being?
Nothing in all of my life had prepared me for this feeling.
As a young warrior I had been taught to face many forces,
but nothing had prepared me for this.
I was face to face with Desire, and I was powerless.
Yes, my mothers older sister had taught me many secret things.
That is one of the ways of my Tribe and sometimes I think,
maybe we were punished for these secret ways
because of what happened later.

Young Beaver: Nothing had prepared me for this meeting.
Could she love me?

What would my tribe say if I brought her home with me?

Beaver: namôya konita mâna kehte-ayak e-kî-itwecik,
                        it is not for nothing that the old ones say
eh âyiman ôma pimâtisiwin.   *Life is difficult*

e-papâm moskôtehiyahk	*we go around with crying hearts*
e-pôni-mâtoyahk	*we stop crying*
ekosi, e-pôni pimâtisiyahk	*and that's that, we die*
nikiskeyithten ekwa ewako	*at this point, I know this*
kikitimâki sinânaw nôsisim.	*We are so pitiful my grandchild*

Young Beaver: There I stood, afraid,
wondering if she would take me.
âstam, ki-nôhte pe-wîcewin?
Come, do you want to come with me?
e-nitaweyihtamân ka-pe-wîcewiyan.
I want you to come with me to my home.

She came! she waded into the water
against the cries and warnings of her countrymen.
I reached out my hand.
The roar of their thundersticks was loud to my ears,
the smell of the gunpowder harsh to my nose.
The thud of their bullets around my body made me brave.
There was no turning back and I abandoned my body to Death.
Nothing lasts forever!

I let out my warrior cry!
Yiy yiy yiy yiyyyyy!
I took her hand.
Hold on tight! hold on tight! Hold on!
and we dove.

Her people will have a great story to tell about me.

We swam along the rocks
at the bottom of the creek.
We met some of my relatives
who were swimming for safety
from the sounds of War.

We came bursting into the sunlight
with a big gasp for air,
into my world, the land of my tribe.

She was weak and collapsed in my arms.
She was even more beautiful
as I gazed upon her, my prize, my love.

Mother: They say we came from the land of the Sunrise,
there where the lands, sky and water meet.
It is there where it all began.
This is where the Muskrat brought up land
from the depths of the water.
The little piece of earth was clutched in his hands
as he emerged dead from his efforts.
From this we learn that
all earthly actions are accomplished with a sacrifice.

Kistesinaw, our Elder Brother, the Son of the Creator
was floating on a raft, destroyed by grief.
The previous world had been destroyed by the Great Flood
as the Great Spirit wanted to begin anew.
He delicately opened the hand of the muskrat
and retrieved the little piece of earth
that had cost the muskrat his life.
He placed the earth into his own hands,
blowing upon it all the while.

The land began to grow and grow,
and soon it made a little island,
then a larger island. ôma ministik.
Until the land became as we now know it.

Young Beaver: Mon amour, my love, nisâkihâkan
    ôta ôma e-wikiyân   *This is where I live*
    ôta ôma e-kî-pe-ohpikihikawiyân *This is where i grew up*
    ôta kista ka-wikin.   *This is where you will live also*

Act 2
    Far away, in the land of the Twilight,
    there is a vast plain.
    A cool wind constantly sweeps across this land;
    In the centre, there is a Tree,

a Tree of Souls.
These souls rest on the branches
and sing like the birds.
The souls closer to the top of the tree
are those whose destiny is to be great,
those souls who have lived and died many times.

At the top is a nest and
in this nest, the souls we call prophets sleep,
awaiting to arrive in our world as babies.
Those souls that come into our lives
and transform us and our Religions.

Beaver: *Nôsisim,* you have no idea of the joy
I had when I brought her home with me.
Nobody had ever felt the pain
Of this foreign love as I did then.

Nobody.

Surely the Heavens saw fit to bless me on that day.
This was yet another honour being bestowed upon me.
I, who was soon to be the Master of my Tribe
as my father before me, and his father, and so on.

It is only the very few who receive
the honour from the Heavens.
It is an honour
that transforms the spirit.

Such as fool I have been.

It is hard to imagine my former greatness
as I sit here at your feet,
seeming to be begging for mercy and pity.
Nôsisim, forgive me for burdening you like this,
I have come only to open the door to my heart
so that I can be free.
e-kî-pâstâhoyan, I have sinned
and I am paying the price.

Rose: *Môsôm,* I pity you.
   It is a great blessing you have given
   by coming to my door.
   Niya, a lonely old woman who has lost her husband
   and whose children and grandchildren have abandoned.

   My grandchildren live in the cities.
   They give themselves needles in the arm
   and drink alcohol and stand on the streets
   selling their bodies and souls.
   Playthings of the whiteman!

   Many are lost forever and never seen again.
   One of my great grandchildren's body was found in a river!
   Huh...huwooo... *(sobbing)*

Mother: And she wept, the tears of an old woman,
   as did the beaver, great heart rending sobs.
   Tears for her lost people
   and that which was and will never be again.

   They sat quietly for some moments.
   Rose went into the next room, returned
   with tobacco and many coloured ribbons
   which she placed at the beavers feet,

   She knew how to treat visitors
   such as this old beaver,
   with ribbons, tobacco and tears.

   Tears, the greatest gift of all.

Young Beaver: We stood on a hill overlooking our valley.
   You humans think that our lodges are dark and damp,
   But it is not so.

   The arc of our lodge is the arc of our sky.
   The floor of our lodge is the soil of our earth,
   the walls are the horizons of our skies.

Here, everything is plentiful and rich,
fish, berries, willows and poplars,
and all manner of nations share our lodge
and have their place, like they do in your world.

Our lodges were strung out along a river valley.
Our young swam playfully in the water,
the men were in the forests, preparing for the winter
which we could feel in the crispness of the dawn.

We made our way slowly to my village.

A great cry arose from the villagers
when they saw me and the stranger,
and all rushed out to look closer.
I introduced her to my people
And said than now, she and I, would be husband and wife.

The young males nodded with approval,
some old ones looked worried.
The young females whispered amongst themselves.
The little ones looked up in wonder.

That night there was a feast,
and I told of how I faced the guns and bullets
and escaped with my wife on my back.
There was singing and dancing
and I danced with joy to the light of the stars.

(dance)

There was only one pair of eyes which mattered to me
and it was the eyes of my new wife.
Her eyes shone brightly in the firelight.

Woman: (singing)
It was a rich summer.

We exchanged breath,
looked into each others eyes, shared feelings,

laughed, talked of the joys and tragedies of our lives
in the delicate manner of new lovers.

My love, this is where all loves end.
This is where all loves end.

It was a rich summer.
It was a rich summer.

Mornings came, our eyes struggled to open.
Our souls like newborn birds,
ever fragile, ever new.
Reborn in love, baptised in desire.

It was a rich summer.
It was a rich summer.

It was a rich summer.

Beaver: Summer turned into autumn,
   autumn into winter,
   the time of the Frost Exploding Trees Moon.
   She became unwell.

At first I thought she was missing her people.
She was pale, and could not leave our lodge
for the cold air hurt her lungs.

She developed a cough,
a cough which racked her thin breast
and which brought blood to her lips.

Our healers tried doctoring her.
All through the night their prayers and songs
beseeched the night heavens,
and their helper spirits travelled far, seeking answers.
Exhausted the spirits returned and said:

"It is a sickness we have no cure for
because we have never seen it before.

It comes from across the Big Water.
Maybe she should go back to her own People."

(cry)

You must go back, my love, mon amour.
Niwîkimâkan   My wife.

piko ka-sipwehteyin   you must leave
kiyâm nipîkotehân   It does not matter that my heart is broken
pok ka-kîweyin   You must go home
ahpwetikwe ka-miyomâhcihon   maybe you will get better
kiskiyihta, kâkike ka-sâkihitin Please know that I love you.

I told her this because I loved her,
and it made me suffer to say it.
But that is how things are with lovers.

After she left, I got sick.
I coughed and I coughed and I coughed.

So I married again, a female from my tribe.
We had many children.
I thought spring would bring me better health.
But my wife began to cough,
and so did my little ones.
Soon, all of my relatives became sick.

Spring normally is the time of new life,
when we are happy to be free from the grip of winter.
That time it was filled with the cries of our people
and the fear of not knowing the cause of this illness.

"It is from exchanging breath with the human!", one said.
How could the beauty of our breath cause
something as terrible as this?

I recovered but my family did not.
The snows melted, and I buried all of my loved ones.

Then, all of my tribe.
ALL OF MY TRIBE!

As it was meant to be, I became the Master.
I accomplished my duties.
I fulfilled my destiny as the Master,
not to the living, but to the dead.
The crown of willow leaves that I wore as the leader,
I wore not with pride, but with mourning and shame,
like a crown of thorns.

Song for a Dead Tribe

I did not know the proper rights of the dead.
I could not help their journeys to the Land of the Dead.
I fear they have not made it to this Land
and are lost somewhere in the In Between Land.
Waiting for the day, when a true Master
can help them cross over.

What have I done? will I be forgiven?
What have I done? will I be forgiven?

That spring I sat alone in my village
surrounded by the bones of my tribe,
and the fluttering of the magpies and crows
picking at my loved ones bones.

The dew they say is the tears of the Creator.
I am only the Master of the Dew,
the tears of the Creator for my dead tribe.
Crying for my dead tribe.
Crying for my dead tribe.

What have I done? will I be forgiven?
What have I done? will I be forgiven?

Rose: *Mosôm*, you have been forgiven many times over.
Through death, we have all re-found life.

Mother: With that, the beaver cried and cried,
his tears seemed to be made up of
all of the bird songs, all of the laughter
of the brooks and streams of the world.

It was a sound from the beginning of time.
The sound of our Elder Brother as he opened
the little hand of the muskrat from which the
World was created.

This world of suffering and forgiveness.

The beavers tears opened the doors of Rose Billy's heart,
and she cried the tears of the old woman.
As she cried, she took the ribbons which lay at
the old beavers feet and wrapped them
around his head like a crown,
then around his wrists and neck.

For this is how you treat visitors from other worlds,
Like Kings and Queens.

Narrator: I think that's how the story goes;
Its been so long since I heard it.
It's from another time, another place,
Before I became a man
in this whorehouse of the world.

The old woman who told this story
Has passed on,
As did my mother,
This is in memory of them.

The End

—1999; revised January 2016. Poundmaker

Gregory Scofield

Métis · b. 1966 · Kinosota, Portage la Prairie

Gregory Scofield was born in Maple Ridge, British Columbia. He is of Cree, Scottish, English, and French ancestry, and was raised in Saskatchewan, northern Manitoba, and the Yukon. He began his writing career with the radio drama "The Storyteller," produced by CBC.

He has published several collections of poetry, including *The Gathering: Stones for the Medicine Wheel* (1993), *Native Canadiana: Songs from the Urban Rez* (1996), *Sakihtowin-maskihkiy ekwa peyak-nikamowin/Love Medicine and One Song* (1996), *I Knew Two Métis Women* (1999), *Singing Home the Bones* (2005), *Kipocihkan: Poems New & Selected* (2010), *Louis: The Heretic Poems* (2011), and *Witness, I Am* (2016).

The selections below evoke the range of Scofield's poetry, including autobiography, protest, exploration, acceptance, erotica, politics, and the use of Cree language.

Not All Halfbreed Mothers
for Mom, Maria

Not all halfbreed mothers

drink

red rose, blue ribbon,
Kelowna Red, Labatt's Blue.

Not all halfbreed mothers
wear cowboy shirts or hats,
flowers behind their ears
or moccasins
sent from up north

Not all halfbreed mothers
crave wild meat,
settle for hand-fed rabbits
from SuperStore.

Not all halfbreed mothers
pine over lost loves,
express their heartache
with guitars, juice harps,

old records shoved
into the wrong dustcover.

Not all halfbreed mothers
read *The Star, The Enquirer,*
The Tibetan Book of the Dead
or Edgar Cayce,
know the Lady of Shalott
like she was a best friend
or sister.

Not all halfbreed mothers
speak like a dictionary
or Cree hymn book,
tell stories
about faithful dogs
or bears
that hung around or sniffed
in the wrong place.

Not all halfbreed mothers
know how to saddle
and ride a horse,
how to hot-wire a car
or siphon gas.

Not all halfbreed mothers

drink

red rose, blue ribbon,
Kelowna Red, Labatt's Blue.

Mine just happened
to like it

Old Style.

—*1999*

I've Been Told

Halfbreed heaven must be
handmade flowers of tissue,
poplar trees
forever in bloom,

the North and South Saskatchewan rivers
swirling and meeting
like the skirts, the hands
of cloggers
shuffling their moccasined feet.

I've been told

Halfbreed heaven must be
old Gabriel at the gate
calling, "Tawow! Tawow!"
toasting new arrivals, pointing
deportees
to the buffalo jump
or down the Great Canadian Railroad,
like Selkirk or MacDonald.

I've been told

Halfbreed heaven must be
scuffed floors and furniture
pushed to one side,
grannies giggling in the kitchen,
their embroidered hankies
teasing and nudging
the sweetest sweet sixteen,
who will snare the eye
of the best jigger.

I've been told

Halfbreed heaven must be
a wedding party

stretched to the new year,
into a wake, a funeral
then another wedding,
an endless brigade of happy faces
in squeaky-wheeled carts
loaded with accordions, guitars
and fiddles.

I've been told

Halfbreed heaven must be
a rest-over for the Greats:
Hank Williams, Kitty Wells,
The Carter Family
and Hank Snow.

It must be
because I've been told so,

because I know
two Métis women who sing
beyond the blue.

Tawow! Tawow!: Come in, you are welcome!

—*1999*

Women Who Forgot the Taste of Limes

ni-châpan, if I take ki-cihcânikan,   my ancestor, your fingerbone
press it to their lips,
Will they remember the taste of limes,
sea salt bled into their grandfathers' skin?

If I pull from this bag of rattling bones
the fiddle, the bow bone,
if I go down to the lazy Red,
lay singing in the grass

will the faces of our ancestors
take shape in clouds

and will the clouds name themselves,
each river-lot stolen?

If I take ki-tôkanikan, ni-châpan,   your hipbone
place on them a pack to bear
will they know the weight of furs,
kawâpahtamiwuk chî   will they see?

the city is made of blood, wîni   bone marrow
stains their grandmothers' aprons,
swims deep in the flesh, a grave of history,
a dry bone song.

ni-châpan, if I take ki-kiskatikan   your shinbone
will they offer up the streets,
lay open their doors and say I'm welcome?
Or if I take ki-tâpiskanikan,   your jawbone

place it scolding on Portage and Main
will all the dead Indians
rise up from the cracks, spit bullets
that made silent our talk?

If I take ki-mâwikan, ni-châpan   your backbone
I could say to them
I'm not afraid of gunshots, stones
or the table I sit at—

this table where I drink tea with ghosts
who share my house and the words
to keep it clean.
ni-châpan, if I take ki-cihcânikan,   your fingerbone

press it to their lips
will they remember the taste of limes,
hold silent their sour tongues
for once?

—2005

The Sewing Circle

Monsieur Riel,
I am most anxious to avoid killing women and children and have done my
best to avoid doing so. Put your women and children in one place and let me
know where it is and no shot shall be fired on them. I trust to your honour
not to put men with them.
    —Fred Middleton, Com' N.W. Field Force (May 11, 1885, the third day of
        the resistance at Batoche)

Sisters,

Now the lamps are adjusted
And it is only fitting
In the glow of your faces

To call faithfully your names as if
I was to pray to Our Lady of Lourdes,
nohkom apihkesis,

Grandmother Spider, Our Mender of Holes.
Yes, the lamps are adjusted
And I ask unto you

My good blood women,
My country sisters
To take up your implements,

Hold steady your hands
As if you are nursing your children,
Polishing the bones of our men.

To Sister Caron, I say take this thread
And sew shut the lips of the government
Whose tongue is as black

As the thread you are given.
To Madame Tourand, I say take this measuring tape
And set down from here

To the queen's grand house
The worth of your man, your sons,
The goods of your home, your cattle.

Dear sister, I say take this measuring tape
And set down from here
That of which to be multiplied

As one would count the beads of Mary,
Our Mother, Queen of All Eternal Losses.
To Sister Parenteau, Madame Fisher

I say take this sewing bird and
Make haste to the bluffs,
There on the eastside of the river.

Set free the timid-looking thing
Whose beak is the mouth of Magdalene.
To it say sing up the redcoats

And when they are resting
Pin down their hearts, hold down their feet
One by one

As we would count the stations of Jesus,
Our Lord, King of all Sweetly-kissed Men.
To Sister Riel, I give this most inconsolable gesture.

To her I say take these buttons
And feed them to Macdonald.
He will think them candy,

Giddy as a schoolboy. To her I say
The bastard will be fermented in festivity.
Savour sweet his choking.

To Madame Fidler, Sister Gariepy
I say take this thimble,
This chalice of conviction.

Come with your hymns, grieved as they are.
Drink from it
This most unspoiled land.

To Sister Letendre, Sister Dumont
I say take this pincushion
And rest there the heads of our sick,

The hearts of our wounded.
To Madame Champagne, dear woman I say
Take this needle and through its slim silver head

Pass as you would a thread of hope
Which I then say to Sister Delorme
Take this, this rope of life

Onto which we shall tie our spirits
That you, Sister Ross shall take to our men,
Be they victorious or their eyes fixed upward

Set upon this new endless sky.

—2011

Gabriel's Letter

*The good Lord did not want me to see my poor Riel again. I wanted to
tell him not to give himself up, but he might very easily have converted
me to his point of view.*
        —Gabriel Dumont

May 26, 1885

Mon frère, nisīmis   my brother, my little brother

How is it I can tell you the sadness your resignation brings me. I can tell you only
I have with me Michel Dumas, my horse and my rifle Le Petit with its ninety car-
tridges and the revolver I took from Albert Monkman, and in it are forty rounds.
    That we have set out by the grace of God and have reached the American
border is nothing short of victory. I think, mon frère, how you would fall on
your knees and cry tears of joy. And how the thieves of our country, our homes
would possess nothing more than the weeds in the rectory garden.

Still I am at a loss. I have sent Madeleine to stay with my father. As for the others I pray for them, as I do you, the swift hand of justice. It seems to me only accurate we are granted immunity. We are offered more than a plate of leftovers.

nisīmis, when now I think of you and the six hundred miles I have worn between us, I stop in moments of contemplation and ponder if it was you who had taken Monkman's revolver, the one with forty rounds. And then I laugh. I see you, my Riel, aiming the cross as if God and the Virgin, all three of you in golden light, will defeat their gun and the anglais who feed it.

That said I miss your unwavering faith. I should be so fortunate a Christian. By the love of Christ we are brothers, Louis, and by the love of our country. Wherever you are I imagine they keep you under lock and key, the jewel of the half-breeds, our ruby, mitehnan.   our heart

Mon frère, when next I see you—in Heaven some say—I will give you the revolver I took from Albert Monkman, the one with forty rounds. And while I am taking tea with the old ones and those I do not know but from stories, I shall pause and to you, dear brother, I will make my way to the side of Heaven where one is able to peer over the edge as if looking from old Madame Tourand's place, to see not the flowing river and swaying trees nor the clouds that are fat with rain, but into the pit of hell where I am told the devil plays poker with Sir John himself.

Then you will laugh. You will see the coward holds an ace, king, queen, jack and ten, all of the same suit. On the table he will have our country. Then you will laugh and say you are not much for gambling. But you will have spent six rounds: five on the devil's deck and one for our country.

You will laugh like a man given a baby. And I will laugh to see you so free.

Yours in friendship,
Gabriel

—2011

Warren Cariou
Métis · b. 1966 · Meadow Lake

Warren Cariou was born in Meadow Lake. He is of Métis and mixed European heritage. He has published numerous stories and poems, and two books, *The Exalted Company of Roadside Martyrs* (1999) and *Lake of the Prairies: A Story of Belonging* (2002). He has also co-directed and co-produced two films, *Overburden* and *Land of Oil and Water* (2009). In 2008, Cariou was awarded a Canada Research Chair in Narrative, Community and Indigenous Cultures at the University of Manitoba, where he also directs the Centre for Creative Writing and Oral Culture.

An Athabasca Story

One winter day Elder Brother was walking in the forest, walking cold and hungry and alone as usual, looking for a place to warm himself. His stomach was like the shrunken dried crop of a partridge. It rattled around inside him as he walked, and with each step he took the sound made him shiver even more.

Where will I find a place to warm myself? he wondered. Surely some relations will welcome me into their home, let me sit by the fire.

But he walked for a very long time and saw none of his relations. Eventually he traveled so far west that he didn't know the land anymore, and even the animals wouldn't dare to help him because they knew how hungry he was. They kept a safe distance. So he shivered and rattled his way further and further, without anything to guide him except the lengthening shadows and his unerring radar for trouble.

When he was nearly at the point of slumping down in a snowbank and giving up, Elder Brother thought he smelled something. It was smoke, almost certainly, though a kind of smoke he'd never encountered before. And though it was not a pleasant odour at all, not like the aromatic pine-fire he had been imagining, he knew that it meant warmth. So he quickened his frail pace and followed the scent, over one hill and then another and yet another. And eventually he came to the top of one more hill and he looked down across an empty valley and saw the source of the smoke.

A huge plume billowed from a gigantic house far in the distance, and between himself and the house there was a vast expanse of empty land. Empty of trees, of muskeg, of birds and animals. He had never seen anything like it. The only things moving on that vacant landscape were enormous yellow contraptions that clawed and bored and bit the dark earth and then hauled it away toward the big house. And the smell! It was worse than his most sulfurous farts, the ones he got when he ate moose guts and antlers. It was like being trapped in a bag with something dead.

Elder Brother knew he should turn away and get out of that smell as soon as he could. But that would mean spending the night by himself, freezing and chattering and rattling, and he couldn't bring himself to do it. There was warmth up there in the big house, he could see it floating away on the breeze. In places he could even see the heat rising in fine wiggly lines from the newly naked earth itself. So despite the smell he stepped forward and made his way out into that strange expanse.

The house was further away than it had seemed. He walked and walked across the empty space, stepping over dark half-frozen puddles, holding his nose, following the tracks of the great yellow beasts. He attempted to stay far away from the beasts themselves because they didn't look the least bit hospitable. But by the time he got halfway across the open land, he strayed close enough to these creatures that he could see each of them giving off its own smaller stream of smoke. And as he stood there studying them, he realized something else: there were people inside.

Maybe they were houses, he thought. Warm, comfortable houses that by some magic were also capable of digging and hauling the earth. Certainly they were big enough to be houses. He got closer and watched again as one of them rumbled past, shaking the ground at his feet. The man inside was bare-armed, as if it was summer. And he was chewing on something.

Of course Elder Brother was scared by the noise and the smell and the shuddering earth. But his hunger and his shivering were stronger. When the next gigantic thing came rumbling down the track he bounded out in front of it and stood there, waving his right hand desperately while his left hand remained clamped on his nose.

The thing squealed and snorted and eventually came to a stop just before it touched him. A man immediately leaned out from a window near the top of it and shouted, Who in hell are you? Where's your machine?

Oh my brother, my dear relation, Elder Brother said. I'm very cold and hungry and I was hoping … to come and visit you in your house.

The man didn't say anything for quite a while. He scanned the blank horizon, as if looking for something. Finally he leaned further out the window and yelled, You're saying you're not with the company?

Uh, company….

Are you Greenpeace?

I'm cold, Elder Brother said.

The man took off his strange yellow hat and gazed into it for a moment, placing one hand over his forehead as if to keep something from bursting out.

Well you'll be a lot worse than cold, the man said, if you don't get the hell out of my way and off this goddamn property.

Well, *that* was rude, Elder Brother thought, but he tried not to betray his disappointment. This man talked as if he had no relations at all.

Okay, he said to the man. I won't come visit you right now, but could I please ride along on the top of your house? I want to go to the big house over there, where I'm sure they'll let me come in and get warm.

The man laughed a little, and glanced up at the sky for a moment.

I don't know what you're on, buddy, the man said. But you need to snap out of it right this goddamn minute. Cause if you don't step aside I'm gonna call Security, see, and they're gonna come out here and throw your ass in the slammer with all those other yahoos from last month and the month before.

I should've called them already. But on the other hand, I could save a little time if we just had a bit of an accident here. Nobody'd ever know it happened.

The man's house made a roaring sound that made Elder Brother step back.

Oh, there's no need for that! Elder Brother said. Don't worry, I'll move aside. But before I go, I just want to know one thing: what are you doing with all that earth?

We're burning it, the man said. Burning. But earth doesn't—

This stuff does, the man interjected. You really are a moron, aren't you? It's very special dirt, this stuff. We dig it up and take it over to the big house, as you call it, and we mix it around in there and after a while it's ready to burn. Fuel to heat your house, if you have one, which I doubt. Gas to power your car. Diesel to move this big rig here. All of it comes right out of the ground. You can tell that by the smell of the air around here. Just like napalm in the morning!

The man took a deep breath through his nostrils and then laughed, but his face turned sour when he saw that Elder Brother didn't understand.

Yeah, we got real big plans for this place, the man said. There's more of this special dirt here than anywhere else in the world. Everybody wants it, and we're happy to sell it to them of course. And all those people around the world are going to help us burn this very dirt that you see here, from under your feet all the way to the far horizon. We're gonna burn it, and burn it, and burn it, until we make so much heat that the winter never comes back! And then even you and the rest of your sorry kind won't be cold anymore. So how do you like that?

When will that be? Elder Brother asked, rubbing his hands together.

Fifty or sixty years. Maybe forty.

Oh. Not to complain, but I was hoping for something a little—

Elder Brother was interrupted by an explosion of noise from the front of the big yellow house-thing, and it lurched toward him with surprising speed. He was barely able to leap out of the way before it rolled right over his footprints.

Now get off this land! the man yelled as his house roared away. It doesn't belong to you. Go back to the bush or wherever it was you crawled out from. I'm calling Security right now!

Elder Brother stood there for a while and watched the house labouring over the hillocks and through the black puddles in its way. He was more than a little scared of this mysterious Security that would soon be coming after him, but he was also angry. How could this man tell him that the land wasn't his? How could this "company" keep all the magical dirt for itself? If there was so much of it, Elder Brother reasoned, there should be plenty to share with visitors.

Though he knew he should probably be running for his life, Elder Brother found himself unwilling to move. He was held there by an idea: if these people wouldn't give him any of this magical dirt, maybe he should take some for himself. Yes, what a fabulous plan! Since the man and his company were so rude, they deserved to have their precious dirt stolen. And the best part was that if Elder Brother gathered enough of this magic dirt for himself, he could burn it for years and keep warm until the winter was gone for good.

So instead of fleeing the empty land, Elder Brother began walking toward the place in the centre where the largest of the yellow contraptions were tearing away at the earth. The snow had all been cleared away there, and he could see how black this magical dirt really was. He watched the beasts moving this way and that, and he waited for his opportunity. Finally he saw an opening, and he darted between a couple of the great mobile houses toward a spot where the ground had recently been opened. It looked softer there, and warmer too. Yes, this was the place. He lifted his right hand and thrust it as hard as he could, right down into the soil, up to his elbow.

Ayah! a voice said. What are you doing, Elder Brother? Sssshhhhhhhh, he answered. I'm taking what's mine.

And he reached deeper and deeper into the ground, spreading his fingers as wide as he could in order to hold the largest armload of dirt. A year's supply in one hand, he imagined! He reached so far that his cheek rested against the redolent earth itself. He nearly gagged at the smell but he didn't loosen his grip. He could already feel the warmth coming out of the soil and it made him a little stronger.

Elder Brother, you're hurting me! the voice cried out.

Not nearly so much as they are, he said, and with that he began reaching in with his other arm, tunneling in with his fingers, opening his arms wide in a desperate embrace. His nose was raw with the fumes, and particles of grit were getting in his mouth. He was about to heave the huge armload of dirt out right then and begin his run for the bush, but one thought stopped him. What if it wasn't enough? What if he ran out and then the winter came back?

So without another hesitation he kicked off his moccasin and began tunneling in with the toes of his right foot. He clasped and clawed until he was more than thigh-deep in the earth, and then he tilted his toes upward to hold as much as he could. Then quickly he kicked off his other moccasin and tunneled with that foot, squirming and worming until that leg too was embedded in the earth. Ass-deep and shoulder-deep in the magical soil! Surely this would be enough to last him for decades, until the winter had been vanquished for good.

You are a genius, Elder Brother, he said to himself. You deserve all the warmth you're going to get.

But when Elder Brother tried to lean back and lift the great clump of dirt out of its place, he discovered that he had no leverage. He pulled and pulled at the soil, flexing his arms and his legs all at once, but nothing moved. The only thing that happened was his limbs seemed to sink a little deeper into the ground. He grunted and panted, flexed again, shimmied his buttocks for extra oomph. However it didn't make a bit of difference.

Well, he thought, I guess I should just take a little less of this stuff, maybe make two trips. I'll just wiggle my legs out of these holes and settle for a nice big armload of magic dirt.

I imagine you can guess how that worked out. Right. It didn't. Elder Brother was stuck fast in that Athabasca tar. By this time he couldn't move a finger or a toe.

Instinctively he called out to the voice that had spoken to him earlier. Help me! I'm sorry I didn't listen to you. I'll leave now without taking anything at all.

But the voice didn't answer. And Elder Brother was stuck there in the ground all night, and all the next day and the following night. He howled to the voice, asking it for forgiveness. He yelled to any of his relations who might be in earshot. He even screamed to the men in the huge yellow creatures that, from their sound, seemed to be moving closer and closer to him. (Of course he couldn't see what was going on back there. All he could see was the clump of oily dirt that his nose was resting on.) If those men in the contraptions heard him, or saw him, they gave no sign of it.

Late in the afternoon of his second day of being stuck in the ground, the sound of the contraptions became much louder, and a dark shadow suddenly closed over Elder Brother. Then he was being lifted, along with his armload of dirt and a great deal more, and he felt himself falling with the thunderous sound of everything else falling around him. He cried out but he knew it was hopeless; no one would hear him over a cacophony like this. When he landed, the dirt closed over him. It pressed into his nostrils, his ears, his mouth, even into his clenched bum. The weight of it pushed down and down until he couldn't even move an eyelid. Soon the thing began to move, and it hauled him slowly across the wasteland, encased there in the tar as if he was a fossil. And eventually the truck reached the edge of the huge smoky refinery, where it dumped him and many tons of tar sand into the yawning hopper that was the beginning of the processing line. And inside the refinery he was made very warm indeed.

Of course Elder Brother can't die, luckily for him. Or perhaps not so luckily. He's still alive even now, after everything he's been through. It's true that people don't see him much anymore, but sometimes when you're driving your car and you press hard on the accelerator, you might hear a knocking, rattling sound down deep in the bowels of the machine. That's Elder Brother, trying to get your attention, begging you to let him out.

—2014

Satan Rouses his Legions on the Shores of Syncrude Tailings Pond #4

Inhale, my friends: breathe deep
the bitumen air. I give you
a waveless lake,

stacks blowing brimstone,
the slick earth itself
turned out, spilled like troubled guts

into the pipeline of need.
The stink that lingers on the back
of your tongues

is the scent of our conjuration.
We are wanted here.
The heavy-haulers drone our names,

the pit-sumps wail to us, desperate
as sirens, and mile-long flags
drape from the mouths of smokestacks

waving us in. I for one will enter
and plant my ensign here.
Which among you hordes will follow?

Come then, hurry!—
wings unfurled, torches on high,
past evaporators and bright

ziggurats of sulfur, past even
the unstanchable pits themselves
to the waiting world.

This time, the ground is laid for us
wide open. Sniff and you know:
all of it was made to burn.

—2014

Louis Speaks to Gabriel Through the Ground

They're building a museum, old friend,
across the river from my bones.
The pilings reach deeper than history
and the cranes stretch higher
than the echo of a drum.
Night and day the cement trucks roll
as if there was no one beneath them.

It makes me envy you:
your place beneath the stone, your
tranquil riverbank that once absorbed
the thwack of the Gatling gun.
Bullets are less dangerous
than pile-drivers, believe me.
The only museum near you
has something of you in it.

But here I see nothing I recognize,
only flashing lights and punctured earth
and a bland directionless goodwill
that crushes the bones of our dead.

They say all the walls will be glass
so soon I'll watch the tourists
staggering through the exhibits
sick with the iniquities of elsewhere.
A crystal palace, they call it,
transparent cathedral of light.
But to me it's just a glass house.

With so many windows, I wonder
if anyone will ever look outside
and see our people walking here
leaving sage and tobacco
for the old ones.

—2014

Randy Lundy

Cree-Irish-Norwegian · b. 1967 · Barren Lands, Manitoba

Randy Lundy was born in Thompson, Manitoba. He is of Cree, Scots and Irish, and Norwegian ancestry, and is a member of the Barren Lands First Nation. He moved to Hudson Bay, Saskatchewan, when he was a child; it was there he began writing poetry. In 1987, he attended the University of Saskatchewan and completed an M.A. in English. His poetry has appeared in numerous anthologies and journals, and he has published two collections of poetry, *Under the Night Sun* (1999) and *Gift of the Hawk* (2004), with a third collection, *Blackbird Song* forthcoming in 2018. His poetry reflects the connections, both spiritual and physical, between humans and nature.

deer-sleep

this place does not require your presence
and beneath the staring stars
you have discovered
your offerings are meaningless

you are left with nothing
but silence
you have forgotten why you came here
you were looking for something

the wind wanders among willows
muttering forgotten stories
it has been everywhere and cannot
keep quiet

you must learn
to listen, to be alone
only then
will you bed down with the deer
to sleep in the long, deep grass
wrapped in the warmth
of slender bodies
of slow-moving breath

each time you awaken with the dawn
stars and moon fading memories
the deer will be gone

all day you carry with you
the sound of their sleeping

the howling song of coyotes
the common dream
that binds you

—1999

Bear
(*for Susan G.*)

Late-summer sunlight, reflected off the river's slow flow
afternoon aurora on patient river stones;

when the bear emerges onto the bank
to dip its muzzle and drink

stones exhale warm breath into dusk
sigh in wet, clay-heavy sleep;

the animal lifts its heavy head in a broad-nostril flare
its senses leaning to the far-bank stir of leaves;

your breathing   hesitates
while the bear's mouth spills mist, and he snorts

the first stars into the darkening eastern sky.

—2004

For Kohkum, Reta

Might as well settle
in a hard-heavy chair,
with a mug of steaming
green tea and some Powwow or
plainchant turned up loud.
Stare out the window
into the glare of sun glazing
the snowfield south of the house.

Remember the butter-glazed, golden
crust of bread fresh from the oven.
Remember the oven door
creaking, heat blasting
your six-year-old face.

Your body's a canvas and bone lodge,
stone-glow hot in your belly.

Low sun at noon falls lower.
Sparrows huddle at the feeder at dusk.

Tonight, a mile north of here,
a train engine will groan and then roar,
a biblical beast, a wihtikow come for the feast.

Memory is an uncomfortable skin.

Your mind like a sapling, bent,
curved like the earth.
Curved like a question mark.

Remember that woman.
It's always a woman
with white hands or brown hands.
The kitchen, mid-winter frost on the windows
as you wait for the school bus,
that smell: yeast and wheat.
Love, was it?
Birth?

—2013

Son

Do you remember waking up
in the middle of that boulevard,
in that northern Saskatchewan city?

Leaves stuck to your face,
the broken twigs of Dogwood in your hair,

the smell of shit and piss
clinging to you
like black mold.

Do you remember falling,
falling first on your knees and then crawling,
trying to get to wherever it was you were trying to go?

Do you remember falling asleep,
the image of your mother's face
staring down at you?

Poverty is the natural condition of our souls.

She came from another place, not so different,
a broken, falling, sleeping land
800 miles north of what people call civilization.

Someone once asked,
Whatever happened to the blues?

Nothing ever happened to the blues,
they simply packed their bags
and moved north.
They moved into every Indian bar in Canada.
They moved into The Imperial in downtown Winnipeg,
where your mother sold her dark skin,
her almond eyes,
her Mediterranean looks.

The river where you went down to pray
is the same river where you threw your hooks,
when you were just learning how to throw a lure.
You would take one out of your tackle box
attach it to the leader at the end of the line,
and occasionally you would catch a pike,
a long-bodied, freshwater fish
its slow, pale-white belly
dragged across the river bottom

the river's silt-middle-of-the-continent spine.

One day the river decided to sleep,
with its hips turned, slowly gnawing
its way into the land,
first this way, then that.

This past autumn the cone-flowers
dropped their petals like flames.

This afternoon you heard a Merlin,
you didn't see the bird,
but immediately you knew
it wasn't supposed to be here,
not at this time of the year.

There was only one,
no mate to accompany it.

How does a person understand anything
before they translate the noun to a verb?

Though the geese have left,
the chickadees are still here.
The large birds have left.
The small, inelegant, almost-infinitesimal-
beneath-the-prairie-sky birds
are still here,
with their tiny hungers that mean everything.

The natural and the supernatural
are both inexplicable.

What you are left with is the question of what you will do.

Pine Siskins, those finches, disappear
as soon as they appear.
Nests at the broken ends of Spruce branches.
This loose nest made of hair, feathers, and seed-fluff.

The one thing you have never been able to see is yourself.

Everywhere you turn your eyes
there is an absence,
there is no *you*.

Perhaps this why you developed
an affection for looking at the world.

As some point,
you must eat your own bones.

You hear a voice
then the vision,
the feathered bodies arrive.

You wish you could tell this to your mother.

Genealogy is a record of where you have come from
and what you haven't done for yourself—
you haven't washed your body for three weeks—
take it to the river.
It doesn't matter which river—
the Euphrates, the Tigris, the Nile,
the Fur, the Etamomi, the Red Deer—
just get it there.

Body, mind, spirit—
this is called trinity.

When there are no buffalo left,
the people leave—
they pack their deer-hide bags,
take down the pine-poles that held the roof
through those long winter nights
—stars that never asked permission to be here—
then they gather their children around them,
and the dogs,
there are always the dogs,
and then they leave,

knowing everything they leave behind
won't save them.

Your mother's mouth opens in the darkness
perhaps a star falls down her throat.

What will be
is not what you think
and nothing you would recognize.

Once upon a time,
let's invoke that beginning
because invocations matter.
Every time, it's locating the correct register
by which a human voice finds a way to begin a story.

She says to you
I drew your body from water,
I stood beside the dusty road,
I sold my body to feed you—

why do you refuse
to forgive me?

Your lover has a lump in her breast,
not in her breast exactly
but writhing its twines like a snake
through her ribs.
How much does this scare you?
How much does it scare her?

Everything is possible,
but you must open that door.
When you reach your arm forward,
there is nothing there
no hand, no knob.

The webs of spiders this December morning
are gathering moisture from the air,
gathering around their emaciated bodies

a bit of frost like a blanket.
The spiders now long gone,
what you are left with are those spines
they have spun out of themselves.

Because we cannot face that empty place
we always see when we look for our selves
we are willing to spill the blood of others.

We all want to speak like Old Testament prophets.

The light from the sun right now
glowing through flakes of snow
blowing off the Cottonwoods
is as hard as diamonds.

How deep and hard is this light?
What is the clarity?
How was the stone cut—
like the throat of your mother?
The wrist of your sister?

How do we value this or that angle of refraction?
How much weight did it take to make this light?

—2014

Creation Story
(for Isadore Pelletier)

This is how it begins,
not with a word, but
with a single breath.

Something our bodies do, not
involuntarily, but without
the intervention of our wills.

Something our bodies do
to save us
from consciousness and death.

Still it is there—death—in that moment
between inhalation and exhalation,
in the time between the separate
beatings of our separate hearts,
in the infinitesimal time
our minds allow our bodies to be.

But, of course, it is our bodies that allow our minds to be,
for a brief time, and always, it is there—
death, like a bird that preys
upon another bird
in mid-flight.

—2015

Joely BigEagle-Kequahtooway

Nakoda-Cree · b. 1969 · White Bear

Joely BigEagle-Kequahtooway is Nakoda-Cree from White Bear First Nation. She is an emerging writer, artist, and engineer. Her passions include fashion design, painting, and buffalo. She is obsessed with Tatanka and bringing back the buffalo spirituality, mentally, emotionally, and physically. The selection below originally appeared in *Briarpatch Magazine* in 2017.

Obsidian Stone Wiya

I come from a long line of buffalo hunters.

The blood and spirit memories from our ancestral buffalo hunts course through my veins to prepare me for today. I feel the sweat dripping down my forehead. The dust is dry and thick, kicked up by thundering buffalo hooves. I crouch, my legs aching from waiting for the signal from the hunters. I watch them get into position. Some of the hunters are dressed in wolf fur—they are nimble and run bent low. They chase the buffalo toward the hunters that are lined up facing each other. These are the brave ones, chosen by the Elders within our community, for they stand in the path of the buffalo. They jump up and down, waving their buffalo robes to keep the buffalo from veering off the path. The route is wide enough for a small herd of buffalo to flow through, guided toward the jump. The buffalo in the front of the herd realize too late that the ground is no longer beneath their feet. The others behind them push the ones in front to the edge. They quickly tumble off the cliff. It's too late for any of them to turn back; they are frightened from the wolf-robed hunters in chase behind them.

I saw this buffalo hunt manoeuvre played out many times as a child, although I was never allowed to help; I needed to observe it first to know what to expect. I have now inherited my grandmother's, my *unci's*, obsidian stone. Its black sheen and pointed flint edges make it the perfect tool for its intended deed. This stone is the sharpest tool known to our people, and if used properly it can cut through anything, including the thick hide of a buffalo.

My *unci* would take me to watch the hunters chase down the buffalo and lead them to the jump, telling me that it was my destiny to eventually help with the buffalo kill at the bottom of the cliff. My mother, my *ina*, would wait at the bottom of the cliff with her own obsidian stone. She was a skilled buffalo killer and was one of the few trusted to skin buffalo hides. I was to follow in her place when I was old enough. Until then I watched from afar with my *unci*.

My most prized possession as a child was my obsidian stone. The stone had been carved into a sharp tip and attached to an antler so I could hold it in my hand. When I was younger, I would help my *unci* as she skinned gophers. Then I graduated to deer, elk, and moose. It was all preparation to be a buffalo hunter and to help with the final kill at the bottom of the jump.

Only the most skilled buffalo hunters were allowed at the hunt. The buffalo robes were the most prized possessions of our people. To kill and skin a buffalo, you must be careful not to make any holes in the fur hide. The robes would be used to keep our people warm on the coldest of winter nights. I feel honoured to be taught these old ways. I was proud to be chosen to help alongside the other hunters. It is humbling to be present when the buffalo spirit takes its last breath—the sacrifice made for our people to continue living.

I have infinite respect for our buffalo brothers and sisters, and I wanted to make sure I honoured their spirits by making sure they did not suffer needlessly. If the buffalo did not die from the fall, then it was my duty to ensure a just and swift final blow for the sake of its spirit. It was a contract we made with our buffalo brothers and sisters, to ensure their journey to the spirit world was completed as painlessly as possible. We wanted them to journey to the spirit world in a good way, knowing their sacrifice was not made in vain.

My *unci* and my *ina* started preparing me when I was a baby, singing the buffalo songs to me. As soon as I could speak, I sang to the buffalo spirit. The dreams didn't come easy at first. First I heard the rumbling, the loud hum-mmph and the wind howling as they ran past. At times I would dream I was running with them, darting between them, one of them. Other times I would fly above them, soaring high overhead and watching, learning, wishing to be close. I loved their animal stench, and their fur felt downy near the neck and rugged at their hump—I wished I could stroke their fur. I felt at ease only when in their presence or as I watched them prance. I looked forward to the buffalo hunt each year because it was when they returned to us.

I loved the energy in the air from my people, when we would begin preparing for the hunt. The men would send scouts out to find where the buffalo shook the ground. We would break camp and travel miles to set up camp near the grazing buffalo. The men would prepare themselves mentally, emotionally, and spiritually for each buffalo hunt. The boys wanting to shed their innocence would be called upon to challenge themselves and prepare to hunt their first buffalo. The hunters would paint symbols of their animal or spirit protectors on their bodies with mud and earth paints. Their bows and arrows, parfleche shields, and obsidian spears would be smudged with the smoke of sage and sweetgrass, and the wooden handles painted to ensure their target was found. The women would sing the buffalo song to advise the buffalo to prepare themselves for the sacrifices to be made. We relied on the buffalo for life—they sustained us. We needed the buffalo to nourish and carry us forward for future generations. We had to think of our unborn children, grandchildren, and those yet to come. We needed to be strong for those yet unborn. These ways have been passed down to us through the generations, and our method was always the same to ensure a successful hunt. There was ceremony, but also protocol that we followed. Each hunter knew their place in the hunt, and we laid tobacco down when a kill was complete in order to honour the buffalo's sacrifice and their life with one of our most valued medicines.

Our community was large and filled with strong men and women, so we hunted in waves. One buffalo could feed 50 people. We would make buffalo pemmican, mixing their meat with berries and animal lard. The pemmican would last us through the winter. The best parts of the buffalo—the tripe, the tongue, the liver –were saved for the babies and the sick Elders. The buffalo noses were saved for the *heyokas*—the noses would appease the spirits and these healers carried special medicines when they performed the buffalo ceremonies for the people and danced the buffalo dance. Every part of the buffalo was salvaged and used by someone in our village.

I am older now, and I feel ready to help in my first buffalo hunt. I talk to my Elders and tell my unci and ina that I want to help my people. They tell me I must prepare myself through a purification ceremony. It's an enormous burden to take the life of a buffalo. We are so connected that when the buffalo spirit leaves the animal, sometimes it wants to take the human spirit with it. So, we have to guard our spirits during the buffalo hunt.

The women and men sweat separately for this purification ceremony. The songs are different, and the Elders have specific instructions for the men and for the women on their duties during the hunt. We each sing our buffalo songs in the sweat lodges. We pray and sing, pray and sing, and tell stories of previous successful hunts. In between sweat lodge rounds, we joke, and some tell stories of heroic acts or misguided adventures during the hunts. Laughter fills the camp. The children run, jump up and down, and crouch, pretending to be buffalo hunters. They take turns, one being the hunter the other being the buffalo, then switch roles. One day it will be their turn to be on the prairie hunting real buffalo.

I cry hard in the sweat lodge. I am happy, but also sad because I don't want to take my buffalo brother or sister's spirit away. I love watching them run free and play with one another. It makes my spirit feel free. It keeps my dreams alive. But the Elders tell me that the buffalo love us and that they want our people to live forever, so they are willing to sacrifice their life and happiness for our survival. It has been that way since the beginning of time. I have to believe I am fulfilling my destiny and that they are too. It is the only way to continue and to take my role in the tribe as a buffalo hunter and robe skinner.

I run with a group of women toward the bottom of the hill as the buffalo tumble and fall from the cliff above. Some buffalo jump up and run, limping away. I have only one chance for my obsidian tool to find its mark, and I must act swiftly to plunge my obsidian into the buffalo's neck. The stronger men and women pull the heavy animals away from the bottom of the hill. As the other buffalo are dropping from the cliff, we have to be quick and kill intently to ensure our food stays in place. We carry the burden of guaranteeing that we have enough buffalo meat for our people to survive the long, frigid winter on the plains.

I meet my first buffalo brother at the bottom of that cliff. I look into his eyes as he rolls toward me. I know I've been waiting for this moment all of my life—but now, faced with the task at hand, I can't do it. I'm frozen. I look into his eyes and start crying.

Then I hear him. He tells me, "You need to take away my pain. If you are my sister, you will do the right thing. Take your obsidian tool and plunge it into my neck. Do it quick, as I must leave this earth. I am one of the chosen ones, and I will take my rightful place where I came from. Then you must eat my heart. I will be yours forever and you will be mine forever. I will live on through you. Never forget me. Tell your children and grandchildren about me so that they will honour my spirit after you have passed on to the spirit world. This is what has been told to me by my brothers and sisters. Our destinies are tied together for eternity. Do it! Take your obsidian and strike now!"

I leeleeleelee as loud as I can to give me strength, and to honour what has been said by my buffalo brother. I remember my unci's and ina's words and I leeleeleelee *again and again. Four times I leeleeleelee as I strike the spot I know will end his life. I take a deep breath in and out quickly so I do not force the buffalo spirit into my body. I can eat only his heart, and I save some of it for my unci and ina and the other hunters who are watching me, encouraging me. It all happens in a blink, but to me and the buffalo spirit, it lasts a lifetime. I feel the blood entering my blood as I take my initial bites of my first buffalo kill. The heart is still beating.*

We will always be one with the buffalo. They are in our blood and we are a part of their spirit. Forever connected, forever bonded. No force alive in the universe will separate us, for as long as the wind blows, the rivers flow, and the sun shines.

I am a buffalo hunter.

—2016

Andrea Menard
Métis · b. 1971 · Flin Flon

Andrea Menard was born in Flin Flon, Manitoba. She is of Métis descent, and is an accomplished actor, jazz singer, and performer, based mainly in Saskatchewan. Her television work includes *Moccasin Flats* (2003–2006), *Rabbit Fall* (2007–2008), *Wapos Bay: The Series* (2005–2010), and *Blackstone*. In 1998, Menard wrote and composed *The Velvet Devil*, a one-woman musical play, and she has also released four albums. Menard says of her songs: "I just want to make music that makes me feel good. I want to speak impeccable words, as taught to me by my Elders, so that when I sing them joy radiates from my heart and affects the people around me in a good way."

The Halfbreed Blues

I was born the privileged skin.
And my eyes are light, light brown.
You'd never know there was Métis blood
Raging underground.
Let me tell you a story about a revelation.
It's not the colour of a nation that holds the nation's pride.
It's imagination.
It's imagination inside.

I was told that my skin would allow me to walk
On the streets where the people are free.
So I left my soul in my loved ones' hands

And I turned my back and walked away.
With my head held high in my high-heeled shoes
I could yell and scream and make my noise.
Then one day I met a man. He looked like me
But he had soft beaded skins upon his feet.

He looked right through me with his weathered eyes
And he asked me if I was free.
He said, "Sister, sister."
He said, "Sister, don't walk away."
I said, "Brother, brother."
I said, "Brother, don't bother me today!"

He looked right through with those weathered eyes
And he asked again if I was free.
"Damn rights I'm free!"
"Of course I'm free!"
"Oh yeah I'm free!"
"I think I'm free."
"I hope I'm free."

Oh, please, let me be free.

—2002

Lift (a Tribute to Gordon Tootoosis)
(by Andrea Menard and Robert Walsh)

"We're just passing through," he said,
"We're all just passing through
No need to get all worked up, girl
'Cause I'll see you on the other side someday soon
But for now, you gotta feel what you're feeling
Let the tears cloud your eyes
Yes I'm leaving this world behind.
But when I do, I'm not leaving you."

"Let me, Lift, the weight off your shoulders
Lift, the veil from your eyes,
Shift, to a brand new perspective
Lift, you higher, where you can see for miles and miles and miles."

I rest my head in a field of grass
Beneath Poundmaker's sky
It's been years since you've been gone
I'm lying here, I'm trying here, to say goodbye
But right now, I gotta feel what I'm feeling
I can't let you go, are you there,
Can you find a way to let me know
I beg of you, to pull me through

Help me Lift, the weight off my shoulders
Lift, the veil from my eyes,
Shift, to a brand new perspective
Lift me higher, where I can see for miles and miles and miles

Wait a minute…Did I just hear your voice in the wind
Just a minute…Did I just see your face in a cloud
I rub my eyes,
It disappears,
But I see clearly now

Lift, the weight off my shoulders
Lift, the veil from my eyes,
Shift, to a brand new perspective
Lift me higher,
Lift, the weight off my shoulders
Lift, the veil from my eyes,
Shift, to a brand new perspective
Lift, me higher,
Where I can see for miles and miles and miles,
I can see for miles and miles and miles

—2012

Jesse Archibald-Barber
Métis-Cree-Scottish-German · b. 1972 · Regina

Jesse Archibald-Barber was born and raised in Regina. He is of Métis, Cree, Scottish, and German ancestry. He is an associate professor of Indigenous literatures at First Nations University of Canada. He is also involved in Indigenous performance and was the co-director of the *Performing Turtle Island Gathering* in 2015, and the artistic director of *Making Treaty 4* in 2017. He has published in *Mitewâcimowina: Indigenous*

Science Fiction and Speculative Storytelling and the selection below is a creative nonfiction piece first published in *The Malahat Review* in 2015.

The Bowl Game

Fields of wheat glowed in the yellow fire of the sun. I curved southward off the Interstate, down to the low hills of the Little Bighorn Battlefield, the shadow of my Gran Torino growing long in the warm air of the fall equinox. I could still hear the words of the Blackfeet teachers back in Bozeman, their stories of the old games, how to craft and play them according to their origins. I had breathed freely in the woods, cutting willow branches and collecting river stones, always leaving tobacco behind. One story stirred something deep in me, from long before my memory had fully formed: a young trickster, born of a distant wind spirit, his mother lost with the rest of the people, madness overtaking them in the land of darkness. The trickster went through his preparations to descend into the earth, to meet the Stone People, his tribe's fate hanging on a game of chance, the stakes increasing with each toss of the bone figures in the wooden bowl.

Homeward now, my eyes swam in the glittering heat, the soft asphalt giving surface to my thoughts. I had made a brief detour to Yellowstone, a patchwork of bubbling acid fields and geysers framed by pine forests and open meadows. I saw the free-ranging buffalo, one of the last pure bison herds on the Great Plains. Now deep in the Crow Agency, pulling up to the Little Bighorn gates, I was nearly too late.

"We're closing up for the day," the park ranger said as he removed his wide-brimmed hat to wipe his brow.

"Ah, but I've come a long way. I'll just be a couple of minutes," I pleaded. He paused, as his eyes scanned me up and down, then, smiling slightly, gestured to the gate, shiny black metal bars offset by the crumbling red brick walls.

Monuments dotted the low hills, the dry grass absorbing the last rays of light. Here Custer made one last discovery. Horse and sky gave way that day, but not the land. He had planned to make it his, had seen the field of battle as one unbroken extension of his own vision, but the Sioux would not yield. He must have held one last image as his vision blurred, the Great Plains rising at the edges all about him, the unending horizon upturned toward the sky, as he hit the ground, bullet in temple and in heart, yellow hair now crimson.

With the click of the lock, the ranger secured the gate and drove off, waving as I returned to my car. I sat alone for a moment, to inhabit the solitude, and then turned the key to start. The engine just growled and sputtered. Opening the hood, I could barely glimpse the motor in the fading light. I saw the fluorescent sign of the village gas station from my vantage on the hill, so I began walking down the narrow road, the oblong shape of the sun slipping entirely below the horizon. My thoughts ran wild in the darkness. I was descending on a curved slope, the hill behind me rising out of sight, as if the earth had no foundation, the young warriors and soldiers dying in the grass around me, emptied of their blood and purpose, stars tumbling from the night sky like bone dice.

When I reached the highway, a car screeched past me and crashed into a lamp post by the gas station. The driver stumbled out of the door, while the two in the back seat clamoured to get out the window. The tribal police were soon at the scene from their station across the road. Blue and red lights pulsed urgency, as dozens of locals began to gather. Some lingered, but most went about their business at the store, the KFC, and the tavern behind the gas station, the crash another sideshow amid the carnival.

The police would be busy with the accident for hours, but I walked over to the station anyway. The office was eerily empty, except for the dispatcher, a young Crow woman, hair pulled back in a ponytail. She briefly looked up at me as she kept taking calls, one after the other. Over twenty minutes passed before I had a chance to speak.

"Tow truck's out. Won't be back till morning." She took a slurp of her coffee as the phone blared again. Her eyes glazed, as if I'd never been there.

I returned to the gas station as two ambulances arrived, the night alive with flashing lights. Carloads of youth circled the scene. Over by the gas pumps, a man filled up his truck, but more gas poured on the ground than in the tank. People continued to arrive in a cacophony of whoops and hollers, music blaring, horns honking, cars swerving everywhere. A black crew-cab truck pulled up to the pumps and a couple of Crow guys hopped out, both in black T-shirts and blue jeans.

"Another Saturday night on the res," the driver laughed, gawking at the crash sight.

"You know them?" the passenger asked me.

"No. I'm kind of I'm stranded here. My car's broke down."

"Where's it at?"

With a quick boost, my car roared back to life and relief washed over me. "Thanks, guys. Here, have one on me," I said, handing them a six-pack from the trunk.

"Thanks," the passenger said. "Better get her looked at right away. Good luck," he waved as they drove off. I sat there for a moment by the gates and stared at the grass in the field illuminated by my headlights, then put my car into gear.

I turned on the radio and settled in my seat for the long hours ahead. The highway hummed with traffic, soft red lights all about me in the darkness. I could smell a pungent odour, like sulphur burning. Soon, the city lights of Billings came into view, as I rounded my way up to the Interstate. I was ascending again, but the car was slowly being filled by the stench of a dying animal.

First to go were my taillights. An angry driver honked as he sped past. Then a truck leaned on its horn, and soon every vehicle did the same. Headlights now dimming, I watched for an exit ramp; the radio slowly faded followed shortly by the dash lights, which by now didn't matter because none of the gauges were working. I slowed down some more, as a convoy of giant semi trucks roared by and nearly shook me off the road. My headlights now nearly gone, I tried the high beams, but there was only a momentary flash, growing fainter until they went out completely. Blind, I could hear the blood in my ears, my eyes desperately adjusting to the darkness. There was just enough radiant light for me to follow the white line at the edge of the road. Then the engine went next, and I braced myself, my entire being focused on that line, eyes squinting for any trace of light.

My salvation at last, an exit sign suddenly appeared, and I swerved to the off ramp. As I coasted downward, I turned the ignition over and over again, my fingers clenching the metal edge of key. Nothing. Not even a click. And the car finally settled at the bottom of the ramp.

I could hear the rush of traffic on the overpass, but I was stranded once again in darkness. Headlights swept from above, falling, illuminating the road about me. I was in the middle of the intersection. I shot for the hazard lights, but they too were dead. Fumbling, I grasped my lighter and started flicking it repeatedly in the window. The car slowed as if to help, but then veered around me and sped away down a long street lined with a row of old houses.

I was at the edge of a small town and could see the light of a gas station sign standing above the low outline of rooftops. I was descending again, pushing the car along the slightly sloped road all the way to the station, which turned out to be closed. I slumped on the hood and caught my breath, as I wiped the sweat from my face and surveyed the desolate streets. A rumble of music and laughter rose from the other side of the station. I pushed my car across the lot, and a saloon came into view, revealing the town's name, the bold letters CUSTER mounted above the archway.

I entered to a flurry of activity. Cowboy hats bounced everywhere, country music cranked out of the jukebox, and rodeo played on every screen. Only a few steps in and everyone turned my way.

"What'll it be, fella?" the bartender said.

"I need a tow … or a mechanic."

"Ain't no tow truck or garage in town. You'll have to go to Billings in the morning." He flung the phone book on the counter. "No bus neither," he laughed. I began flipping the pages, as I gulped down the glass of water he slid in front of me. A man, plaid shirt and big black hat, staggered up to me.

"Got car trouble?"

"Yeah, it's the..."

"Where's it at?" He headed out the door before I could finish.

I was grateful at first, but soon a crowd of cowboys jostled around my car, beers in hand, talking over each other about how to fix it.

"It's probably the alternator," one yelled.

"Let's rip it out right now," boomed another.

"You ain't got no tools, can't fix it tonight," slurred another, his beer spilling over the engine. "Let's get a drink," and he staggered back inside, the others soon following. I lit a cigarette and used the payphone to call home, but there was no answer. I tried again, then wandered back into the saloon and stayed through till closing time.

As I lay in the backseat, I could hear the traffic on the Interstate rushing past the rim of the town, and I felt like I would be stuck down here forever. I exhaled deeply and stared at the back of the front seat, which now seemed to jut out like a huge stone looming over me, and soon the cushion beneath me gave way. My hand slipped to the floor, and my car had become the smooth wood of a playing bowl with stone figures standing about me, some grinning, some downcast, others obscured in the night. Suddenly, a crack along the grain split the wood, and in those depths lay the scattered bones, some picked clean and others still decaying, and around them the circling birds of prey, while beneath the water reflected in the light of the moon the silhouette of bodies swam in the darkness. My hand snapped back to my chest, breaking the surface, as sunlight moved across my eyes.

Combing my hair with my fingers, I strolled up the road to the diner. The clinking of cutlery and the sanity of bacon and eggs on the grill restored my senses. I was sipping on my coffee when a tall man in faded jeans and denim jacket walked in. He had black scraggly hair and a greying beard, and he grunted as he sat down. "Morning," he said to the cook and ordered some breakfast. After a few moments, he looked in my direction and muttered something.

"Pardon me?"

"You look a little worse for wear."

"Yeah. Actually, my car broke down. I think it's the alternator."

"What kind of car?"

"'75 Torino," I replied. He took a swig of his coffee, chewed on a hunk of toast, sat back and thought for a moment.

"I can help you out," he said. "When I'm done here, we'll head to my place."

We jumped in his old Ford truck and headed out of town. The landscape was filled with small farms and fields, the roads covered in red dust, grooved lines stretching to the low mountains on the horizon. I tried to make conversation: "So, you have a lot of spare parts?"

"Yeah, I'm a Ford man," he said. "I got a few different bodies in the back 40." The property was filled with old cars and trucks and some broken down farming equipment. We were removing an alternator from one of the trucks, when a horse with a shaggy mane poked out from behind a shed and let out a pitiful whinny. Then a small cow came out from behind the same shed, along with the two chickens. Setting down his wrench, the Ford man walked over to the little heifer, patted her affectionately on the head, and said, "Yup, I'll be putting her in the freezer this winter."

With alternator in hand, we made the ride back to town, the silence broken only once when we yielded to a young girl on horseback.

"Out here, the horse has the right of way," was all he said. He even worked in silence, grinning only when the car turned over and revved again with renewed life. I tried to pay him, but he would only accept my offer to buy lunch instead.

As I crested the hill, I peered in my rear-view mirror, the town behind me hovering on the prairie until it was lost in the heat. The settlers had built their houses as solid as they could, unaware of the earth below them, holding fast to custom as if what they were could slip forever from their grasp down that long slide to darkness. The folks at the Little Bighorn understood without knowing; their ancestors had paced the land, moving with the grooves of the earth and the great bison that roamed the prairie, before borders, before the dream of permanence.

I drifted with the words of a song on the radio and remembered playing the bowl game with my parents as a child. I imagined my father's madness, leaving with the wind and swallowed up, my mother remarried, moving on, stone figures balanced on the bowl. Hours later, as the sun dipped below the horizon, the fields of Saskatchewan opened up before me. The lights of my city shimmered in the distance, suspended above the earth—Regina, *oskana kâ-asastêki*—a city built upon a pile of bones. I thought of home, of the warm disembodied glow of the TV, and shivered slightly in the cold of the fall equinox.

—2015

Lisa Bird-Wilson
Métis · Saskatoon

Lisa Bird-Wilson's stories have appeared in several periodicals, including *Grain*, *Prairie Fire*, *Geist*, and in the anthology *Best Canadian Essays*. She has been nominated for the Journey Prize. Bird-Wilson also wrote *An Institute of Our Own: A History of the*

Gabriel Dumont Institute, and she has written curriculum materials for the Ministries of Education and Advanced Education, while working as a director of the Gabriel Dumont Institute. The selection below is from her first book-length work of fiction, *Just Pretending*, published in 2010.

Blood Memory

Every pregnant woman dreams of what her baby will be like. But babies shouldn't have to dream of their mothers. It's been more than thirty years, and I still struggle to quell the haunting voice at the back of my mind that urges *Find her find her.* Instead, I invent her.

I want to start at the beginning, but beginnings are slippery to pin down. What would hers look like? Was it the moment she realized her period was late? I can imagine the instant of understanding that her actions, up to then carefree and light, came with real consequences. Or maybe the beginning was the conception itself, when she and my father pushed the limits behind the big barn that housed the cattle in winter, the small heated calf-shack tucked into its shadow. What made her think she was immune to it all, to the fecundity of the land and animals that every day plugged her nose with pungent odours, filled her ears with bawling bleating madness?

More likely, the beginning had something to do with the day the gnarled, squashed fetus (she made herself call it a fetus to avoid thinking of it as a b-a-b-y) squalled its way into her world and she made her way out of its world—a double beginning. Each a newly released hostage, not quite believing she had survived, fleetingly grateful before moving on as though nothing of import had occurred. There's got to be a reason why babies and mothers forget the pain of birth.

I picture it something like this. At the height of the ninth month, swollen like an overstuffed olive, lungs and other internal organs squeezed so tight she felt out of breath on the wide staircase of the antiseptic "home for unwed mothers" (read: "institution for misfits and fuck-ups"), she tried to understand, but she could not find a reason for the mythical underwater creature swirling beneath skin stretched so thin and taut that in her dreams she popped herself with a shiny dinner fork. All the while, inside, the fetus (repeat: *fetus, fetus*) sank and swam in murky depths of blood memory, bonding secret-identity-mother to child. And a word bobbed about in the depths, tickling the tadpole, the word waiting to be picked up and held in the palms of two hands, examined then crushed to the chest rubbed into arms, over shoulders, across the belly, the word more than a word, to be inhaled then expelled bit by bit with every breath—the word *Métis*.

I don't know about the home and the wide staircase; she could have been kept like an animal in a barn for all I know. But going off to a home seems the kind of thing that would have happened, back in the day. I imagine them saying she'd been sent away to live with a sick aunt after her father made an angry visit to the neighbouring farm and scared the hell out of the farmhand, who was really just a boy, while her mother got on the phone with the priest. Sent away for five months before returning deflated, with large leaky breasts, eyes swollen from lying in the back of the family station wagon and bawling all the way home.

"Growing nicely," Dr. Dubious pronounces as he measures my belly from pubic bone to top of fundus—some of the new words I've been learning. What about the words she learned? Not the words of a fantastic and beautiful anatomy to be revealed during the rite of passage through pregnancy and birth toward motherhood. Instead, the words she learned—truly learned in their deep and hurtful meaning, maybe for the first time—those words may have been *shame, wrong, bad, disgrace*—words that made her cover her head and stop her ears to deflect their blows.

I also learned, on my visit to Dr. Dubious, that it's awkward to have a baby when you don't know your medical history. *Any history of heart disease?*

No.

What about in your family?

Nana died when I was nineteen, and my mother struggled to find the words to tell me her mother was dead. That's when I understood that my mother had been a daughter first. But Nana's stroke doesn't count for Dubious's question—he is looking for hereditary conditions. I have nothing to offer, only a great yawning blank. I give him the only thing hereditary I know: *Métis*.

Not a baby, not a baby. She must have willed herself to remain blank and distant from what was right below the sternum. No picturing startled fingers, tiny heels that would fit in her palm, a dark silken bloom of hair, down-covered shoulders. Instead, a fishy eyeless globe, a silent sea monster in the well of her incubator body, gnawing at the base of the cord that attached them, one to the other, trying desperately to escape as a muskrat will chew its own leg off to get out of a trap. She once saw her father open a ripe sturgeon, full of black eggs, and saw him lament the lost potential of those eggs, as though somehow he'd been a careless steward. But her insides harbour only a single shimmery orb shadowed by a thin stretch of tail. She imagines this thing contained; herself a container. She is filled with blue-green water, soft seaweed tendrils undulating in time with her movements, a secret underwater world like a dark aquarium.

There must be a reason we're grown in the dark, submerged in water, hermetically sealed—what is it we're trying to keep out?

She dreams of gigantic garden shears sharpened to a razor's edge, oiled and free of catches, her hands holding the rubber-coated grips and cutting the briny cord, setting herself afloat as the fetus *fetus fetus* drifts lazily away like Huck on his raft, and she is laughing.

In one of her dreams, she finds a small blue jewellery box bobbing in the toilet. She scoops it out and holds it in her palm, wet and messy, leaking onto her bare toes. She's afraid to open it because she thinks it is ticking. She panics and tries to hide the thing before it explodes. She blurts out mock-magic words "*Ababa,*" grievous, faulty in a solemn voice, flicking her fingers over the box, a magician's black-magic flourish, *léger de main*, before flushing. A different type of disappearing act, she conjures me down.

I tell Dubious that I'll have my baby at home with midwives, that my baby must remain with me at all times, particularly during those few first lucid hours when the most intense bonding is said to occur. I mention my anxieties about "attachment capabilities" and "emotional glue." But I don't tell him that I'm teetering on the edge of an insurmountable regret, a loss so large it threatens to smother me—the loss of what was mine by birth, a deficit that I wear like a scar.

I know this because as a child I had two best friends—both adopted, both Native. This seemed incidental, but I now know it wasn't. It was an intuitive recognition of each other's wounds, as though we each saw, like an aura, the pieces that hadn't formed, the missing parts that would have made each of us whole. I only tell Dubious that I want the best for my baby.

"All expectant mothers say that," he laughs.

I don't tell him he's wrong.

During the last months of my pregnancy, my mind becomes watered down with the weight and change in my body. I sit for hours dreamily staring into space while the radio plays softly in another room. I relish the quiet, the peace, the opportunity to do nothing, which those with experience tell me will soon end. I imagine what these months were like for her, in that home, day after day, a prisoner serving a sentence, waiting to be set free.

At the home, there's a girl she has taken to calling Mary K. Mary K is lithe and sexy, even at nine months, while she herself is puffy, toxic with high blood pressure and nauseating headaches. She can envision Mary K sitting on an older man's lap and fiddling with his pants, toying with the idea of being taken advantage of, a spunky, sway-back, streetwise Lolita, her slippery seal's body a horny turn-on. If she'd had something other than sex to peddle, she'd be the queen of snake-oil sales. If life had dealt her a different hand, she'd be driving a big pink Cadillac with vanity plates that read *Mary K.*

As they smoke in the alley behind the home, one girl dares to confess she misses her boyfriend. The rest of them drag on their smokes and say nothing.

The days are long and bleed one into the next. The girls are not allowed out of the nuns' sight. Many resent not being free to walk and shop and pretend to live a different story than the one they do; many are from remote rural places, and being on the edge of the city only to be forbidden a trip downtown vexes them to the point of tears. Only Mary K, looking like a malnourished, pot-bellied orphan, manages to slither out under the cloak of night to secure cigarettes. She brings back small flat bottles of lemon gin, and the girls, with their skewed centres of gravity, tumble one atop the other with shrill delighted screams. The Mother Superior threatens to kick them out; to call their parents. She tells them how lucky they are to be there, how ungrateful.

One evening at the home, as she makes toast, she looks at her bloated reflection in the chrome and dreams of being thin again. The girls can talk of nothing else. As she reaches into the toaster with the point of a knife, she knows that it's a stupid thing to do. So when the shock throws her back onto her ass with a hard *hmph*, she's not surprised. Hours later, after the cold stethoscope with the doctor at the end of it is gone, and her hair still floats about her head with static, she thinks about the pond of dew she might have been standing in were it not enclosed inside her body, and how water and electricity make bad company. She wonders about the cloudy lagoon sloshing about in her distended belly, with its fragments and bits, if it had been electrified, touched the way she once saw a loose live wire send a blue-white spark to skip over puddles in the barn like stones over water.

I was one of those electrified bits, plotting my escape from inside the belly she was forced to wear like a blanket of shame. I know this happened because my own mother, the one who raised me, told me what the social worker had said. "There was an accident. You could have been lost." She told me this in order to impress upon me how much I was wanted even before they knew who I was, even before I was born. I want to be grateful, I am grateful. But still I know she wouldn't understand my feeling that I've always been lost.

As she completes her sentence at the home, waiting for me to be born, shameful words creep up on her. In Cree one word is spoken over and again in her head—*macitwawiskwesis*, a bad girl. Perhaps she had a note from her mother on her birthday, expressing hope for a better year, yet between the lines she reads her mother's desire for a good daughter, not such a bad *nitânis*. My heart twists, half with empathy and half with jealousy, for at least she got to know these words, difficult as they are. At least she was *nitânis*, no matter how *bad*. When my husband returns home from work, I chalk up my tears to hormones and he holds me until I sleep.

I imagine that all her dreams occur under water. The night she goes into labour, she floats peacefully, hair swaying about her face, hands gripping her garden shears, only to be tossed on shore by the insistent tides of her body. She gasps, lying in a puddle. Has she breached the thin membrane between dream and wakefulness, somehow exposing the netherworld to this one? She cries out with her first conscious contraction, and the girl in the next bed says, *Shuddup, fer fucksake*.

Hours into the labour and delirious with pain, does she finally hear me?

"FEE FI FO FUM," I bellow from below.

Her whimpering is lost on me.

"I'LL GRIND YOUR BONES," I holler as I grind my way through her childish pelvis.

A sentimental girl might name the baby. It never occurs to her, before, during or after the birth, that I am anything other than the black-penny-eyed tadpole of her imagination. She fills in the blanks as best she can—there are rules about these things—but no one can make her open her heart, and no one can force her to leave anything behind, not even a name.

I sit in my bathtub at home, riding waves of contractions, soothed by the warm water, two midwives amiably attending, prepared for the long haul typical of most first births. I can't shake the dream-world mother I've created. *Nitânis*, she whispers, as I let my head fall wearily between contractions; one midwife mops my brow with a cool cloth while the other perches on a chair and sips tea. Someone's put soft music on, my husband warms towels in the dryer, and I can hear the excited voices of our families downstairs in the living room.

My mother, real or dreamed, never had any of these things. No one whispered *nitânis* in her ear, mopped her brow, made the tea, warmed the towels, waited in the wings, treated my birth like a celebration. Instead, I imagine harsh words, harsh towels. Maybe a younger nun secretly attempted to soften the punishing experience of most births at the home. I'm confused and angry over the loss of what I needed: identity, blood inheritance, to be Métis, to know where I've come from, something to pass on to my own child, who will also be blind to what ought to be hers by birth.

Hours later, my child is born. "She's a *girl*," I say to my husband, surprised by the awe in my voice. I hold her warm, waxy body, a bent snail, next to my skin, and cover her with my hands. Curled like a comma, punctuation, an exclamation: the end of a sentence, making way for the beginning of something new. I palm her black-capped head, and she looks at me—looks and looks—her eyes wide and serious.

"Hello," I whisper. "Hello, *nitânis*," My first blood relation.

—*2010*

Merelda Fiddler
Métis · b. 1976 · Meadow Lake

Merelda Fiddler is Métis from Meadow Lake. She earned her B.A. in Journalism in 1999 and her M.A. in Canadian Plains Studies in 2010 at the University of Regina. She worked as the current affairs producer for CBC Saskatchewan, producing numerous radio local and network specials throughout her career. In 2013 she received the Métis Award for Journalism.

Powerful Women, Powerful Stories: How I became Métis, and a Journalist

When I look at the world, I see an endless stream of stories. Some give us hope, some serve as a warning, others make us laugh or smile, or even bring tears, but all of them share something with us. Within each story there is an endless amount of power—to teach, change, inspire, instil and guide. That is why listening to, recording and telling stories is as much a part of my identity as being a woman, a mother, a journalist, and, of course, Métis. There are times, as I am listening to someone tell a story, whether it is an interview subject, a friend, an elder or a family member, when I feel as if the rest of the world just melts away. Other times, I am the storyteller, and I know I am doing the story justice in the moment when I look over and the listener cannot break their gaze from me or speak—and their world is melting into my story. Often, there is nothing else in that space but the story, the storyteller or listener, and me. Stories are all consuming—at least for myself—and I believe they are at the heart of everything that we are. So, really, I cannot imagine the world, my world, without stories.

As a little girl, I was surrounded by strong women, who while raising their families (many without fathers), were also born storytellers. My mother, sister, cousins, aunts, and all of their friends were gifted storytellers. Most had not graduated from high school; many, like my mother, had not made it past elementary school. That is the beauty of stories and storytelling, to be good at it you don't need a degree; usually you need to have simply lived. That is how each of those women was able to teach me the importance and beauty of story. They also encouraged me to get an education, and many would encourage me to go on to university. They would also take bets about what I would become. Some, like my mother, hoped for a lawyer—who would eventually become a judge. Others, like my sister, wanted me to act and write. Most didn't worry much about where my career path would go, as much as they wanted all of the things for me that they didn't have the opportunity to obtain. While their love, stern guidance and support all helped me find my way, it was their stories that would have the greatest influence on my future career. I didn't know it at the time, but they were training me to become a journalist, which, in its pure form, is simply a storyteller. When my mother and sister told stories, everyone listened. It wasn't because you were forced to listen; quite honestly, you wanted to listen. Their stories were not just boring anecdotes: they were tales filled with actions, accents, and tiny pieces of humour and family history that said so much more than just 'here's a funny thing that happened on the way to the grocery store.' Sometimes they included eccentric family members, hilarious stories of our grandparents (who all passed away before I turned five), and each other. My mother and father were in their forties when I was born, and my sister was 17 years old at the time. That meant she knew much more about our family, because she had grown up with them. I had come much later, so my grandparents' generation had mostly passed, and stories were one of the things I had to connect with these larger than life people from whom I'd come. I learned what they had to pass on through their stories. I learned about their lives, our history, our legacy, and our struggles through these stories. Stories were also how I learned about my father. He and my mother divorced when I was three, and he moved far away—so I only really saw him a handful of times while I was growing up. Still, the stories my mother and sister told about him, about the family, and my grandparents somehow filled in the gaps, even if they were a little fanciful. So, in the end, my identity was completely wrapped up in and translated to me through these stories.

The journey to become a journalist, part-time academic, full-time wife and mother, and confident Métis woman was not an easy one (and is one I am still working on, frankly). When I was growing up in Meadow Lake, Saskatchewan, being a halfbreed was not an easy thing. You weren't quite Indian enough, and you definitely weren't white enough. I remember being confused, being lonely, and, at times, wanting nothing more than to break free of a history I didn't quite understand and was being punished for. I now realize that had I had the history, I would have understood why some people lived on one side of town, on the reserve, or across the tracks. If I had known about Louis Riel, Batoche, and what the people of that time had been fighting for, I may have understood why some people didn't like Indigenous people, why there are times when First Nations and Métis people have common roots but an inability to find common ground in the present day. That history was lost to me. All I knew was the structures and hierarchy I was forced to live in in that small town didn't fit my dreams or goals. I wanted to tell stories, I wanted to learn, and I wanted to be free of the stories that I believed were holding me back. So I went to university, took writing classes, graduated from the School of Journalism and Communications, did internships in television and radio, made independent documentaries, and finally came to work full-time with the Canadian Broadcasting Corporation.

The world opened up when I first started working with CBC. As an intern, I learned the ropes, how to use the equipment, edit, direct radio shows, do live hits and write for a listening audience. It was like a dream, filled with people who knew so much about the world, both here at home and everywhere else. As CBC is a cross-country public broadcaster, there is always someone, somewhere, within the system who knows something about a story you are working on, or who was there watching it unfold first-hand. As a storyteller, I couldn't have been luckier. The people who brought me into the system started as teachers, mentors and guides, and soon grew into colleagues and even friends. They opened up a world to me that I had seen and heard only from the outside, a world that allowed me to talk about almost anything, anywhere and at any time. At first, it was overwhelming: one day I'd tell stories about the environment or farming, the next about business, development, and then on to health and politics. Every day, I struggled to learn as much as possible about curling, football, arts, social issues, and the people making the news. There was so much, and I wanted to be able to tell it all. First Nations and Métis issues and stories were also in the mix, although initially I didn't tell my colleagues everything about my cultural background. The other thing that happened in this first year after graduating was I met Mervin Brass and Shannon Avison.

If there are two people to whom I owe a deep debt of gratitude in my early career it is these two. Mervin was helping Shannon set up a summer journalism institute and was looking for someone to assist him. He had recently started working at CBC, and he knew who I was before I had told anyone. He and Shannon recruited me, and I spent almost two months working with Indigenous students who wanted to follow in our footsteps. That summer changed my life. My aunt had often told me that my job as a Métis woman, with all of my education and new-found privilege, was to be a role model. I was so young at the time I really didn't understand what she meant. I spent my junior high and high school years trying to escape. What kind of role model did that make me? In some ways, I had all but walked away from my identity. When I walked into the classroom and Mervin introduced me as a Métis journalist, one of the only ones in the province, and probably the country, it all fell into place. Even though I had only graduated a few months before I came to work with Indian Communication Arts, I was a journalist—and an Indigenous one at that! There are so few Indigenous people in the mainstream media in Canada. If you look at each major daily newspaper, television and/or radio station, each may have one or two Indigenous people on staff, while others have none. That summer, as I watched students pitch stories from their communities, be it the reserve, the inner city or the small Indigenous communities on the edges of the mainstream, I realized that I had not heard many of these stories in the media anywhere. In my first few years with INCA, I struggled to understand why I hadn't heard these stories. Each year, students with really great stories would end up pitching them to my colleagues at CBC, and every year those stories would get bought, played and replayed. So, a lack of interest on the part of CBC or our audience was not the issue. That's when I realized something—many of these stories were not reaching the people because there was no conduit. Stories had been my lifeline, my connection to my history, identity, community and family. But those stories could live, be shared, and continue only if I shared them. In the same way that stories saved my identity, I had to help save them. I had to share them. In doing so, we could all begin to understand one another. That understanding does not happen overnight. It will likely take many years, many stories and many more conduits to make that happen. Eventually though, I truly believe that stories will help us find a connection where government policies, agreements and promises never will.

In my career, I have met hundreds of people and worked on countless stories, for radio, television and print. However, when I look back, I can't remember each one. There are, however, moments that I will never forget, stories that were shared, and stories that I told that changed my life. One of those stories is about a woman named Bonnie Moosemay. Bonnie's story was one that stuck with me. That year, I covered two gruesome court cases. One was about a woman who was killed by her estranged ex-husband. The other was about an 18-month-old boy who died, likely from abuse, at the hands of his grandparents with whom the foster care system had placed him, for safety. In the midst of these two stories, which included testimony from what would be a convicted killer and a woman who went free, Bonnie Moosemay's story stood out. Bonnie and her daughter were killed in their home on the Gordon First Nation. The story rocked that community, but quickly disappeared from the headlines, as senseless acts of violence often do. Almost a year after she died, I realized that I knew very little about her, what happened, or what had happened to her remaining children. I knew I was not the only person who could have these questions. So I contacted a friend and fellow graduate student who I worked with at the First Nations University of Canada, and who was also a member of Gordon First Nation. I told her I wanted to do a story about what had happened since Bonnie's death. At first, my friend, someone with whom I had had many conversations and classes with, was suspicious. "Why?" she asked. "Why would you want to tell that story? What do you hope to accomplish?" My answer not only convinced her, but also Bonnie's mother and myself, that telling this story not only made sense, but was also desperately needed. The sad truth is Indigenous women are expected to go missing. They are expected to be victims of violence. Statistics show us that poverty and addiction are partly to blame. We know that Indigenous women are far more likely to meet a tragic end than their non-Indigenous counterparts. While there is hope these statistics will turn around, what we need to do, and what I knew needed to happen then, was to show that no matter whether or not this was a reality in Indigenous communities, it didn't make Bonnie less human. In fact, her story could be any woman's story. Eventually, I was put in contact with her mother and sister. In the chief's office on Gordon First Nation, Bonnie's mother told me about her daughter, not just about her struggles (which had been a focus in early news stories), but also her successes and her life. She told me about a young girl she had raised, who smiled and laughed, and how she and her daughter spoke on the telephone every day. She was a woman whose remaining children were now being raised by their grandmother—Bonnie was a real person. She wasn't just another murdered woman, or victim, but a woman who had family, friends, hopes, and dreams. Her death, and that of her eldest daughter that night, sparked change in the community. They set up a response team in cooperation with the neighbouring reserves; they formed community action plans, held vigils, and elders got involved. Her story had continued past her death, in the form of change. A few months after the story aired, I received a letter from Bonnie's mother. This is what it said:

> *Dear Merelda,*
> *Just a short note to thank you for the C.D. I really appreciate it. I*
> *listened to it and had a good cry. I think of my babies every day. We*
> *had a sad Christmas, when we were cooking we talked about them.*
> *We talk a lot about the girls, tell stories about them. I know we'll be*
> *hurting for the rest of our lives and missing them.*
> *Once again, thank you very much,*

I have kept that letter in my desk ever since. On days when I wondered what I was doing working as journalist, working in a big corporation, working in the mainstream instead of in a more supportive Indigenous community or organization, and even now as I teach journalism to both Indigenous and non-Indigenous students, I pull it out. I have read it many times, and it never fails to inspire me. To know that someone heard something I wrote, that they felt the story honoured that person's life, and that they shared something so deeply personal with myself and every listener, is not only a gift, it's an honour. It's not that another, non-Indigenous journalist couldn't have thought to do this story, or maybe one day would have. It's that it was my first thought and that those people, the way I interviewed them, the way I told the story, it came from a different place. It came from growing up in the same dysfunction, and knowing that that story could have easily been about myself, or my own sister; that I would have wanted that story told and that I would see the power in it. Maybe that story didn't change many people's perspectives, but, then again, maybe it did. I know that story helped one mother see the media in a different light, helped my friend see the media could tell a story of hope out of tragedy, and that our perspectives can be shared, because there are some Indigenous people telling those stories and seeing those perspectives.

Not long after, I found myself and a colleague (who is Ojibwa/Irish) heading out to Standing Buffalo First Nation, in the Qu'Appelle Valley. We were dressed in floor length skirts even though my colleague had to haul a camera and shoot this story for television, and even though it was the middle of winter and the roads weren't great. Did I mention the event was being held in the evening—so we were driving on winter roads, in skirts, at night? However, this story was worth all of the effort and late night work. We were on our way to a feast being held for Amber Redman. The young woman had gone missing in July 2005, and her remains would not be found, and the case would not be solved, for several years. Both myself and Carey had met Amber's family several times doing stories about her disappearance. On this night, the family was holding a feast for Amber, and many still held out hope that she would be found alive. There were no other journalists at this event; just us, in our skirts, carrying tobacco. We interviewed family, friends, cousins, and while Carey was gathering cover shots, I looked over and saw a familiar face. In the middle of the gym sat an elder, Ken Goodwill. I knew him from the First Nations University of Canada, where he was a resident elder. We had met several times, both through my teaching and at a time in my life when I had more questions than answers about my own identity. As an elder, he had helped me see who I was and why I didn't need others to reinforce my identity. On this night, however, I discovered he was also the grandfather of Amber Redman. I stared a long time at him, watching everything move around him—food, people talking, tears and laughter—and yet, he seemed so still. I was terrified. Should I go and try to interview him? Was this the right time? After what seemed like an eternity of fear-filled debate, I decided this is why I had tobacco, in case I wanted to speak with an elder. So I slowly walked toward him and sat down beside him. I gave him the tobacco and asked if he would do an interview with me. He agreed. So I turned on my radio equipment and asked—"Can you tell me about Amber?" This is how he responded.

> Yes, I think of her as a grandchild. I have many grandchildren and I think of her in terms of the things that she was involved in. She was bright and happy, she was involved in sports, but I think mainly I think of her as being involved in our Sundance. She was a pipe girl, I remember her during those hot days and during the heat and everything and she did really well. I remember her also as a young, vivacious girl, her whole life ahead of her. I really don't know what to expect. From our own perspective, the Elders say, we as First Nations people, we believe a lot in the power of prayer, but we also place a great deal, place a great deal of faith in the power of collective thought and as a community with the help of people from outside the community, we want to think in positive terms. Because as I said, the Elders say that enough thinking positive or thinking about something, then, the universe shifts a little bit to accommodate that. It's been a long time since Amber went missing. And as time goes on it becomes more difficult to remain positive, positive in the hopes for her return. But, nonetheless, this community and the people around it, we have Sundances, we have family circles, we pray at pipe ceremonies, for Amber, for the family, all her relatives and friends, and I don't think we've lost hope yet. And as I say, we try to remain positive, it does become difficult from time to time, but nonetheless, we hold at least a positive outlook that she will return.

Up until then, the story I'd heard most about Amber Redman was a girl who went to a bar and disappeared. I had never heard about her community connections, her place in the order of things. I had heard about her as a young woman and a daughter, but not any of the things her grandfather, Elder Goodwill, shared. The entire tape was played the next day, no edits. This story serves as an important reminder to me. I asked one question, he gave me one answer, and that was all that was needed. But it also reminds me—that you need to be strong, to be assertive, to ask, because people may want you to ask, in a respectful way, a way that shows you understand there is a good way to ask. It also reminds me that there are perspectives, many different perspectives that need to be shared. And that as a woman, as an Indigenous woman, there are many stories and perspectives that I see, that are not so obvious to everyone and that those perspectives need to be shared.

These moments are just two amazingly powerful stories that have changed my career, my view on what a journalist can and should do, and what my role as a Métis woman is in the media. I have continued to work with students, earn a Master's degree, and push more Indigenous people—of all ages—to engage with the media. The media can only do what you ask it to. The media cannot save humanity—it can only reflect humanity back to itself. And in that sense, teach, inspire and guide. We can learn from our actions, but only if we know what those actions are.

At the beginning I said that stories have changed my life, that they are the basis of my identity. In some ways, though, they kept things from me too. My parent's divorce, being Métis, how our family fought in the 1885 Resistance at Batoche, these things were in stories, but the stories were confused, left out details and sometimes left me wondering. The best example I have is one from my aunt, Cecil Gibson. She told me the following story when I asked why the family didn't openly and publicly talk about being Métis.

> *Because more or less they didn't want to tell the kids too much. You never even asked where a baby came from in them days. I remember when Leona was born. And you know to this day I wish grandma was alive, because I'd call her a liar. They lived next door to us about from here to the garage (points) maybe closer. And I hadn't been over there for quite awhile, the kids (her siblings and Grandma and Grandpa's youngest child) were at our place. So, mom dressed me up so I could go. So I went up there and walked into the house and Grandpa come into the kitchen. He had the stove just so hot, he took my coat off and told me to warm up there in front of the stove before I went to the bedroom. And I remember when I walked into that bedroom, and grandpa, he was a good man, all the walls were lined with sheets so no air could come in there. And the bedding on grandma's bed she always had feather ticks, hey? And grandma had on a white nightgown, and she was laying in bed covered up to here (gestures to her neck) and I was walking towards her and all of a sudden I spotted a cradle with a baby in it. Here it was Leona (who is sitting beside her in this interview). I said to grandma, I said, 'Grandma, are you sick?' She said, 'Grandma was chasing this rabbit 'cause it had a baby on its back. I tripped and fell and hurt my ankle.' And you know, I believed her. (laughs) I'll never forget that. You know I*

used to believe her and then I'd go home and tell mom that grandma
got hurt chasing this rabbit with a baby on its back.

I love this story. But it took me a long time to understand it—to understand its purpose. As a child, you don't need to know everything. What you need is to have your imagination inspired. You need to hear things that later make you ask questions, those questions motivate you to look for answers yourself. As a journalist, this is essential. If you don't have this, you're not very good at your job. One day after I heard this story, and was writing my thesis, something occurred to me. To regain my identity, I had to want to find and remember the stories. I had to work for it. And then share those stories with those who wanted to hear them. I'm still working on being a good journalist, a confident Métis woman and a role model. There are stories that I've heard and retold that have broken my heart, as well as stories that have given me hope in the face of staggering statistics that show how far Indigenous people have to go in order to just survive. There are days when I've wondered why I do this job—that sometimes has ridiculous hours, is so heavily criticized both internally and externally, and can seem like it makes very little difference. It's then that I go back to the stories for strength. If being a journalist were easy, I wouldn't love it. If gathering these stories and retelling them were easy, then we wouldn't really need it. If you want to know the truth about who you are, and where you come from, you have to go and find out for yourself. If you want to know how you fit in the world, you have to find that place. So as I said in the beginning, I found that place reflecting the world, and sometimes the part that is Aboriginal, back to itself. It isn't always pretty or perfect. It is, however, as real as the people in the stories, as inspiring as they are, and as hopeful as I am most days. Stories are everywhere. And when I look at the world, my world is one endless stream of stories—stories that give me strength every day.

—2016

Kevin Wesaquate
Cree · b. 1977 · Piapot

Kevin Wesaquate is from Piapot First Nation, and is a spoken word artist based in Saskatoon. He has worked as the Aboriginal Arts Leader for Saskatoon Community Youth Arts Programming, where he founded the Indigenous Poetry Society. He has also served as artist/writer-in-residence at Saskatoon Polytechnic Campus. He has previously published in *Cîhcêwêsin: New Poetry from Indigenous Saskatchewan*.

Like a Scene from a Movie

He rose to his feet with blood on his hands
Broken bottle dripping
Bystanders blink of frustration confusion
Not out of fear or concern they stare blindly
Like mutants on firewater

He was immediately pummeled
Take him to the hospital
I just brought that truck no fucking way
And he lay there to die

The minions danced around
Flames grew higher and sneers aimed ever so inwardly
Yes it's us out here
Come and dance with us

So he stood up and walked away into the pouring
Rain drops large like bombs splitting your brow
Walked into the cold black rain
Taking his cries with them
Through doors into it

Stepping out into dark
Alone with blood tumbling down his chest
His shirt dangled off him like wet tarp
His hands still red and vibrant
A man lay on his side

The ashes cooled off the next day
Charred remains of crimes left
Behind closed doors made of
Bars Bricks and Barbed Wires
And another man back to his Mother

—2010

Drop a Pound on My Table, Brother

My friends are higher than the Re/max
Sitting in basements on hot afternoons

Coughing insulting and laughing
So drop a pound on my table, brother
Let our minds mesh
In exile
High walking on paradigms
Of trip wire and tight ropes

To scrutinize the perceptions
Of tic tocs and
Lost meanings scrambling
Through confusion

Let the scales add ounces to your flavour
While black ooze filters through and
Burns your lips closed and
All you can do is smile

While the world floats on by

So drop a bound on my table, brother
We'll smother smoke signals through
Pollution and smog
Send it rising
To better places

—2010

That Picture in Black and White

Black white brown and red
Staring at me from the dead.

Perhaps you
Are you a part of my broken bones
A part from of my scarred body
I know you are, but I ask anyway
What do you teach with that face of stone?

Black white brown and red
Staring at me from the dead.

Burnt charred hair hanging off your crown
Black feathers that sing flyaway songs
Folds that scar and weave below your eyes
Which lead trails to your pursed lips
Trails that whisper to us
Like wind over the prairie
To your lips that never smile at me
An unbroken nose slicing the open sky like an eagle
Those attached lobes hearing my warriors scream
Your handsome brow above that far away stare
Your unseeded chin
And your jaw that pubescent jaw
Appeals to me, it impresses me
It depresses me it has undressed me

Brown white brown and red
Staring at me from the dead.

What was said to you?
    Were you paid with a rifle and a pint of rum?
      What did you teach them?
        What holds you?

Black white brown and red
Staring at me from the dead.

—2009

Brad Bellegarde (InfoRed)
Nakoda-Cree · b. 1978 · Regina

Brad Bellegarde is of Nakoda and Cree heritage and is a member of the Little Black Bear First Nation. Also known as InfoRed, Bellegarde is a hip-hop artist based in Regina. He has released two albums, *Knowbuddy* (2009) and *Rediculous Stories* (2015), and two Eps: *Prairie Poet* (2001) and *No Stickers on My Disc* (2006). He also released an album with The Local Onlyz, *Kings Among Klowns* (2010). In 2009, he was a guest artist in Vancouver for the 2010 Winter Olympics as part of the Cultural Olympiad, which featured hundreds of artists from across Canada. He has given spoken word performances at UBC and the Mackenzie Art Gallery, and he performed for the Prince of Wales in 2012. Bellegarde's lyrics address contemporary First Nations issues from a hip-hop perspective. His song "I Remember" was included in the documentary *RIIS from Amnesia* (2015), about the Regina Indian Industrial School.

Running from Existence

I'm running from existence
Travel to the edge of the world
To make a difference
Lost in the light, life in the dark
Feeling ain't right

The feeling ain't right but I'm right here
In the lime light trying to make the night clear
So many days and so many years have passed
To reach the path of amazement, amazing
What about the dirt road? Save it!
The past is the past now it's pavement
I'm driving on the highway till I make it
Nobody in the world going to take it
Hard headed I quote it the way I read
I said it the way I wrote it
I wrote it to not forget it
Embedded upon the middle
Like medicine for the riddle
When Louis was playing the fiddle
Some problems are never little
So why do you figure middle fingers rise
When another brother dies
And the cops don't try
Take another life when they asked
And they lie
Tell my people why
We're living in poverty until we die
I'm telling my people to unify
Until we fly to the edge of the world
We don't cry.

—2015

Old Wood Bridge

Once upon a time not long ago
When the fish were abundant where the rivers would flow
I heard a lot of stories how the days would go
Picking buckets full of berries at a pace that's slow

Nowadays it's industrial change
Productivity margins and pie charts for the pay
It ain't the same even poisons in our park lakes
They used to drink rainwater now it's not safe
From swimming in the water to the water that's not there
It's hard to earn a dollar cause today the kids don't care
Taking everything for granted grid roads instead of granite
Horses are a thing of the past how did they manage?
Pop bottles were a nickel now a nickel's worth two bucks
City life changed the way
It's drop tops instead of trucks
Awwwwwww shucks!!
Another generation's gone
Let's take them all home in a memorable song, come on!

And when my dad was a kid my grand dad was just a dad
You had to walk where you wanna go you couldn't call a cab
And if you said you're gonna be there
Then you'd be there fo sho though
You couldn't call them up and say maybe tomorrow
Self sufficient no text messaging systems
One room, one school, not one television
No talking back because they all had to listen
Do what you're told otherwise you got lickings
And now its slim pickings
Parking lots are new buildings
And 20 dollars can't get myself a bucket of chicken
Mercury's rising affecting the fishing
Crown lands have gone commercial
Government makes commission!

—2010

I Remember

I was playing outside just a little man
With the world in the palm of my hand
A little kid living life with innocence
I remember everything with images
A red truck and a man in a black robe
They told my mom, call him father Joe

So we called him father Joe
I saw a tear in my mother's eye
I let out a cry
But I didn't know why
Piled up on the back of a truck
It had a flatbed on it and the road was rough
My hands were shaking
Feeling sick to my stomach
Where are they taking us?
Who could have done it?
My body is nervous
Why am I leaving?
What is the reason?
What is the purpose?
Now I'm just a lost little kid
Looking for my mother in this life that I live
All alone
On the road that I'm travelling
And I really want to do is go home

I remember,
Walking through the doors of the school
It was cool in September
They gave us clothes, put numbers on our sweaters
Said this will be your name 'til your home in December
They put powder on my head
Threw me in the shower
Then lined us up for bed
They took my braid away,
They took our braids away.

Cold night feeling shackled to my bed
I remember hearing whimpers from the kids
Whispers across the room
Talking things like, "I hope we go home soon!"
And this is just the first night
In my life, I think this is the worst night
I'm just a kid and they're testing my will
When we'd hear the jingle of the keys
We'd all lie still

I'd close my just to block out where I'm living
With an image on a cloud that I'm sitting
I want to fly away, I want to fly away

I can't cry, I can't sleep
They even took away a kid for trying to speak
I remember thinking that we'd never get to meet
Then my mind drifted off and fell asleep
My first morning brought food I couldn't eat
And if we didn't we'd get punished in our seat
This is the life that I had to live in Residential School as a kid

Now it's sixty years later looking back
Kind of funny how my mind remembers that
All the little things that I can't forget
But I'm thankful that I made it every step
And through the years
Confronted so many fears
My feelings have been adjusted
I'm telling it to your ears
The elements of my tears
Are sentiments of the years
That I spent with my peers,
I remember.

—2014

Thomas Roussin

Métis · b. 1979 · Gerald

Thomas Roussin was born in Gerald. He is a Métis singer and songwriter based in Regina. He has been actively writing and preforming for over fifteen years with an assortment of groups, most notably with the Nancy Ray-Guns (political folk-funk-fusion), the Local Onlyz (folk hip-hop) and most recently, Grain Report (old-tymey pop). He has written and preformed songs for film and television, including the theme song "Neechi Funk" for the Bionic Bannock Boys, which originally aired on APTN. Roussin comes from the modest roots of rural Saskatchewan as a self-proclaimed "village-kid with farm-boy sensibilities." He completed his B.A. in Indigenous Studies at the First Nations University of Canada, and his writing reflects his personal and academic quest for musical and poetic imagery.

Cutarm Creek

When I was younger I wanted to grow old
Learn every story my grandparents ever told
I come from a village of a hundred and fifty or so

Horseback holy men followed Father Albert LaCombe
And made Catholics out of Indians
They called him the Black-Robed Voyageur
He inspired settlers around to put up a home of the Lord
But the house burned down and now it's just a story

In life we learn to grow
In love we learn to grow
In death we learn to grow
And the Cutarm Creek still flows

Grand Trunk Railroad pounded one stake at a time
And brought in enough work with it
Up until they built the potash mine
A half a mile away, created a salt pile
Three-quarters of a mile long and 50 stories high

There was a story I heard about back in World War Two
The racism in town was so high one man didn't know what to do
They said he took his own life in the fear that someone else would
His shot's still up in the rafters and its all but a story

In life we learn to grow
In love we learn to grow
In death we learn to grow
And the Cutarm Creek still flows.

When I was younger I wanted to grow old
Learn every story my grandparents ever told
I come from a village of a hundred and fifty or so

—2009

All Those Years of Heart (1867–1905)

Lately I've been doing some reading of my own
And it seems to me there's a lot of things I was never told or never taught
　　to know.
Maybe we'll just have to write history of our own
And bring to light the story right of all those years of heart we've never known.

It was the Indians that wanted Treaties (and they got some)
But they got the *Indian Act* too that the Canadians could amend at their
　　own free will
And they damn well did!
Outlawing ceremonies of tradition and class
Locked up on the rez without a permit or a pass (how fair is that)
Forced into peasant farming for the better of the economy
Forced into dire poverty while the Crown got prime living

Whoa, Canada, our home's on Native land—it's time to take another look
　　again

The stories I've heard of what we call Saskatchewan
Sound more to me like age old open sores
Glory—the battle was won for Western Canada
Resistance was hung out at the Pile O' Bones

Day to day we can go back minding our own
But past generations depend on us as do the future ones we'll never know

There was a shovel in the ground 'fore they snipped the ribbon
Surveyed the land where the people were living
Consider it a take-over when you cut up the land and its original homes
Education is the new buffalo (it's what we know)
Got Google.com (we're good to go)
But we need more stories of the old ones
Stories of the old times
Stories of the old places before they were renamed

Whoa, Canada, our home's on Native land—it's time to take another look
　　again
The stories I've heard of what we call Saskatchewan

Sound more to me like age old open sores
Glory—the battle was won for Western Canada
Resistance was hung out at the Pile O' Bones

—2010

The Gift

In a plastic bag I picked up in the street
In a plastic bag I picked up in the street
I found a skirt
A children's book
An old cowboy shirt
And some bannock from a feast that tasted a lot like sweet grass

I put that bag on my handlebars and rode a while down Saskatchewan Drive
I came to an abandoned school, sat on the step to see what was inside
I opened up the bag and I held it high.

Gave the skirt to my mother-in-law,
She likes used stuff and wore it out with pride, nothing to hide.
Gave the book to a child—it had stickers inside she thought she hit a mine.

The cowboy shirt fit just right and the bannock (oh yeah)
I shared with the love of my life.

—2010

Mika Lafond
Cree · b. 1981 · Muskeg Lake Cree Nation

Mika Lafond is a member of the Muskeg Lake Cree Nation in Treaty 6 Territory. She lives in Saskatoon with her two children, Kane and Emberlee. She has a B.Ed. and M.F.A. in Writing from the University of Saskatchewan. Lafond has worked as a high school teacher, and as an instructor/mentor for ITEP at the University of Saskatchewan.

Lafond is a strong advocate for Cree language preservation, and the three poems included below are each in Cree (left column) and in English translation (right column).

sipwêtêyani	**when I die**
mistikwaskihk ta pêtâkosiw	don't expect fancy
kâya tâhkotahik	no stage to put me on

kâya mâtok
kâya wîhik

no crying faces

mistikwaskihk piko ta mat-
    wêwaw
thump-thump, thump-thump

I only need the heartbeat of the
    drum
thump-thump, thump-thump

kâya ta mîcêtwinânawiw
kâya ni ka wîhikawin
namôya kisipipayin

don't expect a crowd to gather
no mention of my name
no ending

thump-thump, thump-thump

thump-thump, thump-thump

kâya iytatêyita atâmaskamik ta
    pimisinîyin
kâya ayimota kikway ta kî hikik
kâya pakicîtota mihtâtamowin

don't expect to lie beneath the
    ground
don't talk of what might have been
no submission to sorrow

thump-thump, thump-thump

thump-thump, thump-thump

namôya iskwêyâni katamiskawin
niyaw piko pakicîmakan
kâya kîmohc pîkiskwê ka tipiskâk
namôya kiwanihin

don't expect to say goodbye
only my body surrenders
no whispers in the night
no you have not lost me

thump-thump, thump-thump

thump-thump, thump-thump

ispîhk kanîtâwikîyan
kiskinohtahin, tâpiskohc
    nikâwiy otêh kêsi
pahkahokot nânâskomot
kâpê isi pimâtisiyan êkosi nikêsi
    ponâyitin

guide me as my mother's heart
pulsing with gratitude

the day my life began
show me that I die as I have lived

thump-thump, thump-thump

thump-thump, thump-thump

namôya ayiwak, nikawî yêmi-
    kan, kikway
namôya nik pîkiskatên

free of sadness

free of pain

namôya môsitân wîsakêy-
itamowin
nika pakicîtotên kâkikê pima-
tisiwin

thump-thump, thump-thump   *thump-thump, thump-thump*

nika nîmihiton   I will dance

itâpi   **look**

mîtos namoya kostam   the tree is not afraid
ta mêskocît   to change

ispihk ê-kisipwêk   when warmth embraces bark
wâskwapoy pimiciwan   sap runs
mâchi sâkihpakâw   bud shoots and curls
pîyisk nîpîya nôkwanoh   twisting open into leaf
otinam sâkâstêw mina   soaks up sunrise
nipayastêw   receives each moon
                                          flips unrest in storms

kwêkwêskâso miyikîsikâ   when days grow short
takwâkiyawêw   damp autumn air
mêskocinâkwnoh nîpîya   displaces green
oskaskosîwâwa, osâwâwa,   smears yellow
mina mikosâwâwa   paints orange
wêwepâstanoh kâ yôtik   swaying in cutting gusts

mîtos wâwâstahikêw   the tree
kakwêskinâkwaki nîpîya   proudly waving
pêyatik   the colours of caution
wî pipon   predicting winter
pakitinam   letting go
mitosâcikos namoya miciminam   no stem clings to falling leaf
pinipakaw

katapowakêyitami   winter is worn with trust
kâwi ta kisipwêw   that warmth will reemerge

kâ-wâpamiyin

kiwâpamâw cî iskwêsis
   ê-pimohtêt
ê-wîcêwat omosôma
yoski nêhiyaw kâkîsimowin

kiwâpamâw cî oskâyaw ê-tapasît
wîkihk ôchi
iskotêwâpoy ê-tâkona
kaski tipsikâw
sisonê mêskanâhk ê-apit
ê-mamâtot tipiskahk

kiwâpamâw cî okâwîmaw
   ê-nîpawit
âpîhtâw nohtêkwasiw âpîhtâw
   âpisîkwasiw
pêyak osit iskwâhtemihk
pêyak ocîcî miciminam
   âsîyâniwat
nitotamawêw
   okiskinohamâkêma
têpiya pêyak kîsikaw

kiwâpamâw cî wîkimakan kâkwê
   pimacihot
ê-kanowsimwâkêk
   kwâmwâcisiwin
kîkâtowin
kâkwêyitamowin ascîkêmowin
konta asomisow ta-wanihisot

kiwâpamâw cî oksikinohamâkêw
awâsis mamitoneyicikan
   ê-sakâpihta
kâkwê micimâhpita
mâka mîkosowina
ohpaho makanwa

when you see me

do you see a little girl walking

with moshom
soft Cree words blessing air?

do you see a teenager running
away from home
bottle of vodka in hand
blackout nights
sitting on the side of a road
crying in dark?

do you see a mother standing

half asleep, half awake

one foot in the door
one hand on a diaper bag

begging her teacher

for one more day?

do you see a wife weathering

under umbrellas of silence

storming arguments
jealous accusations
threatening to lose herself?

do you see a teacher holding
kite strings of a child's mind

tying reason to ground
while gifts
catch wind and soar?

kiwâpamâw cî iskwêw ê-ayapit   do you see a woman sitting
sîpâ iykwaskwanoh   below rolling marshmallow clouds
ê-nitoska tânisîsi kwayask   searching for the right way
kêsi âcimot   to tell her story?

kawâpamiyan nîya   when you see me
wâpamin nîya   see me

Tenille Campbell
Dene-Métis · b. 1984 · English River

Tenille Campbell is Dene and Métis, and is a member of the English River First Nation. She has extensively studied Dene oral storytelling at the University of Saskatchewan, where she earned her Ph.D. The selections below are from her collection titled *#indianlovepoems*, which celebrates "positive sexual narratives for Indigenous women."

love poem #98

he was
my best friend's ex
the one who made her cry made her laugh
made her crazy

he was
sitting in the first light of morning
smoking a cigarette
watching me
with those dark eyes
that had once watched her

no good he was
living in his mom's basement
driving on two spares
drinking the cheap beer
and watching me
like a wolf watched
a wounded deer

the chill of late august hung in the air
as he put his arm around me
and leaned down
nose to nose
lip almost to lip

I'm going to kiss you he said
I waited
a moment frozen
in a field of northern Saskatchewan
lost in the golden light of dawn
fading shadows and rising mist

and when his lips finally
lowered down to mine
I glanced up at his closed eyes
laughed and leaned back.
not today baby
not today

—2014

love poem #58

you may be my favorite mistake
the one I should have steered clear of
the one whose name
will never be uttered again

you were a whim
a taste
that never went away
despite your 12 week stint in rehab
and those charges
that were a total fake anyways

those neck tattoos though
keep drawing me in
waiting for the minute
that my name stands
permanently into your flesh

like your taste is permanently
in my mouth

you promise me moosemeat
and a trip to meet your family
and I laugh
we will
never
ever
be that couple
instead
after the dark has fallen
and before dawn has risen
we forget
for a couple hours at least
that a PhD student
and a rezgangster from the big city
are only a good story

—2014

love poem #7

the only neechie I know
that rocks the manbun instead of a braid
casual and effortless
as he saunters through campus
like it's the grassy plains of yesterday
using words like
indigenous worldviews and
decolonization of classroom education
and I want

I just *want*

to make him stutter through a sentence
to make him ache
to make him forget
what he has learned
and to go by instinct only
an instinct that will drive us
under the covers and into the dark

for the winter
discovering
playing
decolonizing our own worldviews
as we make treaty
cree to dene
nehiyawehwin to denesuline

make treaty with me...

—2014

Shannon McNabb
Cree · b. 1987 · Peepeekisis

Shannon McNabb is from Peepeekisis First Nation. She is a graduate of the First Nations University of Canada, having completed her degrees in English Literature and Indigenous Education. McNabb draws her creative inspiration from her family and mentors and students. She is also a singer-songwriter and recording artist at Nashville's Newsun Records. Her poems and music reflect everyday life and the human condition.

Little Red School House

They say, "educate the primitive"
divide and conquer is the root to success
I've learned from many books, you know
didn't know Indians were famous in Hollywood
let alone the entire world
little red school house taught me much about society
browness is dirty, unfit for civilized worlds
yep, them brick buildings are a sanctuary

My grandma told me she would cry every night
she spoke the devil's tongue
she was wet-ragged by the holy sisters
you can call her a saint now
virginity prized and taken by the holy fathers
yep, she's a winner
alcohol is your saviour and she learned how to live well
could not love and learned how to hurt her children
yeppers, I must say that little red school house

taught her the ways of the lord and how to get to heaven
taught her that Indians were less, having no soul
that God will only love her if she learns to pray
in the white man's tongue

Here I am now in the present generation
a survivor, a seventh generation
is it true that God wants us all to be white?
have a brain like the Canadian government?
have an intent to incarcerate?
never mind self-determination
Yep, dumb little red school house
has taught my people to drink and repress feeling
taught us all the art of manipulation well
Wow! who would have thought
a brown child so clever
compromise truth favouring the lies

O wait! I hear something
what's this?
a blue building with a glass teepee
is it safe I wonder
this school house is not red, but blue
I hear singing over there
sounds like a heartbeat
Indians speaking their own languages
they teach each other about harmony and equality

I feel safe here
all people of every race coming together
the old teach the young and the young teach the old
I think I hear them calling to me
my grandmother's happy now
no more tears
my ancestors' ways are beautiful
I hear their voices echoing through these halls
they dance across the sky where King Thunderbird lives
my new friends and family don't drink or yell at me
I think I am home

—2010

Earthly Womb

Into the earthly womb, the spirit goes
Innocence and self belief now flows
Divine essence is the guide
Exposing all things we try to hide

This is where the journeys begin
Worlds between worlds we are let in
Apart from the physical
Sailing to and fro, absorbing the mystical

Souls lead back to the eternal flame
Changing; from staying the same
The purpose; to find yourself in moving places
Searching deeper, you seek familiar faces.
The ancestors cry! Honouring your try!
You take a dive and begin to fly

We hear the cracklings of our grandfathers
Feel the warmth and strength of our grandmothers
Through the heat, the soul reborn
No longer stripped no longer torn

Like children we begin to play
With wisdom, we are not led astray
Through our grandfathers and grandmothers as they talk
They send our little messages on the wings of the hawk

Watch the rocks as they heat
They waited for us, to greet
Waiting for the mystery of prayer
Through any circumstance, they will prepare

We now have something that they stole
Which today! on this plane makes us whole
This practice so humble, and once forbidden
Brought to light, rekindled, no longer hidden

—2016

Permissions and Sources

acāhkosa kā-otakohpit (Star Blanket): "Letter to Governor General" from Dominion Archives, DIA RG 10 Black Series, No. 422752, October 1912.

Janice Acoose: *Paul Acoose: Man Standing Above Ground*. Radio play, first broadcast on "Ambience," CBC, 8 February 1986. Copyright © 1986 by Janice Acoose. Reprinted by permission.

Howard Adams: Excerpt from *Prison of Grass*. Saskatoon: Fifth House Publishers, 1989. Copyright © 1989 by Howard Adams.

Alice Ahenakew: "The Priest's Bear Medicine" from *Ah-ayitaw isi e-ki-kiskeyihtahkik maskihkiy: They Knew Both Sides of the Medicine*. Ed. and trans. H.C. Wolfart and Freda Ahenakew. Winnipeg: University of Manitoba Press, 2000. Copyright © by University of Manitoba Press. Reprinted by permission.

Edward Ahenakew: "That Fatal Day at Frog Lake (No. 5)" from *Voices of the Plains Cree*. Regina: Canadian Plains Research Centre Press, 1995. Copyright © 1995 by CPRC Press.

Freda Ahenakew: Excerpt from Sarah Whitecalf's *kinêhiyâwiwininaw nêhiyawêwin / The Cree Language Is Our Identity: The La Ronge Lectures of Sarah Whitecalf*. Ed. H.C. Wolfart and Freda Ahenakew, as part of the *Publications of the Algonquian Text Society*. Winnipeg: University of Manitoba Press, 1993.

Jesse Archibald-Barber: "The Bowl Game." Copyright © 2015 by Jesse Archibald-Barber. First published in *The Malahat Review* #193.

atāhkakohp (Star Blanket): "Speeches at Treaty Six" from *The Treaties of Canada with the Indians of Manitoba and the North-West Territories*. Alexander Morris. Toronto: Belfords, Clarke & Co., 1880; Saskatoon: Fifth House Publishers, 1991. "Speech at Treaty Six" from *Buffalo Days and Nights*. Peter Erasmus. Trans. Henry Thompson. Glenbow-Alberta Institute, 1976; Calgary: Fifth House Publishers, 1999.

Gabriel Dumont: "Batoche" and "The Fourth Day" from *Gabriel Dumont Speaks*. Trans. Michael Barnholden. Vancouver: Talonbooks, 1993. Copyright © 1993 by Michael Barnholden. Reprinted by permission.

Jo-Ann Episkenew: Excerpt from *Taking Back Our Spirits: Indigenous Literature, Public Policy, and Healing*. Winnipeg: University of Manitoba Press, 2009. Copyright © 2009 by Jo-Ann Episkenew. Reprinted by permission.

Floyd Favel Starr: *Master of the Dew*, originally *Governor of the Dew*, in *The Great Gift of Tears*. Ed. Heather Hodgson. Regina: Coteau Books, 2002. Copyright © 2002, 2016 by Floyd Favel Starr. Reprinted by permission.

Merelda Fiddler: "Powerful Women, Powerful Stories." Copyright © 2016 by Merelda Fiddler. Printed by permission.

Connie Fife: "i have become so many mountains" and "the knowing" from *Speaking Through Jagged Rock*. Fredricton: Broken Jaw Press, 1999. Copyright © 1999 by Connie Fife. "Berries and Ripened Poems" from *Poems for a New World*. Vancouver: Ronsdale Press, 2001. Copyright © 2001 by Connie Fife. Reprinted by permission.

Arsene Fontaine: "The Story of the Bear" from *The Dene Elders Project: Stories and History from the Westside*. Ed. Lynda Holland. La Ronge, SK: Holland-Dalby Educational Consulting, 2002. Copyright © 2002 by Lynda Holland. Reprinted by permission.

Bevann Fox: *Abstract Love*. Self-published, Amazon Digital Services, 2011. Kindle. Copyright © 2011 by Bevann Fox. Reprinted by permission.

Helen Francis: "Life on the Trapline" and "Bombardier" from *Struggle to Survive: A Metis Woman's Story*. Copyright © 1997 by Helen and Tommy Francis.

Kim Soo Goodtrack: "Joe Flyingby's Tape Recorded Story." Copyright © 2010 by Kim Soo Goodtrack. Printed by permission.

Hubert Gunn: "A Lamp to Read By" in *Our Bit of Truth: An Anthology of Canadian Native Writing*. Ed. Agnes Grant. Winnipeg: Pemmican Publications, 1990. Copyright © 1990 by Agnes Grant.

Louise Bernice Halfe: "Crying for Voice," "Nōhkom, Medicine Bear," and "Der Poop" from *Bear Bones and Feathers*. Regina: Coteau Books, 1994. Copyright © 1994 by Louise Halfe. Excerpt from *Blue Marrow*. Regina: Coteau Books, 2004. Copyright © 2004 by Louise Halfe. "*tipiyawewisw*—ownership of one's self" and "*aniskostew*—connecting." Regina: Coteau Books, 2015. Copyright © 2015 by Louise Halfe. Reprinted by permission.

Tom Jackson: "Blue Water," "Vacation," and "Elder" from Ballads Not Bullets album, released 2015. Copyright © by Tom Jackson. Reprinted by permission.

Charlie Janvier: "A Man and a Wolf" from *The Dene Elders Project: Stories and History from the Westside*. Ed. Lynda Holland. La Ronge, SK: Holland-Dalby Educational Consulting, 2002. Copyright © by Lynda Holland. Reprinted by permission.

Harold Johnson: Excerpts from *Charlie Muskrat*. Saskatoon: Thistledown Press, 2008. Copyright © 2008 by Harold Johnson. Reprinted by permission.

kā-kišīwē (Loud Voice): "Speeches at Treaty Four" from *The Treaties of Canada with the Indians of Manitoba and the North-West Territories*. Alexander Morris. Toronto: Belfords, Clarke & Co., 1880; Saskatoon: Fifth House Publishers, 1991.

kā-miyēstawēsit (Beardy): "Speeches at Treaty Six Special Meeting" from *The Treaties of Canada with the Indians of Manitoba and the North-West Territories*. Alexander Morris. Toronto: Belfords, Clarke & Co., 1880; Saskatoon: Fifth House Publishers, 1991.

kā-miyo-kīsikwēw (Fine Day): "Song for Returning Warriors," "Big Bear's Last Thirst Dance," and "The First Person" in *Fine Day: Plains Cree Warrior, Shaman and Elder*. Garry Radison. Calgary: Smoke Ridge Books, 2013.

kamooses: "Speeches at Treaty Four" from *The Treaties of Canada with the Indians of Manitoba and the North-West Territories*. Alexander Morris. Toronto: Belfords, Clarke & Co., 1880; Saskatoon: Fifth House Publishers, 1991.

Jim Kâ-Nîpitêhtêw: "The Pipestem and the Making of Treaty Six" from *Ana ka-pimwewehahk okakeskihkemowina: The Counselling Speeches of Jim Kâ-Nîpitêhtêw*. Ed. and trans. Freda Ahenakew and H.C. Wolfart. Winnipeg: University of Manitoba Press, 1998. Copyright © University of Manitoba Press. Reprinted by permission.

kā-papāmahcahkwēw (Wandering Spirit): "Council Speech" and "Speech to Warriors" in *Kā-pēpāmahchakwēw: Wandering Spirit: Plains Cree War Chief*. Garry Radison. Yorkton, SK: Smoke Ridge Books, 2009.

Erroll Kinistino: "Kokom's Kaddillac." Copyright © 2008 by Erroll Kinistino. Printed by permission.

George Klyne: "The Trapper and the Snare." Copyright © 2015 by Jesse Archibald-Barber. Printed by permission.

Mika Lafond: "sipwêtêyani," "when I die," "itâpi," "look," "kâ-wâpamiyin," and "when you see me." Copyright © 2015 by Mika Lafond. Printed by permission.

Ernie Louttit: "Young Man Frozen." This excerpt is reprinted with permission of the Publisher from *Indian Ernie* by Ernie Louttit © University of British Columbia Press 2013. All rights reserved by the Publisher.

Randy Lundy: "deer-sleep" from *Under the Night Sun*. Regina: Coteau Books, 1999. Copyright © 1999 by Randy Lundy. "Bear" from *The Gift of the Hawk*. Regina: Coteau Books, 2005. Copyright © 2005 by Randy Lundy. "Son." Copyright © 2015 by Randy Lundy. "For Kohkum, Reta" and "Creation Story" from *Blackbird Song*. Regina: University of Regina Press, 2018. Copyright © 2018 by Randy Lundy. Reprinted by permission.

Shannon McNabb: "Little Red School House" and "Earthly Womb." Copyright © 2010 by Shannon McNabb. Printed by permission.

Gloria Mehlmann: "Pin Cherry Morning." First printed in *Atlantis Magazine*, 30.1, 2005. Copyright © 2005 by Gloria Mehlmann. Reprinted by permission.

Andrea Menard: "The Halfbreed Blues" Copyright © 2002 by Andrea Menard. "Lift" (with Robert Walsh). Copyright © 2012 by Velvet & Hawk Productions. Reprinted by permission.

Augie Merasty. Excerpts from *The Education of Augie Merasty*. Regina: University of Regina Press, 2015. Copyright © 2015 by Joseph Auguste Merasty and David Carpenter. Reprinted by permission.

Marie Merasty: "The Wetiko Mother," "A Race for Life," "The Last Laugh," and "Experience as a Medium" from *The World of Wetiko*. Trans. Bill Merasty. Ed. Candace Savage. Saskatoon: Saskatchewan Indian Cultural College, 1974. Copyright © by SICC. Reprinted by permission.

mistahi-maskwa (Big Bear): "To Rev. George McDougall" and "Speeches at Treaty Six" from *The Treaties of Canada with the Indians of Manitoba and the North-West Territories*. Alexander Morris. Toronto: Belfords, Clarke & Co., 1880; Saskatoon: Fifth House Publishers, 1991. "Speech at the Council of Duck Lake," in *The Birth of Western Canada: A History of the Riel Rebellions*. George F.G. Stanley. Toronto: University of Toronto Press, 1961. (This document is among the Confidential Papers of the Department of Justice relative to the Trial of Louis Riel.) "Letter to Sergeant Martin, N.W.M.P." from *Saskatchewan Herald*, 4 May 1885. "Address to the Court" in *The War Trail of Big Bear*. W.B. Cameron. London: Duckworth Overlook, 1926.

mistawāsis (Big Child): "Speeches at Treaty Six" from *The Treaties of Canada with the Indians of Manitoba and the North-West Territories*. Alexander Morris. Toronto: Belfords, Clarke &

Co., 1880; Saskatoon: Fifth House Publishers, 1991. "Speech at Treaty Six" in *Buffalo Days and Nights*. Peter Erasmus. Trans. Henry Thompson. Glenbow-Alberta Institute, 1976; Calgary: Fifth House Publishers, 1999.

SkyBlue Mary Morin: "As You Lie Sleeping" in *Faces of Feminism: Photo Documentation*. Ed. Pamela Harris. Toronto: Sumach Press, 1992. Copyright © 1995 by SkyBlue Morin. "Legacy of Residential Schools." Copyright © 2016 by SkyBlue Morin. Reprinted by permission.

Joseph Naytowhow: "Subtle Energy as Seen through the Eyes of a Nehiyo (Cree Person)." Copyright © 2016 by Joseph Naytowhow. Printed by permission.

nêhiyaw (Glecia Bear): "Lost and Found" from *Kohkominawak otacimowiniwawa: Our Grandmothers' Lives as Told in Their Own Words*. Regina: Canadian Plains Research Centre Press, 1998. Copyright © 1998 by Freda Ahenakew. Reprinted by permission.

Yvette Nolan: Excerpts from *Medicine Shows: Indigenous Performance Culture*. Toronto: Playwrights Canada Press, 2015. Copyright © 2015 by Yvette Nolan. Reprinted by permission.

Bertha O'Watch: "Big Snake" and "Įktómi and Fox" from *A Grammar of Assiniboine: A Siouan Language of the Northern Plains*. Transcription and dissertation by Linda A. Cumberland, 2005. Printed by permission.

payipwāt: "To the Superior-General of the Oblate Order," "Defending the Sundance to Indian Commissioner A.E. Forget" and "Response to Father Hugonard's Offer of Baptism" in *Story of Piapot*. Z.M. Hamilton. 1945. Saskatchewan Archives Board, SHS file no. 49, 13–15; *First People, First Voices*. Ed. Penny Petrone. Toronto: University of Toronto Press, 1983.

peopeo kiskiok hihih (White Bird): "The Nez Percé War." Walsh Papers, May 22, 1890, in *Portraits from the Plains*. J.W. Grant MacEwan. Toronto: McGraw-Hill, 1971.

pītikwahānapiwiyin (Poundmaker): "Speeches at Treaty Six" from *The Treaties of Canada with the Indians of Manitoba and the North-West Territories*. Alexander Morris. Toronto: Belfords, Clarke & Co., 1880; Saskatoon: Fifth House Publishers, 1991. "Letter to Riel" in Confidential Papers, Department of Justice. "Letter to Middleton" in Middleton, Special Report, May 19, 1885. "Address to the Court" Sessional Papers, 1886. No. 52, 336.

piyēsiw-awāsis (Thunderchild): Selections from *Voices of the Plains Cree*. Regina: Canadian Plains Research Centre, 1995. Copyright © 1995 by CPRC Press. Reprinted by permission.

Plains Cree Texts (selections). Trans. Leonard Bloomfield. New York: AMS Press, 1974 (1934); Saskatoon: Fifth House Publishers, 1993.

Charles Pratt: "CMS catechist meets Cha-wa-cis, Saulteaux Medicine Man" in "The Journals of a Church of England Native Catechist: Askenootwo (Charles Pratt), 1851–1884." Winona Stevenson. In *Reading Beyond Words: Contexts for Native History*. Ed. Jennifer S.H. Brown and Elizabeth Vibert. Peterborough, ON: Broadview Press, 1996.

Solomon Ratt: kohkominanihk / "Grandmother's Bay," and paskwawi-mostos mitahtahkwana / "Buffalo Wings" from *Woods Cree Stories*. Regina: University of Regina Press, 2014. Copyright © 2014 by Solomon Ratt. Reprinted by permission.

Margaret Reynolds: "The Snow Man," "The One Who Crossed," and "Crowhead" from *Dene Stories*. Saskatoon: Saskatchewan Indian Cultural College, 1979. Copyright © 1979 by SICC. Reprinted by permission.

Louis Riel: "Message to the Métis of Battleford" in *Footprints in the Dust*. Douglas Light. North Battleford: Turner-Warwick Publications Inc., 1987. "Revolutionary Bill of Rights" in *Riel: A Life of Revolution*. Maggie Siggins. Toronto: HarperCollins, 1994. "Palpite! o mon esprit!" "Shudder, My Spirit." English translation © 2011 by Warren Cariou. "Margaret: be fair and good" and "Robert Gordon!" in *The Collected Writings of Louis Riel*. Vol. 4. Ed. F.G. Stanley. Edmonton: University of Alberta Press, 1985.

Thomas Roussin: "Cutarm Creek," "All Those Years of Heart (1867–1905)," and "The Gift." Copyright © 2015 by Thomas Roussin. Printed by permission.

Charles Ryder: "The Pipe of Peace" and "A Bear Story." *Carry-the-Kettle Assiniboine Texts*. Dissertation by Valerie Drummond, 1976.

Sacred Stories of the Sweet Grass Cree (selections). Trans. Leonard Bloomfield. New York: AMS Press, 1976 (1930); Saskatoon: Fifth House Publishers, 1993.

Buffy Sainte-Marie: "Now That the Buffalo's Gone" and "My Country 'Tis of Thy People You're Dying." Copyright © by Buffy Sainte-Marie. Reprinted by permission.

Saukamappee. "Life Among the Peigans," from *Travels in Western North America 1784–1812*. David Thompson. Ed. Victor G. Hopwood. Toronto: Macmillan and Co., 1971.

Gregory Scofield: "Not All Halfbreed Mothers" and "I've Been Told" from *I Knew Two Métis Women*. Vancouver: Polestar Press, 1999. Copyright © 1999 by Gregory Scofield. "Women Who Forgot the Taste of Limes" from *Singing Home the Blues*. Vancouver: Polestar Press, 2005. Copyright © 2005 by Gregory Scofield. "The Sewing Circle" and "Gabriel's Letter" from *Louis: The Heretic Poems*. Gibsons, BC: Nightwood Editions, 2011. Copyright © 2011 by Gregory Scofield. Reprinted by permission.

Paul Seesequasis: "Republic of Trieksterism" in *Grand Street* 61.56 (1997). Copyright © 1997 by Paul Seesequasis. Reprinted by permission.

James Settee: "An Indian Camp at the Mouth of Nelson River Hudson's Bay" from "James Settee and His Cree Tradition." Jennifer Brown. In *Actes du huitieme congress des algonquinistes*. Ed. William Cowan. Ottawa: Carleton University Press, 1977. "Wars between the Sioux and Saulteaux" from Public Archives of Canada, Bell Papers, MG 29, B-15, vol. 33; *First People, First Voices*. Ed. Penny Petrone. Toronto: University of Toronto Press, 1983.

Priscilla Settee: Introduction to *The Strength of Women: Ahkameyimowak*. Regina: Coteau Books, 2011. Copyright © 1985 by Priscilla Settee. Reprinted by permission.

A. Blair Stonechild: Excerpt from *The New Buffalo: The Struggle for Aboriginal Post-Secondary Education in Canada*. Winnipeg: University of Manitoba Press, 2006. Copyright © 2006 by A. Blair Stonechild. Reprinted by permission.

tatanka iyotake (Sitting Bull): "Arriving at Wood Mountain" and "To the American Commissioners" in Sessional Papers, 1878, no. 4, Appendix E. "To Major Walsh" in Walsh papers, March 24, 1879. All in *Portraits from the Plains*. J.W. Grant MacEwan. Toronto: McGraw-Hill, 1971.

James Tyman: Excerpts from *Inside Out*. Saskatoon: Fifth House Publishers, 1989. Copyright © 1989 James Tyman.

Peter Vandall: "Social Control" from *waskahikaniwiyiniw-acimowina: Stories of the House People*. Ed. and trans. by Freda Ahenakew. Winnipeg: University of Manitoba Press, 1987. Copyright © University of Manitoba Press. Reprinted by permission.

Herbert Walker: "Mink and Coyote." *Elicitation and Analysis of Nakoda Texts from Southern Saskatchewan*. Dissertation by Emily Kay Schudel, 1997.

Abel Watetch: "The Meaning of the Rain Dance" from *Payepot and His People*. Regina: Canadian Plains Research Centre Press, 2007. Copyright © 2007 by CPRC Press. Reprinted by permission.

wāwikanihk kā-otāmahoht (Strikes Him On The Back): "Speech at Treaty Six Negotiations" from *The Treaties of Canada with the Indians of Manitoba and the North-West Territories*. Alexander Morris. Toronto: Belfords, Clarke & Co., 1880; Saskatoon: Fifth House Publishers, 1991. "Become Farmers." *Saskatchewan Herald*, 13 May, 1882.

Kevin Wesaquate: "Like a Scene from a Movie," "Drop a Pound on My Table, Brother," and "That Picture in Black and White." Copyright © 2015 by Kevin Wesaquate. Printed by permission.

wīkasko-kisēyin (Sweet Grass): "Messages from the Cree Chiefs of the Plains to His Excellency, Governor Archibald, our Great Mother's Representative at Fort Garry, Red River Settlement," encl. in Christie to Archibald, April 13, 1871: C.S.P. 1872, Vol. VII, No. 22. "Speech at Treaty Six" from *The Treaties of Canada with the Indians of Manitoba and the North-West Territories*. Alexander Morris. Toronto: Belfords, Clarke & Co., 1880; Saskatoon: Fifth House Publishers, 1991.

Bernelda Wheeler: "Our Beloved Land and You" from *Prairie Fire* 22.3 (2001). Copyright © 2001 by the estate of Bernelda Wheeler. Reprinted by permission.

Winona Wheeler. "Calling Badger and the Symbols of the Spirit Language: The Cree Origins of the Syllabic System" in *Oral History Forum/Forum d'histoire orale*. Vol. 19–20, 1999–2000. Copyright © 1999 by Winona Stevenson. Reprinted by permission.

Vicki Wilson: "It was to me like we had lost our childhood" and "You'd be exposing yourself" from *The Strength of Women: Ahkameyimowak*. Regina: Coteau Books, 2011. Copyright © 2011 by Priscilla Settee. Reprinted by permission.

Alexander Wolfe: "The Sound of Dancing" from *Earth Elder Stories*. Calgary: Fifth House Publishers, 2002. Copyright © 1988 by Alexander Wolfe.

Index of Authors

Index of Topics